Managing with Power

MANAGING
with
POWER

Politics and Influence
in Organizations

JEFFREY PFEFFER
Graduate School of Business
Stanford University

HARVARD BUSINESS SCHOOL PRESS

Boston, Massachusetts

96 95 94 93   5 4 3

Library of Congress Cataloging-in-Publication Data

Pfeffer, Jeffrey.
    Managing with power : politics and influence in organizations /
Jeffrey Pfeffer.
        p.   cm.
    Includes bibliographical references and index.
    ISBN 0-87584-314-X (alk. paper) :
        1. Decision-making.   2. Power (Social sciences)   3. Organizational
behavior.   I. Title.
    HD30.23.P47   1992   91-26237
    658.4'095—dc20   CIP

The paper used in this publication meets the requirements of the
American National Standard for Permanence of Paper for Printed Library
Materials Z39.49–1984.

CONTENTS

Acknowledgments

I wrote this book mostly because of Gene Webb and Hal Leavitt, colleagues at Stanford. Leavitt had urged me for many years to write a book that would be more accessible to students and managers than much of my other writing. I ignored his advice for a long time. When Webb left the associate dean's office at Stanford, he began teaching sections of the course, Power and Politics in Organizations, which I had originally developed and taught. He brought new literature and new ideas to the course, but one year he stopped using the text, *Power in Organizations*, which I had written some years ago and which I use regularly in the course. Gene Webb had served on my thesis committee in the early 1970s when I had been a doctoral student at Stanford. I considered him a friend. When a friend stops using your book, it is clearly time to do something.

For some years, I had been developing new ideas and insights about power in organizations. I was teaching in corporate executive programs, and saw what issues were important and how executives reacted to various ideas and material. I continued to teach the elective course at Stanford, and over the years I had obtained numerous anecdotes and a great deal of feedback from students. For several years, Mike Tushman of Columbia, Charles O'Reilly from UC Berkeley, and I had taught a one-week program entitled, Managing Strategic Innovation and Change, for various companies both in the United States and overseas. From Mike and Charles I had learned a lot about the political dynamics of innovation and change, and the role of power and politics in that process. They, and my students, were also urging me to write a new book.

All of these groups paid a price for their nagging. My students in the course, Power and Politics in Organizations, had to use an earlier draft of the manuscript. Former students, in particular Fran Conley, read a copy. My colleagues who had so vigorously urged on the writing now had the task of providing me with comments, and the help I received from Chip Heath, Dan Julius, Roderick Kramer, Kotaro Kuwada, Charles O'Reilly, Donald Palmer, Michael Tushman, and particularly Gene Webb was extraordinary. Even doctoral students who were working with me at the time were drafted into providing feedback and assistance. Beth Benjamin provided examples and comments, even when she should have probably been working on her thesis. I owe much to these students and colleagues. I have benefited enormously from their feedback and their insights.

I also owe a great deal to the secretaries who have helped so much on this project, particularly Nancy Banks and Katrina Jaggears. One has to work at the Graduate School of Business at Stanford to appreciate the enormous support faculty are provided, in so many ways. I really do thank the school for the many forms of support and for having me on the faculty.

In January 1985, I met Kathleen Fowler. Kathleen had never dated a faculty member before, and wanted to know what I did. I told her I wrote. She said, "Show me something you have written." I gave her an autographed copy of *Power in Organizations*. She read it and stayed awake doing so, mostly. But she, too, said, "Can't you write something people can read?" We were married in July 1986. She gave me a watch as a wedding present. This book is her present—a little late, but then, life has been more interesting recently.

PART

I

Power in Organizations

1

Decisions and Implementation

At 5:04 P.M. on October 17, 1989, a large earthquake struck northern California. The earthquake destroyed or severely damaged several sections of freeway and a number of freeway off-ramps, as well as a portion of the San Francisco Bay Bridge. The vivid pictures of the damaged section of the bridge and the collapsed freeway section in the East Bay, which accounted for most of the fatalities, were flashed around the world. Most people recall that repairs to the bridge began immediately, and since the work was literally done around the clock, the bridge was reopened about six weeks later. What most people do not realize, even many living in the San Francisco area, is that some 18 months later, the opening of the San Francisco Bay Bridge was the *only* completed repair. Not one other damaged highway structure, not one off-ramp, not one other section of freeway had been repaired a year and a half after the quake. Indeed, in the case of the other two major portions of roadway that had been closed by the quake—the so-called Cypress Structure in Oakland and the Embarcadero Freeway in San Francisco—there was still no decision on exactly where, how, or whether to make repairs.

Technical or engineering complexities do not account for the delays, nor do they explain why the Bay Bridge was repaired while nothing else was. San Francisco's and California's response to the earthquake presents a situation that is

3

repeated often in both public and private sector organizations—a paralysis that reflects an inability to mobilize sufficient political support and resources to take action. Confronted with a problem, in this case—or opportunities, in some other instances—organizations are often unable to get things accomplished in a timely manner. This inaction can have severe consequences. The continuing closure of the Oakland section of the freeway costs some $23 million per year in extra transportation costs and fuel, while the continuing indecision about the repair of the freeways and off-ramps in San Francisco has cost much more in terms of lost business in the city.

It is, perhaps, not surprising that there is delay and indecision when the issue is as inherently ambiguous as the location and repair of roadways. Even in cases of life and death, however, there are failures to effectively mobilize political support and get things done that have serious consequences. Consider the chronology of the discovery of transfusion-transmitted AIDS, and the subsequent delays in getting anything done about it:

In March 1981, an "Rh baby" received a transfusion of blood provided by a 47-year-old donor at the Irwin Memorial Blood Bank in San Francisco.

In July 1981, epidemiological evidence led many members of the medical community to conclude that the so-called Gay Cancer was a contagious disease, spread by both sexual contact and through blood.

In September 1981, the child who received the transfusion in March was sick, suffering from immune dysfunctions; the donor, also sick, went to his doctor at about the same time and noted that he was a regular blood donor.

In December 1981, Don Francis, an epidemiologist at the Center for Disease Control (CDC) wanted to put blood banks on the alert. He argued that if the disease spread like hepatitis, it would be spread by blood transfusions.

In January 1982, the CDC learned that hemophiliacs were dying from a disease with symptoms similar to those spreading through the gay community, and that transfusions seemed to be the mechanism of transmission.

In November 1982, Dr. Selma Dritz, assistant director of the Bureau of Communicable Disease Control at the San

Francisco Department of Public Health, was concerned about protecting the integrity of the blood supply; she had documented, at least to her satisfaction, the first case of AIDS transmitted by blood transfusion.[1]

The reaction by the blood-bank industry was denial. "The first public announcement that AIDS might be in the blood supply brought an angry reaction from blood bankers in the East. . . . Dr. Joseph Bove, who . . . served as an officer of the American Association of Blood Banks, went on network television to say flatly that there still was no evidence that transfusions spread AIDS. Privately, some blood bankers thought the CDC was overstating the possibility . . . to get publicity and, therefore, more funding."[2]

On January 4, 1983 (more than a year after it was first suspected that AIDS could be spread by blood transfusions), at a meeting of an ad hoc advisory committee for the U.S. Public Health Service, Don Francis of the CDC was angry. "How many people have to die?" shouted Francis, his fist hitting the table again. "How many deaths do you need? Give us the threshold of death that you need in order to believe that this is happening, and we'll meet at that time and we can start doing something."[3]

In March 1983, the hepatitis antibody screening sought by the CDC was rejected because of opposition from the blood banks, although donor screening was introduced to try to eliminate high-risk donors.

In May 1983, Stanford University Hospital became the only major medical center in the United States to decide to begin testing blood for evidence of AIDS infection. "The rest of the blood industry was stunned. . . . Some said it was a gimmick to draw AIDS-hysteric patients to Stanford from San Francisco hospitals."[4]

In January 1984, the blood industry was continuing to stonewall. The cost of AIDS screening would be high; moreover, the industry was afraid of what it would do to both the supply of donors and the demand for blood from nonprofit blood banks. "In early January, Assistant Secretary for Health Ed Brandt set up a conference call of blood bankers and CDC officials to discuss the AIDS problem. The upshot of all the talk was no new FDA policy; instead the blood bankers agreed to form a task force to study the issue."[5] The careful reader will have noted that two years have passed since transfusion-transmitted AIDS was diagnosed and one year since Don Francis asked, "How many must die?"

By late 1984, even though there was no longer any real debate about whether AIDS could be spread by blood transfusions, widespread screening for hepatitis or other blood abnormalities still had not begun.

"An estimated 12,000 Americans were infected from transfusions largely administered after the CDC had futilely begged the blood industry for action to prevent spread of the disease. 'How many people have to die?' Francis had asked the blood bankers in early 1983. The answer was now clear: thousands would."[6]

The battle between the scientists and the blood bankers was far from an even match. The blood bankers were sophisticated users of language, symbols, and all the techniques of interpersonal influence. The very existence of that industry depended on motivating volunteers to support the work of organizations such as the American Red Cross. The blood banks and associated organizations had years of experience in working with the media. They had experience, too, in working the corridors of power in Washington, particularly the government health establishment. The scientists and the epidemiologists felt that truth would triumph, if the data were presented forcefully. But they were not at first influential enough to gain the upper hand in the struggle to change policies on AIDS. By contrast, the blood-bank industry cultivated allies, was shrewd in its use of language to make the risks appear negligible, and mustered all its resources to stall and delay policies that might harm the industry. Of course, those involved in these early struggles, and particularly the gay community, learned their political lessons. Today there is substantial research and public policy attention, and those fighting AIDS have mastered political skills and tactics. Indeed, the recent success—some claim disproportionate success—of efforts to obtain funding for AIDS research suggests that the early failure of the authorities to act occurred not so much because AIDS was a gay disease (although this was clearly a part of the story), but rather as a consequence of the lack of political will and expertise on the part of those fighting the traditional medical establishment. As they developed both the determination to make changes and the knowledge of how to do so, the outcome of the political struggle changed accordingly.

A distressing story, some will say, but what does this have to do with organizations in the private sector, which, after all, have the profit incentive to ensure that they make smart, rational, and timely decisions? Just this: Do you know which corporation invented the first personal computer as we know it today, the first word processing program applied in publishing, the mouse, the idea of windows on a computer screen, the use of icons rather than commands to make computers work, and which corporation was the first to run a television advertisement for a personal computer? If you answered, Apple Computer, you are partly right, in that the Macintosh, built and marketed by Apple, was the first computer to have these features and be commercially successful on a large scale. But it was, in fact, the Xerox Corporation, at its Palo Alto Research Center (PARC), that accomplished all these things in the mid-1970s, years before the introduction of the Lisa in 1983 and the introduction of the Macintosh in January 1984.[7] We all know that the first company to invent or develop a technology does not necessarily reap the economic benefits from that technology—Ampex Corporation's development of the technology for the VCR is another commonly cited example. What we don't often recognize is that failures to capitalize on innovations are, in actuality, failures in implementation, the same sort of failures in the ability to get things done that we saw in the case of rebuilding San Francisco roads and in protecting the nation's blood supply. Accomplishing innovation and change in organizations requires more than the ability to solve technical or analytic problems. Innovation almost invariably threatens the status quo, and consequently, innovation is an inherently political activity.

The inability to get things done, to have ideas and decisions implemented, is widespread in organizations today. It is, moreover, a problem that seems to be getting worse in both public and private sector organizations. It has led to calls for better leadership, and laments about the absence of leadership in many spheres. It is my thesis that problems of implementation are, in many instances, problems in developing political will and expertise—the desire to accomplish something, even against opposition, and the knowledge and skills that make it possible to do so. Today more than ever, it is necessary to study power and to learn to use it skillfully, since we cannot otherwise hope to gain individual success in organizations or the success of the organizations themselves. As Richard Nixon wrote:

> It is not enough for a leader to *know* the right thing. He must be able to *do* the right thing. The . . . leader without the judgment or perception to make the right decisions fails for lack of vision. The one who knows the right thing but cannot achieve it fails because he is ineffectual. The great leader needs . . . the capacity to achieve.[8]

POWER IN ORGANIZATIONS

Norton Long, a political scientist, wrote, "People will readily admit that governments are organizations. The converse—that organizations are governments—is equally true but rarely considered."[9] But organizations, particularly large ones, are like governments in that they are fundamentally political entities. To understand them, one needs to understand organizational politics, just as to understand governments, one needs to understand governmental politics.

Ours is an era in which people tend to shy away from this task. As I browse through bookstores, I am struck by the incursion of "New Age" thinking, even in the business sections. New Age can be defined, I suppose, in many ways, but what strikes me about it are two elements: 1) a self-absorption and self-focus, which looks toward the individual in isolation; and 2) a belief that conflict is largely the result of misunderstanding, and if people only had more communication, more tolerance, and more patience, many (or all) social problems would disappear. These themes appear in books on topics ranging from making marriages work to making organizations work. A focus on individual self-actualization is useful, but a focus on sheer self-reliance is not likely to encourage one to try to get things done with and through other people—to be a manager or a leader. "Excellence can be achieved in a solitary field without the need to exercise leadership."[10] In this sense, John Gardner's (former secretary of

HEW and the founder of Common Cause) concerns about community are part and parcel of a set of concerns about organizations and getting things accomplished in them.[11] One can be quite content, quite happy, quite fulfilled as an organizational hermit, but one's influence is limited and the potential to accomplish great things, which requires interdependent action, is almost extinguished.

If we are suspicious of the politics of large organizations, we may conclude that smaller organizations are a better alternative. There is, in fact, evidence that the average size of establishments in the United States is decreasing. This is not just because we have become more of a service economy and less of a manufacturing economy; even within manufacturing, the average size of establishments and firms is shrinking. The largest corporations have shed thousands, indeed hundreds of thousands of employees—not only middle managers, but also production workers, staff of all kinds, and employees who performed tasks that are now contracted out. Managers and employees who were stymied by the struggles over power and influence that emerge from interdependence and differences in points of view have moved to a world of smaller, simpler organizations, with less internal interdependence and less internal diversity, which are, as a consequence, less political. Of course, such structural changes only increase interdependence among organizations, even as they decrease interdependence and conflict within these organizations.

I see in this movement a parallel to what I have seen in the management of our human resources. Many corporations today solve their personnel problems by getting rid of the personnel. The rationale seems to be that if we can't effectively manage and motivate employees, then let's turn the task over to another organization. We can use leased employees or contract workers, or workers from temporary help agencies, and let those organizations solve our problems of turnover, compensation, selection, and training.

It is an appealing solution, consistent with the emphasis on the individual, which has always been strong in U.S. culture, and which has grown in recent years. How can we trust large organizations when they have broken compacts of long-term employment? Better to seek security and certainty within oneself, in one's own competencies and abilities, and in the control of one's own activities.

There is, however, one problem with this approach to dealing with organizational power and influence. It is not clear that by ignoring the social realities of power and influence we can make them go away, or that by trying to build simpler, less interdependent social structures we succeed in building organizations that are more effective or that have greater survival value. Although it is certainly true that large organizations sometimes disappear,[12] it is also true that smaller organizations disappear at a much higher rate and have much worse survival properties. By trying to ignore issues of power and influence in organizations, we lose our chance to understand these critical social processes and to train managers to cope with them.

By pretending that power and influence don't exist, or at least shouldn't exist, we contribute to what I and some others (such as John Gardner) see as the major problem facing many corporations today, particularly in the United States—the almost trained or produced incapacity of anyone except the highest-level managers to take action and get things accomplished. As I teach in corporate executive programs, and as I compare experiences with colleagues who do likewise, I hear the same story over and over again. In these programs ideas are presented to fairly senior executives, who then work in groups on the implications of these ideas for their firms. There is real strength in the experience and knowledge of these executives, and they often come up with insightful recommendations and ideas for improving their organizations. Perhaps they discover the wide differences in effectiveness that exist in different units and share suggestions about how to improve performance. Perhaps they come to understand more comprehensively the markets and technologies of their organizations, and develop strategies for both internally oriented and externally oriented changes to enhance effectiveness. It really doesn't matter, because the most frequently heard comment at such sessions is, "My boss should be here." And when they go back to their offices, after the stimulation of the week, few managers have either the ability or the determination to engineer the changes they discussed with such insight.

I recall talking to a store manager for a large supermarket chain with a significant share of the northern California grocery market. He managed a store that did in excess of $20 million in sales annually, which by the standards of the average organization makes him a manager with quite a bit of responsibility—or so one would think. In this organization, however, as in many others, the responsibilities of middle-level managers are strictly limited. A question arose as to whether the store should participate in putting its name on a monument sign for the shopping center in which the store was located. The cost was about $8,000 (slightly less than four hours' sales in that store). An analysis was done, showing how many additional shoppers would need to be attracted to pay back this small investment, and what percentage this was of the traffic count passing by the center. The store manager wanted the sign. But, of course, he could not spend even this much money without the approval of his superiors. It was the president of the northern California division who decided, after a long meeting, that the expenditure was not necessary.

There are many lessons that one might learn from this example. It could be seen as the result of a plague of excessive centralization, or as an instance of a human resource management policy that certainly was more "top down" than "bottom up." But what was particularly interesting was the response of the manager—who, by the way, is held accountable for this store's profits even as he is given almost no discretion to do anything about them. When I asked him about the decision, he said, "Well, I guess that's why the folks at headquarters get the big money; they must know something we don't." Was he going to push for his idea, his very modest proposal? Of course not, he said. One gets along by just biding one's time, going along with whatever directives come down from the upper management.

I have seen this situation repeated in various forms over and over again. I talk to senior executives who claim their organizations take no initiative, and to high-level managers who say they can't or won't engage in efforts to change the corporations they work for, even when they know such changes are important, if not essential, to the success and survival of these organizations. There are politics involved in innovation and change. And unless and until we are willing to come to terms with organizational power and influence, and admit that the skills of getting things done are as important as the skills of figuring out what to do, our organizations will fall further and further behind. The problem is, in most cases, not an absence of insight or organizational intelligence. Instead the problem is one of passivity, a phenomenon that John Gardner analyzed in the following way:

> In this country—and in most other democracies—power has such a bad name that many good people persuade themselves they want nothing to do with it. The ethical and spiritual apprehensions are understandable. But one cannot abjure power. Power, as we are now speaking of it . . . is simply the capacity to bring about certain intended consequences in the behavior of others. . . . In our democratic society we make grants of power to people for specified purposes. If for ideological or temperamental reasons they refuse to exercise the power granted, we must turn to others. . . . To say, a leader is preoccupied with power, is like saying that a tennis player is preoccupied with making shots his opponent cannot return. Of course leaders are preoccupied with power! The significant questions are: What means do they use to gain it? How do they exercise it? To what ends do they exercise it?[13]

If leadership involves skill at developing and exercising power and influence as well as the will to do so, then perhaps one of the causes of the so-called leadership crisis in organizations in the United States is just this attempt to sidestep issues of power. This diagnosis is consistent with the arguments made by Warren Bennis and his colleagues, who have studied leaders and written on leadership. For instance, Bennis and Nanus noted that one of the major problems facing organizations today is not that too many people exercise too much power, but rather the opposite:

> These days power is conspicuous by its absence. Powerlessness in the face of crisis. Powerlessness in the face of complexity. . . . power has been sabotaged. . . . institutions have been rigid, slothful, or mercurial.[14]

They go on to comment on the importance of power as a concept for understanding leadership and as a tool that allows organizations to function productively and effectively:

However, there is something missing . . . POWER, the basic energy
to initiate and sustain action translating intention into reality, the
quality without which leaders cannot lead. . . . power is at once the
most necessary and the most distrusted element exigent to human
progress. . . . power is the basic energy needed to initiate and sustain
action or, to put it another way, the capacity to translate intention
into reality and sustain it.[15]

Such observations about power are not merely the province of theorists. Political leaders, too, confirm that the willingness to build and wield power is a prerequisite for success
in public life. In this consideration of power and leadership,
Richard Nixon offered some observations that are consistent
with the theme of this book:

Power is the opportunity to build, to create, to nudge history in a
different direction.

There are few satisfactions to match it for those who care about such
things. But it is not happiness. Those who seek happiness will not
acquire power and would not use it well if they did acquire it.

A whimsical observer once commented that those who love laws and
sausages should not watch either being made.

By the same token, we honor leaders for what they achieve, but we
often prefer to close our eyes to the way they achieve it. . . .

In the real world, politics is compromise and democracy is politics.
Anyone who would be a statesman has to be a successful politician
first. Also, a leader has to deal with people and nations as they are,
not as they should be. As a result, the qualities required for leadership are not necessarily those that we would want our children to
emulate—unless we wanted them to be leaders.

In evaluating a leader, the key question about his behavioral traits
is not whether they are attractive or unattractive, but whether they
are useful.[16]

OUR AMBIVALENCE ABOUT POWER

That we are ambivalent about power is undeniable. Rosabeth Kanter, noting that power was critical for effective managerial behavior, nevertheless wrote, "Power is America's
last dirty word. It is easier to talk about money—and much
easier to talk about sex—than it is to talk about power."[17]
Gandz and Murray did a survey of 428 managers whose re-

sponses nicely illustrate the ambivalence about power in organizations.[18] Some items from their survey, along with the percentage of respondents reporting strong or moderate agreement, are reproduced in Table 1-1.

Table 1-1

Managers' Feelings about Workplace Politics

Statement	Percentage Expressing Strong or Moderate Agreement
The existence of workplace politics is common to most organizations	93.2
Successful executives must be good politicians	89.0
The higher you go in organizations, the more political the climate becomes	76.2
Powerful executives don't act politically	15.7
You have to be political to get ahead in organizations	69.8
Top management should try to get rid of politics within the organization	48.6
Politics help organizations function effectively	42.1
Organizations free of politics are happier than those where there are a lot of politics	59.1
Politics in organizations are detrimental to efficiency	55.1

Source: Gandz and Murray (1980), p. 244.

The concepts of power and organizational politics are related; most authors, myself included, define organizational politics as the exercise or use of power, with power being defined as a potential force. Note that more than 90% of the respondents said that the experience of workplace politics is common in most organizations, 89% said that successful executives must be good politicians, and 76% said that the higher one progresses in an organization, the more political things become. Yet 55% of these same respondents said that politics were detrimental to efficiency, and almost half said that top management should try to get rid of politics within organizations. It is as if we know that power and politics exist, and we even grudgingly admit that they are necessary to individual success, but we nevertheless don't like them.

This ambivalence toward, if not outright disdain for, the development and use of power in organizations stems from more than one source. First, there is the issue of ends and means—we often don't like to consider the methods that are necessary to get things accomplished, as one of the earlier quotes from Richard Nixon suggests. We are also ambivalent about ends and means because the same strategies and processes that may produce outcomes we desire can also be used to produce results that we consider undesirable. Second, some fundamental lessons we learn in school really hinder our appreciation of power and influence. Finally, in a related point, the perspective from which we judge organizational decisions often does not do justice to the realities of the social world.

Ends and Means

On Saturday, September 25, 1976, an elaborate testimonial dinner was held in San Francisco for a man whose only public office was as a commissioner on the San Francisco Housing Authority board. The guest list was impressive—the mayor, George Moscone; Lieutenant Governor Mervyn Dymally, at that time the highest-ranking Afro-American in elected politics; District Attorney Joe Freitas; Democratic Assemblyman Willie Brown, probably the most powerful and feared individual in California politics; Republican State Senator Milton Marks; San Francisco Supervisor Robert Mendelsohn; the city editor of the morning newspaper; prominent attorneys—in short, both Democrats and Republicans, a veritable who's who of the northern California political establishment. The man they were there to honor had recently met personally with the president's wife, Rosalynn Carter. Yet when the world heard more of this guest of honor, some two years later, it was to be with shock and horror at what happened in a jungle in Guyana. The person being honored that night in September 1976—who had worked his way into the circles of power in San Francisco using some of the very same strategies and tactics described in this book—was none other than Jim Jones.[19]

There is no doubt that power and influence can be acquired and exercised for evil purposes. Of course, most medicines can kill if taken in the wrong amount, thousands die each year in automobile accidents, and nuclear power can either provide energy or mass destruction. We do not abandon chemicals, cars, or even atomic power because of the dangers associated with them; instead we consider danger an incentive to get training and information that will help us to use these forces productively. Yet few people are willing to approach the potential risks and advantages of power with the same pragmatism. People prefer to avoid discussions of power, apparently on the assumption that "If we don't think about it, it won't exist." I take a different view. John Jacobs, now a political editor for the *San Francisco Examiner*, co-authored a book on Jim Jones and gave me a copy of it in 1985. His view, and mine, was that tragedies such as Jonestown could be prevented, not by ignoring the processes of power and influence, but rather by being so well schooled in them that one could recognize their use and take countermeasures, if necessary—and by developing a well-honed set of moral values.

The means to any end are merely mechanisms for accomplishing something. The something can be grand, grotesque, or, for most of us, I suspect, somewhere in between. The end may not always justify the means, but neither should it automatically be used to discredit the means. Power and political processes in organizations can be used to accomplish great things. They are not always used in this fashion, but that does not mean we should reject them out of hand. It is interesting that when we use power ourselves, we see it as a good force and wish we had more. When others use it against us, particularly when it is used to thwart our goals or ambitions, we see it as an evil. A more sophisticated and realistic view would see it for what it is—an important social process that is often required to get things accomplished in interdependent systems.

Most of us consider Abraham Lincoln to have been a great president. We tend to idealize his accomplishments: he preserved the Union, ended slavery, and delivered the memorable

Gettysburg Address. It is easy to forget that he was also a politician and a pragmatist—for instance, the Emancipation Proclamation freed the slaves in the Confederacy, but not in border states that remained within the Union, whose support he needed. Lincoln also took a number of actions that far overstepped his constitutional powers. Indeed, Andrew Johnson was impeached for continuing many of the actions that Lincoln had begun. Lincoln once explained how he justified breaking the laws he had sworn to uphold:

> My oath to preserve the Constitution imposed on me the duty of preserving by every indispensable means that government, that nation, of which the Constitution was the organic law. Was it possible to lose the nation and yet preserve the Constitution? . . . I felt that measures, otherwise unconstitutional, might become lawful by becoming indispensable to the preservation . . . of the nation.[20]

Lessons to Be Unlearned

Our ambivalence about power also comes from lessons we learn in school. The first lesson is that life is a matter of individual effort, ability, and achievement. After all, in school, if you have mastered the intricacies of cost accounting, or calculus, or electrical engineering, and the people sitting on either side of you haven't, their failure will not affect your performance—unless, that is, you had intended to copy from their papers. In the classroom setting, interdependence is minimized. It is you versus the material, and as long as you have mastered the material, you have achieved what is expected. Cooperation may even be considered cheating.

Such is not the case in organizations. If you know your organization's strategy but your colleagues do not, you will have difficulty accomplishing anything. The private knowledge and private skill that are so useful in the classroom are insufficient in organizations. Individual success in organizations is quite frequently a matter of working with and through other people, and organizational success is often a function of how successfully individuals can coordinate their activities. Most situations in organizations resemble football more than golf, which is why companies often scan resumes to find not only evidence of individual achievement, but also signs that the person is skilled at working as part of a team. In achieving success in organizations, "power transforms individual interests into coordinated activities that accomplish valuable ends."[21]

The second lesson we learn in school, which may be even more difficult to unlearn, is that there are right and wrong answers. We are taught how to solve problems, and for each problem, that there is a right answer, or at least one approach that is more correct than another. The right answer is, of course, what the instructor says it is, or what is in the back of the book, or what is hidden away in the instructor's manual. Life appears as a series of "eureka" problems, so-called because once you are shown the correct approach or answer, it is immediately self-evident that the answer is, in fact, correct.

This emphasis on the potential of intellectual analysis to provide the right answer—the truth—is often, although not invariably, misplaced. Commenting on his education in politics, Henry Kissinger wrote, "Before I served as a consultant to Kennedy, I had believed, like most academics, that the process of decision-making was largely intellectual and all one had to do was to walk into the President's office and convince him of the correctness of one's view. This perspective I soon realized is as dangerously immature as it is widely held."[22] Kissinger noted that the easy decisions, the ones with right and wrong answers that can be readily discerned by analysis, never reached the president, but rather were resolved at lower levels.

In the world in which we all live, things are seldom clearcut or obvious. Not only do we lack a book or an instructor to provide quick feedback on the quality of our approach, but the problems we face often have multiple dimensions— which yield multiple methods of evaluation. The consequences of our decisions are often known only long after the fact, and even then with some ambiguity.

AN ALTERNATIVE PERSPECTIVE
ON DECISION MAKING

Let me offer an alternative way of thinking about the decision-making process. There are three important things to remember about decisions. First, a decision by itself changes nothing. You can decide to launch a new product, hire a job candidate, build a new plant, change your performance evaluation system, and so forth, but the decision will not put itself into effect. As a prosaic personal example, recall how many times you or your friends "decided" to quit smoking, to get more exercise, to relax more, to eat healthier foods, or to lose weight. Such resolutions often fizzle before producing any results. Thus, in addition to knowledge of decision science, we need to know something about "implementation science."

Second, at the moment a decision is made, we cannot possibly know whether it is good or bad. Decision quality, when measured by results, can only be known as the consequences of the decision become known. We must wait for the decision to be implemented and for its consequences to become clear.

The third, and perhaps most important, observation is that we almost invariably spend more time living with the consequences of our decisions than we do in making them. It may be an organizational decision such as whether to acquire a company, change the compensation system, fight a union-organizing campaign; or a personal decision such as where to go to school, which job to choose, what subject to major in, or whom to marry. In either case, it is likely that the effects of the decision will be with us longer than it took us to make the decision, regardless of how much time and effort we invested. Indeed, this simple point has led several social psychologists to describe people as rationalizing (as contrasted with rational) animals.[23] The match between our attitudes and our behavior, for instance, often derives from our adjusting our attitudes after the fact to conform to our past actions and their consequences.[24]

If decisions by themselves change nothing; if, at the time a decision is made, we cannot know its consequences; and if we spend, in any event, more time living with our decisions than we do in making them, then it seems evident that the emphasis in much management training and practice has been misplaced. Rather than spending inordinate amounts of time and effort in the decision-making process, it would seem at least as useful to spend time implementing decisions and dealing with their ramifications. In this sense, good managers are not only good analytic decision makers; more important, they are skilled in managing the consequences of their decisions. "Few successful leaders spend much time fretting about decisions once they are past. . . . The only way he can give adequate attention to the decisions he has to make tomorrow is to put those of yesterday firmly behind him."[25]

There are numerous examples that illustrate this point. Consider, for instance, the acquisition of Fairchild Semiconductor by Schlumberger, an oil service company.[26] The theory behind the merger was potentially sound—to apply Fairchild's skills in electronics to the oil service business. Schlumberger wanted, for example, to develop more sophisticated exploration devices and to add electronics to oil servicing and drilling equipment. Unfortunately, the merger produced none of the expected synergies:

> When Schlumberger tried to manage Fairchild the same way it had managed its other business units, it created many difficulties. . . . resources were not made available to R&D with the consequence of losing technical edge which Fairchild once had. Creative . . . technical people left the organization and the company was unable to put technical teams together to pursue new technological advancement.[27]

A study of 31 acquisitions found that "problems will eventually emerge after acquisitions that could not have been anticipated. . . . both synergy and problems must be actively managed."[28] Moreover, firms that see acquisitions as a quick way of capturing some financial benefits are often insensitive to the amount of time and effort that is required to implement the merger and to produce superior performance after it occurs. Emphasis on the choice of a merger partner and the terms of the deal can divert focus away from the importance of the activities that occur once the merger is completed.

Or, consider the decision to launch a new product. Whether that decision produces profits or losses is often not simply a matter of the choices made at the time of the launch. It also depends on the implementation of those choices, as well as on subsequent decisions such as redesigning the product, changing the channels of distribution, adjusting prices, and so forth. Yet what we often observe in organizations is that once a decision is made, more effort is expended in assigning credit or blame than in working to improve the results of the decision.

I can think of no example that illustrates my argument as clearly as the story of how Honda entered the American market, first with motorcycles, and later, of course, with automobiles and lawn mowers. Honda established an American subsidiary in 1959, and between 1960 and 1965, Honda's sales in the United States went from $500,000 to $77 million. By 1966, Honda's share of the U.S. motorcycle market was 63%,[29] starting from zero just seven years before. Honda's share was almost six times that of its closest competitors, Yamaha and Suzuki, and Harley-Davidson's share had fallen to 4%. Pascale showed that this extraordinary success was largely the result of "miscalculation, serendipity, and organizational learning," not of the rational process of planning and foresight often emphasized in our efforts to be successful.[30]

Sochiro Honda himself was more interested in racing and engine design than in building a business, but his partner, Takeo Fujisawa, managed to convince him to turn his talent to designing a safe, inexpensive motorcycle to be driven with one hand and used for package delivery in Japan. The motorcycle was an immediate success in Japan. How and why did Honda decide to enter the export market and sell to the United States? Kihachiro Kawashima, eventually president of American Honda, reported to Pascale:

> In truth, we had no strategy other than the idea of seeing if we could sell something in the United States. It was a new frontier . . . and it fit the "success against all odds" culture that Mr. Honda had cultivated. I reported my impressions . . . including the seat-of-the-pants target of trying, over several years, to attain a 10 percent share of U.S. imports. . . . We did not discuss profits or deadlines for breakeven.[31]

Money was authorized for the venture, but the Ministry of Finance approved a currency allocation of only $250,000, of which less than half was in cash and the rest in parts and motorcycle inventory. The initial attempt to sell motorcycles in Los Angeles was disastrous. Distances in the United States are much greater than in Japan, and the motorcycles were driven farther and faster than their design permitted. Engine failures were common, particularly on the larger bikes.

The company had initially focused its sales efforts on the larger, 250cc and 350cc bikes, and had not even tried to sell the 50cc Supercub, believing it was too small to have any market acceptance:

> We used the Honda 50s . . . to ride around Los Angeles on errands. They attracted a lot of attention. One day we had a call from a Sears buyer. . . . we took note of Sears' interest. But we still hesitated to push the 50cc bikes out of fear they might harm our image in a heavily macho market. But when the larger bikes started breaking, we had no choice. We let the 50cc bikes move. And surprisingly, the retailers who wanted to sell them weren't motorcycle dealers, they were sporting goods stores.[32]

Honda's "you meet the nicest people on a Honda" advertising campaign was designed as a class project by a student at UCLA, and was at first resisted by Honda. Honda's distribution strategy—sporting goods and bicycle shops rather than motorcycle dealers—was made *for* them, not *by* them. And its success with the smaller motorbike was almost totally unanticipated. It occurred through a combination of circumstances: the use of the motorbike by Honda employees, who couldn't afford anything fancier; the positive response from people who saw the bike; and the failure of Honda's larger bikes in the American market.

Honda did not use decision analysis and strategic planning. In fact, it is difficult to see that Honda made any decisions at all, at least in terms of developing alternatives and weighing options against an assessment of goals and the state of the market. Honda succeeded by being flexible, by learning and adapting, and by working to have decisions turn out right, once those decisions had been made. Having arrived with the wrong product for a market they did not understand, Honda spent little time trying to find a scapegoat for the company's predicament; rather, Honda personnel worked vigorously to change the situation to their benefit, being creative as well as opportunistic in the process.

The point is that decisions in the world of organizations are not like decisions made in school. There, once you have written down an answer and turned in the test, the game is over. This is not the case in organizational life. The important actions may not be the original choices, but rather what happens subsequently, and what actions are taken to make things work out. This is a significant point, because it means that we need to be somewhat less concerned about the quality of the decision at the time we make it (which, after all, we can't really know anyway) and more concerned with adapting our new decisions and actions to the information we learn as events unfold. Just as Honda emerged as a leader in many American markets more by accident and trial-and-error learning than by design, it is critical that organizational members develop the fortitude to continue when confronted by adversity and the insight about how to turn situations around. The most important skill may be managing the consequences of decisions. And, in organizations in which it is often difficult to take any action, the critical ability may be the capacity to have things implemented.

WAYS OF GETTING THINGS DONE

Why is implementation difficult in so many organizations, and why does it appear that the ability to get decisions implemented is becoming increasingly rare? One way of thinking about this issue, and of examining the role of power and influence in the implementation process, is to consider some possible ways of getting things done.

One way of getting things to happen is through hierarchical authority. Many people think power is merely the exercise of formal authority, but it is considerably more than that, as we will see. Everyone who works in an organization has seen the exercise of hierarchical authority. Those at higher levels have the power to hire and fire, to measure and reward behavior, and to provide direction to those who are under their aegis. Hierarchical direction is usually seen as legitimate, because the variation in formal authority comes to be taken for granted as a part of organizational life. Thus the phrase, "the boss wants . . ." or "the president wants . . ." is seldom questioned or challenged. Who can forget Marine Lieutenant Colonel Oliver North testifying, during the Iran-contra hearings, about his willingness to stand on his head in a corner if that was what his commander-in-chief wanted, or maintaining that he never once disobeyed the orders of his superiors?

There are three problems with hierarchy as a way of getting things done. First, and perhaps not so important, is that it is badly out of fashion. In an era of rising education and the democratization of all decision processes, in an era in which participative management is advocated in numerous places,[33] and particularly in a country in which incidents such as the Vietnam War and Watergate have led many people to mistrust the institutions of authority, implementation by order or command is problematic. Readers who are parents need only reflect on the difference in parental authority between the current period and the 1950s to see what I mean. How many times have you been able to get your children to do something simply on the basis of your authority as a parent?

A second, more serious problem with authority derives from the fact that virtually all of us work in positions in which, in order to accomplish our job and objectives, we need the cooperation of others who do not fall within our direct chain of command. We depend, in other words, on people outside our purview of authority, whom we could not command, reward, or punish even if we wanted to. Perhaps, as a line manager in a product division, we need the cooperation of people in human resources for hiring, people in finance for evaluating new product opportunities, people in distribution and sales for getting the product sold and delivered, and people in market research for determining product features and marketing and pricing strategy. Even the authority of a chief executive is not absolute, since there are groups outside the focal organization that control the ability to get things done. To sell overseas airline routes to other domestic airlines requires the cooperation of the Transportation and Justice Departments, as well as the acquiescence of foreign governments. To market a drug or medical device requires the approval of the Food and Drug Administration; to export products overseas, one may need both financing and export licenses. The hierarchical authority of all executives and administrators is limited, and for most of us, it is quite limited compared to the scope of what we need in order to do our jobs effectively.

There is a third problem with implementation accomplished solely or primarily through hierarchical authority: What happens if the person at the apex of the pyramid, the one whose orders are being followed, is incorrect? When authority is vested in a single individual, the organization can face grave difficulties if that person's insight or leadership begins to fail. This was precisely what happened at E.F. Hutton, where Robert Fomon, the chief executive officer, ruled the firm through a rigid hierarchy of centralized power:

> Fomon's strength as a leader was also his weakness. As he put his stamp on the firm, he did so more as monarch than as a chief executive. . . . Fomon surrounded himself with . . . cronies and yes men who would become the managers and directors of E.F. Hutton and who would insulate him from the real world.[34]

Because Fomon was such a successful builder of his own hierarchical authority, no one in the firm challenged him to see the new realities that Hutton, and every other securities firm, faced in the 1980s.[35] Consequently, when the brokerage industry changed, Hutton did not, and it eventually ceased to exist as an independent entity.

Another way of getting things done is by developing a strongly shared vision or organizational culture. If people share a common set of goals, a common perspective on what to do and how to accomplish it, and a common vocabulary that allows them to coordinate their behavior, then command and hierarchical authority are of much less importance. People will be able to work cooperatively without waiting for orders from the upper levels of the company. Managing through a shared vision and with a strong organizational culture has been a very popular prescription for organizations.[36] A number of articles and books tell how to build commitment and shared vision and how to socialize individuals, particularly at the time of entry, so that they share a language, values, and premises about what needs to be done and how to do it.[37]

Without denying the efficacy and importance of vision and

culture, it is important to recognize that implementation accomplished through them can have problems. First, building
a shared conception of the world takes time and effort. There
are instances when the organization is in crisis or confronts
situations in which there is simply not sufficient time to develop shared premises about how to respond. For this very
reason, the military services rely not only on techniques that
build loyalty and esprit de corps,[38] but also on a hierarchical
chain of command and a tradition of obeying orders.

Second, there is the problem of how, in a strong culture,
new ideas that are inconsistent with that culture can pene-
trate. A strong culture really constitutes an organizational
paradigm, which prescribes how to look at things, what are
appropriate methods and techniques for solving problems,
and what are the important issues and problems.[39] In fields
of science, a well-developed paradigm provides guidance as
to what needs to be taught and in what order, how to do
research, what are appropriate methodologies, what are the
most pressing research questions, and how to train new students.[40] A well-developed paradigm, or a strong culture, is
overturned only with great difficulty, even if it fails to account for data or to lead to new discoveries.[41] In a similar
fashion, an organizational paradigm provides a way of thinking about and investigating the world, which reduces uncertainty and provides for effective collective action, but which
also overlooks or ignores some lines of inquiry. It is easy for
a strong culture to produce groupthink, a pressure to conform
to the dominant view.[42] A vision focuses attention, but in that
focus, things are often left out.

An organization that had difficulties, as well as great success, because of its strong, almost evangelical culture is
Apple Computer. Apple was founded and initially largely
populated by counterculture computer hackers, whose vision
was a computer-based form of power to the people—one
computer for each person. IBM had maintained its market
share through its close relations with centralized data processing departments. IBM was the safe choice—the saying
was, no one ever got fired for buying IBM. The Apple II was
successful by making an end run around the corporate data
processing manager and selling directly to the end-user, but
"by the end of '82 it was beginning to seem like a good idea

to have a single corporate strategy for personal computers, and the obvious person to coordinate that strategy was the data processing manager."[43] Moreover, computers were increasingly being tied into networks; issues of data sharing and compatibility were critical in organizations that planned to buy personal computers by the thousands. Companies wanted a set of computers that could run common software, to save on software purchasing as well as training and programming expenses. Its initial vision of "one person–one machine" made it difficult for Apple to see the need for compatibility, and as a consequence:

> The Apple II wouldn't run software for the IBM PC; the PC wouldn't run software for Lisa, Lisa wouldn't run software for the Apple II; and none of them would run software for the Macintosh. . . . Thanks largely to Steve [Jobs], Apple had an entire family of computers none of which talked to one another.[44]

Apple's strong culture and common vision also helped cause the failure of the Apple III as a new product. The vision was not only of "one person–one machine," but also of a machine that anyone could design, modify, and improve. Operating systems stood between the user and the machine, and so the Apple culture denigrated operating systems:

> The problem with an operating system, from the hobbyist point of view, was that it made it more difficult to reach down inside the computer and show off your skills; it formed a barrier between the user and the machine. Personal computers meant power to the people, and operating systems took some of that power away. . . . It wasn't a design issue; it was a threat to the inalienable rights of a free people.[45]

Apple III had an operating system known as SOS for Sophisticated Operating System, which was actually quite similar to the system Microsoft had developed for IBM's personal computer—MS. DOS (Microsoft Disk Operating System), except it was even better in some respects. Yet Apple was too wary of operating systems to try to make its system *the* standard, or even *a* standard, in personal computing. As a result the company lost out on a number of important commercial opportunities. The very zeal and fervor that made working for Apple like a religious crusade and produced extraordinary levels of commitment from the work force made it difficult for the company to be either cognizant of or responsive to shifts in the marketplace for personal computers.

There is a third process of implementation in organizations—namely, the use of power and influence. With power and influence the emphasis is on method rather than structure. It is possible to wield power and influence without necessarily having or using formal authority. Nor is it necessary to rely on a strong organizational culture and the homogeneity that this often implies. Of course, the process of implementation through power and influence is not without problems of its own; the last section of the book treats some of them and offers some potential palliatives. For now, what is important is to see power and influence as one of a set of ways of getting things done—not the only way, but an important way.

From the preceding discussion we can see that implementation is becoming more difficult because: 1) changing social norms and greater interdependence within organizations have made traditional, formal authority less effective than it once was, and 2) developing a common vision is increasingly difficult in organizations comprised of heterogeneous members—heterogeneous in terms of race and ethnicity, gender, and even language and culture. At the same time, our ambivalence about power, and the fact that training in its use is far from widespread, mean that members of organizations are often unable to supplement their formal authority with the "unofficial" processes of power and influence. As a result their organizations suffer, and promising projects fail to get off the ground. This is why learning how to manage with power is so important.

THE MANAGEMENT PROCESS:
A POWER PERSPECTIVE

From the perspective of power and influence, the process of implementation involves a set of steps, which are outlined below. This book is about the details of these steps. At this point, however, it is useful to provide an overview of the process:

1. Decide what your goals are, what you are trying to accomplish.
2. Diagnose patterns of dependence and interdependence; what individuals are influential and important in your achieving your goal?
3. What are their points of view likely to be? How will they feel about what you are trying to do?
4. What are their power bases? Which of them is more influential in the decision?
5. What are your bases of power and influence? What bases of influence can you develop to gain more control over the situation?
6. Which of the various strategies and tactics for exercising power seem most appropriate and are likely to be effective, given the situation you confront?
7. Based on the above, choose a course of action to get something done.

The first step is to decide on your goals. It is, for instance, easier to drive from Albany, New York to Austin, Texas if you know your destination than if you just get in your car in Albany and drive randomly. Although this point is apparently obvious, it is something that is often overlooked in a business context. How many times have you attended meetings or conferences or talked to someone on the telephone without a clear idea of what you were trying to accomplish? Our calendars are filled with appointments, and other interactions occur unexpectedly in the course of our day. If we don't have some clear goals, and if we don't know what our primary objectives are, it is not very likely that we are going to achieve them. One of the themes Tom Peters developed early in his writing was the importance of consistency in purpose: having the calendars, the language, what gets measured, and what gets talked about—all focus on what the organization is trying to achieve.[46] It is the same with individuals; to the extent that each interaction, in each meeting, in each conference, is oriented toward the same objective, the achievement of that objective is more likely.

Once you have a goal in mind, it is necessary to diagnose who is important in getting your goal accomplished. You must determine the patterns of dependence and interdependence among these people and find out how they are likely to feel about what you are trying to do. As part of this diagnosis, you also need to know how events are likely to unfold, and to estimate the role of power and influence in the process. In getting things accomplished, it is critical to have a sense of the game being played, the players, and what their positions are. One can get badly injured playing football in a basketball uniform, or not knowing the offense from the defense. I have seen, all too often, otherwise intelligent and successful managers have problems because they did not recognize the political nature of the situation, or because they were blindsided by someone whose position and strength they had not anticipated.

Once you have a clear vision of the game, it is important to ascertain the power bases of the other players, as well as your own potential and actual sources of power. In this way you can determine your relative strength, along with the strength of other players. Understanding the sources of power is critical in diagnosing what is going to happen in an organization, as well as in preparing yourself to take action.

Finally, you will want to consider carefully the various strategies, or, to use a less grand term, the tactics that are available to you, as well as those that may be used by others involved in the process. These tactics help in using power and influence effectively, and can also help in countering the use of power by others.

Power is defined here as the potential ability to influence behavior, to change the course of events, to overcome resistance, and to get people to do things that they would not otherwise do.[47] Politics and influence are the processes, the actions, the behaviors through which this potential power is utilized and realized.

The next two chapters in the first section of this book provide some help both in diagnosing the extent to which situations are going to involve the use of power and in figuring out who the major political actors are and what their points of view are likely to be. The second section of the book has a series of chapters directed at answering the question, where does power come from, and why are some units and people more powerful than others? Implicitly, this section will also help the reader figure out how to get more power, if that is desired. The third section considers the strategies and tactics through which power and influence are used. We need to know not only where power comes from, but how it is employed. The final section of the book addresses issues of power dynamics—and particularly how power, once gained, is lost. It also examines the consequences of power, both positive and negative, for organizations and the vital and necessary role of power in the process of implementation and change. The final summary draws much of this material together by giving some examples of people who used power successfully, and others who did not.

2

When Is Power Used?

Although power plays an important part in organizational activity, not all decisions and actions within an organization involve power to the same extent, nor are conflicts of power equally common in every organization. It is important to be able to recognize and diagnose the context if you are to implement your plans effectively. Not understanding the degree to which the situation is politicized may cause a person either to use power and influence when it is unnecessary, and thereby violate behavioral norms as well as waste resources, or to underestimate the extent to which power needs to be employed, and fail in the task of implementation.

An example of the failure to manage politics and use power skillfully is provided by Xerox. The corporation realized that it had missed exploiting the personal computer technology it had invented, that the Palo Alto Research Center was really a treasure trove of ideas, and that there was a gap between great research and the development of a marketable product. In an attempt to commercialize PARC technology more effectively, Xerox established the Express project, a co-development effort with Syntex, a pharmaceutical company. A team of researchers, working with marketing and product development personnel, as well as with the customer, Syntex, set out to develop a system designed to meet the needs of the pharmaceutical industry, and to do it rapidly.

The task was viewed, for the most part, as one of technical

coordination, in which the major challenges were to find the right organizational structure and to create a common perspective on the development effort. But the effort was highly politicized, in part because of its high visibility. Departments maneuvered for position, and this political maneuvering was neither well recognized nor well managed.

Marketing did not get involved early on, in part because it was understaffed, and in part because it did not view the co-production effort as critical—this was just an experiment, after all. When the project attained high visibility and it became clear that upper management was very interested in its outcome, marketing decided to get involved. Having come in late, it had to do something to justify its importance—otherwise, it might lose out in future efforts of this type. So with the project already well under way, marketing conducted a study of the product's ability to be sold more broadly to the rest of the pharmaceutical industry, and also put together a business plan to evaluate the product's financial attractiveness. The co-production group had already done both of these tasks. However, the marketing group used different assumptions about market penetration and margins (even though the co-production group had used some estimates originally supplied by marketing) and, naturally, came to different conclusions. The marketing group, although late into the fray, had the power of its legitimacy and presumed expertise—after all, who knows more about markets than marketing? The marketing people convinced a group of higher corporate executives, already nervous because of the unusual nature of the project (an interdisciplinary team co-developing a project with a customer), that the effort should be stopped before more money was spent. The incident shows that the political nature of the new product development and innovation process was not fully apprehended or successfully managed at Xerox. Not being aware of the importance of power and its use in the context, the project champions lost the project.

This chapter explores the conditions under which power is more or less important in organizational life, and the implications of power for our own career management activities. Finding a position in which the requirements for exercising power are compatible with our interests and abilities is crucial for our individual success and for the success of the projects we sponsor.[1]

OCCURRENCE OF POWER
AND INFLUENCE ACTIVITIES

There is some limited empirical evidence that can help set the framework for a discussion of the conditions under which power is used. The evidence comes primarily from two types of studies: examinations of actual decision making, and surveys of managers and executives about their perceptions of power and influence activities in their organizations.

A study of some 33 purchase decisions in 11 firms provides useful background information on the importance of influence in decisions of this type.[2] The study revealed that, first of all, in 27 of the 33 decisions, there was some disagreement during the decision-making process that required resolution. It also turned out that the more important the decision, the more people involved in it. For decisions of moderate or major importance, almost 20 people on average were involved, while for decisions of less significance, an average of only eight people were involved. With the relatively large number of people involved in a major decision, it is scarcely surprising that differences of opinion emerge. But the real significance of the number is this: think about the task of trying to affect a decision in which 20 or so people are involved. It will clearly be important to carefully map the political terrain, understand the points of view, and spend time and effort on the process. With a smaller number of people involved, one's attempts at influence can be more ad hoc and still have some chance of success.

From a survey of 428 graduates of a Canadian business school, we learn what types of decisions are perceived to most involve power and influence.[3] In Table 2-1, we see that interdepartmental coordination, promotion and transfer decisions, and decisions about facilities and equipment allocation were thought by many respondents to be highly involved with power. By contrast, work appraisals, hiring decisions, personnel policies, and grievances and complaints were less involved with power.

Table 2-1

Survey Responses about What Organizational Level and
What Decisions Most Involve the Use of Power

Situations	% of Respondents Saying That Situation Always or Frequently Involves the Use of Power
Interdepartmental Coordination	68.4
Promotions and Transfers	59.5
Facilities and Equipment Allocation	49.2
Grievances and Complaints	31.6
Personnel Policies	28.0
Hiring	22.5
Work Appraisals	21.5

Amount of Political Behavior at Various Levels

Level	Mean Amount of Use of Power
	(3 = always; 2 = frequently; 1 = rarely; 0 = never)
Top Management	1.22
Middle Management	1.07
Lower Management	.73

Source: Gandz and Murray (1980), pp. 242, 243.

The same survey provides some interesting information about the amount of power and influence required at various hierarchical levels. This is also displayed in Table 2-1. Not surprisingly, the data show that there is a more political climate, involving the more frequent use of power, at the higher organizational levels.

Another study interviewed three managers in each of 30 organizations, including the chief personnel or human resource officer, the chief executive officer, and one lower-level manager.[4] The data from that study permit us to rank both functional areas and situations in terms of the frequency with which power and influence are used. These rankings are displayed in Table 2-2.

Table 2-2 shows that marketing, sales, and the board of directors are the three areas in which power is most used; by contrast, production and accounting and finance are functional areas in which power is less important. In terms of the

Table 2-2

What Functions and What Decisions Most Involve
the Use of Power

Functional Area	Amount of Organizational Politics
Marketing Staff	4.27
Board of Directors	3.88
Sales	3.74
Manufacturing Staff	3.05
Personnel	3.01
Purchasing	2.67
Research and Development	2.62
Accounting and Finance	2.40
Production	2.01

Type of Decision	Amount of Organizational Politics
Reorganizations	4.44
Personnel Changes	3.74
Budget Allocations	3.56
Purchase of Major Items	2.63
Establishing Individual Performance Standards	2.39
Rules and Procedures	2.31

Note: Responses are to the question, "How frequent is the occurrence of organizational politics?" Answers range from 1 = "very low" to 5 = "very high."
Source: Madison et al., pp. 88, 90.

importance of power in various situations, reorganizations, personnel changes, and resource allocations entail greater use of power, while establishing individual performance standards and changing rules and procedures involve power and political activity less frequently.

All of these data together suggest that power is more important in major decisions, such as those made at higher organizational levels and those that involve crucial issues like reorganizations and budget allocations; for domains in which performance is more difficult to assess such as staff rather than line production operations; and in instances in which there is likely to be uncertainty and disagreement. We need to understand why these conditions seem to be associated with the use of power and influence. In exploring this subject, we will also discover some of the nuances of power and influence processes in organizations.

INTERDEPENDENCE

Power is used more frequently under conditions of moderate interdependence. With little or no interdependence, there is little or no need to develop power or exercise influence. By the same token, when interdependence is great, people have incentives to work together, forge common goals, and coordinate their activities. If they ignore these incentives, then their organization or group is likely to fail.

My colleague Jerry Salancik and I have defined interdependence as follows:

> Interdependence is the reason why nothing comes out quite the way one wants it to. Any event that depends on more than a single causal agent is an outcome based on interdependent agents. . . . interdependence exists whenever one actor does not entirely control all of the conditions necessary for the achievement of an action or for obtaining the outcome desired from the action.[5]

The essence of organizations is interdependence, and it is not news that all of us need to obtain the assistance of others in order to accomplish our jobs. What is news is that when interdependence exists, our ability to get things done requires us to develop power and the capacity to influence those on whom we depend. If we fail in this effort—either because we don't recognize we need to do it or because we don't know how—we will fail to accomplish our goals.

In the first chapter, we saw that Xerox's Palo Alto Research Center invented the first personal computer, the Alto, and also made "the first graphics-oriented monitor, the first hand-held 'mouse' inputting device simple enough for a child, the first word processing program for nonexpert users, and the first local area communications network, the first object-oriented programming language, and the first laser printer."[6] There are, of course, a number of reasons why Xerox failed to capitalize commercially on its inventive technology, but one source of difficulty was the relationship of

PARC personnel to the rest of Xerox. Bringing a new product to market requires the interdependent activity of many parts of the organization; this interdependence was not recognized at PARC, and even when it was recognized, the people involved did not see the need to develop power and influence. It was presumed that the magnificence of the technology would speak for itself and compel the development and introduction of successful products.

PARC was physically removed from the rest of Xerox—the Xerox of Rochester, New York and Stamford, Connecticut. PARC researchers had a healthy dose of arrogance, which led them to cultivate a we/they attitude toward the rest of Xerox, including SDS, the computer company that Xerox had purchased to help it enter the computer business:

> "PARC suffered from a whole lot of arrogance," remarks Bert Sutherland, one of a series of managers of PARC's Systems Science Laboratory. "If you didn't understand automatically, you were 'stupid.' It's hard to get a good hearing that way."[7]

By not appreciating the interdependence involved in a new product launch and the skills required to manage that interdependence, PARC researchers lost out on their ambition to change the world of computing, and Xerox missed some important economic opportunities.

It is especially important to develop power and influence when the people with whom you are interdependent have a different point of view than you, and thus cannot be relied upon to do what you would want. Thus, for example, a study of the process of selecting a dean in 40 colleges located in large state universities found that the greater the interdependence, the greater the amount of political activity on the part of the faculty.[8] However, when interdependent faculty were in agreement, there was less political activity. The study indicates that interdependence increases the need for exercising influence, but, of course, the exercise of influence is important primarily when those with whom you are interdependent are not going to do what you want anyway.

Interdependence helps us understand the evidence presented in Tables 2-1 and 2-2, which show where power is most used in organizations. There is more interdependence at higher levels in the organization, where tasks are less likely to be either simple or self-contained.[9] There is more likely to be interdependence in staff positions, in which getting things done almost inevitably requires obtaining the cooperation of others in line management. Interdepartmental coordination is obviously a situation of extreme interdependence, and decisions about reorganizations typically involve a large number of units. Functional units also vary in their interdependence with other units, but it is often the case that sales and marketing stand between engineering or product development, on the one hand, and manufacturing or production on the other.

Resource Scarcity

Interdependence results from many things, including the way in which tasks are organized. One factor that is critical in affecting the nature and the amount of interdependence is the scarcity of resources. Slack resources reduce interdependence, while scarcity increases it. As an example, consider the case of promotions. If an organization is growing rapidly and there are many promotional opportunities, the competition for promotions will be less intense. Individuals will feel that their chance for promotion depends mainly on their own performance, rather than on the performance of their co-workers. If, however, the organization stops growing and promotion opportunities decline, candidates find themselves in a so-called "zero sum game," in which each person's gain is another's loss. What happens to me in the contest for promotion is now much more contingent on what happens to my competitors, and thus, the degree of interdependence is greater.

This example illustrates why most people prefer to be in situations of plentiful resources. Not only is each person's chance for obtaining what he or she desires increased, but interdependence is reduced and there is, therefore, less need to develop power and influence in the situation. Since many, although not all, people find the task of developing power and exercising influence difficult or uncomfortable, they prefer situations with as little interdependence as possible.

A study at the University of Illinois explored the effect of power on the allocation of four resources that varied both in terms of their scarcity and their importance to the various academic departments.[10] The study indicated that, according to every measure of departmental power employed, departmental power was most strongly related to the distribution of the most scarce resources, and least strongly related to the least scarce resources. Indeed, departmental power negatively predicted the allocation of the least scarce resources, once objective criteria were statistically controlled. The most straightforward interpretation of this result is that the powerful departments, having obtained a disproportionate share of those resources that were scarcest, gave the losers in the struggle, as a partial payoff, a disproportionate share of the resources that were not really contested anyway.

There is other evidence consistent with the argument that scarcity increases the use of power in organizational decision situations. A study at the University of Minnesota examined the allocation of budgets to academic departments over time.[11] The study found that there appeared to be a greater effect of departmental power on resource allocations at times when resources were scarcer. Another study examined resource allocations to academic departments on two University of California campuses.[12] Between 1967 and 1975, on one campus the total budget increased 52% and 11.9% of the faculty positions were lost, while on the second campus, the budget increased by almost 80% and faculty positions actually grew slightly (by .4%). The study observed that departmental power was more strongly associated with budget allocations on the campus facing scarcer resources.[13]

We can also see that in the interviews reported in Table 2-2, budget allocations were considered among the most political of decisions. To the extent that most organizations customarily face scarce rather than plentiful resources, it is not surprising that the allocation of these resources involves the use of power and influence.

DIFFERENCES IN POINT OF VIEW

The fact that people are interdependent is not sufficient by itself to create the use of power and influence in organizations.

After all, the players on sports teams are interdependent, but we seldom see them stopping to negotiate with each other while the clock is running. If everyone has the same goals and shares the same assumptions about how to achieve those goals, there will be a minimum of conflict. With consensus about what to do and how to do it, there is no need to exercise influence or develop the power to affect others, since they will do what you want in any event.[14]

But agreement about how to do it is the key. Goals alone are not a reliable index of political activity in a given situation. At first glance, one might think that goals are fundamental to all action, and that disagreement about goals inevitably leads to the use of power and influence. Although there is no comprehensive evidence on this point, observation suggests that it is not invariably true. There is often intense political activity in business firms, in which there is presumably shared agreement about the goal of making a profit. And, there are frequently cordial compromises in the world of governmental politics, where goals are inconsistent but deals can be struck in which the same means are employed to reach several ends.

The greater the task specialization in the organization, the more likely there will be disagreements. This is simply because, when work is divided into different specialties and units, it is more likely that the organization will have people whose differences in background and training will cause them to take different views of the situation. Lawyers are trained to see the world in one way, engineers another, and accountants yet another. Moreover, holding a particular position in an organization causes one to see the world through the information that comes with that position. Marketers get data on sales and market share, production folks on manufacturing costs and inventory levels. Moreover, different positions often have different incentives—sales maximization, cost minimization, innovation, meeting budgets—and these various incentives provide reasons to see the world differently. The aphorism I often use to describe this situation is: where you stand depends on where you sit.

David Halberstam's history of Ford Motor Company vividly illustrates how education and functional background can condition the ways in which people view their environment.[15] The conflict at Ford (and at other automobile companies as well) between finance and engineering was, at its heart, a conflict about how to view the world. Engineers fundamentally see cars and engines as technological challenges, as things to be built. They are interested in developing a technological advantage over their competitors and in being the first to introduce new features. They want to design and build cars that have elements of engineering excellence. Finance analyzes cars less in terms of their aesthetics or their engineering wizardry than in financial terms such as payback period, return on investment, and the amount of capital required to launch new car models or to introduce new technologies of engines or transmissions. The two groups look at the same project from different perspectives, and therefore come, in many instances, to very different conclusions. Ford developed front-wheel drive and numerous other engineering innovations, but it was often one of the last automobile companies to actually put these innovations into its cars. Introducing a totally new transmission and redesigning the car accordingly cost a lot of money, and, unable to prove that such expenditures would produce enough additional revenues to make them profitable, engineering often lost out, at least in the 1960s and 1970s, to finance.

Serious disagreements among people with differing points of view are more likely to emerge in the absence of clear objectives or in the absence of an external threat or competition sufficient to cause subunits to work together. In the 1960s and 1970s, General Motors dominated the automobile industry. It is hard to believe now, but in the late 1950s GM's biggest concern was antitrust—whether it would be broken up, not whether it could withstand competition. The lack of external competitive pressure, along with its large size and differentiated structure, produced an environment that was prone to organizational politics. John De Lorean noted, for instance, that "objective criteria were not always used to evaluate an executive's performance."[16] What seemed to be valued more were being a good team player, not standing out too much, and being loyal to one's boss. De Lorean provided many details of the extremes to which people went to prove loyalty to their boss: hiring a crane and removing a hotel window so that a refrigerator, too large to get in the door, could be placed in the hotel room of a GM executive who liked late-night snacks; picking up their boss at the airport; organizing retinues of people to meet and accompany the boss on tours; finding out the culinary likes and dislikes of their boss, and making sure that every need or desire was accommodated.

The politicking that occurs in the absence of real competitive pressure rarely promotes the success of the organization. It is, consequently, not surprising that political leaders, whether of nations or organizations, like to find a common enemy or an external threat that they can use to make organizational citizens put aside their differences and work together more effectively. For Apple Computer, for a long while, this was IBM, for the Japanese copier companies at the beginning, it was Xerox, and for U.S. automobile companies today, it is the Japanese. It is not coincidental that cross-functional communication and coordination in U.S. automobile firms increased as the Japanese competition intensified.

IMPORTANCE OF THE ISSUE

Power is a valuable resource—as such, it is not used wantonly. Rather, those who have power typically conserve it for important issues. In the study I mentioned earlier, which described the effect of resource scarcity on the use of power to allocate those resources, it was impossible to estimate separately the effect that the importance of the decision had on the use of power.[17] Not surprisingly, scarcity and importance were correlated—if something is important, it will be sought by many, making it scarce.

It is necessary to recognize that importance has both a substantive and a symbolic component. We are sometimes perplexed as to why so much effort and energy are expended over seemingly unimportant decisions such as the location or size of one's office. When Pacific Telephone began building office facilities outside the city of San Francisco and closing down some of its buildings in the city, many executives spent a lot of time trying to ensure that they would remain in the headquarters building rather than be banished to the suburbs. As we will see, the appearance of power can actually provide power, and thus these efforts to maintain the symbols of power are significant.

Because important decisions activate the processes of power and influence, and because at least some people find power and influence aversive, it is not at all uncommon to observe organizations or subunits avoiding important issues. For example, in a study of the *New York Times*, Argyris described how a decision about a new feature for the newspaper was delayed for almost four years.[18] The management of the newspaper was afraid to open up certain political issues, such as who would be in control and who would gain and lose space in the paper. To avoid these confrontations, it simply delayed making the decision and introducing the feature. A study of political reporting at the *Los Angeles Times* observed a similar phenomenon.[19] The newspaper had difficulty coordinating political reporting, particularly of national campaigns, since it was typically split between the national and metropolitan desks. A proposal to create a new, political desk, which would have overall responsibility for campaign coverage, was delayed because of conflicts over space in the paper and status. A political desk was finally established, but it was disbanded as soon as that particular election was over. Reluctance to confront territorial issues caused the Los Angeles paper to avoid an innovation that might have enhanced the coordination and quality of its political reporting.

SOME IMPLICATIONS FOR CAREER PLANNING

On Wednesday, September 1, 1976, W. Richard Goodwin, president and chief executive officer of Johns-Manville Corporation, was forced to resign. While preparing to attend a board meeting in New York, he was surprised by three outside directors who told him that the nine outside directors on the company's board wanted him out. This event, predating Manville's difficulties with asbestos litigation and its subsequent bankruptcy, stunned many, including Goodwin. Under his leadership, the corporation's revenues had risen 91% between 1970 and 1975, and net profits had increased 115% between 1970 and 1974. During the first half of 1976, earnings had set a company record.[20] The two inside directors on the board were surprised by the move. Goodwin was apparently well liked by senior corporate management, and he had done a number of things, including moving the company's headquarters to Denver, to give the organization new life.

Goodwin's rise to the position provides some clues as to why he did not keep his job longer. He received his Ph.D. in experimental psychology (sometimes called "rat psychology" because of its reliance on experiments to uncover principles of learning) at Stanford University. He worked 10 years for the RAND Corporation and its spin-off, the System Development Corporation. He was running his own consulting firm and teaching an evening course for New York University's business school when he was retained by Manville to provide help on a strategic planning effort. The effort was so successful that he was offered the full-time position of vice president for corporate planning. Some 20 months after assuming that position, he was appointed president. If we consider Goodwin's career, we see someone who is clearly very smart and highly educated, but who has spent almost his entire working life either in situations in which he worked alone or for himself, or on tasks (such as the design and software development for the Strategic Air Command's command and control system) that had a high intellectual component. Nothing in his background, experience, or training prepared Goodwin for the task of managing relations with his board of directors, or for the rough-and-tumble world of large company politics. John Schroeder, vice chairman of Morgan Guaranty Trust Company at the time and one of the outside directors who met with Goodwin to tell him he should resign, made the same point:

> "We had here a fellow who had no experience working with a group of people who held ultimate responsibility for the company," explains Schroeder. "He was used to working as an individual before he joined Johns-Manville. . . . he had trouble working with a board."[21]

Contrast the situation of Goodwin at Johns-Manville with that of William Agee at Bendix. In 1981, Agee was also in a struggle with his board of directors, in spite of excellent financial performance. The outcome, however, was somewhat different: "Before Purcell [a director] departed [in August], Agee engineered the resignations of three other outside Bendix directors in a maneuver that wiseacres at the company's headquarters in Southfield, Michigan came to call 'the midnight massacre.'"[22] Agee graduated from the Harvard Business School and, prior to joining Bendix, had risen rapidly through the financial organization at Boise Cascade. Both his training and his experience left him better prepared for successfully coping with organizational power struggles.

One of the reasons why general management may not be so general—in terms of the ability of high-level managers to move from one organization to another—is that power dynamics differ across oganizations, and certainly across types of organizations. Aptitudes and skills developed in one setting may leave one unprepared for successfully operating in an entirely different context. High-level corporate executives, for instance, often assume deanships of business schools. In two fairly well-known instances, the results were actually quite disastrous. In one instance, the head of Conrail became the dean at Cornell's business school, and in the other instance, the chief executive officer of a major manufacturing company, widely considered to be a model of effectiveness, took on the deanship at another leading business school. In each case, the executives had come from organizations in which the use of hierarchical authority was more prevalent. Neither had any particular experience dealing with a more collegial, or peer form of governance. In one instance, the person behaved strongly, thereby offending the faculty and being driven out; in the other, the person was overwhelmed by the administrative and political complexities and was ineffective in getting things accomplished. But in both cases, the new deans lacked the ability to get things done, because neither was skilled or experienced at the particular forms of power required by the situation.

These examples illustrate the more general point: your success in an organization depends not only on your intelligence, industriousness, and luck, but also on the match between your political skills and what is required in the position you occupy. Individuals have different skills as well as aptitudes for developing and using power. For some, such activities come naturally—they enjoy it, and are good at it.

For others, the idea of engaging in informal influence and the task of worrying about sources of power and how to develop them is anathema. It is not surprising, then, that people rarely prosper in their jobs if their skills and aptitudes don't match the requirements of the situation.[23]

My experience is that most people are neither very self-reflective about this particular dimension of the person-job match nor very realistic in guiding their actions on the basis of it. Most people search for positions in which their particular intellectual competencies and interests will be useful and important. But they seldom analyze jobs in terms of power and influence.

Moreover, it is not the case that jobs that require lots of political aptitude necessarily pay more. Many jobs that primarily entail individual, analytic effort, including those in fields such as consulting, tax law, and investment banking, pay extraordinarily well. The issue is thus not one of trading off an uncomfortable situation for a high salary, but rather, simply of finding a place in which one can do one's best.

3

Diagnosing Power and Dependence

To be successful in getting things done in organizations, it is critical that you be able to diagnose the relative power of the various participants and comprehend the patterns of interdependence. One needs to know and understand not only the game, but also the players. After studying power and influence in a British organization that was purchasing a computer, Andrew Pettigrew observed that "an accurate perception of the power distribution in the social arena in which he lives is . . . a necessary prerequisite for the man seeking powerful support for his demands."[1] As we will see in the next section of the book, which treats sources of power, knowledge of the power distribution is itself an important source of power. A study of power in a small entrepreneurial firm found that the individuals within the firm who had more accurate information about the actual network of advice-giving and influence were more powerful.[2] A study of resource allocation to academic departments at the University of Illinois came to the same conclusion: namely, that to the extent department heads had more accurate perceptions of the power distribution within the university, they could obtain more resources for their departments. This positive effect of knowledge on the ability to obtain budgetary resources was particularly important for the heads of less powerful departments. It was these individuals who most needed to know the power distribution in order to form coalitions and effectively deploy what leverage they did possess.[3]

There are three tasks required to assess power distributions in an organization. First, the relevant subunits or subdivisions must be identified. Then, one must come up with some indicators of power and apply them to the identified units to assess their relative power ranking. Both these tasks require judgment and experience, as well as knowledge of the particular situation, but there are some general ideas that can help. Finally, after units and their relative power are identified, the patterns of dependence and interdependence among them must be considered in order to determine an effective course of action. This chapter covers all three of these tasks.

DEFINING RELEVANT POLITICAL SUBUNITS

Suppose you had been hired by E.F. Hutton in the early 1980s, and you wanted to understand the political structure of the organization. The first task would be to determine the most important political divisions or subdivisions—most important in terms of giving you the ability to understand what is going on in the organization. At Hutton, as in many other organizations, there were a number of options. One set of subdivisions could be drawn by geography, showing where the various offices and branches were located. Another set of subdivisions could be drawn by age or tenure in the organization, distinguishing older and longer-tenured employees from those who were younger and more recently hired. Yet another set of subdivisions might have followed departmental lines, dividing the firm into political groupings such as retail brokerage, investment banking, and the various corporate administrative units. Yet another way of cutting up the organization would have made only two subdivisions: headquarters and administrative on the one hand, the revenue-producing line organizations on the other. There could also be political units defined by rank—for instance, officers of the corporation, managers, and rank-and-file workers. And, in organizations more demographically heterogeneous than Hutton used to be, subdivisions might be defined by gender or ethnic groups, or, perhaps, by academic background and training.

In Hutton's case, several of these ways of carving up the organization were relevant, depending on both the time and the issue. In terms of promotion to the very top management positions, religious subdivisions were once crucial, at least for the first cut:

> Throughout the firm's history, an unwritten rule had barred Jews from holding down the top spot. Sylvan Coleman had evaded the rule by camouflaging his Jewish identity under a false name and a membership in the Episcopal Church. . . . "There was a streak of anti-Semitism there that you had to be blind to miss," says Goldberg, now a partner with the brokerage firm Neuberger and Berman.[4]

But Hutton was characterized by other divisions as well, such as geography:

> The East vs. West schism that had lain beneath the surface for years grew more apparent when the Wellin [president] regime launched a burst of retail expansion. . . . Hutton's "California mafia" had always cheered for bold expansion of the retail network, but in this case the pins on the map were dotting the East Coast rather than the West. This, they feared, would further dilute their power base.[5]

These religious, ethnic, and geographical divisions were most important in Hutton when retail brokerage, its traditional strength, still held unchallenged sway over the company. As the 1980s progressed, the retail department came into conflict with new activities in investment banking, public finance, and capital markets. Some conflict arose over the salaries paid to bring in people to staff these new areas. Rivalry between departments over which of them was more important was also a source of discord. For instance, the head of capital markets said that "he wasn't going to take a single position to accommodate the retail system unless they paid him to do it."[6] Finally, in the waning days of the firm, when many in the field felt the company was squandering its resources on a fancy new corporate headquarters and too much management overhead, the relevant political division was between the field and headquarters.

How do we decide which of the many ways of drawing the political map is the most appropriate? The first step to recognize is that there is no final answer to this question, even within a single organization, let alone across different organizations. The second is to recognize the importance of categories and labels for understanding social behavior. We all interact with others in our environment at least partly on the basis of categories. The principal function of categorization is to systematize the environment and thus to facilitate action.

Categorization has profound consequences for intergroup interaction. For example, persons sharing a category will be judged more similar to each other, and persons in different categories will be considered more different than they would if the categories were not known.[7] Categorization also affects an individual's self-image. Brewer and Kramer, reviewing the literature on intergroup behavior, concluded that "group membership influences the attributions we make about our own and others' behavior, intentions, and values."[8] The question not answered fully in the existing research on categorization is, which of the various categories predominate?

What category is meaningful depends on the political question at issue. Consider, for example, the recurrent bargaining in professional sports between the players, represented by unions and agents, and the owners. Age and ability come to define categories in this context. Older players want to obtain long-term, no-cut contracts that insure them against both injury and skill loss, each of which is correlated with age. Younger players are more concerned about minimum salary levels and the provision to negotiate raises through some form of free agency as soon as possible. Star performers are less concerned about minimum salaries and more about freedom and control over movement among teams, while average performers are more concerned about pension rights and benefits and other forms of nonwage compensation.

The best way to identify the meaningful political categories for a given issue is to choose categories that are: 1) as inclusive as possible and 2) internally homogeneous with respect to the issues under study. Identifying the political categories is, in other words, a problem of clustering, in which the criterion is to cluster people together to maximize their homogeneity in opinions and preferences that are relevant to the questions being studied. This involves the exercise of judgment, to discern whether the differences between given sets of people are important enough to justify considering them as separate political groups.

Another, more formal method for identifying political categories is to use a social network analysis, in which ties among social actors are explicitly measured and the structure of such ties is uncovered using one of the available network analysis algorithms. In both the formation and analysis of political groups, interests are not the only things that are important—social ties are too. At times, political interests coincide with friendship patterns, but when friendship or social ties are at odds with self-interest, often the social and friendship ties will be the better predictors of action.

Categories are not just accidental, but are often purposely created. Thus, for instance, some organizations have fewer hierarchical and horizontal distinctions among individuals, while others have more. Such distinctions are created by giving individuals job titles connoting rank, or specific occupation, naming separate subunits, locating subunits in separate places, and paying people differentially. One of the first things the management of New United Motors did when it took over what was formerly the Fremont plant of General Motors was to negotiate with the United Auto Workers to eliminate most separate job classifications. Moreover, plant management gave up its dining room and ate with the employees, and layers of management were eliminated. Doing away with the signifiers that separate people into distinct categories provides obvious advantages in terms of worker motivation and commitment. It encourages people to take a more common and cooperative point of view and therefore reduces the amount of conflict and politicking that occurs.

Categories may also be more or less salient depending on the actions that individuals take as part of a political strategy. For Marxists to succeed, people have to see themselves in terms of their class position. For there to be a politics of gender, women must be convinced that what happens to them at work and in other social arenas is a consequence of their shared gender. In rivalries among departments, people are encouraged to see themselves according to structural categories—the retail division of Hutton, the Apple II division of Apple Computer, and so forth—and to minimize differences in rank, gender, or training. At other times, the political strategy entails creating the appearance of differentiation and divisions. When the owners negotiate with the players in professional sports, they try to divide the players by pay level, reminding the players that while they are all on strike, some are losing a lot more per day than others. Thus, the very question of the political consciousness of groups or units is often itself the object of influence strategies employed in political contests.

ASSESSING THE POWER OF SUBDIVISIONS

Power is not employed when there are no differences in perspective, or when no conflict exists. As a consequence, power is most readily diagnosed by looking at important decisions, which involve interdependent activity and which lead to disagreements. Such decisions may involve the allocation of scarce resources such as money, status, or jobs, or the strategic direction and focus of the organization.

The second general lesson to keep in mind when trying to diagnose the power of organizational actors is that power needs to be distinguished from foresight. If I know what is going to happen, and adopt that position as the one I favor, I may have great forecasting ability, but little power. Power means being able to get things one wants, against opposition—not predicting what is going to happen anyway and then advocating that outcome.

It is important, in assessing the power of organizational participants, to use multiple indicators or measures such as those described below. Any single instance, any single measure, is likely to be flawed in some way. However, by looking at multiple instances, and by considering many indicators of power, one can arrive at a fairly accurate estimate of the power of the subdivisions one has identified.

Reputational Indicators of Power

One way of finding out who has power in organizations is to ask people. A study of the power of the marketing, production, finance and accounting, and research and development units in 12 industrial firms asked people to rank the four departments in terms of how much power they had within the organization.[9] A study of the power of subunits in breweries in Canada used a similar but more elaborate interview and questionnaire procedure.[10] In studies of the power of academic departments at the University of Illinois and the University of California, department heads were asked how much power they thought various departments possessed.[11] Patchen's study of influence in purchasing decisions in 11 firms interviewed the people who had the most influence in the decision to acquire a particular product.[12]

The critical issue in the process of assessing power by asking people is whether this process produces reliable and valid information. More specifically, will all the people being questioned define and measure power in the same way? One indicator of the quality of the information produced is whether there is consensus among informants. In the University of Illinois study, department heads were asked to rate, on a seven-point scale, the power of all of the departments being studied. Only one department head even asked for a definition of what was meant by the concept of power. Although not all heads were familiar with all of the departments, and therefore did not answer for those with which they were unfamiliar, for those that were rated, there was enormous consistency in the responses. No department that was judged, overall, to be in the top third of the departments in terms of power was rated by a single individual as being lower than the top third. Similarly, no department that, overall, was rated in the bottom third in terms of power was rated by a single person as being higher than the bottom third. This consensus provides at least some evidence for a shared social definition of both the measurement and meaning of power.

One must also consider the reactivity of the process in determining whether the information is reliable. Does the act of asking itself produce the phenomenon being studied? As Polsby, a scholar of community power, has noted, when individuals are asked about the power of various social actors, "any response short of total unwillingness to answer will supply the researchers with a 'power elite' along the lines proposed by stratification theory."[13] There may not have been, in reality, differential power at the University of Illinois, but the appearance of differences in power may have been produced by the process of asking about it.

Another potential problem is that in asking about power,

one must assume that those being questioned are 1) knowledgeable about organizational power distributions and 2) willing to share that knowledge. Neither of these assumptions is infallibly correct. It is often the case that politically adept actors attempt to keep the extent of their power secret. This means that those most likely to be in the know, who also often happen to hold the most power, are precisely those with the least incentive to divulge what they know about the organization's power distribution. And, asking about power, particularly given societal norms about rationality, may get one labelled as a troublemaker or a Machiavellian. Consequently, reputational indicators of power are most readily used in highly politicized settings, in which power has greater visibility and in which discussing the topic is not off-limits.

Representational Indicators of Power

Reputational measures of power are not always reliable enough to be used as the sole method of obtaining information about power relationships. As I have noted, questions about power may be met with suspicion, and the people you question may not be able or willing to give accurate information about power in their organization. Also, reputational indicators of power and influence can be collected, with any accuracy, only contemporaneously, which means if you want to see how power and influence have shifted in the organization over time, you will need some other method.

Representational indicators of power show what political subdivisions are comparatively overrepresented in critical organizational roles such as membership on influential boards and committees or in key administrative or executive positions. As long as the backgrounds or affiliations of people can be identified from organizational records, one can use this information to assess power in organizations and how it has evolved over time.

Representational indicators are useful indices of power because some positions endow their occupants with specific and defined powers, whether it be control over resources, control over information, or formal decision-making authority.

In other words, the holders of some positions are given the ability to ratify or signify their power to the world at large. If we can identify critical roles in organizations, we can see who occupies those roles, and use this information to understand power distributions.

When the retail brokerage community lost power at E.F. Hutton, the change was visible in the highest-level administrative positions—the CEO no longer came from retail, and people from retail occupied fewer positions on the board of directors and other high-level administrative posts. When power at major public utilities shifted from engineering to finance and law, this was visible in the backgrounds of the top corporate officers, as well as in the composition of key organizational boards and committees. The rising importance of business skills in hospitals can be observed by noting that high-level hospital administrators are frequently either non-physicians or physicians who have additional training in business or hospital administration, and that hospital boards of directors increasingly consist of people with business and administrative skills, with proportionately fewer positions being occupied by other community groups. The power of academic departments in a university can be assessed by examining departmental representation on critical university committees such as those dealing with budgets and with promotions and appointments.[14]

Nor is the department the only political subdivision for which power can be diagnosed in this fashion. Representational indicators also provide useful information about age, rank, and training. At the University of Illinois in the early 1970s, assistant professors held all but one position on the elected executive committees of the four departments in the College of Commerce and Business Administration. By contrast, at Berkeley at the same time, committees were appointed by the dean, not elected, and assistant professors held no positions. These data provide some information about the relative power of various ranks and age groupings in the two settings. People will tell you that Apple Computer is (or at least was) a young company. That assertion can be empirically verified by looking at the ages of senior management in the firm. Are companies dominated by one school or another? One way of assessing the importance of educational background and training is to examine the backgrounds of the people who occupy key positions.

As a more detailed example, suppose you wanted to test your hunch that attorneys had gained power at electric and gas utilities in recent years, for instance, at Pacific Gas and Electric, the utility that serves northern California. Without asking anybody, you could obtain annual reports and count the number of attorneys in officer- and manager-level positions and determine how this count has changed over time. These data for PG&E are displayed in Table 3-1.

Table 3-1

Attorneys in Officer- and Manager-Level Positions
at Pacific Gas and Electric, 1950–1980

Year	CEO	President	Other Officers on Board of Directors	Exec. VP	VPs	Gen. Counsel	SR Counsel	Total
1950	0	0	0	0	1	1	1	3
1955	0	0	0	1	0	1	2	4
1960	0	0	0	1	0	1	2	4
1965	1	0	0	1	1	1	9	13
1970	0	0	1	1	2	0	9	13
1975	0	0	2	0	4	0	8	14
1980	1	0	0	5	3	0	9	18

Source: Annual reports for corresponding years.

The data indicate that between 1950 and 1960, nothing much changed in the governance of the company. But between 1960 and 1970, lawyers gained substantially more power in the corporation—power they held and expanded slightly during the 1970s. Moreover, one can observe that attorneys acquired power in two ways—first, by obtaining positions in the organization formerly held by engineers or operations personnel, and second, by having positions they would hold automatically, such as senior counsel, expanded in number. Comparative data on other utilities would permit one to see to what extent the process taking place at PG&E was repeated elsewhere. And, of course, one could do a similar type of analysis in any organization for which one had the data.

Diagnosing Power by Observing Its Consequences

Power is used to take action, and one way to determine who has power is to observe who benefits, and to what extent, from organizational actions, particularly decisions or actions that are contested. Of course, it is rarely in the interest of either the winners or the losers of organizational power struggles to make their success or failure known. For those who have fared poorly in the influence contest, the announcement of their failure would only confirm their loss of stature and, by this very confirmation, make it more permanent. To lose a struggle is to lose face, and unless the publication of such a loss can be used to mobilize allies, there is little to be gained by revealing it. Even the more influential, who have fared well in the contest for resources, have little to gain by making their success public. It is considered unseemly to boast, and more important, if others see how well you are faring, they may unite against you, or at a minimum, demand some of the spoils. Thus, it is often the case that the results of organizational influence are kept secret, which makes diagnosing power by this means more difficult.

Nevertheless, many of the results of organizational power and politics are visible. Interestingly, salaries may be known, particularly as they differ across units. A student of mine once received three offers from different departments of a large, consumer products company. The offers differed substantially, there being about a 50% difference between the largest and the smallest. Although this occurrence may not have made the organization's human resource staff very happy, the student had a nice, concrete example of the differences in power across the units in question. At E.F. Hutton in the 1980s, when investment banking was gaining power at the expense of the traditional retail side of the house, this shift was reflected in salaries:

> Hutton's finance department was hardly setting Wall Street on its ear, but that didn't stop executives in the department from . . . winning enormous salaries. For example, in 1984 Jim Lopp [in charge of corporate finance] earned $262,461 in salary and an $800,000 bonus, for a grand total of $1,062,461. At the same time Jerry Miller [in charge of the retail brokerage operation] was earning . . . $665,000.[15]

Salary can also help us to diagnose the relative power of various levels in the organization's hierarchy. Whisler et al. argued that the concentration of salary in an organization is a good surrogate measure of the concentration of power.[16] There is less concentration of power and authority in universities, in which the difference between the lowest- and highest-paid faculty member in a department is on the order of two to three times, compared to corporate environments where the differences approach 100 times. The insight of Whisler and his colleagues is a good one, and to the extent that salary data are available, it can help us understand the distribution of power across political subdivisions.

Salary differentials can likewise help us to understand more informal distributions of power within organizations. As the distribution of influence at Pacific Gas and Electric shifted from engineers to lawyers, this shift was reflected in the salaries paid. For instance, in 1982, lawyers with the title of vice president made, on average, $148,755, while engineers with vice presidential titles earned, on average, $110,018, according to documents filed with the California Public Utilities Commission. Furthermore, with only 90 lawyers out of 25,000 total employees in 1982, the number of lawyers in the upper salary brackets of PG&E exceeded the number of engineers in officer or manager positions within similar salary ranges and also exceeded the number with other backgrounds.

Some readers are probably thinking, salaries reflect the operation of market forces, so how can salaries tell us much about the distribution of power in an organization? The key is to compare salaries across organizations, to get a sense of the relative power of various groups. New MBAs earn, on average, more than graduates from bachelor's programs in business. But this difference is not constant across organizations, and in those settings in which MBAs earn comparatively more, it is likely that they have comparatively more influence and power as well. Business school faculty earn more than faculty in many of the humanities because of the comparative scarcity of business school faculty. But, again, this difference is not constant across settings—at the University of California at Berkeley, business faculty earn only slightly more than faculty in other social sciences, while at other universities (particularly private ones such as Harvard and Stanford), the difference is greater. If the inference is drawn that business schools have comparatively more power at those private universities, I would maintain that the inference is correct. In some universities, the football coach earns more than the university president. Although it doesn't mean that he necessarily has more power, it does reflect his comparative power, in contrast to more modestly paid football coaches in other schools. I recall talking to a colleague who was the NCAA faculty representative at Stanford and who participated in the hiring of a football coach. He noted that Stanford's comparatively lower salary made it difficult to attract some coaches. Why, I inquired, when coaches could earn additional income from doing television shows, advertising, product endorsements, speaking, and so forth, and when such earnings were often much larger than the official salary? The applicants knew that, my colleague replied, but they also understood that the comparative salary of the football coach (or the athletic director) at Stanford said something about the power and autonomy they would enjoy.

Salaries are, of course, not the only resources whose allocation can shed light on the power of various political units. The allocation of funds for expansion, capital budgets, operating budgets, and even titles can all be used to help assess which groups are more influential.

Symbols of Power

Although people often attempt to hide the extent to which power and influence have affected organizational decisions and actions, it is not always easy to hide the symbols of power. Such symbols can be used to gauge the distribution of power in the organization. For instance, I was making arrangements to meet a former student who at the time was the head of management development for a large California bank headquartered in San Francisco. I thought I knew where he was—in the named headquarters building. But he gave me another address, and I arrived at his office many blocks from headquarters in an older building. It was clear in an instant that at least at that time, training had very little power in the firm.

Physical space is one of the more readily discernible symbols of power. Some professional service firms have more egalitarian office arrangements, at least for the professional staff, reflecting the collegial interaction that characterizes their environments. But in many organizations, the size, location, and amenities of offices say something about the relative power of various groups. At Salomon Brothers, "the equity department wasn't on 41, the principal trading floor, but on the floor below. The fortieth floor had low ceilings, no windows, and the charm of an engine room."[17] Moreover, it was served by a separate bank of elevators. The Transamerica Pyramid is an even more striking physical manifestation of the corporate hierarchy, narrower at the top than at the bottom, with the highest-level executives occupying space higher up in the building.

Physical indicators of power include height in the structure, view, size of office, and office decoration. Indeed, some firms, to avoid continual haggling, have set policies and rules that translate status into office accoutrements. In one organization in San Francisco, managers above a certain rank were entitled to carpets on the floor; below that rank, they settled for linoleum. Some offices were shared. In one instance, when someone who was entitled to carpet moved out of an office and was replaced by someone who was not, the carpet for that half of the office was removed from the linoleum, so that each of the occupants could have the floor covering appropriate to his managerial rank. When I have told that story at various talks, I have had people from other organizations tell me that I must be talking about their firm—so apparently this type of practice is not rare. At PG&E, a friend visited the recently appointed manager of the organization development department in his new office. Several weeks later, when he visited again, he noticed that some of the more elaborate office furnishings had been removed, and that the office had been provided with a smaller, less imposing desk. The new manager had not come in with the same rank as his predecessor, and his status did not entitle him to the office furnishings of the person he had replaced.

We have seen that at PG&E during the 1960s and 1970s, attorneys were gaining power and engineers and operations personnel were losing it. This change in the power distribution had a physical manifestation as well. In the new corporate headquarters building, which was first occupied in 1971, the law department was given the floor just below that occupied by top management. By 1983, the corporation had moved all of its design engineering and drafting personnel from the general office to new space located outside of San Francisco in the suburbs. This further loss of status on the part of engineering resulted from the growing importance of the finance and regulatory staff, which required more space in the headquarters building.

Of course, symbols of hierarchical power are often conveyed by insignia, such as the ones used by the military or the airlines. Other symbols of power include corporate limousines, jets, country club memberships, and so forth. By determining what units or what ranks are entitled to these symbols of power, one can learn a lot about the relative status of various groups in the organization.

Using Multiple Indicators

Any single indicator of power may be misleading in a specific case. Salaries may reflect market forces rather than internal political dynamics, and corporate offices may have evolved unintentionally or be left over from a bygone era. Consequently, the best way to diagnose power in organizations is to use multiple indicators. For instance, to assess the relative standing of the power of various departments within a firm, one might consider the following indicators:

Departmental representation in general management positions; what proportion of all top-level managers are from that department.

Departmental representation on the board of directors.

Salary of the executive in charge of each department.

Starting salary offered to people in each department.

For positions in common across departments (e.g., secretaries), the salaries earned by people of comparable experience.

Is the department located in the headquarters building?

Where in the building the department is located, and the average size of offices for people working in the department.

Growth in personnel in each department in the recent past.

Level of the department's reporting in the formal structure.

Representation of the department on important interdepartmental

task forces, teams, and committees such as those involved in new
product development, capital budgeting, and strategic planning.
Rate of promotion for people in the department, compared to that
in other units.
Reputation for influence in the firm.
Allocation of the budget.

If you do this exercise in your own organization, you may
discover some interesting patterns. You are likely to find that
the various indicators are tightly correlated, although not perfectly correlated, and that a distinct pattern emerges of the
most influential subdivisions.

Assessing Power in Different Cultures

In diagnosing power cross-culturally, one must be careful
not to import, without question, the same indicators one
might use in the United States, or at least not to interpret
them in exactly the same way. Information provided by a
colleague in Japan, Kotaro Kuwada, nicely illustrates this
point. It is commonly known that salaries are more equal in
large Japanese corporations than they are in comparable U.S.
corporations. It is also the case that power in Japanese corporations is widely distributed. However, it does not necessarily follow that the less extreme salary differentials mean that
power is less concentrated as well.

In Japanese society, and in Japanese corporations, the appearance of equality is an important value, and references to
power and influence are taboo. In the United States, both
power and salary are related to the status and capability of
the individual. French and Raven noted that one source of
power was expert knowledge; in a study of influence in 33
purchase decisions in 11 organizations, expertise was the
second-most important source of influence.[18] However, in
Japanese organizations, power and salary distributions are
based on somewhat different criteria, and therefore are more
independent. Salary is determined largely by the age, length
of service, and specific task of the individual, with the differences based on task being quite small. Power, in Japanese
organizations as in American firms, is based on the expertise
of the individual. Consequently, it is often the case that an
older executive in a higher position, with less power and

expertise, will receive a higher salary than a younger person with more ability and more real power. Note that in this situation, the more senior executive is content with his salary and ranking because, even though he may have less power than he seems to have, he saves face. On the other hand, the more junior executive gets less salary but more effective power. Power and salary, rather than being correlated, are used to balance the exchange so that each feels relatively equal, although the equality is achieved in different ways.

The distribution of physical space is also quite equal in most Japanese organizations, and in a way analogous to the salary distribution; it can also hide the actual distribution of power. Space has a different meaning in Japanese organizations. In Japan, who a person is depends on the specific situation, especially on one's relationship with others. Sharing space with another person is thus a way to identify oneself. Although the shared space leads to good information-sharing among people, it is, in fact, the result, not the intended cause, of open office arrangements. The evidence suggests that the custom of setting up open offices arises first from the high cost of land and office space in Japan, and second, from the need to define one's own role and identity in terms of the relationship to others. Sharing space on an equal basis camouflages the real power distribution and maintains a sense of equality among participants, even if that equality is not real. And the open access to information that shared space provides makes it possible for those with power to gain access to more information without having to resort to formal authority.

The best way to diagnose power in Japanese corporations is not, therefore, to look at the formal distinctions conveyed by salary, rank, or office space. These are all quite equal, often based on age or seniority, and in many instances, they have been designed intentionally to mask the real distribution of power. Rather, particularly because of the importance of consultation in decision making, the best diagnostic tool is the pattern of interaction among individuals involved in the decision. Who gets consulted, at what point, and with what result provides information about where power resides.

The cross-cultural differences shown here between Japan and the United States reinforce the importance of using multiple indicators of power. They also show the necessity of understanding the societal and organizational cultural distinctions around status and power before diagnosing power in organizations.

Diagnosing Patterns of Dependence and Interdependence

Knowing the power of various organizational members and subunits is important, and so is understanding whose help you need in order to achieve your goals. Failing to properly account for patterns of interdependence can result in grave difficulties for both you and your organization.

Successful sales representatives whose customers are other organizations recognize the importance of diagnosing the political structures within the organizations to which they sell. In order to target key decision makers in the purchase process, one must first be able to recognize them. For example, Xerox Corporation trains its account representatives to identify who makes technical recommendations within the customer organization, as well as who has influence over capital budgeting decisions. A technical innovator or a particular department within the customer's organization may want a particular piece of equipment, but the sales representative realizes that he or she must convince the person who allocates the funds for the equipment. In order to do this, successful account managers try to assess who the budget allocator depends on for advice, and to work through these influential advisers to turn the decision in Xerox's favor.

The importance of being able to effectively diagnose patterns of dependence and networks of power was also evident in the Express project. In "co-producing" innovation with a customer organization, Xerox needed to diagnose patterns of interdependence in order to understand fully how the introduction of technological change would reverberate through that organization. Such a diagnosis was also important to identify who needed to be convinced of the effort's value and to obtain the necessary funding and support in the customer's firm.

Much like sales representatives, co-producers have to be sensitive to the critical decision makers and dependencies within the customer's organization. Working at the wrong level, dealing with problems considered unimportant by those responsible for funding the project, or not being sensitive to the effects of the project on power dynamics can doom a project to failure.

Such problems were endemic in the Express project, in which Xerox worked with Syntex on a product development effort to get new technology to the marketplace quickly. The co-production group failed to adequately diagnose patterns of interdependence in Syntex. As a consequence, the group worked with a relatively powerless set of individuals in the information processing department at Syntex; they also focused on a customer need that was not deemed critical by higher-level executives. The Express group failed to identify important power relationships at Syntex—for instance, that clinical information processing was dependent on the medical research department for capital allocations. Express also did not fully understand how decisions were made at Syntex and which organizational issues were most critical to the top managers in the medical research group. Many times, instead of doing diagnosis, they simply assumed that Syntex was similar to Xerox—they saw Syntex through "Xerox-specific" lenses. So, although the project may have identified a viable technological solution to a key customer problem, its importance was not conveyed to critical decision makers within Syntex. Without this sponsorship, it was difficult for the project to maintain its funding and support.

Similar problems in diagnosing interdependence often doom the implementation of new management information systems. Almost any innovation, of either a product or a process, inevitably changes power structures and requires the mobilization of support. Innovators who pay no attention to the patterns of interdependence will be successful only if they are unusually lucky. In order to diagnose interdependence, it is necessary to ask a series of fairly straightforward questions:

1. Whose cooperation will I need to accomplish what I am attempting; whose support will be necessary in order to get the appropriate decisions made and implemented?
2. Whose opposition could delay or derail what I am trying to do?
3. Who will be affected by what I am trying to accomplish, in either

a) their power or status, b) how they are evaluated or rewarded, or c) in how they do their job?
4. Who are the friends and allies of the people I have identified as influential?

Be conservative in your estimates; it is preferable to overestimate potential dependencies rather than to be surprised at the last minute by a person or group you failed to consider; the best surprise is no surprise.

Understanding the pattern of interdependence you confront can be helpful in anticipating problems and heading them off. Much of the conflict that occurred when new functions such as municipal finance and investment banking were introduced at E.F. Hutton might have been avoided if the right questions had been asked; it would have been useful to anticipate the effects of these activities on the other units in the firm and to bring them into the planning and implementation.[19] If the interdependence among the various computers and peripherals developed at Apple Computer had been more adequately recognized, there might have been less conflict in the organization and also more effective product development. Apple's culture, which replicated its theory of machines (one computer for each person), and which stressed independence rather than interdependence, caused trouble as the firm began to compete in a more systems-oriented marketplace.

This first section of the book has focused on why power is important, the conditions under which power and influence matter most in organizations, and how to diagnose political subdivisions, patterns of interdependence, and the comparative power of individuals within the organization. The task has been to understand the context, or the game, and to be able to identify the players. The next section of the book considers where power comes from, or why some people and some subunits have more power than others. In so doing, it offers implicit lessons on how to acquire more power and influence for ourselves.

PART

II

Sources of Power

Power comes from being in the "right" place. But what is the right place? A good place or position is one that provides you with: 1) control over resources such as budgets, physical facilities, and positions that can be used to cultivate allies and supporters; 2) control over or extensive access to information—about the organization's activities, about the preferences and judgments of others, about what is going on, and who is doing it; and 3) formal authority. Much of being in the right place comes from being in the right organizational subunit.

Why is it that some people in organizations are in a good place to develop and exercise power, and others are not? In fundamental terms, does the person make the place, or does the organizational place make the person? This question, still tirelessly debated, is consequential for focusing our attention and efforts on changing individual attributes or locating situations where those attributes can be most effectively employed to obtain power. It is an issue about which it is easy to be misled, because of basic cognitive biases that affect how we see the world.

In this section, which addresses the sources of power, our first task is to determine whether the most critical source of power is individual characteristics or location in the organization. Although individual attributes are important, my view is that being in the right place is more essential. After considering this issue, the section proceeds to examine the factors that create the power of an organizational position: control over resources, control and access to information, and formal position. Next we will consider how each of these critical sources of power is affected by the subunit that surrounds it. We want to understand first why some people are powerful, and then use that insight to explain why some units are more powerful, and how being in those units provides more power to the people within them.

Not everyone is equally effective in making the most out of his or her place in the organization, or for that matter, in getting into a favorable set of circumstances at all. The section concludes, therefore, by outlining the individual characteristics that reflect the ability to reach good organizational locations and to make the most out of the resources at hand.

4

Where Does Power Come From?

Long-term studies of companies in numerous industries ranging from glass and cement manufacturing to the mini-computer industry "show that the most successful firms maintain a workable equilibrium for several years . . . but are also able to initiate and carry out sharp, widespread changes . . . when their environments shift."[1] These so-called discontinuous or frame-breaking changes always alter the distribution of power. Consequently, organizational innovation often if not inevitably involves obtaining the power and influence necessary to overcome resistance.

To be successful in this process, we need to understand where power comes from. It is critical to be able to diagnose the power of other players, including potential allies and possible opponents. We need to know what we are up against. Knowing where power comes from also helps us to build our own power and thereby increase our capacity to take action. It is useful to know that getting a new product introduced may involve power and politics, and to understand the pattern of interdependence and the points of view of various participants. But, to be effective, we also need to know how to develop sources of power and how to employ that power strategically and tactically.

We all have implicit theories of where power comes from, and we occasionally act on these theories. For instance, we may read and follow the advice of books on "power dressing," pondering issues such as whether yellow ties are in or out and whether suspenders are a signal of power. The cosmetic surgery business is booming, in part, at least, because some executives are worried that the signs of aging may make them appear to be less powerful and dynamic. People attend courses in assertiveness training, go through psychotherapy, and take programs in public speaking for numerous reasons, but among them is the desire to be more powerful, dynamic, and effective.

Many of our theories about the origins of power emphasize the importance of personal attributes and characteristics—which are very difficult to alter, at least without herculean efforts. We sometimes overlook the importance of situational factors over which we may have more direct influence. If we are going to be effective in organizations, we need to be skillful in evaluating our theories of the sources of power, as well as sensitive to various cognitive biases. This chapter briefly outlines some issues to think about as we observe the world and try to diagnose the sources of power. It also sets the stage for the consideration of personal characteristics and situational factors as sources of power, which will occur in the later chapters of this section.

PERSONAL ATTRIBUTES AS SOURCES OF POWER

When we walk into an organization, we see people first, not situations. People are talking, moving around, and doing things. People have personalities, idiosyncrasies, and mannerisms that engage our attention and hold our interest. Our preoccupation with the vividness of the people we meet leads to what some psychologists have called "the fundamental attribution error"—our tendency to overemphasize the causal importance of people and their characteristics, and underemphasize the importance of situational factors.[2] The phenomenon is pervasive, and there are many examples. One striking manifestation of the tendency to ignore situational factors in evaluating people is provided in an experimental study done by a colleague.[3] The study entailed assessing the performance of a speaker—a situation not dissimilar to assessing the power of someone we encounter in an organization. In the study, evaluators asked questions that were either positively or negatively biased—and moreover, they were aware of the bias when asked about it later. Nevertheless, evaluators were themselves affected by the answers they elicited through their biased questions. They "underestimated the potential effect of their own behavior [the situation] in drawing conclusions based on potentially constrained answers."[4] Instead of discounting the diagnostic value of the behavior they had affected, evaluators used that information in making assessments both of the performance and (in other studies) of the attitudes of others. In other words, even when we know that the behavior we observe is strongly affected by situational factors, we readily make attributions and evaluations about others based on that behavior.

Not only do we overattribute power to personal characteristics, but often the characteristics we believe to be sources of power are almost as plausibly the consequences of power instead. Interviews with 87 managerial personnel (including 30 chief executive officers, 28 high-level staff managers, and 29 supervisors) in thirty southern California electronics firms assessed beliefs about the personal characteristics of people thought to be most effective in the use of organizational politics and in wielding power.[5] The percentage of all respondents mentioning various characteristics is displayed in Table 4-1.

Table 4-1

Personal Traits
Characterizing Effective Political Actors

Personal Characteristic	*Percentage Mentioning*
Articulate	29.9
Sensitive	29.9
Socially adept	19.5
Competent	17.2
Popular	17.2
Extroverted	16.1
Self-confident	16.1
Aggressive	16.1
Ambitious	16.1

Without, for the moment, denying that these characteristics are associated with being powerful and politically effective, consider the possibility that at least some of them result from the experience of being in power. Are we likely to be more articulate and poised when we are more powerful? Are we likely to be more popular? Isn't it plausible that power causes us to be extroverted, as much as extroversion makes us powerful? Aren't more powerful and politically effective people likely to be perceived as more competent? Certainly power and political skill can produce more self-confident and even aggressive behavior. And considering that people usually adjust their ambitions to what is feasible, people who are more powerful are probably going to be more ambitious, and to be viewed as such.

Why is the causal ordering of more than academic interest? The answer is that we may try to develop attributes to help us attain power, and if those attributes are ineffective or dysfunctional, we can get into trouble. Most of us can recall people who acted "out of role" and behaved as if they were more powerful and important than they were. This behavior typically only erodes support and makes one ineffective, even if the same behavior, exhibited by someone holding power, is accepted and enhances that person's effectiveness.

A third problem in drawing inferences from personal attributes lies in the fact that people are seldom randomly assigned to their situations. External factors often have a direct bearing on the success or failure of an individual, and yet many studies of power fail to take account of such factors. Consider David Winter's study of the effect of three individual dispositions—the power motive, the need for achievement, and the affiliation-intimacy motive—on various indicators of leader effectiveness, including one measure closely related to a common definition of power: the ability to get one's way in terms of appointments or initiatives.[6]

Winter's sample is the U.S. presidents, a nonrandom sample if there ever was one. Each president's personality traits were assessed by scoring the first inaugural address for imagery that represents the underlying motive. Winter's results are correlations between presidential scores on the three traits and several outcome measures such as being reelected, having court and cabinet appointments approved, and avoiding or entering war.[7] The analysis does not consider the possibility that the type of person elected to office is not independent of the times and conditions that bracket the election, and that perhaps these factors, not just motive profiles, help explain outcomes such as avoiding or entering war.

Errors of this type are made routinely. For instance, in evaluating own-recognizance bail programs, studies often don't account for the fact that the people are not randomly released on their own recognizance; only the less dangerous prisoners are likely to be released.[8] Thus the tendency of those released without bail not to commit crimes does not necessarily mean that if the program were extended to all prisoners the same results would hold. The wider point here is that we need to understand and account for how people wind up in various situations, and to use this information in evaluating their power and their effectiveness. In general, we need to be thoughtful when we analyze personal characteristics as sources of power, particularly if we intend to take action based on those insights.

STRUCTURAL SOURCES OF POWER

Structural perspectives on power argue that power is derived from where each person stands in the division of labor and the communication system of the organization. The division of labor in an organization creates subunits and differentiated roles, and each subunit and position develops specialized interests and responsibilities. Further, each subunit or position makes claims on the organization's resources.[9] In the contest for resources, those who do well succeed on the basis of the resources they possess or control as well as the ties they can form with people who influence allocations.[10] Control over resources, and the importance of the unit in the organization, are derived from the division of labor, which gives some positions or groups more control over critical tasks and more access to resources than others.[11] Power, then, comes from the control over resources, from the ties one has to powerful others, and from the formal authority one obtains because of one's position in the hierarchy.

For instance, in a study of 33 purchase decisions, the most

frequently mentioned characteristic of those perceived to have influence over the decisions was that the choice would affect them:

> ... in a company which makes musical instruments, the choice of a tractor truck was said by one informant to have been influenced most by the traffic supervisor. "He lives with the situation, so he must have the choice," he said.[12]

Who is affected by a decision is determined, obviously, by the division of labor. According to those interviewed in the study, people with formal responsibility for the unit where the product was to be used, or with responsibility for the performance or output of the product were also viewed as influential. Although interviewees were asked to judge who had the most influence "regardless of who had the final authority," authority and responsibility were often-mentioned sources of influence in these purchase situations.[13] Authority and responsibility, too, are conveyed by one's position in the formal structure of the organization.

Or consider the power sometimes possessed by purchasing agents.[14] They stand between engineering, production scheduling, and marketing on the one hand, and outside vendors on the other. Some purchasing agents were able to use this intermediary position to obtain substantial influence over other departments that, in many instances, possessed more formal status and authority than they did. By relying on purchasing rules and procedures (which they often had developed themselves), the agents made it necessary for other departments to accede to their power—as is evidenced by the willingness of other departments to provide favors to those in purchasing in exchange for preferential treatment.

The point about situational sources of power is that one possesses power simply by being in the right place—by being in a position of authority, in a place to resolve uncertainty, in a position to broker among various subunits and external vendors—almost regardless of one's individual characteristics. Authority and responsibility are vested in positions, and one's ability to broker is affected significantly by where one sits in the structure of interaction. Of course, not all people in the same situations are able to do equally well.

Some purchasing agents, for instance, were much more successful than others in raising the power and status of their departments, in spite of the fact that virtually all wanted to do so, and some of this difference resulted from variations in political skill among the purchasing agents in the various companies. This suggests that while situations are important, one's ability to capitalize on the situation also has decisive implications.

THE FIT BETWEEN SITUATIONAL REQUIREMENTS AND PERSONAL TRAITS

An important source of power is the match between style, skill, and capacities and what is required by the situation. For instance, in a study of influence at a research and development laboratory of 304 professionals, the participants were questioned about influence in their organization. Was influence primarily related to being 1) an internal communication star, someone who had extensive contacts within the laboratory but who was not linked to external sources of information; 2) an external communication star, someone linked primarily to external information and not well connected in his own unit; or 3) a boundary spanner, someone linked both to others within his own unit and to external sources of information?[15] Influence was measured with respect to technical, budgetary, and personnel decisions. The principal finding was that the type of person who was influential depended on the nature of the project: in technical service projects, with less task uncertainty, internal communication stars were most influential, while in applied research units, boundary spanners carried the most weight.

Another illustration of the contingency between situations and the characteristics that provide influence comes from a study of 17 organizations that had recently purchased a piece of offset printing equipment.[16] For some organizations, the purchase was new and therefore totally unfamiliar; for others, it involved the replacement of an existing piece of equipment; and for still others, it involved adding a piece of equipment. Clearly, the amount of uncertainty differed, it being greatest for those buying offset printing equipment for the first time, and posing the smallest problem for those firms that were merely acquiring another piece of the same equipment they already had. Individual experience was most highly related to influence in the case of purchasing an additional piece of equipment. Internal communication and the number of different sources of information consulted were most strongly related to influence in the case of new purchase decisions. Those who were able to affect perceptions of need were most influential in adding a piece of equipment, while those who gathered external information were more influential in the situation in which new equipment was being purchased. These two studies, as well as other research, strongly suggest that:

> The influence of a subunit or individual on a decision is a function of (1) the kind of uncertainty faced by an organization, (2) the particular characteristic or capability which enables reducing organizational uncertainty, and (3) the degree to which a particular subunit [or individual] possesses this characteristic. As decision-making contexts vary, so do the sources of organizational uncertainty, and consequently, the bases for influence in organizational decision-making.[17]

The necessity of matching personal characteristics to the situation can be seen in politics as well as in business. Ronald Reagan, the former movie actor and U.S. president, came to office at a time in which mass communication, through the medium of television, was essential. Reagan had no skill in dealing with details, but was a "great communicator." Lyndon Johnson rose to power at a time when television was less important, and party organizations were stronger. The ability to pay attention to small details and the willingness to do favors for colleagues and constituents were critical. Had Reagan and Johnson been able to exchange decades, it is likely that neither one would have been elected president. Johnson's difficulty in responding to the rise of the media in his administration shows his inability to flourish in an era of mass communication. And Reagan would have been unsuited for the continual attention to detail that was required of old-style party politicians. Not only are particular kinds of knowledge and skill differentially critical across time and settings, but personal attributes also become more or less important, depending on the setting.

Can Charisma Be Transferred?

Charisma is perhaps the best illustration of the fit between situations and personal attributes. The concept of charisma came into social science from theology, where it means "endowment with the gift of divine grace."[18] Charismatic leaders often emerge in times of stress or crisis. They create an emotional (rather than purely instrumental) bond with others; they take on heroic proportions and appeal to the ideological values of followers.[19] President John Kennedy, Martin Luther King, and Gandhi were all charismatic figures.

Some have asserted that charisma is a characteristic of the individual, based on the person's need for power, achievement, and affiliation, as well as on his inhibitions in using power.[20] Moreover, charisma and personality are said to explain the effectiveness of leaders—for instance, that of U.S. presidents.[21] A careful longitudinal study of a school superintendent in Minnesota provides some interesting evidence on the interaction between charismatic properties and situational constraints.[22]

While serving in a large, suburban school district in Minnesota, the superintendent exhibited both charisma and effectiveness. Her work drew attention in the media and the legislature. She "gained wide acclaim for her massive grassroots program to cut $2.4 million from the budget while at the same time successfully avoiding the 'bloodletting' of retrenchment."[23] School personnel described her in interviews as "a mover, a shaker, a visionary . . . who had made a dramatic, unprecedented impact on the district. People believed that she had extraordinary talents."[24] She developed an extremely loyal following, unlike the superintendents who had preceded her. She involved many people in the process of change in the district, forming task forces to investigate district policy and budget problems, hiring consultants to conduct workshops to develop a vision of the future, and redesigning jobs and the administrative structure of the district office. Her effect on the district was striking:

> Budget reductions were scheduled without acrimonious debate. The school board unanimously approved the superintendent's budget reductions after only a brief discussion. Teachers awarded her a standing ovation, despite her recommendations to cut support jobs and

program funding. Innovative ideas poured in from district personnel . . . At the end of her two years as superintendent, the district
had catalogued over 300 suggestions for innovative ventures.[25]

Then she was appointed by the governor of Minnesota to
be the head of the state Department of Education. She
brought to this new position the same modus operandi she
had used as district superintendent: "Begin with a mission
and a vision that outline where one wants to go; generate
enthusiasm and support for the vision at the grass-roots
level; . . . create a structure for change at the Department of
Education that will serve to channel the interest and energy
into innovative programs."[26] During her first year in her new
job, she personally visited almost every one of the 435 school
districts in the state. She initiated town meetings held in 388
public school districts, which drew about 15,000 citizens. She
sponsored public opinion polls. She replaced the top five
assistant commissioners with her own team of nine people,
all formerly outsiders to the Department of Education.[27] And
what were the results of all of these efforts?

As one might imagine, efforts to restaff and restructure the
Department of Education were immediately opposed by
those already well served by the existing structure. Five of
the new assistants were either fired or resigned from office
within the first year.[28] The press soon heard of morale problems, departures of key middle managers, and confusion over
routine tasks and job assignments. Instead of being able to
focus on long-term change, she now found herself "em-
broiled in the day-to-day details of established bureaucratic
order."[29] Charisma, so evident at the school district level,
clearly did not transfer to her new position at the state level,
nor could it be created at will.

The administrator had more success in her role as superintendent because it gave her more control and more autonomy
over educational matters. She was also able to have closer,
more personal relationships with those she wanted to influence when she operated at the local level. As the governor's
political appointee, she had to worry about what her actions
would mean for him. As head of a large state department, she
"was embedded in a much more complex web of relations
among the legislature, state executive departments, constit-

uents, interest groups and networks, and state and national educational communities."[30] Her freedom of action was constrained, and her personal contacts were worth much less; in short, she needed to rely more on bureaucratic politics and less on emotional appeal than she had been accustomed to.

As situational factors change, the attributes required to be influential and effective change as well. That is why it is important not only to find positions with the political demands that match our skills and interests, but also to tailor our actions to the circumstances we confront. In any event, we can probably best understand the sources of power as deriving from individual characteristics, from advantages the situation provides, and from the match between ourselves and our settings.

5

Resources, Allies, and the New Golden Rule

Some years ago *Life* magazine ran a pictorial series on the hundred most influential people of the twentieth century. Included were Roosevelt, Churchill, Gandhi, Einstein, and other major figures of politics, science, and the arts—along with a parks and bridges commissioner, Robert Moses. I suspect that if I asked you to choose a position in which you could wield enormous power, you would probably not pick the job of parks commissioner. But Robert Moses was arguably the most powerful public official in the United States during the twentieth century. During his 44-year career, he built 12 bridges, 35 highways, 751 playgrounds, 13 golf courses, 18 swimming pools, and more than two million acres of parks in New York. His public works displaced more than 500,000 people.[1] Table 5-1 lists some of his most prominent projects. In addition to what he acomplished directly, he had indirect influence over several generations of city planners and urban development specialists, both in this country and overseas. This meant that public works all over the world were affected by his thinking.

Like the other powerful figures we will discuss in this chapter, Robert Moses recognized the truth of the so-called New Golden Rule: the person with the gold makes the rules. They realized that various kinds of resources, including allies, are vitally important as sources of power. This may not seem like a big revelation. It is crucial, however, when coupled with an understanding of how resources can be created,

Table 5-1

A Partial List of Public Works Built by Robert Moses

Public Structures	Roads
Lincoln Center for the Peforming Arts	Cross-Bronx Expressway
United Nations Headquarters	Cross-Island Expressway
Shea Stadium	Henry Hudson Parkway
New York Coliseum	Long Island Expressway
New York World's Fair 1939	Major Deegan Expressway
New York World's Fair 1964	Grand Central Parkway
	Southern State Parkway
Bridges and Tunnels	Staten Island Expressway
Triborough Bridge	Van Wyck Expressway
Verrazano-Narrows Bridge	
Throgs Neck Bridge	Beaches
Brooklyn Battery Tunnel	Coney Island
Henry Hudson Bridge	Rockaway
Bronx-Whitestone Bridge	Jones Beach
Queens Midtown Tunnel	Orient Beach
Robert Moses Causeway	

how control over resources can be gained and maintained, and finally, how to use incremental or temporarily unallocated resources in order to build power.

CREATING RESOURCES

Over the years, I have come to marvel at the skill of those who can create resources virtually out of thin air. The key to this skill seems to be the ability to recognize the fundamental things that people in a given situation want and need, and then to create a resource that will give one access to and control over them. There are many examples of this ability, but perhaps none so strikingly illustrates the capacity to make something out of nothing as Lyndon Johnson's development and use of the Little Congress.

When Johnson arrived in Washington in 1931 as Congressman Richard Kleberg's secretary, the Little Congress was almost worthless:

It was a moribund organization. Formed in 1919 to provide secretaries with experience in public speaking and a knowledge of parliamentary procedures, it was modeled on the House of Representatives and held debates under House rules. But it had degenerated into little more than a social club, whose desultory meetings . . . were attended by no more than a few dozen secretaries.[2]

But Lyndon Johnson saw in it an opportunity. The press corps was eager to get advance information on how the major issues of the day were to be decided. This was, after all, the depths of the Great Depression, and much important legislation was being considered. Politicians, of course, coveted press coverage and exposure. Congressional secretaries, although not all as ambitious and aggressive as Johnson, did frequently seek advancement and prestige.

First, Johnson got himself elected Speaker of the Little Congress. It was an organization in which few were interested anyway, and he packed the election meeting with his allies and won the vote. Once elected, he transformed the Little Congress, and his position as Speaker, into a much more important resource. He changed the monthly meetings to a schedule of once a week, and altered the format to include not only debates on the issues, but also speeches by "prominent figures."[3] In extending invitations to speak, Johnson could offer access to prominent politicians, and more important, he had an excuse to talk to them himself. He organized formal debates on bills, lined up speakers on both sides, ran the debates according to the rules of the House, took straw votes on the bills at the end, and invited the press to cover the debates. The press soon figured out that the debates offered previews of congressional positions on the issues. Once the press came, it was easy to get congressmen to come, and to have more and more people interested in participating in the organization.

> Soon, 200 or more congressional aides were crowding into the Caucus Room every week. . . . In a remarkably short time . . . Lyndon Johnson had, through an organization in which advancement had previously depended on longevity on the Hill, lifted himself dramatically out of the anonymous crowd of congressional aides.[4]

The Little Congress became, under Johnson, an important resource and the beginning of his substantial power base. Yet it was a highly unlikely position from which to obtain this leverage. Johnson recognized that the press wanted information and access, the politicians wanted coverage, and the aides wanted publicity and a sense of being part of the action. He figured out a way to use the vehicle of the Little Congress so that he could reap the publicity and the benefits, and still provide each group what it wanted.

And how could Robert Moses, beginning as a parks commissioner, amass such influence? First, he accumulated positions that often initially appeared to be of little importance. In the years after World War II, Moses held the following posts, often simultaneously: 1) chairman of the New York State Council of Parks; 2) president of the Long Island State Park Commission; 3) chairman of the Jones Beach Parkway Authority; 4) chairman of the Bethpage Park Authority; 5) commissioner of the New York City Department of Parks; 6) member of the New York City Planning Commission; 7) chairman of the Triborough Bridge and Tunnel Authority; 8) construction coordinator for the City of New York; 9) chairman of the New York State Power Authority; 10) president of the 1964–1965 World's Fair; 11) director of the Lincoln Center Area Development Project; and 12) chairman of the Federal Title I Housing Program. Each job entailed building, and building involved getting contracts for the actual construction, the purchase of insurance policies and performance bonds, and the use of legal services and banking services—in short, the expenditure of a vast amount of public money. Moreover, Moses's inside knowledge of where roads were to be located, and where slum clearance was to take place, could make entrepreneurs rich if he passed it along to them. During his career, Moses traded both information and contracts not for money for himself—he died with a very small estate—but rather, for power. The thousands of union members, construction firms, legal firms, and bankers dependent on his largesse constituted an army of people more than willing to do his bidding. And at least some of his positions, such as the Triborough Bridge job, brought him direct control over resources—the tolls from the bridges and tunnels, and also the bonding authority that he used to obtain large amounts of debt. Because Moses held so many different positions, with so many different sources of power, people were reluctant to fight him in any one place, knowing he could exact retribution in some other arena. Moses's genius was in seeing the opportunity to control the expenditure of enormous sums of money through parks, roads, and bridges, and in using these development resources to obtain a degree of power almost unparalleled in public life.

The parks department and the Little Congress shared some things in common. At the time they were used to build power, they were political backwaters, which attracted almost no interest from powerful individuals. In product markets, an effective strategy is often to go where the competition isn't. In political markets, the same principle holds: begin by building a power base in a niche that is largely uncontested. Then, having obtained a position of influence in an organization, figure out how to use that organization to obtain resources that are more consequential and substantial. This requires determining how to create resources and to make others dependent on you for things that they need.

Similar processes occur in business firms. To an uninformed observer, it is not obvious that finance should be the most important function in a company that makes automobiles. After all, finance does not design or engineer the cars, solve problems in their manufacture, or distribute and sell them. And, indeed, the dominance of finance has scarcely been healthy for either Ford or General Motors.[5] Finance came to power in both companies because that function was able to first gain control over the planning, capital budgeting, and operations research processes, and then convince others that these were the critical functions in the operation of the company. After Ford went public in the 1950s, and after antitrust action, also in the 1950s, forced Du Pont to sell off its substantial equity stake in General Motors, finance argued that the companies needed to cultivate the investment community in order to attract outside capital and maintain the stock price of the firms.

Resources can be almost anything that is perceived as valuable—from building contracts to press exposure to control over systems and analysis. When Xerox faced product introduction delays, quality problems, and substantial budget overruns, the response was to institute more planning, more budgets, more reviews, and more schedules. Each of these processes was controlled by finance or by those with financial backgrounds.[6] At Burgmaster Machine Tools, difficulty in building machine tools that sold well at a good price and problems in meeting delivery dates were attacked with elaborate material planning systems and cost control systems.[7] These systems were designed and implemented by people who, for the most part, had never built a machine tool or run a factory, and the systems, at least in this instance, seemed to do more harm than good. However, the ability to find an external constituency interested in the particular resource helped transform something comparatively unimportant—budgets, systems, and planning reviews, not the product being manufactured and sold—into a critical resource. And this transformation gave enormous leverage to those who controlled the resource.

CONTROL OF RESOURCE ALLOCATION AND USE

Jurisdiction over resources is an important source of power, but only to the extent that one actually controls the resource and its use. For instance, one seldom sees the commissioner of Social Security listed as one of the most powerful government officials in the United States. Yet the Social Security tax is a major source of federal revenue, the Social Security trust fund and the question of financing future benefits is a major item on the public agenda, and perhaps most significant, expenditures on Social Security constitute one of the largest items in the federal budget. To offer another example, in 1984 and even in 1985, most of Apple Computer's sales and profits came from the division that made the Apple II. Nevertheless, the Macintosh division was far more powerful than the Apple II unit, which experienced substantial turnover because of its lack of power and respect in the organization. And in many organizations, personnel costs constitute a major portion of the expenses, but it is rare that either payroll or human resources is the most powerful unit.

In each instance, what makes the unit relatively powerless is its lack of control over the resources that it oversees. Social Security pays benefits according to formulas set by law, and although the commissioner operates a large bureaucracy, it is an organization with little discretion over the vast sums of money that pass through it. Similarly, payroll and human resources often have little control over the expenditures on salaries, and the Apple II division did not choose to develop and exercise, if it could, control over the sales and profits of that machine. For resources to be a source of power, several conditions must be met, but control over them is one of the most fundamental. There are several bases for controlling a resource:

> One basis for control over a resource is possession. . . . However . . . ownership is a form of indirect discretion in that it depends on a social-political conception and on enforceable social consensus. . . . Another basis for control is access to a resource. It is possible to regulate access to a resource without owning it. . . . Another important basis for control is the actual use of the resource and who controls its use. . . . The final source of control derives from the ability to make rules or otherwise regulate the possession, allocation, and use of resources and to enforce the regulations.[8]

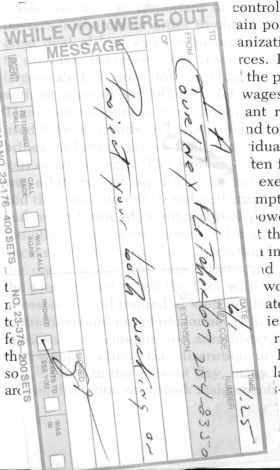

control, and not merely to ain power, there is often a anizations about the right rces. In the early days of the power to hire and fire wages arbitrarily as well. ant resource—jobs—was nd to extract, on occasion, iduals who sought good ten felt that the foreman exercise of this power, mpts to organize unions ower.[9] The owners, on t the foremen were not in the best interests of d high wages profited workers who were not ated. This concern led ies and personnel pro- rules and regulations lower-level supervi- labor disputes center —such as contracting out—and disciplinary issues. The evolution of this so-called bureaucratic control gave workers more security and stability in their work life and owners more effective control over the enterprise, but it was initially resisted by the foremen, who did not want to lose their special privileges. Today foremen are caught in the middle between owners and workers, and they earn comparatively less money than they did in the late 1800s.

Civil service regulations make it more difficult for politicians to obtain jobs for their friends or to dispense patronage as a way of building a network of obligations. It is not surprising, therefore, that the imposition of formalized hiring procedures is often resisted mightily, both in government and in private organizations, by those who will, under these systems, lose discretion over the important resource of jobs. For many years, the postmaster general of the United States was one of the most powerful officials in government. The Post Office was (and is) one of the largest government employers, today employing more than 750,000 workers. When postal jobs were controlled by patronage, the resources of the person who controlled that agency were enormous, and the position possessed tremendous power.

The control of physical space is another resource that can confer great power. Facilities people in corporations often are not powerful in a formal, organization chart sense, but they frequently exercise enormous influence because of their control over large building budgets and the allocation and use of facilities. I know of one organization that decided to lower costs by moving many of its administrative activities out of San Francisco to the suburbs. Of course, it wanted to retain its corporate headquarters, its signature, in downtown San Francisco. When the time came for the move, it turned out that not all of the departments slated to remain in San Francisco would actually fit in the headquarters building. The facilities people played a major role in deciding which functions would be located in that building, and which would be consigned to leased space elsewhere in the city.

The use of control over physical space to develop power is nicely illustrated by the actions Jim Wright took when he became Speaker of the House of Representatives in 1986.[11] "Wright's first step was to take physical possession of his of money that pass through it. Similarly, payroll and human resources often have little control over the expenditures on salaries, and the Apple II division did not choose to develop and exercise, if it could, control over the sales and profits of that machine. For resources to be a source of power, several conditions must be met, but control over them is one of the most fundamental. There are several bases for controlling a resource:

> One basis for control over a resource is possession. . . . However . . . ownership is a form of indirect discretion in that it depends on a social-political conception and on enforceable social consensus. . . . Another basis for control is access to a resource. It is possible to regulate access to a resource without owning it. . . . Another important basis for control is the actual use of the resource and who controls its use. . . . The final source of control derives from the ability to make rules or otherwise regulate the possession, allocation, and use of resources and to enforce the regulations.[8]

Because it is so important to control, and not merely to possess, resources in order to obtain power, there is often a great deal of hue and cry in organizations about the right to exercise discretion over resources. In the early days of large-scale U.S. firms, foremen had the power to hire and fire without review, and often to set wages arbitrarily as well. Their control over a very important resource—jobs—was used to favor friends and relatives and to extract, on occasion, bribes and other favors from individuals who sought good jobs or good wages. The workers often felt that the foreman was arbitrary and capricious in the exercise of this power, and their resentment stimulated attempts to organize unions and other forms of countervailing power.[9] The owners, on the other hand, were concerned that the foremen were not necessarily exercising their discretion in the best interests of the organization. The sale of jobs and high wages profited the foremen but it left the firm with workers who were not necessarily well trained or well motivated. This concern led to the development of personnel policies and personnel professionals to formulate and administer rules and regulations that would delimit the discretion of lower-level supervisors.[10] Even to the present day, many labor disputes center around discretion over work assignments—such as contracting out—and disciplinary issues. The evolution of this so-called bureaucratic control gave workers more security and stability in their work life and owners more effective control over the enterprise, but it was initially resisted by the foremen, who did not want to lose their special privileges. Today foremen are caught in the middle between owners and workers, and they earn comparatively less money than they did in the late 1800s.

Civil service regulations make it more difficult for politicians to obtain jobs for their friends or to dispense patronage as a way of building a network of obligations. It is not surprising, therefore, that the imposition of formalized hiring procedures is often resisted mightily, both in government and in private organizations, by those who will, under these systems, lose discretion over the important resource of jobs. For many years, the postmaster general of the United States was one of the most powerful officials in government. The Post Office was (and is) one of the largest government employers, today employing more than 750,000 workers. When postal jobs were controlled by patronage, the resources of the person who controlled that agency were enormous, and the position possessed tremendous power.

The control of physical space is another resource that can confer great power. Facilities people in corporations often are not powerful in a formal, organization chart sense, but they frequently exercise enormous influence because of their control over large building budgets and the allocation and use of facilities. I know of one organization that decided to lower costs by moving many of its administrative activities out of San Francisco to the suburbs. Of course, it wanted to retain its corporate headquarters, its signature, in downtown San Francisco. When the time came for the move, it turned out that not all of the departments slated to remain in San Francisco would actually fit in the headquarters building. The facilities people played a major role in deciding which functions would be located in that building, and which would be consigned to leased space elsewhere in the city.

The use of control over physical space to develop power is nicely illustrated by the actions Jim Wright took when he became Speaker of the House of Representatives in 1986.[11] "Wright's first step was to take physical possession of his surroundings."[12] The Speaker of the House directly or indirectly controlled the House side of the Capitol, having discretion over every room, hallway, and closet contained in it, along with five office buildings on Capitol Hill.

> Control over real estate provides more than symbolic evidence of the Speaker's power; it *is* power, because information is power and proximity to the floor of the House chamber affects the flow of information. . . . Only the leadership and a handful of the chairmen and ranking members of the most powerful committees have space in the Capitol itself, close to the floor. The House chamber sits on the second floor of the Capitol, and every second-floor office except for one . . . on the entire east front on the House side of this immense, block-long building belongs to the Speaker.[13]

Previous Speakers had not exercised control over all of this space, but determined to increase his power, Wright decided that he would. He took space formerly occupied by the whip's office and "moved into it the staff of the Democratic Steering and Policy Committee, staff who answered to him and who . . . had occupied space a quarter of a mile away."[14] Wright also took space from the Rules Committee—in short, he made sure that his subordinates and the functions he controlled occupied the space nearest the House chamber. He would use the resource of physical space to build his power:

> All this—the real estate, the people who occupied the real estate—extended Wright's person, served as outposts of information and operation, of thought and intelligence, of eyes, and ears; they were the coils and nerve endings of Wright's rule.[15]

As Long Island State Park Commissioner during Al Smith's governorship of New York state, Moses controlled many resources other than those that were officially within his jurisdiction. For instance, he was able to exercise some control over employees of other agencies, because of Smith's support of his park projects. As a state official, he had access to the power and resources of the state, particularly legal resources. One of the reasons he was often able to prevail in his legal battles with those who challenged his plans was that he could delay and fight interminably, since the funds to pay legal fees were state funds, not his own. On the other side, fighting him required the expenditure of personal resources, and eventually his opponents tired of the battle and gave up. What is critical about resources, then, is to have effective control over them, and this control is not always perfectly correlated either with ownership or with official responsibilities. Moreover, those who are most effective in developing and exercising power are sensitive to what resources they do control, and use them vigorously in their efforts to get things done.

Power is vested in us by the dependence of others, and that dependence is a function of how much others need what we control, as well as how many alternative sources for that resource there are.[16] Thus, another strategy for developing power is to ensure that there are no alternative ways of obtaining access to valuable resources we control. For instance, in the past, the data processing department in many corporations had tremendous power because of its influence over computing and information systems. When accounting and data bases were lodged on mainframe computers, and when operations and access to those computing resources were centrally controlled, the data processing department was critical, particularly in firms in which data processing and data base management were important to success. With the advent of distributed computing power, through personal computers and networks, the power of the central data processing department decreased. This is why central data processing units initially did not welcome personal computers and why, when PCs were forced on them, they tried to maintain control over the acquisition of both hardware and software. A similar phenomenon occurred in reprographic departments, when smaller, less expensive copiers diminished the importance and the power of central copying units. Note that computing or copying is not less critical than before, but rather, changes in technology now provide alternative ways of accomplishing the task without relying on the central unit that formerly controlled the function.

HOW RESOURCES BECOME IMPORTANT

We have already noted that the way to gain power is not only to obtain control of a resource, but also to make the resources that one controls more important. In understanding the importance of resources to organizations, the politics of budgeting and the social psychology of commitment are fundamental ideas. For instance, they help us explain how a small amount of money, strategically applied, can be used to generate effective control over much larger resource pools.

Budgets are incremental. The best predictor of this year's budget is last year's, a finding replicated in arenas ranging from the national budget to university budgets.[17] Indeed, the power of precedent is so great that it leads to some strange organizational anomalies. For instance, in most organizations, departments are allocated a budget for salary increases, usually a percentage of their current salary base. Within that budget constraint, raises are then allocated to the various department members. What if the organization's allowance for raises is not sufficient to reward all of the outstanding performers in a given department? In many instances, the salary raise constraint is a binding one. However, when you recruit someone from outside the organization, you are normally given permission to meet competing offers, particularly the salary paid by the individual's last employer. Although the department may have some total budget constraint, this is less frequently the case, and is often less binding. Thus, a department that could not pay its members a given level of salary if they had to be granted raises, could pay replacements an even higher salary, as long as they were hired from outside and paid competitively with market rates. On the one hand, this looks as though organizations are somehow perversely more concerned with attracting people than retaining them. And this conclusion is probably true in part. But it is also the case that budgets are viewed incrementally, and somehow a raise of 10% seems worse than the same amount of money when it is spent to recruit new people from outside the organization. Because of the power of precedent, it becomes quite important to argue about what is and what is not in the budget base (as opposed to a temporary bonus, one-time allocation, and so forth), and because of the power of compound interest, getting one's base augmented on a consistent basis is critical.

For our purposes, what is important is that each unit in an organization considers its current base to be the minimum that it would find acceptable. Kahneman and Tversky's work on risk and decision making shows that a decrease from the current base would be viewed as a loss, and an increase would be viewed as a gain.[18] Moreover, their work shows that a loss of a given amount is viewed as twice as painful as a gain of the same amount. Gains and losses are not viewed symmetrically, and consequently, it is very difficult to reallocate resources, since it means taking them away from those that now enjoy them. Therefore, often the only way to provide incremental resources for new activities is to bring new resources, above and beyond what everyone already expects, into the system. Another way of saying this is to note that it is much easier to add than to subtract—and this is true whether we are talking about salary, staffing, or budgets.

What this observation implies is that the most precious resource in any organization is an incremental resource, not already spoken for, that can then be used to solve the organization's current problems—problems that are more difficult to address using the current resources because of the conflict involved in reallocation. In studying power in universities, I have repeatedly found that governmental grants are one of the best predictors of departmental power, particularly in public universities.[19] This is the case even in organizations in which grants and contracts represent a small proportion of the total budget, compared, for instance, to state appropriations or tuition revenue. The reason that grants and contracts are so crucial is that they carry overhead—a "tax" that the central administration extracts before passing the rest of the funds along to the principal investigator to perform his or her research. These overhead funds are, of course, discretionary. They are available for redistribution to other units and therefore constitute an important source of organizational slack. For much the same reason, universities prize unrestricted donations more highly than funds earmarked for a specific purpose. Unrestricted donations are available for new initiatives at the discretion of those who have control over the funds. Most universities would prefer that such discretion reside in the administration rather than in an outside organization or even in a department within the university. The best source of unrestricted funds is endowment funds, particularly funds provided by a will or trust. Endowment, once given, provides a capital base, which is no longer under the control of the donor; funds from deceased donors are even more desirable, since they are less likely to be monitored.

It is, therefore, quite possible to control, or substantially affect, the operations of a much larger entity, as long as one possesses discretionary control over a source of incremental resources. Before providing some examples of this, we need to understand the second feature of resource expenditures— their committing properties. What was once a luxury soon becomes a necessity, as most of us learned long ago in our personal lives. The same principle applies in organizations. An incremental source of funds will, initially, be perceived as a wonderful bonus, permitting, perhaps, the purchase of additional equipment, the hiring of more staff, the undertaking of new activities, the expansion of opportunities that were heretofore only dimly contemplated. But soon—very soon, indeed—these funds and the new equipment, staff, activities, and initiatives become viewed as the bare necessities of life, without which the organization could not possibly survive. The organization becomes, if you will, addicted to them. Thus, the person or organization offering the incremental resources can obtain tremendous power over the organization to which they have been allocated; this power holds as long as the resources remain truly in the discretionary control of the other.

Two examples, one academic and one corporate, provide compelling illustrations of this point. The university example concerns the leverage that the federal government has exercised over the relative size and development of various academic disciplines. At a university such as Stanford, which is heavily research-oriented, tuition accounts for about 50% of the annual operating budget, and income from endowment and annual giving supports another 20%–30%, depending on the year. Only about a quarter of the budget derives from federal grants and contracts, with overhead providing, obviously, an even smaller proportion of the budget. At most other universities, the contribution of federal research to the annual operating budget is substantially lower, and for many universities, there is no significant research component in the budget at all. But, as researchers noted some time ago, there is evidence that internal allocations of discretionary resources exacerbate, rather than diminish, funding inequalities created by the government's comparatively greater support of certain physical sciences (particularly those in which research may be defense-oriented) over social and other physical sciences.[20] Moreover, this effect occurs even in universities that receive almost no federal funds. DiMaggio and Powell use the phrase mimetic isomorphism—a fancy term for imitation or copying—to describe how, in institutionalized environments in which objective criteria are often absent, organizations decide what to do by following each other.[21] Large, prestigious, research-oriented universities provide visible models for others to follow, and consequently, federal funding—a tiny proportion of total expenditures on higher education—exerts a disproportionate influence both on internal funding priorities and indeed on the very development and research topics chosen in numerous academic specialties.

And the influence does not stop there. Initially, the federal government viewed its support of academic research as a way of developing and building research capabilities at universities and, therefore, the technology base of the society. Over time, the purchase of research has come to be viewed in the same way as the purchase of any other supply from an outside source. It is seen as a procurement problem, with the goal being to purchase a given quality and quantity of scientific research at the least possible cost. As a consequence, the National Science Foundation began to cap the amount of salary their grants would reimburse at the level of about $75,000 per year, and federal agencies negotiated intensely over the indirect cost recovery rate, or the overhead rate, that could be applied to grants and contracts. The first limit provides an extra incentive for the university to restrict professors' salaries. The second intervention provides strong inducements for universities to cut their administrative overhead dramatically. Thus, Stanford, in the spring of 1990, announced a $22 million budget-cutting program (from a base budget of about $175 million), in response to concerns over its rising indirect cost recovery rate. The faculty had complained that the overhead rate, set by the university and added automatically to all contracts and grants submitted from the university, was hurting the competition for research funds.

I am no fan of administrative overhead, and I have often noted that, while student enrollments have remained constant and faculty size has grown in small amounts, administration has increased dramatically. What is most interesting about this move, however, is not that someone finally became concerned about the size of the administrative component at colleges and universities, but rather, that federal government pressure, exerted through the indirect cost recovery rate negotiations, finally caused Stanford (and numerous other universities) to restructure and reorganize their internal administration, at some points cutting activities such as student services in response. A tremendous amount of leverage, albeit often indirect, is exerted over the operations and budgeting of major institutions through the discretionary control of a comparatively small proportion of the total budget.

For the corporate example, consider the case of OPM Leasing Services. Robert Gandossy wrote a book describing the substantial fraud perpetrated by Myron Goodman and Mordecai Weissman of OPM Leasing.[22] OPM (which stands for Other People's Money) was a computer leasing firm that was, according to records, not profitable virtually from its inception. At the time the frauds were uncovered (they included obtaining financing from multiple banks to cover the purchase of the same computer under the same lease, and representing leases prepared by OPM as being prepared by actual lessors of computer equipment), "OPM was accused of fraud amounting to over $200 million by nineteen financial institutions and several of their customers. Another $100 million was owed to others stemming from the bankruptcy."[23] One naturally wonders how such a questionable institution was able to exert substantial leverage over its accountants, its investment bankers (which included Lehman Brothers and Goldman, Sachs), and even its customers, such as Rockwell International. These associations were absolutely essential for OPM's legitimacy, and consequently, for its continued ability both to stay in operation and to continue to engage in fraudulent transactions.

In each instance, the pattern was the same—dependence was created gradually, and it capitalized on some vulnerability in the other organization. For instance, when OPM approached Goldman, Sachs in 1975 to handle the placement of its debt for computer leasing, Goldman and the entire investment banking industry were in the middle of a substantial transformation.[24] In 1973, the investment banking industry had lost $50 million, and the traditional emphasis on securities sales and trading was rapidly shifting to mergers and acquisitions, real estate deals, and private placements. Between October 1975 and March 1978, "Goldman, Sachs received nearly $2.4 million in fees from OPM and . . . it became one of the investment banker's largest private placement customers."[25] What began as a single transaction developed into a relationship that provided OPM's investment banker with substantial revenues in an important new area where it was trying to grow.

A similar picture emerges when OPM's accounting relationships are examined. Their initial accountant, Rashba and Pokart, had discovered fraudulent leases and had refused to issue a certified financial report for 1974. OPM then went to Fox and Company, the eleventh-largest accounting firm in the United States. "Myron's preference at that point was that he wanted to be . . . a big fish in a little pond. . . . So, it had to be a medium-sized firm, a firm a little below the 'Big 8.' "[26] In other words, OPM sought a firm that was large enough to provide respectability, but small enough so that the auditing fees would be a substantial portion of its business, creating, over time, dependence and a willingness to not examine transactions too diligently. From 1976 until 1981, Fox collected over $1 million in fees from OPM, "and the leasing company became one of its largest New York clients."[27]

Perhaps the most dramatic instance of building dependence occurred with one of OPM's largest customers, Rockwell International. The company was created through the merger of Rockwell Manufacturing and North American Aviation in the early 1970s, and afterwards it engaged in a typical post-merger program of cutting costs. Computer costs were a substantial item in the budget, because the company's aerospace business made heavy use of computers, for instance, on the B-1 bomber. Within Rockwell, Sydney Hasin had been appointed to examine the firm's computer procurement practices. He had recently been demoted and had his salary cut because of his poor performance in an information systems subsidiary, so he was looking for a way to recover his stature in the company. He recommended computer leasing rather than purchase as a way to save costs, and OPM made him deals that seemed too good to be true. OPM wrote leases that could be cancelled with 30 days' notice, with the standard seven- to eight-year term specified to keep payments low, on equipment that was going to be obsolete in a year or less as IBM introduced a new line of computers. "In a memo, Hasin wrote that the leases with OPM represented savings to Rockwell of $760,000 over the bid of the nearest competitor . . . and savings of nearly $2.5 million, compared to the equivalent IBM rental over the project period."[28] Hasin was handsomely rewarded for his good work, obtaining more and more responsibility for Rockwell's computer operations. The problem was that in a lease transaction the lessor provides the ultimate security:

> But it was Rockwell, not OPM, that was committed to the lenders on those leases. The banks didn't care what side arrangements were made between OPM and Rockwell as long as they got paid by Rockwell as the financing documents stipulated . . . Rockwell should have been more concerned about OPM's ability to pay.[29]

Gandossy argued that one of the reasons OPM succeeded in perpetrating fraud on such a large scale and for so long was because the 1970s were difficult for business. "The firms in OPM's orbit were greatly affected by the troubled economy, and their growing dependence on the leasing firm caused them to interpret events favorably, neutrally, or even to look the other way."[30] In each instance, the dependence was built incrementally, but once in place, it was, like an addiction, almost impossible to conquer.

Although our previous two examples have focused on dependencies built across organizational boundaries, many of the same principles apply to the building of resource dependence within organizations. Staff groups, such as corporate planning, internal consulting, or, most commonly, accounting and information systems, offer services without internal recharging and help on projects of various types. Over time, dependence on these internal resources grows, and the units involved obtain power over the clients, just as OPM obtained power over the firms that became dependent on it.

Consider how, in a corporation such as Xerox, research obtains power over new product development efforts. Research units often have more discretionary or slack resources than marketing or development groups, which are constrained by continuing projects. Some development groups at Xerox were committed to specific projects as much as two years in advance. This makes it difficult for such groups to take on new projects on short notice, without getting additional resource support. Efforts to persuade research units to invest discretionary funds in co-development projects may thus be less an attempt to collaborate with research than an attempt to obtain funding for tasks that the development groups could not otherwise undertake. By providing the research units with discretionary funds, the corporation forces other units to involve research more closely in the development and marketing activities.

IMPLICATIONS FOR ACQUIRING POWER

The ideas and examples considered thus far have fairly clear implications for obtaining power and influence in organizational settings. First, the control over resources is crucial, and obviously the New Golden Rule gives enormous power to those units and individuals that control budgets and other substantial resources. A study of faculty salaries found that individuals who brought in grants and contracts both earned higher salaries and received more economic returns for their research productivity than those who did not have outside funding.[31] These effects held even when numerous other determinants of salaries were controlled, which indicates that the ability to bring in resources provides an independent and important source of power.

However, it is often possible to develop and exercise power by finding unexploited resource domains. Rather than contending over budget authority, power might be acquired by developing operative control over facilities, equipment, time and schedules, or other potential resources even less visible. In other words, power can often be increased by finding underutilized resources and exploiting them.

Resources are useful in the development and exercise of influence only to the extent one has discretion over them, and only to the extent that the dependence of others can be developed. The latter step often requires building commitments incrementally, and understanding how the opportunities with which one begins can be developed to provide resources that are crucial to the major actors one is seeking to influence. In this effort, the skills required are the ability to understand what is important to various constituencies, what currently underexploited resources are available to be mustered, and how to build dependencies.

From the other side of the equation, one can use these ideas to avoid becoming dependent on resources in the control of someone who may be untrustworthy and to be aware of the leverage that others may be developing. Dependence is inevitable in social life and certainly in organizations; social interaction always involves looking to others for advice, information, and other resources. But by paying attention to patterns of dependence and to the potential agendas of those who have power, one can at least avoid being surprised by power plays.

ALLIES

One of the most important resources that any member of an organization can have is allies or supporters. Organizations are frequently large, interdependent, and complex systems, in which it is difficult to get things done by yourself. It is essential to have loyal, trusted supporters to help carry out your plans. Although this may appear obvious, I often see managers at all levels who overlook the importance of coalitions of support and who therefore fail to cultivate allies. In thinking about this topic, it is important to consider how coalition partners can be identified, how alliances are built through promotions and hiring decisions, how alliances are built by providing resources and doing favors for others, how and why allies are lost, and the consequences for managers who don't have as many friends as they would like.

Succession at Nissan: The Rise of Kawamata

In the late 1940s and early 1950s, Japanese industry was still reeling from the war and its effects. Many industrial leaders had been stripped of their posts by the allies, factories were in disrepair, and much of industry was demoralized. Moreover, the allies had installed a labor relations system based on the U.S. model, and an energetic working class was organizing itself into powerful unions to take on a weakened industrial structure.[32] This was the situation that prevailed at Nissan. The founder, Yoshisuke Ayukawa, had been purged because of his role in the colonization of Manchuria, and several other top leaders had also been removed from the company. A powerful, left-leaning union of Nissan workers under the leadership of Tetsuo Masuda virtually ran the factories.

In 1947, the then-president of Nissan, Taichi Minoura, facing terrible problems that he was ill equipped to solve, asked the Industrial Bank of Japan to send him a financial man. The bank sent Katsuhi Kawamata, at the time 42 years old, who not only knew nothing about running a large manufacturing plant, but in fact did not even know how to drive a car.[33] He knew money, however, and as it turned out, he knew how to build power through alliances. His association with the IBJ gave Kawamata a certain amount of leverage, since the bank was a powerful force, along with the Ministry of International Trade and Industry, in the reindustrialization of Japan. He could count on the bank's support during his campaign to break the union, even if it meant waiting out long and violent strikes. The bank and its government contacts could build an alliance of other manufacturers and automobile companies willing to stand with him as he took on the union. Their backing was valuable, since it meant that they would not try to profit by seizing sales during periods of labor unrest.

Kawamata began to develop his power by obtaining support from the IBJ to withstand a strike that would almost certainly occur when he announced layoffs for almost 2,000 employees in 1949.[34] The 40-day strike was met with a new and harder line on the part of management, and the loan for $220,000 from the IBJ and two local banks began to cement their commitment to Kawamata and to Nissan. They had backed him and loaned him money, and now would be compelled to stand with him.

In 1951, when a new president was to be chosen, Kawamata sided with Asahara, a weak individual who he knew would not stand in his way. In further developing his power base, Kawamata relied extensively on building alliances, both externally and internally:

> Kawamata let everyone know that he was the bank and the bank had power over the company. . . . Soon Kawamata was reaching out to recruit his own people. Young management men had the distinct impression that very quietly a Kawamata team was being formed. . . . he started going around the factory giving out small sums of money to workers who might be working exceptionally late. . . . This was an executive letting the workers know that he was the main man.[35]

To further solidify his power in the firm, and to break the power of the union, Kawamata designed a brilliant strategy. He would not simply attack the old union, but rather, he would help create a second, competing union, which he would support and which would therefore become his ally:

> Even as Kawamata was looking for a second union, one had been forming at Nissan under a man named Masaru Miyake. In a way Kawamata had been looking for Miyake, and Miyake had been looking for Kawamata. They found each other in the spring of 1953.[36]

With the behind-the-scenes support of Kawamata, Miyake and his ally Ichiro Shioji built a strong union and crushed the old union that Masuda had built. Through this successful strategy, Kawamata put himself in a position to take over control of Nissan:

> Until the strike he had been a somewhat solitary figure at Nissan, an outsider sent over by the bank. . . . But Kawamata, as it turned out, had both crushed a union and at the same time . . . taken over the whole company. His power base was the Miyake union. . . . they were union leaders, but they were white-collar men of middle management, and their ambitions were managerial. . . . In terms of loyalties, they were very much Kawamata's men. Some had been encouraged to go to the union by him, others had turned to him. . . . Now Kawamata began to place them in important jobs throughout the company. They formed a cadre loyal first and foremost to him.[37]

Over the years, Kawamata maintained his position by maintaining his alliance with Shioji, and Shioji, in turn, held his position of power both in the union and in the company through his alliances with Nissan's management. Each side remained in power and enjoyed its perquisites in return for helping the other, on occasion quite secretly.

Many of the lessons in developing allies are apparent in the tale of Kawamata's rise to power at Nissan. One of the most important is the significance of finding others with common interests and building long-term relationships with them. "Coalitions survive over time because each element recognizes a commonality of interests. Deals are onetime, one-shot transactions, with no commitment on anyone's part for the future."[38] Kawamata recognized this distinction, and his masterful use of coalitions was the source of his success in the firm.

Obtaining Allies through Appointments and Promotions

One of the ways in which we can build alliances and coalitions is by helping people with whom we have ties to obtain positions of power. The ties may derive from previous working relationships, or from the fact that the people owe their very jobs and positions to our having promoted or hired them. Although we often like to think of the hiring and promotion process as based primarily on merit, ambitious managers understand quite well the necessity of ensuring that the organization is liberally salted with people who are obliged to them.

When Nabisco merged with the Standard Brands firm headed by Ross Johnson, Johnson set out to consolidate his power in the new organization. He arranged to have his own people placed in positions of influence, even though he was not yet formally the chief executive:

> Johnson had Standard Brand's Dean Posvar named planning director—a job that put Posvar—and thus Johnson—in charge of board presentations and enabled the Johnson troops to define and thus control board discussion. Johnson's crony Mike Masterpool took over public relations, giving him control of the outward dissemination of information as surely as Posvar's planning group and the financial apparatus regulated the inner flow. . . . Within three years, twenty-one of the company's top twenty-four officers were Standard Brands men.[39]

When Jim Wright was building and consolidating his power as Speaker of the House, he used the appointment and staffing process to help him. His own staff was hired primarily for their personal loyalty, rather than for their intellectual accomplishments or other skills:

> Wright used staff as an extension of himself, as executors of his will, not as advisors. . . . loyalty was the first requisite for employment. Indeed, only one senior member of his majority-leader staff had finished a four-year major college at all.[40]

He also made sure that the committee members he appointed knew to whom they owed their jobs. For instance, he controlled appointments to the powerful Rules Committee:

> Rules was one of three "exclusive" committees, meaning that members served only on it. Anyone removed and placed on other committees would start dead-last in seniority. . . . a few days before the organizing Caucus in which Wright would formally name Rules members, he hosted a luncheon for committee Democrats. He explained that he intended to use the committee as a tool, and sometimes they would have to obey the leadership. Then he said, "I assume you all want to be reappointed."
>
> There was a still moment. They would not forget again whose appointees they were.[41]

Wright made appointments to other committees, placed his allies in other leadership positions, and "made appointments to more than one hundred commissions. Each appointment had purpose, advanced his agenda. It was the minutiae of power."[42]

In very much the same way, the finance division at General Motors during the late 1950s established and maintained its power through a system that John De Lorean referred to as "promotion of the unobvious choice":

> This means promoting someone who was not yet regarded as a contender for the post. Doing so not only puts "your man" in position, but it earns for you his undying loyalty because he owes his corporate life to you. The "unobvious choice" is a devoted follower of the system who has nothing noteworthy in his background to mark him as a promotable executive. . . . Once in a position of power, a manager who was promoted by the system is insecure because, consciously

or not, he knows it was something other than his ability to manage
and his knowledge of the business that put him in his position.[43]

De Lorean detailed the importance of loyalty, and how
executives sponsored "unobvious choices" for positions as a
way of building a cadre of loyal, committed allies in key
positions within the corporation. A study some years ago
found that the appointment of an outside chief executive was
accompanied by more turnover in the upper executive ranks
than when an insider received the top job.[44] This is exactly
the result one would expect, since the outsider would want
and need to put his own people in place.

Building Alliances by Doing Favors

Alliances are built not only by putting people in critical
positions, but also by doing favors for others whose support
you want and need. The idea here is to capitalize on the
norm of reciprocity, which says that we are *obligated* to future repayment of favors, gifts, invitations, and so forth.[45] It
is a norm that is important in the development of society, for
it tends to facilitate transactions both among individuals and
across time. The development of the reciprocity norm meant
that one individual could give something such as food, shel-
ter, or assistance to another, without having to worry about
the resources being lost, since reciprocity would ensure the
person would be repaid. This meant that cooperation and
exchange could develop more readily, to the advantage of
the larger society.

It is important to distinguish reciprocity from more
straightforward exchange relationships. If I give you money
and in return you give me a product such as a vacuum
cleaner, there has not been reciprocity, but rather, a market
transaction. Similarly, when Robert Moses gave contracts and
inside knowledge to powerful Long Island Republican leaders in return for their support on specific park projects, the
exchange was a straightforward one.[46] What distinguishes the
development of allies through reciprocity are the following
features: 1) the favors are not necessarily sought or even desired by the individual receiving them; 2) the extent of the
obligation is not specified at the time the favors are granted;
and 3) the gift therefore creates, not a specific expectation

(such as a vote in return for money), but a diffuse, generalized obligation.

When Ross Johnson worked for Nabisco Brands as president and chief operating officer, Robert Schaeberle was the chairman and chief executive officer. In addition to insisting that Schaeberle's country club dues be paid by the company, making sure he drove a fancy car, and arguing for high pay for Schaeberle as well as himself, Johnson "deferred to Schaeberle in every regard, obsequiously addressing him in meetings as 'Mr. Chairman'. . . . Johnson donated $250,000 to Pace University to endow a Robert M. Schaeberle chair in accounting."[47] Although the company paid for the chair in accounting and for the new research center that Johnson had named the Robert M. Schaeberle Technology Center, "Schaeberle was moved."[48] Johnson was given the title of chief executive of Nabisco.

William Agee's ability to win a showdown with a group of unfriendly board members depended significantly on social ties with other board members and on the favors he had done for them:

> Jack Fontaine's law firm, Hughes, Hubbard, & Reed, received almost $600,000 in fees from Bendix during 1981. Jonathan Scott . . . is an old Idaho acquaintance of Agee's, and Agee sat on the A&P board when Scott was there. Hugo Uyterhoeven, 50, a professor at the Harvard Business School . . . drew more than $40,000 in directorial and consulting fees from Bendix in 1980. Given Equitable's so-so financial performance, Eklund [the CEO] seemed likely to need all the support he could get. . . . Agee now sits on several Equitable board committees, including the compensation unit that works out the financial packages of retiring senior executives of the company.[49]

Unlike Agee and Johnson, who cultivated allies by doing favors, Tylee Wilson, did not do favors for members of the board of directors while he was chief executive of RJ Reynolds Industries. This left him vulnerable to being ousted by Johnson after Nabisco and Reynolds had merged. For instance, one member of the board was Paul Sticht, the former Reynolds CEO:

> On his retirement, Sticht remained a powerful board member— maybe the most powerful. . . . Wilson did everything possible to freeze him out. Sticht's life revolved around corporate jets, but when

> Wilson felt his trips were for personal business, he made sure Sticht
> was charged for them. A retired chairman was entitled to an office . . .
> and Sticht got one—but in the old headquarters downtown.[50]

Wilson didn't treat other board members much better. Vernon Jordan, formerly director of the Urban League, was now a partner in a major Washington law firm. When he pressed for more legal work, "Wilson would cooly reply that as a non-lawyer, he couldn't judge whether there was anything appropriate; he referred Jordan to Reynolds' general counsel."[51] John Macomber, chief executive of Celanese, was also on the board. Although Reynolds paid Celanese about $25 million a year for material used in cigarette filters, Macomber wanted more business. Wilson rebuffed him. When a showdown with Ross Johnson finally came, Wilson found he had few friends on the board. Johnson's favors had earned him good will and obligations; Wilson's refusal to do favors had left him with little support for a political contest.

It is easy to see the building of a network of support, either through the appointment and promotion process or through personal favors, as activities that are somehow illegitimate or inappropriate. Such a view would be incomplete at best. The development and exercise of power in organizations is about getting things accomplished. The very nature of organizations—interdependent, complex systems with many actors and many points of view—means that taking action is often problematic. Failures in implementation are almost invariably failures to build successful coalitions. Although networks of allies can obviously be misused, they are nevertheless essential in order to get things done. And, allies must be put in place through whatever practical means are at hand.

How Allies Are Lost

One way of showing the importance of allies is to consider instances in which the managers did not do what was required to build and maintain coalitions of support. Most often, this failure resulted in the executives losing their positions. One thing we can be sure of: when an executive loses his or her position in the organization, it is impossible for the organization to benefit any longer from that person's insights, experience, and abilities. Simply put, keeping your job is a prerequisite for getting anything done. And keeping one's job involves having supporters in the firm.

Steve Jobs, one of the founders and for a long time the chairman and technical leader of Apple Computer, had numerous skills as a technical visionary and motivator of people. But his wisdom was lost to the company when he was forced to resign, a situation that arose largely from this own arrogance and his inability or unwillingness to cultivate support within the firm, particularly the board of directors:

> While some of the board members . . . took a paternal interest in Steve, his relationship to them, complicated as it was by fame and money, was something other than filial. He was at least twenty years younger than all of them except Markkula and Sculley. . . . He listened to their advice; but in strategic matters . . . he also did what he wanted to do. And he certainly never went out of his way to cultivate them or curry favor or ingratiate himself with them. . . . He simply managed to be more restrained around them than he was with most people.[52]

The problem is often one of ego. Getting something accomplished frequently involves sacrificing a bit of the limelight, and people who are unwilling to make this trade-off find it difficult to build coalitions. It is really as simple as asking yourself the question: Would you like to sign up to help me with my project, to achieve my success, or would you rather help a group of us achieve some collective goal and share in the credit? Most colleagues want their egos cared for and fed, which means involving them, sharing credit, and making sure they feel important and secure.

Peter Peterson joined Lehman Brothers in 1973 and within several months became the managing partner. He was superb in bringing in business, and under his stewardship, Lehman grew and prospered. But he did almost nothing to build alliances within the firm, especially among his partners, and so he was vulnerable to being thrown out in a power struggle with Lew Glucksman:

> But the attention Peterson could lavish on clients was rarely turned toward his partners, much less to those who worked in the trenches. . . . He would call partners at home at all hours, summon them to ride uptown in his chauffered Oldsmobile and then ignore them as he talked on the telephone or scanned a memorandum. Many partners thought him self-centered, haughty, unfeeling, uncaring. . . .

Peterson is a man of many talents, but few associates would say that sensitivity to people is among them. He was unaware that many of his partners, including some he felt close to, while respecting him, did not like him; they had tired of his one-sided conversations.[53]

Contrast Peterson's behavior with that of Katsuhi Kawamata or Ross Johnson, both of whom worked to build and maintain coalitions of support. Respect, competence, and intelligence are not enough. One needs friends and allies to attend to the many details of implementation, which are often too much for one person. One also needs allies to help fend off attacks from rivals for power. In getting things done, building coalitions of support, as well as finding and developing resources, are essential activities. Allies and resources are important sources of power, and as such, should not be wasted.

6

Location in the
Communication Network

There is an old saying that knowledge is power, and it certainly holds true in organizations. The knowledge that produces power in organizations is not only technical knowledge about the work process itself, but also knowledge of the firm's social system. One's access to social knowledge depends on one's position in the network of communication and social interaction. People who are well placed in the communication network also tend to be the central players in terms of power and influence. Those who have valuable social connections within the organization are also fortunate. Powerful people have powerful friends, it is said, both because they may offer advice and assistance and because we learn by watching others. Consequently, we can say that power is a function of one's position in the network of communications and social relations, where this position is assessed not only simply in terms of structural centrality, but also in terms of the power of the people with whom one is connected.

The measurement of a person's position in the communication structure is of both practical and theoretical concern. Many different measures of network centrality have been developed. Freeman has described three related conceptualizations of centrality: betweenness, connectedness, and proximity or closeness.[1] Betweenness is a particularly useful indicator of information control; it assesses the extent to which a person falls between pairs of other individuals on the communication paths that link them. Connectedness simply describes the number of others with whom one has contact, and it is more a measure of communication activity than of one's centrality in the network. Finally, closeness measures the distance between the focal individual and all other individuals in the communication network, using the shortest communication paths that exist between them. Closeness indexes which of a group of people can reach all the others in the fewest number of steps, and Freeman has suggested that it serves as an indicator of independence, because one who is close to all the others in the communication network cannot as readily have his or her access to those others controlled by someone else.[2]

EVIDENCE ON COMMUNICATION STRUCTURES

The importance of position in the communication network is a very old idea, which was studied by Bavelas and Leavitt some time ago.[3] In these early experiments, people were placed in a communication structure created by the experimenter. Some representative structures are shown in Figure 6-1. The effect of these structures on the task performance of the group, as well as on the influence attributed to the various individual members, was then studied. The results indicated that 1) the more centralized structures were more efficient for well-structured tasks, and the all-channel network was better for highly unstructured tasks; and 2) the individual with the highest degree of structural centrality tended to assume a leadership role, particularly in the structured tasks, and was perceived as being more influential by the other members of the group.

Subsequent research demonstrated that structures were themselves determined by the nature of the task.[4] A group that could reorganize itself would soon evolve to a centralized structure, like the star, when confronted with a routine task that did not impose complex information processing requirements; it would organize itself into something resembling the all-channel network when the task changed to one

Figure 6-1
Communication Networks

Star

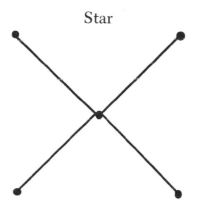

Wheel

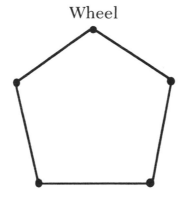

All-Channel

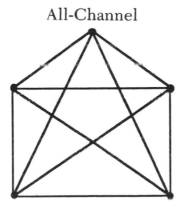

of more complexity. The theory that more centralized systems are more appropriate for routine tasks, and more decentralized structures are more efficient for coping with complex tasks, which require the active involvement of more people, has been extended to the literature on organizational design.[5] Thus, the general prescription has emerged that more hierarchical, centralized organizations are fine for dealing with situations that do not require a lot of information processing capacity, but that more complex, uncertain tasks require structures that facilitate information handling, such as lateral coordination, task forces, and teams.[6]

That structural centrality and control over communication provide power has been demonstrated in numerous contexts. Hickson et al. argued that in addition to the ability to cope with uncertainty, one of the attributes that enabled a department to gain power was its centrality in the work flow of the organization.[7] Andrew Pettigrew examined issues of communication and leverage in his study of a firm's decision to buy a particular computer system. In the firm being studied, the board of directors had the formal authority to make the decision. Jim Kenny, the head of management services, was under the board of directors, and under Kenny were the systems department and its manager and the programming department and its manager. It was the task of the management services group to recommend, with appropriate documentation and analysis, which of the computer manufacturers should receive the order:

> As it turned out, the decision process within the Management Services group developed into a competitive struggle for power between Kenny and his systems manager, Reilly, and between Reilly and the programming manager, Turner. . . . within three months of the onset of the decision, Kenny, Reilly, and Turner had each identified with a particular manufacturer. . . . Kenny possessed a major strategic advantage in the power conflicts because of his placement as a gatekeeper along two communication channels: . . . Firstly, the channel between his technical subordinates and the . . . board; and secondly, between the computer manufacturers and the . . . board. By sitting at the junction of the communication channels between his subordinates, the manufacturers, and the board, Kenny was able to exert biases in favor of his own demands and at the same time feed the board negative information about the demands of his opponents.[8]

Pettigrew further showed, in an analysis of actual documents used during the decision process, that Kenny mentioned his favored manufacturer more often than the others, and that the ratio of positive to negative comments in the documents was much higher for the favored manufacturer than for any of the others. Through his control over the communication channels that were used to convey information about the decision, Kenny was able to exercise substantial control over the outcome of the decision process.

In order to examine similar issues, Brass studied nonsupervisory employees at a newspaper publishing company. He identified employees' positions within three social networks: "(1) the work flow network, (2) the informal communication network, and (3) the friendship network."[9] He also suggested that "being included in the informal communication and friendship networks of supervisors and top-level executives will be more instrumental in a person's acquiring influence than being central in nonsupervisory networks."[10] Using three measures of influence—promotion to supervisory positions and both supervisors' and nonsupervisors' ratings of the individual's influence—Brass found evidence for the importance of the communication position in obtaining influence. He found that "being in a position to control communications within the department is particularly important to being promoted."[11] Because there was so much overlap among friendship and other communication networks, it was not possible in this study to disentangle the effects of task-related versus social communication. There is, in general, reason to believe that such networks often overlap substantially, and rather than worrying too much about what kinds of communication network centrality produce influence, it is more useful to note that virtually all kinds are related to one another and are sources of influence.

Krackhardt examined the determinants of power in a small, entrepreneurial firm involved in the sales, installation, and maintenance of information systems and communication equipment for client organizations.[12] He measured people's position in both the advice network and the friendship network and their effect on the individual's reputation for being powerful, as assessed by all other individuals in the firm. He found that, controlling for formal hierarchical position (the most important single predictor of power), one's centrality in the friendship network was significantly related to one's power, whereas one's position in the advice network had no effect. Although centrality in the advice network was quite independent of centrality in the friendship network (the correlation was only .22), centrality in the advice network was highly related to one's formal position in the organization—which is probably why advice centrality did not have an independent effect on an individual's power in this setting.

Position in the communication structure can also affect salary and the economic returns earned on other productive attributes such as performance and educational credentials. In a study of salary determination in a large sample of college and university faculty, Alison Konrad and I found that individuals who had more extensive communication with persons in other colleges and universities earned higher salaries, and likewise enjoyed greater returns on their research productivity and experience (in other words, for instance, an additional year of experience was worth more to someone who had more extensive contact with others in the same field).[13] Although the data did not permit us to measure structural centrality precisely, the finding that people with more extensive communication contacts earned more is certainly consistent with the argument that network position is an important source of power.

On occasion, centrality in the flow of communication alone can provide a great deal of influence to otherwise powerless units or individuals. Human resource departments are seldom very powerful, at least traditionally. In an organization such as Apple Computer, which was heavily dominated at first by engineers and later by marketing and (to a lesser extent) finance and manufacturing people, human resources might have been expected to have comparatively little influence. Many of the human resource executives were outsiders hired into the company, which also would tend to diminish their power. Yet human resources developed quite a bit of influence, particularly during the turbulent times at Apple after John Sculley's arrival. This was largely a consequence of the unit's centrality in the flow of communication and of the fact that, at a time when few divisions were talking to each other because of intrafirm rivalry, the human resource people spoke to each other regularly and shared common perspectives. All of this gave them more power than might otherwise have been expected:

> Apple's human resources department was far more than the paper-shuffling personnel bureaucracy of most corporations. . . . For every senior manager in the company, there was a corresponding human resources manager, usually female, forming a sort of shadow management team whose job was to find out what the real management and the people who worked for them were feeling.[14]

After Jobs was ousted in the struggle with Sculley and the corporation was thoroughly restructured, with a large number of layoffs, human resources came to play an even more critical role. The chief of human resources was Jay Elliot, and the head of human resources for the Macintosh group at that time was Mary Fortney:

> Because they headed a network that extended into every crevice of the organization, Jay Elliot and Mary Fortney and her counterparts in the II and sales divisions knew everything that was going on— who was unhappy, who was jealous, and who was saying what to whom. . . . The meetings were thoroughly scripted, and HR had the script. Mary was a facilitator . . . guiding the process, like the psychologist who stays in the background but exerts control with the subtle and well-timed remark.[15]

Caro's biography of the early years of Lyndon Johnson show the important role that Johnson's personal contacts and his centrality in the communication structure played in his acquiring influence in Washington. While he was still Richard Kleberg's congressional secretary, Johnson cultivated the friendship and acquaintance of powerful figures in the Roosevelt administration.

> Not only . . . did Johnson know powerful officials who were in a position to help him, these officials knew him . . . and wanted to help him. A measure of this feeling was the number of patronage jobs Johnson obtained. . . . Such jobs were generally rationed . . . on the basis of a Congressman's importance. The office of the average Congressman might be given four or five, the office of a senior . . . Congressman perhaps twenty. . . . The office of Richard Kleberg, a Congressman with neither seniority nor power, was given fifty.[16]

The story of Lyndon Johnson's early years was very much the story of his cultivation of one man, Sam Rayburn, a fellow Texan, a bachelor, and a very lonely man whom the Johnsons frequently invited to their home. Through his connection to Rayburn, Johnson was permitted to participate in informal gatherings among very powerful and senior congressmen. His friendship with Rayburn also gave him greater influence in the political establishment. As the friend of such a powerful person, Johnson was himself a formidable figure, to be treated with deference. Both in his dealings with other congressional secretaries in the Dodge House where they first roomed, and in his interaction with administration personnel and with congressmen, Johnson was tireless in his effort to know and be known by others. This familiarity served him well on many occasions in his efforts to acquire power and to get things done.

Another example of the importance of being connected to the right person, as a source of power, can be found in the recent history of E.F. Hutton. In 1983, Tom Lynch was made president of E.F. Hutton Group, the holding company for Hutton's subsidiaries. Lynch had been the company's chief financial officer. In a retail-oriented firm, which had derived most of its profit from retail brokerage, and in a firm that was expanding its investment banking and trading activities, it might appear that Lynch, in a staff position, would have little power. But Lynch was the intimate friend and adviser of Robert Fomon, the CEO of E.F. Hutton. Moreover, in the Hutton structure, 17 people reported directly to Fomon. That left Lynch, who was in close and frequent contact with Fomon, in a position to wield extraordinary power:

> Under the crazy-quilt system they had in place, Lynch would sit down with Bob and make decisions with him. . . . Lynch's influence over Fomon was extraordinary. . . . he hardly seemed on the surface like a power broker. But for years he was the second most powerful figure in Hutton: a power that stemmed from his relationship with Fomon.[17]

Physical Location and Centrality

There are many reasons why a given individual or organization is more central in the communication network, but among the most important is physical location in the organization. When I left the University of California at Berkeley to move to Stanford, Charles O'Reilly, a friend and colleague, inherited my office. Charles, many people would say, is one of the more powerful members of the Berkeley faculty. His sources of power are numerous, including his willingness to devote time and effort to the school, his academic reputation, his popularity as a teacher, and his personal style. But not to be overlooked is the fact that his office is located across from the men's room on the sixth floor of Barrows Hall. The Berkeley business school occupies space on the third, fifth, and sixth floors, and there is no men's room on the fifth floor. This means that all Charles has to do is to sit in his office with his door open, and during the day, all the male Berkeley faculty (which is the largest proportion, as there are few women faculty members), except those with very strong kidneys, will pass by his door. That physical centrality affects one's centrality in the communication network is so well known, at least intuitively, that people are almost always concerned about their office location and their nearness to headquarters.

Physical location helps to account for the great power often enjoyed by people in staff or assistant-to positions. Although not necessarily endowed with formal authority, these individuals have power because of physical arrangements. Henry Kissinger wrote, "Propinquity counts for much: the opportunity to confer with the President several times a day is often of decisive importance, much more so than the chairmanship of committees or the right to present options. . . . every President since Kennedy seems to have trusted his White House aides more than his Cabinet. . . . it may be as simple as the psychological reassurance conferred by proximity just down the hall."[18]

Even though there is now great interest in equipping managers in U.S. firms with foreign experience, the issue of physical location creates a paradox. Having an overseas assignment, although undoubtedly important from a developmental point of view, puts one far from the center of power, and often leads to the phenomenon "out of sight, out of mind." To the extent that conscious efforts are not made to overcome this effect of centrality on influence, and hence, on the chance of promotion, people will see overseas assignments as dead-end jobs, and will turn them down. But missing the potential learning that such experience provides will make it difficult for U.S. firms to develop the expertise necessary to truly compete in increasingly international markets.

The effect of physical location on power and influence also helps us understand the attitude toward manufacturing in corporations today. Many of our MBA graduates do not want jobs in manufacturing, and in many firms, manufacturing has little power.[19] The issue is not just the relative importance of the function of manufacturing in the firm; even in firms in which manufacturing is a critical factor for success, another problem arises—manufacturing takes place in the plants and facilities far away from headquarters. Except in a few instances, such as Lincoln Electric, in which corporate headquarters is located in the plant, this means that the manufacturing function, and its key executives, are likely to be physically separated from the administrative core of the organization. Finance, accounting, information systems, the legal office, and other staff functions, which might actually be more ancillary, are often housed in the headquarters building, near the top executives of the firm; this physical proximity gives them an advantage in the contests for influence that can occur.

Central physical locations provide power because of proximity. Out-of-the-way locations both leave people out of the flow of events and symbolize how peripheral their work is considered by the organization. When Roger Smith became executive vice president, finance, of General Motors in 1974, he concluded that GM was sadly out of touch with its marketplace. One remedy was to upgrade the corporation's strategic planning efforts, which until that time had been handled, poorly, in the divisions. Smith and Mike Naylor, an engineer in the transportation systems division chosen as head of a special planning team, were convinced that strategic planning was vital to the company. Smith used to say, "I don't want to run a buggy-whip company when somebody is inventing the automobile."[20] The problem was that Smith and Naylor were not sufficiently attuned to the need to muster political support for the changes, nor were they aware of the critical role the location of the planning group would play:

Both [Smith and Naylor] believed that with the right formula, the organization . . . could be convinced to go along with the plan.

Naylor's planning group consisted of Ph.D.s and computer jocks—an elitist element held in faint regard by the company regulars. They worked in the basement of the GM building. . . . The basement location was chosen for "security" reasons, since the group was dealing with highly confidential information about the company's operations. But symbolically, the fact that the small band of elite computer types were being hustled off to the basement to build their plans made it easier for other executives to ridicule them.[21]

Their location also made it harder for them to integrate themselves into the organization's ongoing work process.

Very often, the most prestigious office is the one in the corner with the best views, or the one on the highest floor. The price paid for occupying that separate and distant space is the price of being removed from the flow of communication. Balancing the status of one's location against its proximity to the flow of information can be crucial to an individual's success. I knew a man who was director of engineering for a division of Genrad Semiconductor Test Equipment located in Milpitas, California. At the time, the division was housed in a typical California R&D building—open plan office, one level, and quite horizontally dispersed. His two predecessors had both been forced to resign, so it was clear that the position was a challenging one. The head of the division and his top managers had private offices along one wall of the building. After carefully studying the facility layouts, the new director of engineering decided not to occupy his office in the so-called Executive Row. He noted that during the course of the day, people walked to the cafeteria and to the washrooms. He found where the two paths tended to intersect, near the center of the open plan office layout, and took that position as his work location. He attributes much of his subsequent success to that simple move, since it gave him much better access to what was going on in his department. He could keep on top of projects, answer informal questions, and in general, exercise much more influence over the activities of the unit than he could had he been off by himself.

The importance of physical arrangements in facilitating or inhibiting interaction should never be underestimated. Where one sits has an important effect on the number and content of one's interactions.[22] And this, in turn, influences what one knows, whom one knows, and one's relationship with others.

TASK INTERDEPENDENCE

In addition to the impact of physical location, communication centrality is affected significantly by the nature of the task and task-related interaction. Some people do jobs that require little interaction with others, and in which they rely primarily on their own skills and abilities; others have jobs in which they necessarily come into frequent contact with others within the organization.[23] Jobs differ not only in their degree of dependence on others, but also, obviously, in terms of the likelihood that their occupants will be centrally located in communication networks. A job that is high in its dependency on others may sometimes be difficult to perform, but it is useful in that it forces its holder to interact frequently with others and, thereby, to gain access to more and better information about what is occurring in the organization.

Ambitious people often evaluate job opportunities in terms of their potential for bringing them into contact with other members of the organization, particularly with powerful ones. Thus, for instance, the opportunity to work on the launching of a possible new publication, *TV-Cable Week* at Time Inc., was viewed as particularly attractive by two Harvard MBA graduates just starting in the company.[24] The launching of a new magazine, after all, would bring these fairly junior employees into contact with senior executives responsible for making the final decisions concerning the launch, as well as with people from marketing, production, and editorial who would be involved in the magazine's design and the analysis of its feasibility and potential.

The daunting aspect is that the very jobs that are more likely to bring a person into contact with others, and therefore positively affect his or her communications centrality, are also the jobs in which success will depend not so much on your own abilities and efforts, as on what others do, and what you can get them to do. Consequently, I often see people seeking out jobs with less interdependence in order to have more control over their own performance. The problem with such jobs is that they are less likely to lead to a set of relationships that will enhance a person's influence.

In law firms, different specialties vary in their degree of interdependence. Tax tends to be comparatively low, whereas litigation and business law tend to be higher in terms of interdependence with others both in the firm and outside of the firm. We would expect, then, that those specialties with the most contact across units would, all others being equal, tend to develop more influence in the firm because of their more central role in the communications structure.

Serving on a task force, team, or committee has some of the same positive effects in broadening as well as deepening one's network of contacts. It is not surprising, then, that such assignments are often considered desirable in terms of development as well as visibility. In fact, often the sole purpose of the task force, team, or committee is to bring people from different parts of the organization together. Viewed in this light, one can tolerate somewhat more readily the occasional inefficiencies and apparently wasted time that occur in these settings. If the real agenda is getting to know and understand other people and other parts of the organization, the ostensible task at hand may be less important.

BECOMING CENTRAL

Some of our centrality, and hence, our power and influence, derives from factors over which we may have limited control—for instance, office location and job assignment. But there are times when we can choose where we sit, where we work, and what types of projects we seek out or avoid. The effects of such choices on communication centrality, and consequently, on power and influence, need to be considered.

There are also things that we can do on our own to increase our access to influential people in the web of social relationships that constitutes an organization. I sometimes say that because I am a university professor, a job that has comparatively low amounts of interdependence, I have the freedom to eat lunch with my friends. What this means is that, as long as I do not desire to exercise a lot of power and influence, the limited amount of required interaction in my job permits me to associate with those whom I like. Most people in business or politics do not have this luxury, however, and no one who covets power and influence can afford it. To develop influence, we need to be plugged into the structure of com-

munication and interaction, and that means seeking out interactions, even social interactions, strategically. Although Lyndon Johnson may have been somewhat extreme in this
practice—dancing with congressmen's wives, playing the
role of the professional son, spending hours meeting and talking with almost anyone who was available—it is the extrem-
ity, not the general content, of his behavior that sets him
apart. The cultivation of social relationships, and the jockeying for position in social as well as physical space, is something that I observe frequently on the part of those seeking
power, simply because it is essential that they do so.

For example, I knew a person who worked in human resources at Apple Computer. At the time the firm was in some
turmoil. Indeed, the Apple II division went through five general managers in less than 18 months. As a nontechnically
trained, human resource professional, whose responsibilities
included helping the general manager to manage the business, she needed to get up to speed and to obtain influence
quickly. She instituted a series of get-togethers early on
Wednesday mornings in which four people from different
levels and units of the division were invited for coffee and
croissants and informal discussion. In about 10 weeks, she
knew 40 key people in the division to whom she could go for
advice, as well as having gathered a lot of information about
the problems confronting the division. John De Lorean, from
a more exalted position, did much the same thing when he
took over the Chevrolet division.[25] By meeting with divi-
sional executives on their own turf and not summoning them
to his office, and by listening to what they had to say, he
communicated effectively that he was interested in their
opinions, and also developed a more elaborate network of
contacts than he might otherwise have had.

Working to achieve centrality is particularly important for
people or groups who would otherwise have little power.
Various forms of discrimination against women, for instance,
have been extensively documented.[26] This means that
women need to be even more conscious of the importance of
networks and proximity, and more willing to be proactive
in overcoming the obstacles and disadvantages that confront
them.

Consider the case of a female neurosurgeon who was also a full professor of surgery at Stanford. When she was in training, there were few women surgeons. She scrubbed with the nurses, thereby missing out on the informal interaction that occurred as one dressed for surgery and undressed afterwards. When she served on call, there were no sleeping facilities for her—so she slept in the room in which fractures were set. The impossibility of having common changing and living facilities put her at a disadvantage both in terms of medical training and in terms of developing influence. When she joined the Stanford faculty as an assistant professor of medicine, she almost immediately ran for a place on the elected Faculty Senate. This job was not widely sought, but it put her in a position to know what was going on in the medical school. Since that time, she was elected chair of the senate and served on numerous committees. If she is asked about this activity, she says that it was important to intentionally obtain access to information and to put herself into influential communication structures.

As another example, the present chief operating officer of Stanford University Hospital, a large medical center, is a woman who formerly served as the director of nursing. She is also sensitive to the importance of serving on committees, task forces, and, in general, doing things that bring her into contact with a broad range of people from the hospital, the medical school, and the larger community. When the hospital was undergoing a major redesign and expansion, she served on the hospital design committee. Also serving on that committee was David Korn, at that time the chair of the pathology department, and today the dean of the Medical School. Committee service usually adds work to an already demanding schedule, but this type of visibility is critical, particularly for those who might otherwise be overlooked.

Social networks are, then, structures that can be built deliberately, and our place in the network of communication is something that is under our own control. We can work the numbers or the halls—and often it is more effective to work the halls.

7

Formal Authority, Reputation, and Performance

On February 6, 1968, Henry Ford surprised the automotive world by naming S.E. Knudsen, at the time the fourth-highest executive in General Motors, to the job of president of Ford Motor. Nineteen months later, on September 11, 1969, Ford fired Knudsen. Lightning struck a second time when, on July 14, 1978, Henry Ford fired Lee Iacocca from the presidency of Ford, in spite of considerable opposition to this move from board members, dealers, and even members of his own family. " 'Never complain, never explain,' Henry Ford II says. Because his name is Ford, he usually doesn't have to."[1] Although Henry Ford had power because of his control over resources, it was his position as chief executive, as well as his reputation and his performance while leading the company, that gave him the power to do with the company, and its executives, as he saw fit. The power of position, and the power conferred by a history of control and performance, was also demonstrated by William Paley of CBS:

> Despite his diminishing share of the company—some 11 percent—Paley acted the omnipotent owner. If he wanted to explain something, he did; if he chose not to, he didn't. . . . His imperious conduct made people automatically regard him as the Boss.[2]

A major source of power is your reputation in the organization—how well you have performed in this and previous positions, particularly in terms of getting things done and holding onto power. Your location in the formal organization structure obviously helps to determine power—it is better to be the boss. But the power of position, and the use of that power, is more than just formal authority. It entails building and maintaining a reputation for being effective, and it entails the capacity to get things implemented. Without these two components, the power of formal position tends to erode.

This chapter describes the power of formal position and tells how and why authority develops in social systems. It then considers the process through which reputations are developed and job performance is evaluated.

FORMAL POSITION AND AUTHORITY

One important formal source of power is position. Some years ago, I worked with a company that constructed cooling towers such as those used by electric utilities. The corporation was, at the time, a division of a larger conglomerate headquartered in the Midwest. The cooling tower company was a comparatively small part of the entire corporation. It was organized along functional lines, with a sales and marketing department, an engineering department, a production department, which manufactured standard parts for the construction projects, and an administrative department, which included finance and human resources. The company was dominated by engineering, in part because the division was run by engineers, and in part because the design and engineering of the projects were the most crucial and problematic features of the work. Even obtaining orders was secondary to getting the work done on a timely basis and to the customer's standards—for that was the surest way to book more business.

The company faced a problem of interdepartmental coordination. Marketing would book an order, but on occasion, engineering would not even start to work on the project until almost the due date for completion. Furthermore, engineering was often surprised by the specifications promised in obtaining the order. And, once engineering had completed its design work, production was often caught off guard by the material requirements and the pace that was expected.

Projects were consistently running behind schedule and over budget, and customers were complaining. It seemed fairly clear to most people in the organization that some form of project management was needed.

The senior management of the division held a meeting at which they discussed options for change. Moving either to a matrix structure or to a form of project management were obvious choices, which would improve cross-department coordination but which would also dilute the power of engineering. In spite of the threat to his power, the engineering vice president seemed sympathetic at the start of the meeting. He agreed with the diagnosis of the problem and admitted that a change was needed. Toward the end of the meeting, however, as consensus seemed to be emerging about a particular structural alternative, the vice president made some remarks that appeared to support the proposal, but that actually killed it. "I agree that the problem of interdepartmental coordination is a severe one," he said, "and that the structural suggestion being proposed is something that might possibly help us solve the problem. However, you know how headquarters is. They are very conservative, traditional folks who like clean lines of authority and responsibility. I don't think headquarters will approve our idea—in fact, I'm sure they won't, because I talked to my counterpart there the other day about this general idea and he expressed his displeasure with these new-fangled administrative notions quite strongly. Thus, even though it might be the right thing to do, it will never pass muster." He then casually introduced a plan that involved having engineering, his department, take on some responsibilities for overall project coordination, and also become more involved both in the bidding process for new contracts and in the scheduling and control of production. His idea carried the day.

Even now, I don't know 1) whether the person had ever spoken to anyone at corporate headquarters; 2) whether personnel at headquarters approved or disapproved of the proposed change; or 3) whether they even cared, as long as the division did something to solve its coordination problems and enhance its profitability. I do know that this strategy of saying, "the boss won't approve" or "headquarters won't approve" is often utilized and seldom challenged.

The fact that this strategy works implies that there is power associated with formal positions. The chairman, the president, the supervisor—all have power as a consequence of their formal position in the organizational hierarchy. We obey the orders of those who have formal authority, or at least if we disobey them, we think carefully about it first. We seldom consider the fact that formal authority is a source of power if and only if we accede to it. Lower-level participants in organizations also have power—the power to resist or refuse the orders of their superiors.[3] And, in fact, if enough of them resist, their superiors will come to have no power at all. The process is well illustrated, although on a grander scale, by what has happened in Eastern Europe and the Soviet Union. As long as most people, and certainly the army and the security apparatus, accepted the authority of Communist leaders, their rule was secure—the few who dissented could be imprisoned or otherwise dealt with. When, however, almost everyone rejects the authority of the existing political leadership, that authority is no longer legitimate, and even in the most totalitarian regimes, the leaders soon have no real power.

The power inherent in a given formal position is, therefore, power invested in that position by all (or at least most) members of the social organization in which the position is located. "Consent of the governed" is a phrase with meaning not only in democracies, but in all forms of organization, including corporations and other bureaucracies. The power to hire, fire, and reward, which comes with many high-level managerial positions, is available only to the extent that the holder's right to exercise that power remains unchallenged. If personnel will not actually fire someone, and payroll will not cut off his or her pay, and security will not bar the person from the building, and colleagues continue to work with that person, then the firing has, in effect, not occurred. John Gardner, writing about leadership, has noted, "Leaders cannot maintain authority . . . unless followers are prepared to believe in that authority. In a sense, leadership is conferred by followers."[4]

If the power that derives from positions and formal authority is something granted by others to the occupant of the position, the next question is, what motivates social organizations and their members to make such grants? Why do people obey, rather than challenge, question, or ignore authority—at least most of the time? This obedience to authority is, at times, quite dramatic. During World War II, German citizens by the thousands participated in the slaughter of innocent people, many of them women and children, simply because they were ordered to do so. When confronted with such events, most people reply that they would behave differently. In part to illustrate that they would not, as well as to explore the foundations of this obedience to authority, Stanley Milgram, a social psychologist at Yale University, ran a series of experiments that are now classic and widely known.[5] Subjects were recruited to participate in a study that ostensibly was designed to explore the effect of punishment on learning. After a drawing of straws (rigged so that the subjects were always given the role of teacher), the subjects were told to read a set of pairings of nonsense syllables to another person (actually a confederate of the experimenter). Then, they were to repeat the list, and when the learner made a mistake, they were to depress a lever administering an electric shock, moving up the panel of levers each time a new shock had to be given. The confederate complained about the pain, begged to be let out of the experiment, and so forth, finally letting out a bloodcurdling scream (the confederates were actually from Yale's drama department) and then making no further response. If the subjects questioned the experimenter, he said only that the experiment required that they continue. They were not forced to continue, nor was their modest payment for participating contingent on their continuing to administer the shocks. Nevertheless, a large proportion of the subjects went all the way to the highest shock level. Although this experiment illustrates influence processes other than obedience to authority (such as escalating commitment to a course of action, once embarked upon), it also illustrates people's willingness to comply with outrageous requests made by authority figures who are virtually strangers.

Obedience to authority is conditioned early in life, and offers, under most circumstances, many advantages to both society and the individual. Consider, for instance, a football team. Suppose, instead of following the play called by the quarterback in the huddle, each player were to decide for himself what play to run. Or what if the players in the huddle debated which was the appropriate play to call? In either case, the result would be uncoordinated or untimely action and a very poor performance in the game. Most activities involving interdependent action will not be successful if the actions are uncoordinated. It is consequently not surprising that we learn from experience to coordinate our activities with others, and that we defer to authority in order to ensure such coordination.

Moreover, we learn early in life that those in authority typically know more than we do. One of the fundamental tenets of Weber's bureaucratic model of organizations is promotion based upon competence and experience.[6] To the extent that promotions are based on merit, it is likely that those in higher-level positions have more knowledge, experience, and ability than their subordinates. This means that obeying their directions is good for the organization as a whole. Furthermore, if we obey people who appear to be in authority, we economize on our information processing requirements. We do not have to reinvent the wheel, but rather, we can act in a fairly automatic fashion.

We not only obey authority, of course, we obey people who possess the symbols of authority. That is why security services dress minimum-wage security guards in uniforms, which often appear to be similar to police uniforms. If they look like police, maybe they will be obeyed as police are. Dress is used to indicate authority and special ability in other domains as well. I knew a woman neurosurgeon who graduated from the Sloan Program at Stanford, with whom I kept in touch because of my interest in women exercising power in typically male environments. On her invitation, I watched her and some of her male colleagues perform surgery. On one occasion, I arrived in the operating theater before the surgeon, dressed, of course, in the green garb of the operating room. Introduced to some people in the room as Dr. Pfeffer (I have a Ph.D.), I took a place at some distance from the patient. A nurse (who didn't know who I was) said, "Over here, doctor," and prepared to hand me a scalpel. It was fortunately not difficult to curb my desire to play doctor, and we all had a good laugh at the incident. But there are documented cases of nonphysicians performing surgery, nonlawyers practicing law, and businesspeople faking their credentials and experience and operating successfully, at least for a while, as high-level corporate executives. We do not bother, in most instances, to examine the person's credentials, or to investigate whether they really have the knowledge and skill to be in the position held—the position itself implies competence, and we treat its occupant accordingly.

When United Artists was purchased by Transamerica, at that time a conglomerate, the CEO of Transamerica, John Beckett, had the authority to issue orders even though he knew very little about the movie business and admitted as much. The first time that United Artists lost money, in 1970: "The order went out: 'All acquisitions cease until we have a management system in place that we can understand and will give us early warnings.' "[7] After the executives running United Artists left to found Orion, in part because of what they perceived as interference by a corporate management that did not know the movie business, Andreas Albeck, United's senior vice president of operations, was appointed president and chief executive of the subsidiary. Albeck was virtually unknown in the industry, although he had worked in it for many years. In spite of the fact that he did not enjoy a significant reputation, his title gave him the power to direct United Artists' operations, and he did so without serious challenge to his authority. His decisions eventually led to the demise of the company as a separate entity, but he had the power to make them because of his position in the corporate hierarchy.

The acceptance of hierarchy, of the chain of command, is so automatic that it makes news when it is violated. Orders are followed, and authority is given deference, in part because of the instability or even chaos that might otherwise result. Authority is also obeyed because it is almost inconceivable not to. The power of leaders and bosses becomes institutionalized, and is thus not questioned or even thought about. To understand the source of this unquestioning attitude, we need to know something about the process of institutionalization in organizations.

Institutionalization

Like the authority conveyed by position, standard ways of doing things come to be accepted automatically as a social fact. Writing about the process of institutionalization, Zucker has commented:

> . . . social knowledge once institutionalized exists as a fact, as part of objective reality, and can be transmitted directly on that basis. For highly institutionalized acts, it is sufficient for one person to simply tell another that this is how things are done. Each individual is motivated to comply because otherwise his actions and those of others in the system cannot be understood.[8]

Methods of operation become institutionalized, not only because new organizational members imitate their peers, but also because those methods are sanctioned by the weight of authority. The authority in question can either be a person higher in the organization, or the generalized authority of tradition in the organization itself.

Zucker's study of the transmission of an arbitrary microculture established in an experimental context is a dramatic illustration of the force of authority. If one stares at a stationary point of light in a darkened room, the light will appear to move. Jacobs and Campbell had conducted a study in which confederates of the experimenter gave initially extreme estimates of the distance the light moved.[9] In successive experimental trials (known as generations), the confederates were removed one at a time and replaced with naive subjects. The question was how long the distance estimates—the cultural norm—would persist under conditions of personnel replacement. Zucker modified the experimental conditions only slightly, introducing, in addition to the original condition of simple replacement, an organizational context condition and an office condition.

In the organizational context condition, the following instructions were given to the subjects:

> This study involves problem solving in model organizations. You will be participating with another organizational member. . . . Most large organizations continue even though individual members, or even whole divisions, may be replaced. . . . The model organization in which you will participate also will have this feature. . . . Thus, performance of any single member may not be important to the organization as long as the job continues to be done.[10]

In the office condition, the organizational context instructions were supplemented with the additional instructions:

> Large organizations also place members in different positions, often according to the amount of time spent in the organization. The model organization in which you will participate also has this feature—the member who has spent the most time in the organization will be the Light Operator. . . . To simplify the recording procedures, the Light Operator will be asked for the judgment first.[11]

Zucker's results were striking. The average subject, doing the task by herself, will estimate that the light moves slightly more than four inches. The initially established "culture" (distance estimate) was eleven inches. Under a simple condition of interpersonal influence, in which new subjects gave their distance estimate last, and then remained as the senior subject left, it took only about six generations for the distance estimates to converge with the number provided by random subjects doing the task alone. However, in the office condition, after six generations the distance estimates had fallen only to ten inches, and the data, extrapolated out, indicated that even after some 36 generations, the distance estimate was still approximately six inches. The organizational context condition also caused the original distance estimates to persist, but not as strongly as in the case of the office condition.

What this means is that merely telling someone that he or she is joining an organization, even an artificial one, and presenting that person with a title, even one that is clearly without significance, like Light Operator, causes the person to act differently. To be specific, subjects conformed much more strongly to the apparent norms that had been established in the mock organization. If we extrapolate these findings to real organizations in which cultural norms are more important, we can readily see how authority comes to have such a profound effect on behavior.

REPUTATION

To know that formal position conveys power is one thing, but it is also vital to understand something of the dynamics through which one advances to such positions. In the process of acquiring power, both through actual promotion and through informal acceptance of one's authority by others, reputation and performance are critical. One wants to develop a reputation as someone who is reliable and predictable, someone who can get things done, and someone who has power and influence—the reputation for having power brings more power.

For the individual, being viewed as powerful or influential may have the effect of changing the person's behavior. There is a large literature on a phenomenon called the self-fulfilling prophecy, which notes the effects of expectations on behavior.[12] People who are expected to succeed tend to do well, while those who are expected to fail often perform poorly. One reason such an effect might occur is through a mechanism called defensive effort. If you don't expect to do very well on a task, you may not try as hard—why waste the effort on a lost cause? Similarly, if you perceive yourself (and are perceived by others) as having little power, you are not likely to try to influence others, or if you do try, your efforts may be halfhearted. Also, being in a powerless position, particularly if there is much to be accomplished, may cause anxiety. Anxiety or tension can be distracting, and can make your attempts to get things done less effective than they might otherwise be.

Another reason why perceptions can become reality is that perceptions affect how others interact with us, and we respond accordingly. Mark Snyder reviewed a number of social psychological experiments that illustrate this point dramatically.[13] For instance, if a subject is told that she or he will be talking on the telephone to a person of the opposite gender who is attractive, the subject behaves differently, thereby eliciting different responses from the person at the other end of the line. Or, if you are told you will be supervising someone who is not competent, you will supervise more closely and engage in more directive behavior, which will then produce different behavior on the part of the person being supervised.[14] In the case of exercising influence, if you are perceived as being influential, you are less likely to be challenged, attacked, or fought. Consequently, you will be able to get things accomplished with less effort, and you will get more things done. And this, in turn, will only further enhance your reputation for being powerful and effective.

Rosabeth Kanter has argued that when people in organizations are difficult, argumentative, and temperamental it may be because they are in positions of powerlessness, in which what they have to do exceeds their resources and capacities to do it.[15] One of the reasons many of us like to work for and with people who are powerful is that they are generally more pleasant—not because it is their native disposition, but because the reputation and reality of being powerful permits them more discretion and more ability to delegate to others.

Not only does the reputation for having power change our own behavior and the way others interact with us, but it also affects how real resources are allocated, thereby transforming reputation into reality. Some years ago, a study followed a group of American Telephone and Telegraph managers over a five-year period, examining the extent to which performance evaluations received at the end of the first year were predictive of performance evaluations five years later.[16] The study found a very strong correlation between the evaluations at the two points in time. One explanation for this result is that the performance evaluation system was quite effective in rating the individual's true abilities, so that first-year evaluations had a lot of accurate information that correctly forecast how people would be doing years later. However, another, more plausible explanation for the findings is that individual's evaluations have consequences in their subsequent careers. People with more favorable reputations are likely to get the more interesting and challenging job assignments with more developmental potential, more training and executive education opportunities, more mentoring and coaching from higher-level managers, and other opportunities that will, in fact, tend to make them more effective performers. Similar feedback processes occur with power and influence as well. People with reputations for being influential and effective will, all other things being equal, find it easier to obtain allies and supporters. They are also more likely to have opportunities to exercise their influence, thereby getting things accomplished and enhancing their reputation.

Roger Smith's career at General Motors nicely illustrates how a reputation is developed, and what elements in that reputation are important. In his 31 years of working his way up the corporate ladder to chief executive, he acquired a reputation for being efficient and industrious:

> Not only would he enthusiastically support the task on the table, he would also make certain that he got it done faster and more masterfully than anyone else. "Whatever the senior people wanted done, he did it," a former colleague told *Fortune* magazine. . . . He was an eager beaver, capable of outworking everyone around him. He put himself at GM's service and developed the reputation of a young comer who would go anywhere or do anything for the company.[17]

Smith also developed the ability to get things done without limiting the credit his bosses received for what were actually his accomplishments. His willingness to work hard, to be loyal both to his boss and to the company, and his capacity for getting things accomplished soon brought him a powerful mentor, Thomas Murphy, who preceded him as CEO:

> It was this instinct for being the "good old boy" in the corporate game that first brought him to the attention of Thomas Murphy . . . who learned, like others before him, that he could depend on Smith. "It wasn't too long before I realized that if you wanted to get something done and you had to be sure it got done on time and accurately, Roger was the guy who could do it," recalls Murphy. . . . "He was a guy who was willing to work at whatever you gave him, whenever it was there, and do well at it."[18]

A reputation like Smith's makes others want to have you work for them, and to bring you along as they move up in the organization. It is also a reputation that helps create opportunities to expand your competence and your sphere of influence.

The career of Frank Stanton, who was to rise to the presidency of CBS under William Paley, was quite similar in many respects to that of Smith at General Motors. He started his career at CBS in 1935, and soon "impressed his colleagues as a diligent, energetic worker and a stickler for detail."[19] He worked almost endlessly, taking little time off for his personal life or for other diversions. Stanton's base of operation was the research department, and he pioneered in conducting surveys to find out who listened to what radio station, which programs they liked, and in discovering facts about the market and about the competitive position of the various stations. His department, and his reputation, grew:

Stanton had his tiny research department churning out facts and figures to salesmen trying to lure advertisers and choice affiliates from NBC. He was establishing himself as an executive with precise methods. . . . Everyone called Stanton "Doc." . . . Before long, his research was used in almost every facet of CBS's business—to help attract advertisers and audiences, to select and build programs, and to help coax affiliates to switch from NBC to CBS. By 1938 he was research director with a staff of one hundred.[20]

Much of Stanton's information was obtained from the *World Almanac*, which was potentially available to anyone. However, through his hard work and his insight and willingness to track down information, he made himself indispensable. "Stanton's bywords around CBS became 'Let's find out.' Whenever there was a vacuum, Stanton would fill it with enthusiasm and dedication."[21] Needless to say, there were more and more such vacuums to be filled, as his reputation as someone who gets things done, in this case, by analysis, grew. By 1942, Stanton was vice president in charge not only of the research department, but also of "advertising, sales promotion, public relations, building construction, operations and maintenance, and supervising the seven radio stations owned and run by CBS."[22]

The reputation for having power is almost as important as the reputation for loyalty and competence, since, as we have seen, the perception of power can help to create power. Early in the first Nixon administration, Henry Kissinger engaged in a battle with the State Department over control of the foreign policy decision-making structure. "State wanted to control the staffing of the interdepartmental machinery; it also insisted on the authority to resolve disputes with other departments and the right to take disagreements to the NSC."[23] Kissinger had proposed a National Security Council system that gave him much more power and control over the process. Nixon sided with Kissinger, and his plan won out. This particular bureaucratic victory had far-reaching effects on Kissinger's career:

This incident was important less in terms of real power than in the appearance and in what it foretold about the President's relations with his principal advisors. The fact that the contest ended in what was perceived to be a victory for me helped establish my authority early on.[24]

A similar struggle occurred at the start of the Kennedy administration in the early 1960s. Again, the contest for power occurred between Secretary of State Dean Rusk and McGeorge Bundy, the special assistant to the president for national security affairs:

> Kennedy was quickly dissatisfied with State, and Bundy, sensing the vacuum, moved deftly to fill it. He began to build his own power, looking for his own elite staff. . . . They could move papers quickly, something State could never do, and through an informal network at Defense and CIA, they could exploit sympathetic friends and thus create an informal inner network in the government.[25]

Rusk resented the growing profile and power of Bundy and his staff, and complained about it often. However, Rusk's complaining served Bundy's interests well:

> . . . . [Bundy] did not worry about the rumors of his growing power and influence; he delighted in them, knowing that the reputation that you are the man to see feeds on itself, and makes you even more so.[26]

There are two fairly straightforward implications that follow from this discussion of the importance of reputation and how it helps build power in organizations. First, what happens early is critical. Note that both Bundy and Kissinger moved quickly to vanquish their principal rival, the State Department, and to establish their reputation for winning. Roger Smith and Frank Stanton began building their reputations as loyal, hardworking, can-do people early in their career. Your reputation is formed soon after you enter the organization, and thus it is essential to start out on the right course.

The second implication concerns the question of when to fight on the losing side of an issue. Because of the importance of reputation as a source of power and as a lever to attain higher-level positions, it is fairly easy to answer a question I am often asked: If I know that I will lose on an issue that I consider important and about which I am convinced I am right, should I carry on the fight anyway? My reply is, in almost all instances, no. Being on the losing side of issues, particularly if it happens repeatedly, gives one the reputation of being a loser. Such an image is quite inconsistent with attaining power and influence. Just as a person is known by the company he or she keeps, we are known by the issues we are associated with, and by what happens to those issues when they are decided.

Note, too, that the question as it is phrased presumes that you will lose regardless of what you do, and that you know this in advance. If you acknowledge your differences with others on the issue and state the reasonable basis for your opinion, but then agree to go along with the opinion of your colleagues, you will get points for being cooperative and a team player. More important, by making it clear that you are, in fact, making a concession, you will obligate the others to reciprocate in some way, perhaps by acceding to your views on a subsequent issue. On the other hand, if you simply continue to resist, the others involved in the decision will owe you nothing and, in fact, will probably come to resent your continued opposition.

Finally, literature in social psychology suggests that people like to think the world is orderly and just. There is, therefore, a tendency to think that if someone suffers a reversal or setback, even if it is a true accident, like a car crash or a fatal illness, that person must have deserved what happened because of something about him or her.[27] To lose on an issue, particularly after one has struggled openly in its favor, can scarcely be considered a random, uncontrollable event. Consequently, the loser is even more likely to be perceived as having deserved this failure. By being on the losing side of an issue, we may activate social perception processes that will produce exactly the worst possible result—a devaluation of our capabilities and our importance.

Jim Wright, as Speaker of the House of Representatives, was aware of the damage that public losses might inflict on his reputation. In his struggles with the Reagan administration over both tax and budget policy and the support of the Nicaraguan contras, Wright pushed his Democratic colleagues to take strong positions, to stick together, and to win votes for bills even if Reagan would veto them later. One of the most difficult debates was over the budget of the 100th Congress. The deficit was growing rapidly. Reagan had opposed new taxes, and the responsibility for formulating the budget rested with a Congress controlled by Democratic chairmen who wanted neither to cut funds from their pet programs nor to commit political suicide by increasing taxes. Wright took some significant political gambles in pushing his own agenda through the Democratic leadership, but he always faced the risk of losing:

> What would a loss mean? If he could not even get a budget out of committee, he and the party would become laughingstocks. If the House rejected the budget it would not be much better. The perception of power gave him power. Perceptions were fragile. If he was perceived not to have power he would lose it.[28]

The importance of reputation means that we must plan our actions carefully and be sensitive to appearances. This is particularly true in the early stages of our tenure in a new organization or a new position—thus Jim Wright needed to be especially careful about how his reputation was perceived in the period just after he assumed the speakership.

PERFORMANCE

Position and reputation are sources of power in part because of what they imply about the individual's ability to perform his or her job effectively. And, in turn, effective performance in the job helps to build one's formal authority and reputation. Thus, position, reputation, and performance are interrelated, and if any of the three is favorable, the others will be positively affected.

It is, however, important to recognize what performance means, and what it does not. In an activity like baseball, for instance, it is fairly easy to assess performance.[29] There are books published regularly with statistics on almost every aspect of the game, and great efforts have been made to derive composite measures of performance for both pitchers and nonpitchers. Moreover, baseball is a game in which individual contributions and skills are readily assessed because the sport involves comparatively little interdependence. None of these conditions holds true in most organizations. It is often not clear what the specific objectives are and how each individual's activities are or are not contributing.

In most organizations, consequently, performance means being knowledgeable, drawing criticism away from the boss, and accomplishing things that make the subunit and the boss look good. We may hope that what we have done has long-term value for the organization, but as I noted already in Chapter 1, evaluating decisions for their quality is often quite problematic. It is easier to fall back on indicators such as short-term practical results and problem-solving ability.

In describing the source of Robert Moses's power during the LaGuardia mayoral administration, many of his contemporaries emphasized his ability to solve problems and get things accomplished:

> Says Judge Jacob Lutsky, who not only served in the LaGuardia administration, but was a top adviser to Mayors O'Dwyer, Impellitteri, and Wagner: "You've got to understand—every morning when a mayor comes to work, there are a hundred problems that must be solved. And a lot of them are so big and complex that they just don't seem susceptible to solution. And when he asks guys for solutions, what happens? Most of them can't give him any. And those that do come up with solutions, the solutions are unrealistic or impractical—or just plain stupid. . . . But you give a problem to Moses and overnight he's back in front of you—with a solution, all worked out down to the last detail, drafts of speeches you can give to explain it to the public, drafts of press releases for the newspapers, drafts of the state laws you'll need to get passed, advice as to who should introduce the bills in the Legislature and what committees they should go to, drafts of any City Council and Board of Estimate resolutions you'll need; if there are constitutional questions involved, a list of the relevant precedents—and a complete method of financing, are all spelled out. He had solutions when no one else had solutions."[30]

Hopefully, the solutions were good ones, involving building the right public works in the right places. But such considerations pale in comparison with the ability to provide answers and to reduce uncertainty at all. Moreover, Moses understood that at that time the mayor (and the governor) ran for reelection every two years, and that a park completed in 20 months was much more valuable than one completed in 26 months.

In much of our thinking about decisions and choice in organizations, we are obsessed with the importance of doing the right thing, making the correct decision. This is a carryover from our days in school, where our grades were determined by our ability to produce the "right" answer. With such a frame of mind, performance becomes defined by the consequences of our actions, measured against an objective standard of correctness. And, from this perspective, we fail to see how and why some individuals get ahead and obtain power by getting things done, since it may look to us as if they are getting the wrong things accomplished.

There are several problems with this perspective on performance. First, history is often ambiguous.[31] The connection between actions and the consequences of those actions is frequently unclear. The delay between making a decision and experiencing its consequences may be so long that the people involved may have either left the organization or been promoted into higher positions. Even more important, responsibility for decisions is often collectively shared so that blame or credit cannot be attached to a single individual.

Second, as John Gardner has recognized, the multiple determinants of outcomes mean that it is not very useful to judge people solely by the consequences of their actions:

> Leaders act in the stream of history. As they labor to bring about a result, multiple forces beyond their control, even beyond their knowledge, are moving to hasten or hinder the result. So, there is rarely a demonstrable causal link between a leader's specific decisions and consequent events. Consequences are not a reliable measure of leadership.[32]

And, I would add, consequences are not a reliable measure of performance.

Moreover, information about consequences is not often sought, and indeed, is sometimes consciously avoided. Few educational programs systematically trace their alumni to see what effect the program has had on their lives. Few physicians keep records of their success in treating patients. And, even in organizations, information systems are often established as much to signal good intentions about measuring performance as to actually assess it.[33]

Performance is an important source of power in organizations. But we need to understand performance for what it usually is—the ability to exercise influence and get something done. We also need to deemphasize our preoccupation with correctness as a measure of performance. Being correct is not always the same as solving problems for the boss and the organization, which are the accomplishments that really define performance in most organizations.

SOME IMPLICATIONS FOR DEVELOPING POWER

Formal position matters because it confers control over certain resources and the ability to take certain implied or specified actions. As I noted in the preceding chapter, resources are crucial in the quest to obtain power. Thus positions with control over resources and with actual decision-making authority are more desirable in terms of developing and exercising power. In this sense, line positions are generally better than staff assignments, even though various staff, internal consulting, and assistant-to jobs can be more interesting, fun, or intellectually challenging. In organizational battles, one needs an army and some supplies, and control over resources is important in securing power.

Because reputation is affected by first impressions, it matters to develop a good track record early. If you get off to a poor start, it may be necessary to switch to a different unit within the organization, or even to a different organization, in order to get your career moving again. Because of the interconnected nature of reputation, performance, and position, it is exceedingly difficult to work yourself out of a hole. It is better to start over somewhere else, presumably having learned some lessons about how to be more effective in the future.

Strategic behavior consciously intended to demonstrate performance and build reputation is helpful in the effort to develop sources of power. Roger Smith, Frank Stanton, McGeorge Bundy, Henry Kissinger, Robert Moses, and Jim Wright were all conscious of the importance of establishing their reputation and performance early in their careers. One of the lessons we learn from reading political and business biographies is that those who maintain power and influence over protracted periods of time do so because they are conscious of how power is developed and what its sources are, and because they work to acquire and maintain these sources through planned effort.

8

The Importance of Being
in the Right Unit

In Salomon Brothers in the 1980s, being in equities put you at a disadvantage compared to being in bonds:

> With the rise of the bond markets, the equity salesmen and traders had been reduced by comparison to small-time toll takers. They made a bit of money and had a few laughs, but not nearly so many as the bond men. . . . An investor could buy shares in IBM from Salomon, but he could equally well buy them from forty other stockbrokers. . . . Salomon was nearly a monopolist in certain bond markets.[1]

This example illustrates the fundamental point that one source of an individual's power is the subunit or organization of which he or she is a member. Not all individuals are equally influential in organizations, and neither are all groups or units. Most of us recognize intuitively that being in a more powerful group will provide us with more power. Business school students interviewing for jobs try to assess the best place to begin in their prospective employer's organization, and that assessment often involves determining which are the most powerful units. In state or national legislatures, being a committee chairperson provides varying amounts of power, depending on the power and importance of the committee involved. In organizational life, we often act as representatives of our subunits as we sit on task forces or as we advocate promotions, budgets, or resources for ourselves and our colleagues. The success of this advocacy is likely to depend partly on whether the subunit we represent is more or less powerful.

After briefly examining evidence that being in a powerful unit provides one with more influence, I will spend this chapter exploring what factors account for the variation in the power and influence of organizational subunits and how subunit power is built. Power derived from subunit membership or identification is power based on one's location in the social structure and the division of labor. In this sense, it resembles power derived from one's position in the communication network or one's formal position of authority.

Although the importance of subunit membership as a source of individual influence seems obvious, it has not been demonstrated to any great degree. There are, however, a few studies that investigate the effect of subunit power on individual salary and other career outcomes. Some years ago, William Moore and I examined the effect of subunit power on the rate of progression through the quasi-civil service of the University of California faculty salary system. The sample under study included faculty in a set of departments on two campuses.[2] Not surprisingly, we found that there were more accelerated promotions in more powerful departments, even when departmental size and rated academic quality were statistically controlled. More recently Alison Davis-Blake and I conducted a slightly different study with a parallel theme.[3] We examined whether certain high-level academic administrative positions (such as director of development, athletic director, public affairs director, and so forth) were compensated more highly in settings in which the function was more critical. Again not surprisingly, we found that positions that were more important to private colleges and universities (such as director of development) were more highly compensated in such settings, controlling for other factors that might account for compensation; positions more critical for public colleges and universities (such as athletic director) were more highly compensated in those settings.

Another study examined all 338 managers who began their careers in a large public utility during the period 1977 to

1987.[4] It found that the power of the department in which a manager began his or her career (categorized by raters within the company as high, medium, or low power) significantly affected both the rate of salary growth and length of time spent in each job, with persons beginning their careers in higher-powered departments showing more rapid movement through the organization. Managers also did better when they were brought into the company as part of its formal trainee program, which is taken to be a signal of the individual's potential for career progress. The study indicated that where managers began in the organization had important effects for subsequent career progress, and that the power of one's initial department played a continuing role in salary and career progression.

These results all suggest that people fare better if they are in favored units in the organization. The task of this chapter is to explain the factors that provide some subunits with more power than others, as well as to show how subunit leaders and members can build the power of their units and, by doing so, increase their own influence in the organization.

UNITY: SPEAKING WITH ONE VOICE

Subunits such as departments are comprised of various individuals, all of whom may, at one time or another, represent the unit to its environment and take part in its decisions. In organizational units, consistency in perspective and action is often problematic. While teaching at the University of California at Berkeley, I was once told about the problems confronting its anthropology department. It seemed that, at the time, there were five different perspectives on anthropology—physical anthropology, cultural anthropology, and so forth—and the department could not agree on which it should build. The department dealt with this conflict by appointing five department heads simultaneously, although since the university would only recognize one, the position rotated frequently. The problem that such a unit would have in pressing its claim for resources is obvious—people are likely to say, if its members cannot even agree among themselves about what they should be doing, then why should anyone take them seriously. Internally divided, a subunit will fare poorly in the contest for resources and status.

Unity of action can help explain why, in the U.S. Congress, the power of some states is out of proportion to the number of their representatives. For instance, "Every week for over half a century the Texas delegation luncheon had gotten together to resolve differences behind closed doors. The resulting unity was one reason for Texas's power."[5] By contrast, the California delegation has often been fragmented, not only between Democrats and Republicans but even within each political party. The inability of the California delegation to act together, except in rare instances (such as right after the San Francisco earthquake of 1989), has meant that its power is less than it might otherwise be, even though it is the largest delegation in the House of Representatives.

In the sociology of science literature, there is a concept called the level of paradigm development, which is useful and relevant to this discussion. A survey of faculty in 80 academic departments in four scientific fields asked about the degree of perceived consensus concerning course and curriculum content, research problems, and research methodologies.[6] The study found that the fields differed dramatically in the extent of consensus on these issues. Highly developed paradigms resemble more explicit technologies, in which what needs to be done and how to go about it are clearer to all concerned. In fields with more highly developed paradigms, the results of action—in this instance, research and teaching—are more predictable and certain.

Consensus and technological certainty can have a number of effects that enhance the power of the subunit. First, with more predictable and certain results, the department's claim on resources tends to be taken more seriously. Those in charge of allocating resources like to reduce risk and to know in advance what they will get for their funds. Lodahl and Gordon, for instance, found that the physical sciences, with their higher levels of paradigm development, received much more money both from federal agencies and through internal allocations within universities than did social science departments.[7] In a study of resource allocation to academic departments on two University of California campuses, William

Moore and I found that the level of paradigm development of the departments contributed a statistically significant increment to the explained amount of variation in funding, with more funds being allocated to higher-paradigm departments.[8] This effect was observed even when other predictors of resource allocations, such as enrollment levels and the academic prestige of the department, were controlled.

Second, consensus and certainty facilitates both internal and external communication. More effective internal communication reduces coordination costs and makes joint action easier to achieve. It also improves communication with outsiders by helping the organization to present a united front and a consistent message. Rosabeth Kanter has argued that one reason that organizations often engage in "homosocial reproduction" is to build trust and produce efficient communication among managers.[9] Managers, by the very nature of their work, often deal with uncertainty and have tasks that are difficult to evaluate and monitor. Certainty is at a premium, as is efficient, tacit communication. If power derives from speaking with one voice, then another reason for hiring others like ourselves is that the resulting unity in perspective can increase the power of the subunit.

That highly developed paradigms promote efficient communication has been established in several studies, again in the domain of science and university governance. Two studies found that in more paradigmatically developed scientific fields, the average length of both doctoral dissertations and dissertation abstracts was shorter.[10] More recently, Alison Konrad and I found that in fields with more highly developed paradigms, a greater proportion of the research publication took the form of articles, with books being comparatively more important in fields that were less paradigmatically developed.[11] Longer dissertations, longer abstracts, and more book-length research all reflect the fact that with less consensus on important research problems, methods, and even terminology, more time and space are required to communicate results so that they can be readily comprehended by others.

If consensus improves communication within the units, it then follows that members of the unit will find it easier to take joint action. This is an advantage both in the internal business of the unit and in its interactions with the environment. Beyer and Lodahl, studying governance in British and American universities, wrote:

> . . . the higher predictability of greater paradigm development tends to increase consensus over means to goals. . . . This serves to reduce conflicts within departments, and may also reduce the potential for conflict and misunderstanding with the administration. Second, faculty members who have more consensus can form stronger and more effective coalitions than those in fields rife with internal conflicts.[12]

Research has found that departments in more paradigmatically developed fields tend to have longer chains of courses. In order to have a chain of courses—with one course serving as a prerequisite for yet another, and with that course constituting a prerequisite for yet another, and so forth—the department has to be able to agree on what are the core concepts of the field and how these ideas and skills are divided among specific courses. In other words, in units in which there is more certainty, it is easier for members to take concerted action and thus it is possible for them to get more things accomplished.

Yet another advantage accrues to units that have consensus: turnover and conflict are reduced. The average tenure of academic department heads was found to be longer in units that were in more paradigmatically developed academic disciplines.[13] This makes perfect sense, particularly in light of our example from the anthropology department. When there is consensus in the department about research methods, curriculum content, and other such issues, it matters less who heads the department, since each individual has views virtually identical with those of his or her colleagues; consequently, there is less contest over the leadership position, and less conflict in general. This unity has obvious advantages for dealing with other units. There is more stability, and the leader knows that his or her position is relatively secure. In the labor-management negotiations arena, we often see that a labor leader who is insecure in his position has a much more difficult time bargaining effectively with management. This is why, when labor unions go on strike, management often tries to sow dissension in the ranks and thereby weaken the leader's ability to speak for the organization.

I have become increasingly convinced that unity, consensus, and technological certainty are not things that just happen—either to academic departments or to subunits within other types of organizations. The way in which members of subunits behave can create or undermine organizational unity. One of the most important behaviors is simply reminding others within the unit of external threats and of the potential competitors for resources and policy outcomes. Often, units that are racked with internal dissension are units that have not fully faced the political realities of the larger environment. Becoming isolated from the outside world almost inevitably leads to a narrow perspective.

How the unit is staffed also affects how it acts. Although I am not going to advocate the practice of hiring people exactly like ourselves, it is clear that having a unit comprised of others with similar backgrounds and perspectives makes cohesive and coherent action more likely. But it is perhaps as important that activities are undertaken to build consensus within the group. Here, as in most other aspects of organizational life, the sad fact is that the rich are often able to get richer. Take the physical sciences in universities, for example. Possessing more highly developed paradigms, they are able to get more research funding. These additional funds are obviously not wasted; rather, they are used to do research, which in turn produces more results, which build the knowledge and technology of the discipline. With this better understanding of the field, these departments can readily ask for even more money, as the predictability of their research grows all the time. By contrast, a field without adequate funding is less likely to be able to advance in its understanding of basic processes, and therefore, it may never be in a position to request additional funds with as much strength.

Similar dynamics occur every day in all kinds of organizations. One of the ways in which finance was able to assume such power at both Ford and General Motors was that its initial capture of resources enabled it to hire the best and the brightest people in adequate numbers to build sophisticated and comprehensive financial reporting systems. Once the systems were in place, they became self-perpetuating, because they were able to produce the kind of numbers and analysis that were impossible for others without access to the same level of resources. I have seen similar dynamics play out with respect to computers and information systems departments. A department that is underfunded cannot produce results, which in turn leads to a lack of reliance on the unit in the organization and an increasing inability to successfully compete for staff and budget. In this sense, building unity and consensus may be a critical first step in a department's strategy for building power.

SOLVING CRITICAL PROBLEMS

David Hickson and his colleagues argued that the ability to cope with critical organizational uncertainties provides a subunit with power.[14] The logic is quite straightforward. All organizations face certain problems or issues that are more pressing than others. Because of the division of labor within the organization, some units have responsibility for coping with these critical concerns, while other units deal with more routine or mundane matters. Those units that have the oversight of critical areas have the potential to become quite powerful. Whether they do become powerful depends, to some extent, on whether the units can actually cope with the critical problems confronting the organization. Such problems vary both over time and across organizations, which means that power shifts as the critical concerns vary, and power may be lodged in different units within an organization depending on the particular problems that arise.

There have been dramatic power shifts in hospitals, as cost containment and patient service have become more critical issues—the first because of the growing involvement of the government in funding medical care, the second because of hospital overcapacity, which has made the competition for patients more intense. Hospitals needing to compete on the basis of patient service and concerned about costs tend to have powerful nursing units. As I noted earlier, Stanford University Hospital's chief operating officer is the former head of nursing and a nurse herself. This makes sense when you consider that physicians are not hospital employees, but merely work in the hospital using its facilities. Nurses are the single largest group of employees in most hospitals, constituting about half the budget and staff. The director of nursing therefore exercises tremendous budget responsibility and controls the largest bloc of employees. As health care costs and service have become increasingly important issues, the power of nursing has grown substantially, and it is expected to increase even more in the future.

The argument that coping with critical organizational problems provides power seems to hold cross-culturally. A study in the early 1980s by a Japanese scholar collected data on the organization of the legal departments of the 36 largest subsidiaries of Japanese manufacturing and trading corporations operating in the United States.[15] Setsuo Miyazawa measured the power of the legal staff in three ways: the number of U.S. in-house lawyers, the proportion of the subsidiary's total legal personnel who were U.S. lawyers, and whether the head of the legal department was a U.S. in-house lawyer.[16] Large Japanese firms seldom have a separate legal department in Japan, nor is it common for departments to be headed by a lawyer. Both occurrences are common, however, in U.S. firms. The argument, then, is that Japanese subsidiaries facing problems specific to the United States are more likely to have a more powerful and professionalized legal staff. "Antitrust and product liability seem to be among the fields in which legal rules are perceived to be significantly different from their counterparts in Japan and plaintiffs are considered to take more legalistic actions than Japanese disputants."[17] Using the industry of activity as a proxy for the kind and severity of legal issues most likely to be encountered, the study found strong support for the argument that the organization of the legal department would reflect the contingencies and problems facing the various firms.

What is, and what is not, a critical issue confronting the organization is, of course, itself open to interpretation. But power entrepreneurs inside organizations work to make sure that their unit handles critical issues and that others in the organization realize the importance of the issues that are within the province of their unit. There are few better examples of this entrepreneurial activity than John Dean's actions in his role as counsel to the president in the Nixon administration. When he started his job on July 27, 1970, the office of White House counsel had little power—and Dean knew it.

> By all White House standards my office was shabby. The walls needed painting and the furniture looked like military discards. . . . From my window I could gaze on an interior asphalt courtyard filled with delivery trucks . . . plus the rear ends of air conditioners in other office windows.[18]

But he had a plan to build the power of his unit by expanding its domain into issues that were critical to the Nixon administration:

> Our conflict-of-interest duties were the key. . . . The work was complicated and boring, but I had already sensed that it would produce new business. "It seems that when you really get to know a man's personal financial situation . . . and then candidly discuss his job here to determine if he has any conflicts, you can end up in his confidence if you play it right. And once you're in his confidence, he sends you business."[19]

Moreover, Dean soon figured out that the counsel's office could perform intelligence work for the White House. This was the same administration so obsessed with intelligence that it would eventually drift into the Watergate scandal—so getting into the intelligence business was clearly a smart way for Dean to expand the importance of his unit:

> We had already assumed the role in our conflict-of-interest investigations. And we had Jack Caulfield, who knew such waters. We advertised our office as the place where questions would be answered. I encouraged this new specialty, figuring that intelligence would be more valued by the policy-makers than would dry legal advice. All through 1971, my "warm-up" year, we were bombarded with intelligence requests. I learned a lot about some of the things my superiors were interested in.[20]

Dean put this learning to good use, increasing the size of his staff and, most significantly, becoming important to Ehrlichman and Haldeman, the two highest advisers to President Nixon. Although he was only in his early thirties at the time, Dean showed enormous skill in increasing the perceived importance of his unit and using this criticality to become a more central player in the administration.

BEING IRREPLACEABLE

Subunit power comes from being unified, being able to deal with critical organizational problems, and from having a monopoly on the ability to solve those problems. The earliest formulations treating the origins of power emphasized that power came not only from having something that other people want or need, but from having control over access to this resource, so that alternative sources are not available.[21] Just as monopoly provides power to firms in product markets, monopoly provides power to units interacting in markets for influence.

A nice illustration of this point, which also reinforces the importance of problem solving as a source of power, comes from Michel Crozier's study of a French tobacco factory.[22] The plant was part of a state-owned monopoly, so neither market demand nor financing were very problematic (this study was done before divestiture of state-owned enterprises and also before tobacco became widely recognized as a health hazard). The only real uncertainty or contingency ever faced by the plant was the breakdown of the highly automated cigarette manufacturing equipment. Their ability to fix this equipment gave the maintenance engineers enormous power—so much so that they were actually able to have a managing director of the operation removed. The obvious question is, if the maintenance staff was abusing its power, why not simply hire other skilled machinists, mechanics, and engineers to replace those now in the plant? There was only one problem with this course of action—it was impossible. Somehow, a "fire" or some other accident had destroyed the manuals and drawings that had come with the machines. Some of the machines were older, many had been modified in various ways, and knowledge about how to repair them, particularly how to repair them efficiently, was effectively controlled by the current maintenance engineers. When new maintenance engineers needed to be brought into the factory, because, for instance, of death or retirement, the new engineers were instructed verbally. Although they were permitted to take notes during their training, they were encouraged to destroy the notes once they had mastered the material and the art of repairing the machines. Through this strategy the engineers managed to make themselves irreplaceable to their employers.

For many years, a similar process helped to maintain the power of computer and systems departments in organizations. Specialized software was written for particular and critical applications, and there was rarely enough time to fully document this software. Many organizations would not spend the resources necessary for documentation, and furthermore, many software programmers were more interested in getting on to the next program than in taking the time to document something that was already completed. How particular systems worked was often handed down from generation to generation, in an oral tradition, and was also acquired, in part, through trial-and-error learning. In such a case, the computer or systems department could demand increases in budget or complete autonomy. Its power derived from the department's control of critical uncertainties, coupled with its virtual irreplaceability, at least where reasonable expenditures of money were concerned.

The desire to be (or at least to appear) irreplaceable helps us understand why units within organizations often jealously guard access to outside consultants, and make it appear as if access can only be obtained through them. By seeming to have a monopoly on information and expertise, these units increase their power. I recall, for instance, being approached some years ago by a person in charge of management training for a large U.S. corporation, who wanted me to help teach an internal executive training program. This individual had assembled the faculty for the program by calling a number of well-known business schools, reading catalogues for external programs, and examining listings of business school faculty—all of which could readily have been done by others. He made it appear, however, as if obtaining the faculty was a matter of some skill (as contrasted with simple market-based negotiation) and made sure that all contacts went through his position. For instance, if someone wanted to use you as a consultant on a project not connected with executive training, the person nevertheless went through the head of training to get in touch with you. I finally remarked to an executive in the program how convoluted the system was, and offered to deal with him directly. Needless to say, I was

never invited to the executive training activities again. Trying to be a one-trial learner, I now always ask permission if
I want to talk to anyone in a client organization other than
the person who brought me in. And in all public settings, I
make sure everyone knows what a special relationship that
person and I have, and how I would only work for that individual!

One of the sources of Robert Moses's power, quite in evidence during the administration of Mayor LaGuardia, was
his control over almost all the planning and engineering staff
in New York City. For a public works project to be built,
plans had to be drawn and engineering performed. Because
Moses had the staff to do the work, he could determine what
would be built and what would not. His monopoly of the
city planners and engineers—a hardworking and competent
team—was one of the factors that made Moses irreplaceable.
Caro has described the situation thus:

> . . . that mayor was not controlling the construction of public works
> in the city to a similar extent. . . . the federal government was paying
> for the bulk of those public works, and the federal government was
> much more interested in speed, in getting something to show for its
> expenditure. . . . because speed of construction depended on the
> existence of detailed plans . . . the Mayor needed plans and needed
> them fast . . . Robert Moses decided which projects those would
> be. . . . Moses had the "large, stable planning force" of engineers
> trained to design urban public works on the new, huge scale. . . .
> Continually, LaGuardia sought to overcome this handicap. "He was
> always prodding other departments to come up with plans," Windels
> recalls. "But it took them so long." And when the plans were avail-
> able, the labor often was not; Moses . . . had tied it up on Park
> Department projects.[23]

Moses's control over public works gave him leverage over
the mayor, not only because public works were a crucial resource in the Depression era, but because LaGuardia's own
goals involved building public works. The only problem was
that the works that were built were those Moses wanted, not
the mayor:

> . . . the Mayor had twenty new firehouses in mind; he was able to
> build three. . . . school houses, jail houses, and police station houses
> were also involved—as were hospitals, sewage disposal plants, sew-

ers and subways. LaGuardia was forced to cut back his planned programs of construction of almost every type of municipal institution
except parks . . . and bridges . . . and roads.[24]

Maintaining a position of irreplaceability involves monop-
olizing resources, controlling access to expertise, and, as we
saw in the case of the French maintenance engineers, making
sure that one's expert knowledge is not readily accessible
to others. In this effort, using jargon or language not easily
understood by others is a useful and often employed tactic.
Many professions use specialized language as a way of making knowledge less accessible to outsiders. In fields where
language is less important, access to knowledge may be controlled by limiting training opportunities. For many years
the building trades (as well as other crafts) maintained their
power through a monopoly on skills training, which could be
obtained only through apprenticeship programs controlled
by the trades involved. These and many other instances indicate that being irreplaceable is a key determinant of why
some organizational entities have power and others do not.

THE PERVASIVENESS OF ACTIVITY AND INVOLVEMENT

Units build power not only by being perceived as irreplaceable, but also through the pervasiveness of their activities in the organization.[25] As we saw in Chapter 6, being
central in the communication structure provides subunits
with more power than they might otherwise have. And being
involved in many of the operations of the organization is likewise an important source of power. Understanding the importance of pervasiveness can help us understand how units
such as finance and legal departments are able to exercise so
much influence in many organizations. The key is to become
involved in administrative and decision processes that might,
at first glance, look far removed from the unit's normal
purview.

Consider Pacific Gas and Electric. Although the process of
energy delivery to customers is handled by operating divisions, which are geographically organized by form of energy

(e.g., gas or electricity), most of the major decisions are made in the general office of the company. Operating personnel are geographically dispersed and are limited in the scope of their actions; their role is simply to ensure quality customer service according to guidelines and procedures that are spelled out in manuals prepared by the general office staff. As a result of geographic dispersion, differences in social background and educational background, and the relatively routine and prescribed nature of the work, operating personnel have only limited access to top management. Thus, control at PG&E is centralized, and the only real issues of power lie in the control of the general office.

How did power in the general office shift from engineering to legal and finance? In part by redefining the core competencies necessary to cope with the corporation's environment. For example, the procurement of natural gas supplies has become more critical and problematic over the past thirty years, as a result of partial deregulation, the oil price shocks, and the increasing volatility of energy prices. The gas procurement function had historically been handled as a department under the vice president of gas operations. The function received elevated status in 1971 when John Sproul, an attorney, was named vice president for gas supply, a new position. At the same time, the manager of the long-range gas supply department, Robert Brooks, with a background in mechanical engineering, was bypassed for the new post. One could argue that gas procurement requires contract negotiation skills, and these skills are more likely to be possessed by a lawyer. Certainly, there has been litigation (although not necessarily just at PG&E) about the enforceability of long-term contracts signed with gas suppliers prior to dramatic price escalations, as well as conflict over relationships with pipeline companies that transport the gas. Thus, it may be that the critical skills have changed, and that the legal perspective is more important for ensuring natural gas supply and delivery.

Nor was gas procurement the only arena in which law and finance expanded their influence. Historically, raising capital for public utilities had been almost routine—demand for electricity and gas grew steadily and predictably, and utility rate regulation ensured an adequate rate of return on new facilities. In the 1950s and 1960s, raising capital was a function performed by low-status people who had infrequent contact with top management. In the early 1970s, however, inflation made raising capital more problematic. The environmental movement and increasing public intervention in the regulatory process made rate hearings more uncertain, and the issue of new energy sources became an increasing focus of public and regulatory concern. Thus, for instance, in the financing of the Diablo Nuclear Power Plant, there was some uncertainty, until the very end, as to how much, or indeed, whether any, of the construction cost would be permitted to be included in the rate base. When cost overruns occurred, there was uncertainty as to how much of these overruns would be paid by the shareholders and how much by the public through higher rates. During this time, the capital markets were also becoming more complex and more competitive. Stanley Skinner, a lawyer with a bachelor's and master's degree in economics, was appointed treasurer in 1973. Within four years, he had moved to senior vice president, and one year later to executive vice president, all in the finance function.

During the 1960s and 1970s, another change was occurring in the environment—consumer rights and consumer activism were new forces at work. Pacific Gas and Electric had a department that interacted with consumers, and its importance grew. John S. Cooper, a lawyer who had previously run the energy conservation and services department, was appointed vice president of customer operations in the late 1970s. Also in 1979, another lawyer, Mason Willrich, was hired from the Rockefeller Foundation to become vice president of corporate planning, a newly created position. With law continuing to dominate regulatory affairs, we can see that the legal function had become pervasive at PG&E, controlling finance, planning, customer operations, regulation, and gas procurement. Engineering seemed to retain control, however, over several critical functions, including facilities planning and procurement and operations.

But this control was short-lived. With the new management team in place, a consultant was hired to develop alternatives for a new corporate planning tool, the Planning Support System. The system was intended to consist of an integrated set of simulation models, which would produce pro forma financial results based on various combinations of capital budgets and operating plans. This system was also intended to complement a new Responsibility Budgeting System that was being developed. Although some details of the proposed system were never implemented, and a proposal to formally shift authority for some functions to finance and legal units was resisted, a major expansion in the responsibility of the finance function had nevertheless occurred. The development of the Budgeting System was placed under the comptroller's office, and planning, already staffed by a lawyer, Willrich, oversaw the development of the new Planning Support System. Now with control over budgets, planning, and financial projections, the legal function had effectively stripped engineering of control over facilities, particularly new facilities. It was the lawyers' budgets that set goals and accountabilities, and their planning models that were used to forecast the impact of new facilities on corporate financial performance. The pervasiveness of the lawyers' influence had expanded substantially, bringing them increased power. In early 1981, as a demonstration of this power, Skinner, the company's chief financial officer, caused a large coal-fired electric generating plant to be dropped, sending a clear signal to engineering that major facilities decisions were now under the control of finance.

In this expansion of influence, the fact that there were ties by background and acquaintance among the lawyers, and that they acted in concert, helped immeasurably. Similar tales of expansion, and of the acquisition of power through involvement in numerous activities and decisions throughout the organization, are to be found in the history of firms such as General Motors, Xerox, and Ford Motor. The scope of operations, as well as the criticality of the functions overseen, provides subunits with power in the organization.

SUMMARY

One of the sources of power is location in the organizational structure. Not all subunits are created equal—some are more influential than others. The power of a subunit comes from its ability to act in a unified, consistent fashion, from its proximity to critical issues, and its ability to cope with those issues, and from achieving a position of monopoly by means of its expertise and problem-solving ability. What the PG&E example should help us understand, however, is that critical issues and their solutions are subject to debate and emerge only in political interplay. The reader could readily write an alternative scenario, in which PG&E's success was not seen as a function of its planning, financial analysis, and regulatory and legal skills, but rather, as a function of its technical proficiency and the ability to deliver energy in a cost-effective manner. Different departments would have come to dominate the organization, and different individuals would have risen to power. The alternative scenario might also have had different implications for the development of the organization and its ability to innovate technically and to operate effectively.

Indeed, just such an alternative scenario occurred at Southern California Edison, a similar-sized utility operating in the same regulatory and economic environment, only in southern rather than northern California. At approximately the same time as PG&E (the early 1980s to mid-1980s), Southern California Edison had an engineer as its CEO, a lawyer as the chief operating officer, one other lawyer serving as vice president and general counsel, an engineer and an MBA as executive vice presidents, seven other engineers as vice presidents, and six other disciplines also represented as vice presidents. Out of the top 20 positions, only two, one of them the general counsel's post, were occupied by lawyers. In 124 other large public utilities covered in Dun and Bradstreet's *Reference Book of Corporate Management, 1982–1983*, there were 1,311 positions of the rank of vice president or higher. Attorneys occupied 132 of these positions, or about 10%, although they held about one-quarter of the chief executive officer positions. The contrast with PG&E, with half of the top 18 positions held by attorneys, is striking. This contrast tells us that changes in the economic and regulatory environment, although important, are by themselves not sufficient to fully account for shifts in power in an organization. The ability to act together provided attorneys at PG&E with leverage they did not have in other organizations, where, for various reasons, there was not the same coordinated behavior.

9

Individual Attributes as Sources
of Power

There are 435 representatives in the U.S. Congress, yet only one is chosen Speaker, and few over the course of their career will ever reach this position. There have been many White House counsels, but few were as skillful at obtaining power quickly as John Dean. There were scores of congressional secretaries, and many of them had more education, sophistication, and poise than Lyndon Johnson, yet few of them succeeded in politics as he did. There were plenty of young executives at CBS and at General Motors, but at CBS no one before or since had a career like Frank Stanton's, and while Roger Smith rose to the top at GM, many others fell by the wayside. The road to power is open to many, but only a few follow it with great success. What distinguishes those who acquire great power from those who don't?

It is, from a scientific point of view, not sufficient to study only those who succeed in acquiring power and to infer from them what characteristics are required, just as it is insufficient to look only at outstanding companies to infer the characteristics of excellent management. For a characteristic to be conclusively shown to be useful in acquiring power, we need to see that it is present in those who acquire power to a greater extent or more often than it is in those who are relatively powerless. Studies examining the individual characteristics that produce power have often emphasized personality traits such as the need for power, achievement, and affiliation. Yet these seem to me not to be the individual characteristics that make the biggest difference.

My experience, research, and observation lead me to emphasize the following characteristics as being particularly important for acquiring and holding great power in organizations: 1) energy, endurance, and physical stamina; 2) the ability to focus one's energy and to avoid wasted effort; 3) sensitivity, which makes it possible to read and understand others; 4) flexibility, particularly with respect to selecting various means in order to achieve one's goals; 5) the willingness to engage, when necessary, in conflict and confrontation, or, in other words, a certain degree of personal toughness; 6) the ability to submerge one's ego, at least temporarily, and play the good subordinate or team player to enlist the help and the support of others. Some of these characteristics may bring one more social approval than others, but all seem to be displayed by people who are able to acquire and wield substantial power.

ENERGY AND PHYSICAL STAMINA

In the so-called information age, a list of individual attributes providing power and influence is more likely to begin with great genius or intellect than with a physical characteristic such as strength, energy, and endurance. But such emphasis would be misplaced, for it is quite often the case that endurance triumphs over cleverness. In a study of general managers in industry, John Kotter reported that many of them worked 60 to 65 hours per week—which translates into at least six 10-hour days.[1] The ability and willingness to work grueling hours has characterized many powerful figures. Christopher Matthews, at one time the spokesman for the Speaker of the House of Representatives and now a political columnist and writer, noted that Senator Ed Muskie was able to get things done in part because of his physical stamina:

> "Muskie's great strength was that he never left the . . . room," Matthews recalled. "I mean he *never* went to the bathroom. He'd go in at nine o'clock and stay until one. Everybody else was getting hungry. If there was a photo opportunity, congressmen and senators would come in and out, get their pictures taken, say a few things, and leave. Muskie would stay—right? That's a great strength. . . .

And if you're hungry and he's not, all the better. He'll wait until one o'clock and if you want to go eat at twelve, fine, leave a proxy. He'll take your proxy, and he'll finish at one-thirty, and he'll have his resolution then."[2]

Lyndon Johnson, too, had enormous energy and physical endurance. The woman who worked with him in Congressman Kleberg's office reported that he ran everywhere: ". . . whenever she saw Lyndon Johnson coming up Capitol Hill, he would be running."[3] He got to work earlier than the other congressional secretaries, and did not stop for lunch. Although most congressional offices closed by 4:30 in the afternoon, Johnson and his compatriots often worked past eight in the evening.[4] After his first assistant left her job, Johnson obtained two young men he knew from Texas as assistants, and worked them even harder. Their willingness to put in long hours and expend tremendous effort was motivated by Johnson's own example:

If they awoke at five, it was because their boss was awake at five, and if they trudged up Capitol Hill before daylight, their boss trudged beside them. The days they spent chained to typewriters, he spent chained to the telephone. . . . And often, after they had returned to their little room and were falling asleep, they would hear their boss tossing restlessly on his narrow bed. "He worked harder than anyone," Latimer says. "His head was still going around when the rest of us had knocked off."[5]

Robert Moses drove himself and his men equally hard. He would leave his New York apartment at 6 A.M. to catch an early train to Albany if he needed to be there for a meeting with Governor Smith and his advisers. "When the session broke up, usually well after the last train back had left at midnight, Moses would ask Smith for the use of a state car and chauffeur. . . . If he drove back at once, he'd be able to start in the morning."[6] Frank Stanton, who rose to the presidency of CBS under William Paley, was another driven individual who worked around the clock. Hard work was important to his success at CBS:

His idea of relaxation was arriving in the office on Sunday wearing a sports coat. He survived on little sleep, usually five hours a night. . . . Stanton was in the office by 7:30 or 8:00 A.M., and by the time everyone else arrived at nine or ten, he was miles ahead.[7]

Energy and strength provide many advantages to those seeking to build power. First, it enables you to outlast your opposition, or to use sheer hard work to overcome others who surpass you in intelligence or skill. Second, your energy and endurance provide a role model for others, something that will inspire those around you to work harder. Working long and hard yourself not only shows your subordinates that such effort is humanly possible, but it also signals the importance of the task. After all, if you are willing to devote so much of yourself to the job, it must be worth doing.

In John Gardner's book on leadership, he wrote, "If one asks people to list the attributes of leaders, they are not likely to mention a high energy level or physical durability. Yet these attributes are essential."[8] Without endurance and the ability to persevere, other skills and attributes are not worth as much.

FOCUS

All of us are limited in what we can accomplish. No matter how great our energies or our skills, they are far from infinite. People who exercise great influence tend to focus their energies and efforts in a single direction. All of us, when we were young, probably did the science experiment in which we took a magnifying glass and allowed the sun to shine through it, causing dry grass to catch fire. What that simple demonstration shows is that by focusing the sun's rays, we can make them much stronger.

The story of Lyndon Johnson is a story of focus, of the single-minded pursuit of a specific goal—the presidency of the United States. Although Johnson was very poor as a youth and wanted badly to make himself financially secure, when he was offered the opportunity to get in on the ground floor of an attractive oil deal, he declined, noting that to have oil interests might harm his career. This occurred in the early 1940s; at the time he was a representative in the U.S. Congress. To have oil interests was not likely to hinder the re-election of a politician in the Democratic Party in Texas, where incumbents, particularly Democratic incumbents, were virtually assured of victory.[9] Nor, for that matter, would being known as a friend of the oil industry necessarily hurt Johnson's chances of being elected senator from Texas, which, after all, was (and is) an oil state. Only if he chose to run for the presidency might Johnson be harmed by an association with oil. We see, then, that even at this early stage in his career, Johnson was focused on a clear objective and was willing to subordinate other interests to that objective. Johnson's focus was also evident in his social life.[10] When he went to social functions in Washington he used them as forums to cultivate political connections, thus forgoing the opportunity to meet eligible young ladies. He proposed to his wife on their first date, and many thought he was attracted to her primarily because of her father's money, which turned out to be helpful in his early political campaigns.

Robert Moses also possessed focus. Throughout his more than 40 years in public life, he was concerned primarily with parks, and then with other public building projects. He did not win elective office, go into national government, or enter business. His power base was the state of New York, especially New York City and its environs, and that is where he concentrated his efforts. He spent all his time thinking about his projects, and his family either participated in activities associated with his work or were ignored. "If he couldn't get home to his wife and children as much as he would have liked, he brought them to work."[11]

In Kotter's study of 15 successful general managers, he found that they tended to have concentrated their efforts in one industry and in one company.[12] He concluded that general management was not general, and that the particular expertise acquired by concentrating on a narrow range of business issues is helpful in building a power base and in becoming successful. Concentrating your career in a single industry and in one or a very few organizations is also helpful because it means that your energy is not diverted, and your attention is focused on a narrower set of concerns and problems.

During his rise to power at CBS, and after becoming president of the corporation, Frank Stanton was extraordinarily focused on the company and his job. This focus meant that he directed his attention to activities that would enable him to do more and be more effective, and this obviously made him more powerful. The following incident indicates Stanton's focus on his job at CBS:

> CBS was Frank Stanton's life. . . . If one incident typifies Stanton's devotion to CBS to the exclusion of his own pleasure, it was New Year's Eve in 1952. During the Christmas season, the playwright George S. Kaufman had made a comment on a CBS comedy show that the sponsor, American Tobacco Company, considered sacrilegious. American Tobacco demanded Kaufman's removal, and Stanton wanted to keep him on. . . . New Year's Eve . . . Stanton and his wife set off for New Hampshire to celebrate their twentieth wedding anniversary. Midway through the eight-hour drive, Stanton seized on a possible solution: CBS would take the time period from American Tobacco and keep Kaufman on the air while it sought a new sponsor. After a truncated celebration, the Stantons returned the next day so he could meet with CBS lawyers.[13]

One aspect of this focus is an obsessive attention to small details. Attention to detail is critical for getting things done, and it is the one characteristic that is often lacking in students and managers I encounter. Many are too smart for their own good, in the sense that they have so much intelligence and such a wide range of interests that they do not focus on one or a very few things. Effort is wasted by being spread too thin, and more important, details that may be significant in the effort to build power and influence are often overlooked. During his career in the House, Jim Wright understood the importance of paying attention to small details and keeping one's efforts focused:

> Minutiae mattered. Members believe one function of the leadership . . . is to service them just as they service constituents. Minutiae measured this service. Wright had thrived on minutiae, had proven his willingess to do little things for colleagues not just on Public Works or on a trip to a district. For years he had learned the names and faces of just-elected members so he could greet them by name. Several members recalled that Wright was the first colleague they met when they arrived in Washington.[14]

Just as focus is helpful in developing power and exercising influence, the absence of focus can hinder even the most worthwhile endeavors. In 1970, Peter McColough, the chief executive of Xerox, knew that Xerox needed to move beyond its copier business. Eventually the patents would expire or become technologically obsolete, and growth in the copier market would slow; hence new avenues for growth and development were required. McColough recognized that Xerox had great strength in research and development, as well as tremendous presence in the offices of America and the world. He also saw, quite presciently, the key role that information would come to play in the economy. He recognized that the office of 1980, or 1990, would look nothing like the office of 1970. His vision for the future role of Xerox was insightful and potentially energizing:

> "The basic purpose of Xerox Corporation is to find the best means to bring greater order and discipline to information. Thus, our fundamental thrust, our common denominator, has evolved toward establishing leadership in what we call 'the architecture of information.' "[15]

Two things conspired to prevent this grand vision from reaching fruition, and both were related to the issue of focus. First, Xerox was sued by the government for antitrust violations in the early 1970s. The suit, which took years to settle, diverted management's attention and almost paralyzed the organization's planning processes. Second, McColough became involved in numerous other activities outside of Xerox:

> He volunteered his own time and effort to the United Way, the University of Rochester board of trustees, the Council on Foreign Relations, the U.S./U.S.S.R. Trade and Economic Council, the Overseas Development Council, the International Executive Service Corps, the Business Committee for the Arts, the National Urban League, and the United Negro College Fund. . . . in 1973 he was named treasurer of the Democratic National Party. . . . The picture of McColough as a distracted leader intensified with Xerox's legal problems. In addition to his high profile in public affairs and his role as Xerox's ambassador to external constituencies, McColough assigned himself the task of directing Xerox's antitrust struggles.[16]

SENSITIVITY TO OTHERS

Power involves the exercise of influence over others; leadership involves inducing "a group to pursue objectives held by the leader or shared by the leader and his or her followers."[17] In this effort to influence others, it is clearly useful to be able to understand them, their interests and attitudes, and how to reach them. This is what I mean when I talk about the importance of being sensitive to others and being a good reader of individuals.

It should be clear that being sensitive to others does not mean that one is necessarily going to act in their interests, in a friendly fashion, or on their behalf. Sensitivity simply means understanding who they are, their position on the issues, and how best to communicate with and influence them. The negotiating context provides a setting in which the importance of this ability is well recognized. In the dispute resolution literature, one of the most common recommendations for reaching agreement is to negotiate over interests, rather than positions.[18] This simply means finding out what the other party in the negotiation really wants and needs, and why, and then, perhaps, accommodating those requirements in ways the person had not even thought about. In order to accomplish this, it is very useful to be able to put yourself in the other person's shoes, assuming his role, for a moment, and seeing the world from his perspective. This is a skill that is often helpful in reaching agreement when there is a potential zone of agreement.[19]

Gardner, writing about the attributes of leaders, notes that "leaders must understand the various constituencies with whom they work. . . . At the heart of skill in dealing with people is social perceptiveness—the ability to appraise accurately the readiness or resistance of followers . . . to make the most of the motives that are there, and to understand the sensitivities."[20] Many people think of politicians as arm-twisters, and that is, in part, true. But in order to be a successful arm-twister, one needs to know which arm to twist, and how.

Jim Wright was sensitive. He was "alert to and remembered everything, he could sense a colleague's needs and weaknesses and what his constituents were like, whom his colleague listened to and how best to approach him."[21] Another Speaker of the House, Tip O'Neill, was similarly perceptive:

> Part of the reason for O'Neill's success is his understanding of human weakness. In a system built on mutual dependence, those with no

insight into the nature of frailty never get very far. . . . As he likes to say, you put the people together, job by job, favor by favor, and you get a program, a bill, a policy.[22]

And, in the corporate arena, Frank Stanton was a sensitive and adept reader of others, particularly William Paley, with whom he worked for so long. Stanton and Paley had little in common.[23] Paley was mercurial and often fired people without warning. To survive so long at CBS, Stanton needed both to understand Paley and to know how to manage him. "Each used the other for his own ends. Stanton wanted operating control of CBS, and Paley wanted someone to operate it for him while he maintained ultimate authority."[24] And Stanton understood how important it was not to threaten or challenge Paley in public, and to maintain Paley's feeling of being in control:

> Although Stanton was only seven years younger than Paley, the two men assumed a father-son manner marked by Stanton's unwavering filial respect . . . in the presence of their subordinates. . . . In meetings, Stanton submerged his ego, never taking issue with Paley. As he grew more experienced, he learned to reflect an opposing viewpoint by attributing it to others. . . . When Stanton expressed his own opinion, it was to agree with the Boss.[25]

Sensitivity to others requires an almost clinical interest in the observation of behavior. It requires not only self-awareness, but more important, awareness of others. These skills are not taught in school or in management education courses, except in a few rare instances. At Stanford's business school, two colleagues offer a course that has come to be nicknamed "touchy-feely." Using groups, students learn how they affect other people and how they are perceived. For most of the students I talk to, however, the goal of the course is essentially self-oriented—to understand themselves better and to understand how they affect others. Few spontaneously talk about learning how to listen to others more effectively, or learning how to read others. To be sensitive to others requires one to be able, at least for a moment, to stop thinking about oneself and one's own needs and beliefs. Somewhat ironically, it is this capacity to identify with others that is actually critical in obtaining things for oneself.

FLEXIBILITY

Sensitivity to others is not worth much unless you are able to use that information to modify your behavior. Great salespeople skillfully pitch the same automobile, for instance, as a luxury car for someone looking for prestige, and as an economical choice because of its safety and resale value for someone with a more practical bent. For politicians, flexibility is essential to success. The first requirement for effectiveness in politics is to get in office and stay there, and that occasionally requires adjusting one's positions to the prevailing climate. As president, Lyndon Johnson showed his willingness to stand up for civil rights. The same Lyndon Johnson who sponsored the Voting Rights Act of 1965 and the Civil Rights Act of 1964, which established the Equal Employment Opportunity Commission and outlawed discrimination in employment, the same Lyndon Johnson who established the Office of Federal Contract Compliance to force federal contractors to develop affirmative action programs, the same Lyndon Johnson who sent federal troops to the South in 1965 to protect peaceful protests of civil rights activists, was a very different Lyndon Johnson in his senatorial campaign of 1948:

> Texas was a segregationist state in 1948. In that year, President Harry S Truman submitted a civil rights program—including a proposal for a Federal law against lynching—to Congress. . . . Lyndon Johnson used the opening speech of his 1948 campaign to make an all-out attack on that program. "The Civil Rights program is a farce and a sham—an effort to set up a police state," he said.[26]

For 11 years in Congress Lyndon Johnson, who later passed more legislation protecting blacks, women, and other minorities than any other president, voted against every civil rights bill including an antilynching bill.

Although flexibility sometimes carries a negative connotation, it is a very important characteristic for those who hope to develop power. It provides the capacity to change course and to adopt new approaches, rather than clinging to actions that are not working. Flexibility also helps one to acquire allies, as it is easier to shift approaches to accommodate different interests. John Gardner noted:

It was said of Kemal Ataturk, the greatest figure in modern Turkish history, that he could shift swiftly and without second thought from a failing tactic to another approach, and if that did not work, to still another. . . . His goals were stable but his tactics flexible.[27]

In a television program profiling David Rockefeller, Bill Moyers probed the issue of flexibility. Rockefeller, as chairman of the Chase Bank at the time, was doing business with various countries, some of them totalitarian. One of the bank's largest clients was the Shah of Iran. Rockefeller had arranged for the Shah to be admitted to the United States for medical treatment for cancer after he was forced to flee Iran, an act that led to the seizure of the U.S. embassy in Tehran and the holding of U.S. hostages for more than a year. How was it possible, Moyers wondered, to do business with someone who was accused of running a police state and of using torture on his political opponents. Rockefeller replied that doing business only with those with whom one agreed would mean having "fewer friends than one would like." Having connections, having allies, is important for developing and exercising influence. This requires one to do business, literally as well as figuratively, with a variety of people from a number of different political systems, regardless of their beliefs.

One way of seeing the importance of flexibility is to consider a crisis that was created by its absence—the case of Frank Lorenzo and his battle with the machinists and Charlie Bryan at Eastern Airlines. Lorenzo and his Texas Air Corporation purchased Eastern in February 1985, and until its demise in 1990, he carried on constant battles with the machinists, which soon took on the aura of a personal vendetta against the union and their president, Bryan. In the struggle, Lorenzo apparently lost sight of the economic goals he was pursuing, and became obsessed with achieving an unconditional victory:

> Even many die-hard Lorenzo supporters thought he had gone overboard. What had started out as economics now looked like a grudge match. Lorenzo had become so obsessed with beating the unions that rational economic decisions had gone out the window. Eastern had lost about a million dollars a day for two straight years while Lorenzo waited to break the machinists. The savings Lorenzo expected from the machinists came to only $150 million a year.[28]

Lorenzo's rigidity caused him to lose $365 million per year to save $150 million, and to eventually destroy the airline.

In a study of the personality of people who were politically very adept—so-called high Machiavellians—researchers observed:

> The dispositional differences . . . are all seen as related consequences of the high's cool detachment. . . . Although their coolness may not be more than skin deep, they appear to be thick skinned enough to withstand the enticements or dangers of interpersonal involvements which might interfere with task achievement. . . . It was proposed that the basic process underlying the high's cool is a tendency on their part to focus on explicit, cognitive definitions of the situation and concentrate on strategies for winning.[29]

The evidence from a number of sources seems clear: flexibility that comes from focusing on ultimate objectives and being able to remain emotionally detached from the situation is an important characteristic that enables one to develop power. Flexibility is particularly important when contrasted with its opposite. It is evident that being rigid hinders the development of support and also inhibits changing tactics and approaches when necessary to achieve one's objectives. We may not always like the characteristic of flexibility in the abstract, but we quite often like what it is able to accomplish.

ABILITY TO TOLERATE CONFLICT

Power has been defined as the ability to overcome resistance, to get others to do what you want.[30] Inherent in this definition of power is the assumption that disagreement is one of the constant realities of the social world. The disagreement may be about the goals to be achieved or the connection between means and ends, or both.[31] Power, therefore, is exercised in situations in which there is conflict. If everyone agrees on what to do and how to do it, there is no need to exercise power or to attempt to influence others. Because the need for power arises only under circumstances of disagreement, one of the personal attributes of powerful people is the willingness to engage in conflict with others.

Not everyone shares the taste for conflict or disagreement.

The aphorism, "to get along, go along," is often inculcated at an early age. Many, if not most, people experience conflict as aversive and unpleasant. Conflict is one predictor of stress in organizations. Robert Kahn and his colleagues studied role conflict and role ambiguity.[32] They reported that various forms of role conflict—such as differing demands from different persons with whom one interacted, demands that conflicted with pressure from others outside of the organization, and demands that conflicted with one's sense of self—were all experienced as stressful. To avoid such stress, some individuals will acquiesce to the wishes of others, or will avoid bringing conflicts into the open, hoping that by ignoring them, they will cause them to disappear.

If you shy away from conflict, you are not likely to get your way very often. Conversely, if you are willing to assert your views, and even to behave in a bullying fashion, you can often obtain power in a situation—albeit occasionally at some long-term cost. Being pliable may win you more genuine liking among your co-workers. But it is not the case that those who are the most liked by others for their pleasant personalities are inevitably the most powerful or able to get things accomplished.

Conflict is a form of deterrence. "Deterrence . . . is concerned with influencing the choices that another party will make, and doing it by influencing his expectations of how we will behave."[33] Deterrence involves letting other people know that if they don't do what we want, the consequences will not be pleasant—and since many people dislike conflict, being willing to do battle, vigorously, with others over something we want provides a strong incentive for them to go along. Writing about the exercise of power in Washington, DC, Smith reported on an interview with Christopher Matthews, the spokesman for Tip O'Neill when he was Speaker of the House:

> "The key is to be a porcupine—have a reputation for being difficult," Matthews told me. "Don't have a reputation for being a nice guy—that won't do you any good. . . . I worked for . . . Ed Muskie for three years. He was the best of them all, the absolute best, because nobody wanted to tangle with him. You know, why tangle with the guy? Why ruin your day? Most people are generally utilitarian; they try to achieve the greater happiness. So why spend your day being miserable?"[34]

Being willing to fight, being difficult, was also a source of power for Averell Harriman. It was something that distinguished him from Chester Bowles, another very intelligent person with a distinguished career in government, particularly in the State Department.

> Thus, while Averell Harriman might stand for the same policy as Bowles, Harriman was not a good target; he was a vicious, almost joyous, brutal infighter, and anyone who tangled with him would do so in the full knowledge that Harriman would remember and strike back. . . . Bowles made a much better target. His career in government thus was limited by the knowledge of potential adversaries that they could strike at him and he would not strike back.[35]

One source of Robert Moses's power was his willingness, indeed some might say eagerness, to contend with others who disagreed with him. His inclination to engage in conflict was evidenced most dramatically in his struggle with Mayor LaGuardia over the city-operated ferry, the *Rockaway*, which crossed the East River every twenty minutes. LaGuardia had agreed to mothball the ferry so that the land its terminal occupied could be used "for the East River Drive approach to the [Triborough] bridge and so that the motorists who had been using the ferry would be forced to drive over the bridge instead and pay tolls to the Authority."[36] The ferry, however, had its supporters, not the least of whom were the 1,700 persons who used it each day. They appreciated both its charm and the fact that it was substantially less expensive than the bridge was going to be. LaGuardia attempted a compromise, ordering the ferryhouse turned over to the Triborough Authority, but also saying that the ferry service should continue for 60 days so that the riders would have time to find other means of transportation. Moses, however, did not want to wait 60 days, or any days at all:

> Defying the Mayor, he decided to stop the service immediately—by tearing down the ferry terminal. . . . On July 21, he waited until the *Rockaway* had . . . pulled away from Manhattan for one of its . . . trips . . . and then . . . ordered the barges towed into the ferry slip . . . so that the *Rockaway* would have no place to dock when it returned. And he ordered the pile driver and crane to pound and pull the slip to pieces. . . . he dispatched crews . . . to tear up . . . cobblestones in front of the ferryhouse to cut off all access to the terminal by land.[37]

LaGuardia was forced to call the police to stop the demolition, and he ordered public works crews to repair the damage that had been done during the day. Caro noted that "On July 23, 1936, readers of the *New York Times* were served . . . a headline reading MAYOR CALLS POLICE TO HALT RAZING OF FERRY BY MOSES." But Moses had the final victory as soon as the headlines had faded; on July 31, near midnight, this time with LaGuardia's acquiescence, the ferry terminal was torn down for good.[38]

This conflict was over the question of who was to be the ultimate authority in matters having to do with parks, parkways, and bridges, the objects of Moses's interest. By demonstrating that he was not afraid either of the mayor's authority or of a public battle with the mayor, Moses was able to win out in the conflict and to become substantially more powerful.

Nor is the taste for confrontation a source of power solely in the public arena. Harold Geneen of ITT was well known for intimidating his managers in the monthly financial performance review meetings. De Lorean tells of a General Motors executive who got his way because he was ugly and mean-looking, and intimidated others. Organizational bullies may get their way simply because others will choose to back down, rather than to stand and fight. The stomach for engaging in conflict, then, provides a source of power in any organization.

Ross Johnson, eventually CEO at RJR Nabisco, demonstrated during his rise through the corporate ranks that he would not shrink from a fight. His willingness to engage in conflict was one source of his influence. The first battle occurred at Standard Brands. Beginning as president of a Canadian subsidiary, he was appointed head of international operations in 1973, a director in 1974, and president and heir apparent to Weigl, the CEO at the time, in 1975. He and Weigl were totally different in style—Johnson being lavish and Weigl quite frugal. Weigl had torpedoed previous potential successors, and now set out to do the same with Johnson. He hired a private investigator to gather information on Johnson's extramarital affairs and dispatched auditors to go over Johnson's expense reports. Johnson, however, was not one who readily shrank from a fight.

Johnson . . . prepared for war. A headhunter who gathered employee intelligence for Weigl became a double agent, also reporting to Johnson. . . . A gathering of conspirators . . . assembled a report showing how Weigl's tightfisted ways were slowly strangling Standard Brands. . . . Soon, Weigl was pretty sure *he* was being followed.[39]

A conflict ensued in front of the board of directors, during which Johnson threatened to resign (a ploy that was also used by Robert Moses). When the board offered to make him president in another year, Johnson turned down the offer, demanding that Weigl retain only the position of chairman with the proviso that his office not be in the headquarters building. "That bit of hardball brought Johnson command of a New York Stock Exchange company."[40]

When Standard Brands was merged with Nabisco, Johnson was once again willing to play rough to get his own people installed at the company and to eliminate any competitors he might have for the CEO position when the present CEO stepped down. For instance, Dick Owens was Nabisco's chief financial officer and apparently at the height of his power, having been made an executive vice president and appointed to the board of directors. But Johnson laid a clever trap for him:

Whatever Owens wanted, Johnson got him. He approved a steady stream of Owens's requests for new aides: a senior vice president here, a vice president there, a veritable raft of assistant vice presidents. In Johnson's warm embrace, Owens's financial fiefdom grew steadily. Then one day Johnson walked into Schaeberle's [current CEO] office with his brow furrowed. "Dick is building up a huge financial organization," Johnson fretted. . . . he laid out the dangers of substituting the analysis and judgment of people at headquarters for those of line managers. . . . "I think Dick is congenitally incapable of decentralizing. . . . I think we need to make a change." And so Owens was shunted aside, replaced, for a time, by Johnson himself.[41]

After Nabisco had merged with Reynolds, Johnson again seized an opportunity to gain power through threats and confrontation. Wilson, the CEO of the combined companies, had expended some $68 million on the development of Premier, a smokeless cigarette, without the authorization of the board of directors. When Johnson heard that the board, now apprised of the product's failure, was unhappy with Wilson, he moved quickly. He told several board members that he was thinking of leaving to head a British food company; as the merger was now complete, his job was over. Several of his allies on the board asked him to delay his decision, and he was soon installed as CEO, with Wilson receiving a generous severance package.

In each of these instances, we see that Johnson was willing to gamble and to fight for a position, on occasion using ruthless tactics. He did not wait to get selected, but pushed hard, and occasionally deposed those who stood in his way. This is not the only way to obtain promotions, and certainly some of Johnson's behavior was unattractive. But the point is that his willingness and indeed eagerness to engage in combat helped his corporate career immeasurably.

In contrast, the unwillingness to fight diminishes power and influence, and often results in our being defeated by someone who is less fastidious. That is certainly one lesson that can be drawn from Lewis Glucksman's successful attempt to oust Peter Peterson from his position as co-CEO at Lehman Brothers.[42] In 1983, Glucksman confronted Peterson and asked him to leave the firm:

> Glucksman . . . was quite explicit with Peterson and wanted him out now. He was surprisingly confident Peterson would leave, sensing he did not have the stomach to fight. Peterson had been through his share of soul-wrenching experiences in recent years—surgery in 1977 for a brain tumor that turned out to be benign, a painful and much-discussed divorce, a happy remarriage clouded by several cancer scares. Glucksman admits he calculated that Peterson would not want to get into a messy public brawl. . . . Glucksman smelled weakness.[43]

Glucksman was right. Having faced medical problems, and not really wanting to run the firm again on a day-to-day basis, Peterson negotiated an excellent severance package, and with that in hand, agreed to turn the firm over to Glucksman. Glucksman won, in part, because he had more stomach for a fight than his opponent.

People who want to be liked by everyone are not prone to

engage in conflict. Consequently, people who are effective in exercising power are those who are independent enough to not need approval or intimacy with others.

SUBMERGING ONE'S EGO AND GETTING ALONG

Sometimes it's important to fight, to be difficult, to make rivals pay for getting their way instead of doing what you want done. At other times, it is important to build alliances and networks of friendship by getting along. People who are able to develop great power often seem to have the knack for changing their behavior according to the needs of the occasion. Ross Johnson of RJR Nabisco was able to ingratiate himself with his bosses at times, and also to fight and move them out of the way at other times. Robert Moses could fight with LaGuardia, but was always the deferential subordinate to Governor Al Smith, the only politician he never called by his first name. The problem in getting along, building alliances, and developing a coterie of supporters is that our ego sometimes gets in the way. Thus, the final characteristic I have identified as a source of power is the ability to submerge one's ego in the effort to get something accomplished. It is related to the characteristic of flexibility, since it entails the ability to trade present restraint for greater power and resources in the future.

At CBS Frank Stanton not only managed his relationship with William Paley masterfully, he also managed his relationships with other senior executives. Stanton was superb at acquiring and using power without lording it over his subordinates:

> Stanton gave his senior executives their own private dining rooms and seats on the CBS board to enhance their prestige in the eyes of the world. He designed generous bonus and incentive plans to encourage their best work. . . . When CBS was crippled by a union strike, Stanton supplied the picketers with coffee; after the strike was over he arranged to have overtime checks delivered by hand to the executives who had replaced the striking workers.[44]

Stanton's consideration won the loyalty and support of many at the corporation. He was able to do these things because he did not feel that by building up others, he was tearing himself down. He was secure enough in himself to submerge some of his own status and to improve the prestige of others in the organization—who then were bound to him with loyal gratitude.

The ability to submerge one's ego to build support is an important source of power. The case of George Shultz and Casper Weinberger as executives in the Bechtel Corporation shows contrasting instances of the ability to build support by treating others as equals.

George Shultz joined Bechtel as a senior executive in charge of the Mining and Metals division in 1974, following the unexpected death of Raphael Dorman, a brilliant and popular executive with the firm. Shultz was an outsider, and his appointment broke a long-standing company tradition. "As with the military, Bechtel executives, including Steve junior, worked their way through the corporate ranks, one painstaking rung at a time."[45] Not only was Shultz an outsider, but he was a nonengineer in a company dominated by engineering. He came to Bechtel from the position of secretary of the Treasury, and he had a long and distinguished career in government and in academia—but he was still an outsider. He would have to build a power base, and do it quickly.

Shultz went out of his way to set aside his status and power and to win the support of people in the company. He was unthreatening, and took time to talk to people, including secretaries, clericals, and whoever else was around. He "scored more points by downplaying his status, through such symbolic measures as choosing an Oldsmobile for his company car rather than the Cadillac to which he was entitled."[46] He went through a crash course presented by the division's senior engineers in the operations of the division. When people played jokes on him, or teased him, he reacted with good humor.

"George Shultz did everything right," Bechtel chief counsel Bill Slusser noted. "Here was a guy who had been secretary of the Treasury and held a post at Stanford. Yet he got down in the trenches and proved himself to a bunch of hard-hats. The fact that he did it, that he enjoyed doing it, that he did it with such goodwill—all of that impressed people."[47]

Shultz was also very helpful, of course, with the company's overseas clients, with Bechtel's contacts in Washington, and with business clients in the United States. In about a year, Shultz became president of the Bechtel Corporation. A lot of his success came from his acceptance within the organization and his consequent ability to get internal people to work with him and carry out his plans.

Just six weeks after George Shultz became company president, the former Health, Education and Welfare secretary, Casper Weinberger, joined Bechtel as its general counsel. Although they had both served in the Nixon cabinet, Shultz and Weinberger were not close, and indeed, Weinberger had resented Shultz's influence in the administration. Weinberger had two immediate problems. First, he was replacing Bill Slusser, one of the best-liked executives in the company. Second, the timing of his arrival was bad. "As the second outsider to join Bechtel's tight-knit senior management team in less than a year, he became the focus of the resentment that had been building since Shultz's appointment."[48]

Weinberger's imperious and aloof style made these problems worse:

> Where Shultz had shown himself to be a relaxed, affable, open manager, Weinberger seemed to many to be guarded and unfriendly. In dealing with subordinates, Weinberger . . . gave the impression of having scant time for lesser mortals. . . . His combativeness . . . did not go down well, especially since his primary role was to provide support and legal guidance to the heads of the operating companies and division chiefs.[49]

He hired a host of lawyers to augment Bechtel's outside counsel, who had worked for the company for 40 years. To tighten up the legal department's loose operating style, he hired another outsider, Virginia Duncan, who was very much in his own image. " 'She ran the department like a butcher shop,' groused one Bechtel observer. 'You took your number and you waited your turn.' "[50] As Bechtel lawyers began leaving the firm in large numbers, Weinberger's support in the firm eroded even further. Anxious to get back to Washington and having few friends or supporters at Bechtel, Weinberger jumped at the opportunity to become secretary of defense in the Reagan administration in 1980.

SUMMARY

The six personal traits discussed in this chapter are, of course, not the only ones that may be sources of power in organizations. However, as we think about the characteristics that provide people with power, we need to keep in mind that organizations almost invariably are characterized by interdependence, and frequently are arenas for competition and conflict among both individuals and subunits. For that reason, it is logical that attributes that are related to the capacity to garner support and allies—for example, sensitivity, flexibility, and being able to submerge one's ego when necessary—are important sources of power. And similarly, attributes that are related to the ability to survive in a competitive arena—such as focus, energy and stamina, and the willingness to engage in conflict—are also significant sources of individual power.

One way to evaluate characteristics as sources of power, then, involves assessing the extent to which they solve the two critical problems that confront individuals seeking to become powerful in organizations—namely, garnering support and triumphing in competition. As situations change, and cultural norms vary, what it takes to win support and to compete effectively will likewise vary. But in most countries and situations, at least at present, these characteristics seem to be important individual sources of power.

Strategies and Tactics for Employing Power Effectively

We need to know more than where power comes from—we need to know how to use it effectively to get things done. The effective use of power involves understanding the social psychology of interpersonal influence. All of us practice influence, and are influenced by others, every day as we go about our lives. Those who are particularly effective in getting things accomplished—for instance, successful salespeople—may have used trial and error to develop informal strategies, which rely implicitly on basic social psychological principles. We learn rules of thumb as we encounter different situations, and are successful in some and less successful in others. Some of this learning may be invalid, in that we may have reached incorrect generalizations based on limited experience. But to the extent that our knowledge of how to employ power effectively can become conscious, we can develop a wider range of behaviors and a better understanding of social interactions, which will enhance our effectiveness in organizations.

This section, which examines how power is used, begins with the topic of framing and the simple point that how we see things depends upon the context in which they are seen.

How we look at things is affected by the principles of contrast, commitment, and scarcity, which emphasize the order in which proposals are presented and their relative availability and abundance. The next chapter continues the consideration of interpersonal influence by examining the impact of what others are saying or doing, the effects of liking, and the use of emotional contrast.

Once we understand these basic interpersonal influence processes, we are ready to consider some strategic elements in the exercise and development of power, including questions of timing, how we use information and analysis, how to make structural changes to wield and solidify power, and finally, how to employ language, ceremony, and settings to influence the heart as well as the head.

Throughout the book, the purpose of the information is always twofold. First, it is imperative that as members of organizations, we become more skilled at understanding the world around us. The information in this section, therefore, will help the reader become more sensitive to and informed about processes of social influence that occur regularly in the world he or she inhabits. Second, the information can be employed in situations in which influence is required, to help develop effective strategies for implementation.

It is not enough to know that power exists. It is also critical to know how power is used—to have an arsenal of strategies and tactics that translate power and influence into practical results.

10

Framing: How We Look at Things
Affects How They Look

In the 1972 presidential election, Richard Nixon's campaign operatives authorized the hiring of five Cubans to break into the Democratic National Campaign Headquarters in the Watergate apartment and office complex in Washington, DC and place listening devices on the premises. The Cubans were apprehended during the break-in, and the subsequent disclosures about campaign activities as well as the attempted cover-up of the Watergate scandal caused Nixon to resign in 1974. One might well ask, with Nixon running as an incumbent in 1972 against George McGovern, who was far from a mainstream candidate, why and how did this misadventure occur? The answer tells us something about the importance of context and framing in understanding how actions occur.

One answer derives from the fact that Nixon had barely defeated Hubert Humphrey in 1968 and had lost the 1960 race against John Kennedy after dropping an early lead. He had also narrowly lost the 1962 California gubernatorial election. He and his staff therefore were inclined to take nothing for granted and were determined to treat McGovern's challenge seriously. Nixon and his people reacted to present circumstances based on a set of assumptions and beliefs derived from the past.

But perhaps more important was the way the idea was presented. The campaign committee had hired Gordon Liddy to help them with campaign intelligence. Liddy initially approached the committee with an elaborate plan. He wanted $1 million to break into the Democratic National Headquarters and place wiretaps, to rent a yacht off the coast of Florida (where the Democratic convention was to be held) and use prostitutes to compromise prominent Democratic politicians, and to equip a surveillance airplane with sophisticated electronic eavesdropping equipment so that Democratic campaign planes could be followed and private conversations overheard. The committee, needless to say, rejected that plan.

Liddy returned later with a scaled-down version: $500,000 for the break-in and wiretapping and the yacht with the call girls, and he would forgo the surveillance plane. He was turned down again. He returned a third time to ask for only about $250,000 for the Watergate break-in. Compared to $1 million for surveillance planes, yachts, and prostitutes, a mere $250,000 for a simple wiretapping and electronic surveillance operation seemed very reasonable. The lesson is that what looks reasonable, or ridiculous, depends on the context—on how it is framed in terms of what has preceded it and the language that is used to present it.[1]

CONTRAST

The Watergate example provides one illustration of the principle of contrast. We see and experience events in terms of what has just occurred. We economize on memory by tending to react primarily to what we have recently experienced. And what is good or bad, what is expensive or inexpensive, what appears reasonable or unreasonable, is profoundly affected by what we have just experienced. The contrast effect is often used in sales situations. If a person comes into a clothing store to buy a suit and a sweater, the salesperson will sell the suit first. After purchasing the more expensive item, the customer will see the sweater—even an expensive sweater—as comparatively inexpensive. Conversely, if the less expensive item is presented first, the contrast principle suggests that the more expensive item will seem even more costly by comparison. Real estate people will use "setup" properties, properties that are both undesirable and offered at inflated prices. After seeing such a property, the prospective buyer is much more likely to react favorably to a nicer house offered at a high price—by comparison it is a bargain. Automobile salespeople are also masters of the contrast effect. It is particularly useful in selling extended service contracts. After spending many thousands on a new car, a few hundred dollars for an extended warranty "to protect your investment" seems cheap by comparison.[2]

The same psychological mechanism that makes it easier to sell an item that is framed to seem inexpensive can work to ensure that not much thought or attention is given to something that is, at the moment, only a small part of the organization's operations. In the late 1960s and early 1970s, Xerox's copier business was growing dramatically. Xerox was very profitable because of its virtual monopoly in the marketplace, and as a consequence, the corporation paid little attention to small products and small markets.[3] Consequently, when the Japanese began to market low-end, inexpensive copiers at reduced prices, they were simply ignored. Xerox leased its machines, and therefore derived its revenues from selling copies, not copiers. The Japanese machines copied in such small volumes that they represented only a fraction of the rapidly growing and highly profitable copying market. By comparison with Xerox's line of business, these small machines for smaller users were not worth thinking about. For much the same reason, corporate management had little time for the computer product ideas that came out of the Palo Alto Research Center. The presumed market and profit potential was small enough, compared to the main copier business, that few were willing to take these innovations seriously.

In these two instances at Xerox, the contrast effect worked against products for smaller markets or those with seemingly small market and profit potential. The contrast principle may, then, help to explain why it is so difficult for large, successful organizations to enter markets that, at least initially, seem small. Compared to their primary line of business, the markets seem not to warrant much attention. Often by the time market potential becomes clear, it is difficult to enter successfully, since other, smaller organizations have already carved out dominant positions.

The implications of the contrast principle for exercising

influence are fairly straightforward. Since the order in which things are considered affects how they are viewed, agendas are important. Xerox, which missed some important opportunities in the personal computer marketplace, now lavishes attention on the Palo Alto Research Center, and products with what may be much less potential get a lot more time and attention. Compromises in governmental politics often occur after a series of unworkable proposals make the final proposal seem much more reasonable. We need to make sure that our proposals benefit by contrast with what has come before, and at the same time that they are significant enough to get noticed.

THE COMMITMENT PROCESS

Previous actions and events not only set the frame of reference by which we judge present possibilities, they also constrain our psychological freedom to take a different course. The principle of psychological commitment suggests that we are bound to actions that 1) we choose voluntarily with little or no external pressure; 2) are visible and public, so we cannot deny being responsible for them; 3) are irrevocable, so we cannot change them easily; and 4) are explicit in their implications about our attitudes, values, and subsequent behavior.[4]

The process of commitment, in which a person is bound to some behavior or choice, occurs for a number of reasons and in a number of ways. One mechanism that binds us to our past behavior is the process of self-perception, in which we look to our own past actions as a guide to our attitudes and beliefs.[5] If we choose a job that pays less than we could otherwise command and that involves a lot of hard work, it must be because we really like the job. And, if we like the job, how can we fail to do it diligently? This process of self-perception, in which we learn what we want by our own behavior, explains why research has consistently indicated that things that are more difficult to attain are valued more highly. For instance, groups that are more difficult to join are more attractive than ones that do not require such severe initiations. As Aronson and Mills wrote, "Persons who go through a great deal of trouble or pain to attain something tend to value it more highly than persons who attain the same thing with a minimum of effort.[6]

Commitment is also produced by generalized social norms that favor predictability and steadfastness. People who vacillate may be viewed as indecisive, whereas persistence is valued as a trait of leadership.[7] A person in authority may persist in a course of action simply for the sake of appearing to be a consistent and strong leader. Barry Staw and his colleagues have conducted research on consistency and escalation, often using an experimental paradigm in which subjects are confronted with a business case and asked to make an investment decision, for instance, allocating funds to research and development. Some subjects are then given information indicating that their past decisions are not succeeding, and are asked to make additional decisions. The studies often find that subjects facing failure escalate their investments, committing more resources to endeavors that aren't doing well, in an attempt, presumably, to turn them around.

In a study that sheds light on the normative basis of commitment, people were given a case in which an administrator behaved in either a consistent or inconsistent fashion, allocated either many or few resources, and achieved either success or failure.[8] The subjects had to evaluate the administrator and recommend the size of the raise that he or she should receive. As one might expect, all three conditions affected the perceived ability of the administrator: success, behaving consistently, and using the minimum resources were all positively associated with the evaluation given. The study used different sets of subjects—some were undergraduate business students, some were psychology undergraduate students, and some were students earning an MBA in an evening program, which meant they had full-time jobs during the day. Who did the evaluating affected the emphasis placed on consistency versus performance. Evening MBA students, the practicing managers, gave performance the smallest weight in evaluating the administrator; they also showed the greatest difference in their evaluations of consistent and inconsistent administrators. Practicing managers gave the lowest ratings of any of the groups to administrators who changed decisions. These results suggest that as one progresses up the organizational hierarchy, one develops a theory of leadership in which consistency and perseverance, particularly in the face of adversity, are valued. Such generalized social expectations about what constitutes effective management help to explain why many organizational leaders strive for consistency.

Consistency also serves to economize on cognitive effort. Once we have made up our minds and embarked on a course of action, if we are consistent and committed, we do not have to revisit the issue again. Consider the alternative. If we continually reevaluated all of our choices, it would be difficult for us, or our organizations, to do anything. There is a time for contemplation and decision, and a time for acting on that decision. Also, the value we place on consistency helps us to avoid rethinking past decisions, a process that might remind us things did not work out as well as we had planned or hoped. Reviewing botched decisions is unquestionably unpleasant, and in many instances, it is not even helpful, since we may not be able to alter the results.

Consistency, then, is a pattern of behavior that is: 1) valued by many people, particularly as an attribute of managers or leaders; 2) used to economize on information processing and decision making; 3) produced by a process of self-perception, in which we become bound to past actions and behaviors because we see them as reflecting something about ourselves; and 4) used to avoid confronting failures or problems with past activities. Consistency and commitment are produced by both intrapsychic and interpersonal processes.

One clear implication of this argument is that the best way to get something accomplished is to begin with any useful action, no matter how small. As long as it is done voluntarily, it will have committing implications. Thus, a door-to-door dictionary salesperson will try to get a prospective customer to look at the book and spend time thinking about it, an automobile salesperson will try to get a customer to test-drive the car (which is why many dealers resist giving prices over the phone; once you have made the effort to come to the dealership and drive the car, you are less likely to leave without buying), and why someone trying to sell a computer may offer it on a rental or trial basis.

The process of commitment means that once a project is under way, it is very hard to stop. I once saw a company test-market a new consumer product. After four months and a $1 million promotion budget, the product was doing poorly. At the meeting to review its fate, the product manager did not recommend that it be scrapped. On the contrary, he said, "How could we expect this product to succeed, given the lack of backing and financial support it has received? Up against entrenched competitors and established consumer tastes, we have not really given it a chance." The firm proceeded to appropriate $10 million to give the product more time and more promotion—and some eight months later it was finally cancelled.

Initial estimates for the movie *Heaven's Gate* projected 69 days to shoot the film, and a budget of $9.5 million.[9] A review by the budget analyst at United Artists indicated that a more accurate figure would be approximately $10 million, or $12 million if some of the extravagances built into the picture were not eliminated. The story of the making of the movie is, of course, a story of these budget estimates being revised gradually upward, as first there were final negotiations on the deal, and then production was actually undertaken. Once a psychological commitment had been made to make the picture, it was difficult to back down. Once millions of dollars had already been spent, it was even more difficult for United Artists to walk away from its investment with nothing, particularly if by spending just a little more money, it could produce a blockbuster hit.

Perhaps an even more dramatic example of escalating behavioral commitment was the decision to choose Isabelle Huppert, a minor French actress, as the leading lady. The director, Michael Cimino, wanted her but she spoke with an accent (a problem in an American western), and from the point of view of United Artists, she would not add any box office draw, a critical issue because the leading man, Kris Kristofferson, had limited name recognition and box office appeal himself. In part, however, because Kristofferson had already been selected, and in part because United Artists was increasingly concerned about budget overruns, the firm found it difficult to get a good replacement. Cimino played the United Artists executives beautifully:

"I can't accept such a decision from executives who have never bothered to see their director's choice on the screen, who have never met or talked with her. You are rejecting her only because she doesn't have a name no matter how right she may be for the part."[10]

Soon two United Artists executives were on the Concorde to Paris, on their way to meet Huppert:

> We had said no to Cimino in California. . . . Michael pressed all his arguments, which were neither inconsiderable nor unreasonable. Flying to Paris for one last meeting seemed excessive, but I had . . . business to conduct there. . . . For Field, the trip was more arduous, but at least it was a respite from the often crushing California schedule.[11]

Note that Cimino made the reasonable request that the UA executives just meet with his proposed leading lady, and so the two flew to Paris, rationalizing the trip as not really being a sign of indecisiveness. Flying to Paris to meet her was, of course, an important behavioral commitment. When the executives met with Huppert:

> Huppert . . . read indifferently. . . . She seemed to have little idea of the script's content . . . and none whatever of the character of a frontiers-woman. . . . She was simply wrong. Still, as the night wore on and the wine bottles emptied, her charm began to take hold.[12]

By this time they were feeling vulnerable—United Artists was at the time owned by Transamerica, and UA personnel felt pressured to show that they had good artistic sensibilities:

> The line between rationally weighing alternatives and rationalizing them is notoriously fine. . . . it began to seem preferable and somehow nobler to make the wrong decision for the right reasons than the right decision for the wrong. . . . there was always the possibility that Cimino was right, that he saw something in her our vision was not acute enough to see.[13]

Bach and Field convinced themselves that they needed Cimino's cooperation to make the film a success, that Huppert wasn't so bad, and that they should trust Cimino's judgment. But how could they rationalize the choice of a leading lady who was so clearly inappropriate in almost every way? Very simply:

> Then it came, the master stroke of persuasion and manipulated perspective: Who was the real star of this picture? Not Kristofferson . . . not Fonda or any of the others we couldn't have anyway. . . . The star of this picture . . . was Michael Cimino. We weren't betting that this or that actor or actress would add a million or two to the box office. We were betting that Cimino would deliver a blockbuster. . . . Cimino was the star, and if our director wanted Huppert, we had an obligation to back him. . . . The next morning we capitulated. Isabelle Huppert would play Ella Watson.[14]

This example illustrates beautifully, in one of the participant's own words, how one proceeds along the slippery slope of commitment—from doing something almost reasonable, like simply talking to the prospect, to finally convincing oneself that a bad decision is nevertheless the right one. This is a process that unfolds over time, slowly, subtly, and almost imperceptibly.

It is important that the committing behaviors occur with little external pressure, for that way they say more about the individual's own beliefs and values, and provide few external justifications for abandoning the action. Actions taken voluntarily, behaviors chosen when one faces possibly adverse consequences, are the most committing of all. This fact is well known by those who seek to build a committed, hard-working team of employees. Tracy Kidder's book on Data General and the development of a new minicomputer provides a powerful illustration of the commitment process at work. The two project leaders, West and Alsing, needed to find people who were willing to sacrifice themselves and work hard for the project, which was competitive with a design effort going on in another facility in North Carolina. Alsing used a ritual called the "signing up" as a way of building commitment:

> And a successful interview with Alsing constituted a signing up. . . . "Well," says Alsing, "we're building this machine that's way out in front in technology. We're gonna design all new hardware and tools. . . . Do you like the sound of that?"
>
> . . . "It's gonna be tough," says Alsing. "If we hired you, you'd be working with a bunch of cynics and egotists and it'd be hard to keep up with them."
>
> "That doesn't scare me," says the recruit.

"There's a lot of fast people in this group," Alsing goes on. "It's gonna be a real hard job with a lot of long hours. And I mean *long* hours."

"No," says the recruit. . . . "That's what I want to do. . . . I want to be where the action is."

. . . "I don't know," said Alsing after it was all done. "It was kind of like recruiting for a suicide mission. You're gonna die, but you're gonna die in glory."[15]

An earlier discussion showed how we can build alliances by doing favors for others, invoking the principle of reciprocity. Commitment also suggests that we can build alliances by getting others to do favors for us. If a person complies with my request for a favor, self-perception will tend to cause that person to think he or she likes me—why do a favor for someone you don't like? A cycle may begin, in which I do you a small favor, and you feel obliged to repay me. But the very act of your doing something for me helps to commit you to me, and thus further cements the alliance and the relationship.

How did Jimmy Carter, the ultimate outsider, obtain the Democratic party nomination and eventually win the presidency in 1976? The answer is that he was a master at building alliances. He seized upon a simple strategy: "To build an outsider's campaign, recruit some outsiders to run it for you."[16] Every Democrat who lost a primary election in 1974 received a personal letter from the then-governor of Georgia. Carter recognized that people who had lost were going to have a lot of time on their hands, and he wanted them to spend their political energies on his candidacy. His strategy was to bind people to him by identification with the campaign, getting them involved in working for his success.

Contrary to what many people assume, the most effective way to gain a person's loyalty is not to do him or her a favor, but to let that person do one for you. . . . people get a kick out of being propositioned. The smart politician knows that in soliciting someone he is not so much demanding a gift or service, he is offering the person the one thing he himself wants: the opportunity to get involved.[17]

Letting someone do you a favor commits that person to you. Once people have invested in your project, in your candidacy, in your career, they will not want you to fail, and therefore may make extraordinary efforts on your behalf. Thus, we often observe efforts being made to save pet projects and pet candidates, in either corporate or national politics.

How can we counteract the principle of commitment, when we need to get others to change their behavior? To change behavior, individuals must be unbound from their past. One way to do this is to suggest that they were not really responsible for their past decisions—they faced external pressures or information that naturally led them to act as they did, but now, the situation is different, and they are free to do something else. What you should not do is to attack directly, and to ask, "How could you have done something so stupid?" When asked this question, most of us will state the myriad reasons we had for doing what we did. We may not convince the questioner, but we are quite likely to convince ourselves.

One of my favorite examples of the unbinding of behavior occurs in the movie *Twelve Angry Men*. After a court trial, the members of the jury convene in the room in which they are to deliberate. A straw poll is taken, and eleven jurors publicly vote guilty. How can Henry Fonda, the protagonist, change their minds? He argues that although the evidence makes the defendant appear to be guilty, perhaps the defense lawyer did a poor job. After all, he was only a public defender, and may not have enjoyed handling this unpopular case. Fonda says at one point, "The evidence indicates he is guilty; maybe he is; I'm not sure." Then, he asks only if they have doubts about the verdict—he does not have to prove that the defendant is innocent, only that there is some reasonable doubt. Most important, he gets their commitment, not necessarily to change their votes, but at least to talk about the case for an hour. After all, a boy's life is at stake, and there is no harm in a little discussion before they reach a verdict. Because of the way Fonda's character frames his argument, the jurors do not have to admit that they were misled, only that the defense lawyer did a poor job. Furthermore, their agreement to talk commits them to examining the evidence in more detail, and thus creates the opportunity for Fonda to involve them in the discussion and act out critical testimony.

Direct attacks, by contrast, almost always backfire. When

Frank Lorenzo of Eastern Airlines was fighting the machinists, he wanted to have the National Mediation Board declare the bargaining at an impasse, so that after 30 days there could be a strike or a lockout, and he could proceed to hire low-cost replacements. His peremptory treatment of the board, however, only made it more committed to its policy of encouraging further negotiations. The chairman of the board was Walter Wallace, and Wallace and the NMB refused to budge:

> . . . Lorenzo had got off on the wrong foot with Wallace. Then, instead of trying to mend fences, Lorenzo chose to hit him harder and harder. Wallace, not surprisingly, dug in his heels. In the end, he came to see Lorenzo, not the unions, as the primary problem at Eastern.[18]

Lorenzo had begun by trying to meet with Helen Witt, the chairwoman before Wallace, even before a mediator had been appointed. Wallace felt as though he'd been circumvented. Lorenzo got Frank Borman and William Usery, the mediator who had worked out an equity-sharing deal in 1983, to lobby Wallace and the board. He organized a "group called PEACE, for Positive Employee Action Committee at Eastern."[19] Lorenzo had "Tom Matthews, Eastern's labor-relations executive, send a blizzard of letters to Wallace, outlining the airline's case. The letters accused the board of dragging its feet."[20] Eastern management curried favor with the press, who editorialized against the board. But Wallace, who was due to retire in a year, was merely irritated by all the pressure.

> Lorenzo fired wildly at the board. Texas Air even tried to sponsor a bill in Congress that would have expanded it from three to five board members and put a 90-day limit on the length of board-supervised mediation. Lorenzo aides hinted that he was mulling over whether to sue the board for blocking an impasse.[21]

In spite of Wallace's basically pro-business stance, he was so angered by Lorenzo and his heavy-handed tactics that he was to delay for almost two years the showdown that Eastern management had wanted. Pressure had merely hardened the resistance of the National Mediation Board, and had served to make it more committed to its decisions.

SCARCITY

How things look to us also depends on how scarce they are. It is often difficult to value something objectively. However, if many others want it, then we assume that it probably has value. The popularity of the item may be signalled in its price or its comparative unavailability. Thus, price and scarcity—which are, of course, often related because of the operation of the forces of supply and demand—are used as indicators of value or desirability. The scarcity principle, like many of the other principles of interpersonal influence, helps economize on information processing. Do we want a Honda Accord, or a Mazda Miata? If they are scarce, if dealers are charging premiums over list price, then of course we do! If they were available in large numbers, they would not be as desirable. Or consider the example of the selectivity of university graduate schools. In published rankings of graduate business schools, one of the factors often tabulated is how selective they are—how many people apply compared to the number of available slots. The greater the scarcity of admission slots, the better the reputation of the school, and somewhat ironically, the more numerous the applicants. Thus, the rich get richer, so to speak, simply because of the desirability associated with scarcity.

Scarcity as an influence principle also relies on the theory of psychological reactance.[22] "As opportunities become less available, we lose freedoms; and we *hate* to lose the freedoms we already have. . . . whenever free choice is limited or threatened, the need to retain our freedom makes us want them (as well as the goods and services associated with them) significantly more than previously."[23] The term *reactance* comes from the fact that "when increasing scarcity . . . interferes with our prior access to some item, we will *react against* the interference by wanting and trying to possess the item more than we did before."[24]

There are many everyday examples of the scarcity principle at work. Suppose you have been looking for a house and have finally seen one that you like, but it is not perfect and you are having trouble deciding whether you want it. Your decision will be facilitated mightily if the real estate agent tells you that another offer is coming in. Faced with the pros-

pect of no longer being able to freely decide whether to purchase the house, many people will make an offer. Also, you
will now have information that indicates others like the
house as well, thus validating your judgment. Many sales
techniques make use of the scarcity principle in setting deadlines and cutting short supplies—something will be available
only for a limited time, or in a limited quantity. The scarcity
principle means that the country-and-western song entitled,
"The Girls All Look Prettier at Closing Time," actually has
social psychological (as well as possibly alcoholic) foundations to support its theme. Shakespeare's "Romeo and Juliet"
illustrates the power of scarcity to induce passion. Some people argue that the attractiveness of long-distance relationships or of extramarital affairs is enhanced by the operation of
the scarcity principle in both situations. Because restricting
access makes it more desirable, censorship of messages,
books, or information actually increases demand. This latter
effect causes problems in jury deliberations in which some
information is ruled to be inadmissible, and the ruling comes
only after the information has been heard. The jurors are
supposed to disregard the information, but reactance theory
suggests that when told to do so, they will actually consider
it more.

The scarcity principle can explain the dynamics of the process through which Apple Computer and Steve Jobs hired
John Sculley from Pepsico—Sculley, the same person who
would ultimately force Jobs out of the company. In 1982,
Apple decided that it was really in the consumer products
business, and retained Gerald Roche, president of Heidrick
and Struggles, a head-hunting firm, to help it find an appropriate president. Eventually Sculley emerged as a serious
contender. A description of the recruiting process indicates
that it was his aura of being unavailable, but still not out of
the question, that helped get him the offer:

> Jobs and Markkula flew to New York to meet him [Sculley] in De-
> cember, but he was cool during the meeting and afterwards told
> Roche he wasn't interested. That didn't deter Roche. . . . It left Jobs
> absolutely intrigued. . . . In January they showed him Lisa and went
> out to dinner at the Four Seasons. In early March . . . Jobs persuaded
> him to stop in Cupertino. . . . There were a number of reasons why
> Jobs wanted Sculley so much. . . . as time went on, Jobs simply got

caught up in the challenge of luring him to Apple and converting him to Apple's cause. Jobs . . . had so much money it was embarrassing. Nothing made him salivate like the thing he couldn't get.[25]

As with many of the strategies of power we have seen, this example shows the applicability of more than one principle. Scarcity made Sculley attractive to Jobs, and escalating commitment made Jobs more and more eager to convince him to join the company.

The scarcity principle has a number of applications, the most fundamental being that what you advocate should always appear to be scarce. If you are looking for a job, you should appear to be in high demand. If you are pitching a proposal, the proposal should only appear to be feasible for a limited time, after which the opportunity would be lost. Even better, someone else should be on the verge of taking advantage of it. In this regard, the use of deadlines is important. The scarcity principle also has obvious implications for pricing. Sometimes, the higher the price, the greater the demand, which at first glance would appear to violate normal economic assumptions. But high price often signifies scarcity, and as a consequence, desirability. The more desirable the product, the greater its success in the marketplace.

HOW ISSUES ARE FRAMED

We have seen that how things are viewed depends on the context—what they are compared to, whether there is a committing history of action, whether they are perceived to be scarce. In much the same way that pictures are framed, questions and actions are framed, and the context in which they are viewed and discussed determines what gets done. Establishing the framework within which issues will be viewed and decided is often tantamount to determining the result. Thus, setting the context is a critical strategy for exercising power and influence.

Several examples help to make the point. A friend who once worked at SRI, a consulting firm, on a project for Merrill Lynch when Donald Regan was CEO, talked about his experience with the implementation of the Cash Management

Account (CMA). When Merrill introduced this idea in the 1970s, it was a tremendous innovation. SRI had done a study showing how profitable and successful it was likely to be—it would permit the firm to capture a lot of business by offering an integrated system of check writing, credit cards (VISA), money market funds, and traditional brokerage services. It would generate substantial interest income and also generate more business for Merrill Lynch's money market funds.

After the SRI presentation, Regan went around the room getting comments from the other senior executives. They all saw problems. The operations vice president noted that it now cost the firm many dollars to process a transaction. That was fine when the transactions were securities purchases and sales, in which the commissions were large. When the transactions were deposits in money market accounts, check writing on such accounts, and similar things, they would have to be able to process them for only cents per transaction. The systems simply were not able to handle the task. The legal vice president noted that the cash management account idea would in effect turn the firm into a bank, making it subject to much more stringent regulation than it faced as a securities firm. It would have to get charters, regulatory approvals, and so forth, and this would be difficult, given the resistance of potential competitors. The marketing vice president noted that banks were currently some of Merrill Lynch's best customers. They would certainly be offended if the firm became a competitor, and consequently might take much of their business to other securities firms. And so it went around the table, each senior executive stating valid and sensible concerns that showed why the CMA idea simply wouldn't work.

Regan then turned to the vice presidents and said, "The objections that you raised were good ones. However, I decided to go ahead. So, the question now becomes, how do you solve the problems you described so articulately?" A funny thing happened. With the issue now framed not as, should we do this? but rather, we're going to do it, so let's solve the problems, the same vice presidents, sitting at the table, quickly began to come up with solutions for the problems they themselves had articulated. One suggested beginning in Colorado, because of its particular banking laws and relationships. Another suggested letting banks actually process the checks and the transactions, thereby giving them business and helping to solve the company's operations costs problem. Once the question was reframed, the discussion and attitude changed accordingly.

Because the framing of an issue can decide its outcome, it is important to be early in the process of setting the terms of the discussion. The ability to write intelligent memoranda, which then affect how issues are viewed and discussed, can be used effectively in a strategy of influence. McGeorge Bundy, national security adviser in the Kennedy administration, had that skill and used it to advantage:

> . . . to be a good memo writer in government was a very real form of power. Suddenly everyone would be working off Bundy's memos, and thus his memos guided the action, guided what the President would see.[26]

Two other examples, both from U.S. government policy toward Vietnam, also nicely illustrate the point that decisions often depend on how questions are framed. In the early 1950s, when the French were fighting to retain Indochina, the question arose as to whether the U.S. government should aid the French, who were, after all, a colonial power. Many in the government thought we were harming our interests by helping another country to hang on to its empire. However, that was not the way the issue came to be framed:

> . . . the given was not whether it was wise to aid the French, whether this was the right side or not, but whether the French needed the aid. Of course, the French said they needed the aid. Thus began a major new policy of aid to the French in this colonial war, a policy by which the United States would eventually almost completely underwrite the costs, $2 billion worth, and would by 1954 be more eager to have the French continue fighting than Paris was.[27]

Note that not only was the decision affected by how the question was asked, but once the United States began helping, it became committed by that very behavior.

Later on, when the United States was more directly involved, the issues were frequently framed not in terms of whether policy was wise, or whether the United States should be in Vietnam, but rather, whether we were winning.[28] The underlying assumption, the so-called domino theory (if Vietnam fell to the Communists, the rest of Indochina would fall as well) was seldom examined directly. Rather, the issue was always framed in terms of the viability of the current South Vietnamese government, whether U.S. aid was effective, and whether progress was being made.

As these examples illustrate, the frame of an issue is often constructed through the questions that are asked. Do the questions emphasize potential risks, or gains? The costs of something, or the possible benefits? Do the questions assess what is innovative, what is important? The framing of issues also results from the kind of information that is collected and the matters that the information systems emphasize in their data collection and reporting. It is difficult to frame proposals in terms of quality, for instance, if no data about quality are regularly being produced in the organization, and if questions about quality are seldom raised.

Because decisions and actions inevitably have multiple components, which can be viewed along multiple dimensions, the ability to set the terms of the discussion is an important mechanism for influencing organizational behavior. Yet, we often show little foresight or consciousness about how frames of reference are set, and how the questions asked and data gathered tend to determine the outcomes of choice and action. We are, unfortunately, not as sensitive to the context of organizational activity as we should be. Decisions and activities are not begun anew each day. We need to be aware of history—the history of commitments, of past choices that set the context within which present events are evaluated, and of the set of cognitive lenses that affect what we see and how we see it. Being skilled at both recognizing and using these ideas provides great leverage in getting the things that you want accomplished.

11

Interpersonal Influence

We are not simply influenced by the context of the situation, as we saw in the last chapter; we are also influenced directly by the actions of others. Organizations are not collections of isolated individuals making decisions and taking action in splendid solitude. They are, above all, social settings in which people interact with their colleagues. We are influenced by what our colleagues are saying and doing—the effect of social proof—and we are swayed by the things others do to get us to like them and feel good about them. We are also influenced by the emotions that are created and used in social settings. These three topics—the principle of social proof, the use of ingratiation, and the role of emotions in interpersonal influence—form the subject matter for this chapter.

SOCIAL PROOF AND INFORMATIONAL SOCIAL INFLUENCE

What happens when we are confronted by an ambiguous situation? We may join a new organization, and find ourselves uncertain about the norms and customs that govern interaction, how to get work accomplished, and indeed, how to do our jobs. We may face a decision about whom to hire, what capital investment to favor, what new markets to enter. Uncertainty is pervasive in organizational life, and we are constantly being called upon to make judgments and to take action under conditions of ambiguity. Leon Festinger recognized that when confronted with uncertainty and ambiguity, one way people cope is through informal social communication, in which they ask for the opinions of their associates.[1] Attitudes, perceptions, and choices are compared with those held by others, particularly others who are similar and who are in close proximity. These shared views come to influence the person's own view of the situation. Beliefs and judgments, therefore, become socially anchored and reality becomes a consensual social construction. It is useful to distinguish between complying with or publicly confirming the beliefs of others in order to gain acceptance—in other words, engaging in an exchange in which conformity is bartered for social acceptance—and a situation of informational social influence, in which we come to agree with others because we crave the certainty of a shared opinion.

As with many other influence techniques, relying on the judgments of others to help us form our own opinions economizes on our cognitive work. If I learn from my colleagues that a particular job applicant is perceived as quite strong, I do not have to take as much trouble to weigh the individual's strengths and weaknesses and come to my own conclusion.

There is a second advantage to forming our judgments on the basis of the information provided by others. If we use others as a source of our views, then, obviously, we will come to hold the same views as they hold, and vice versa. The literature on interpersonal attraction shows that similarity is an important source of attraction—we like those who are similar to ourselves.[2] Thus, sharing views with others constitutes an important foundation for interpersonal attraction and social solidarity. Social consensus, which emerges from the process of informational social influence, tends to reinforce interpersonal attraction and good feelings among those who share the consensus. A third advantage is that it reduces the likelihood of being ostracized or rejected. Most of us unconsciously strive to agree with others, because we know that it will ensure acceptance in the group.

Cialdini described some results of the principle of social proof, which inclines us to follow the lead of others:

> Our tendency to assume that an action is more correct if others are doing it is exploited in a variety of settings. Bartenders often salt their tip jars with a few dollar bills at the beginning of an evening to simulate tips left by prior customers and thereby to give the impression that tipping with folding money is proper barroom behavior. Church ushers sometimes salt collection baskets for the same reason. . . . Evangelical preachers are known to seed their audience with ringers, who are rehearsed to come forward at a specified time to give witness and donations. . . . The producers of charity telethons devote inordinate amounts of time to the . . . listing of viewers who have already pledged contributions.[3]

The principle of social proof also helps us understand how bystanders in New York could watch Catherine Genovese be stabbed to death and do nothing.[4] Having a lot of people around doing nothing in such a situation has two effects—first, it diffuses responsibility, since each bystander knows there are others around who could potentially undertake the task; second, with no one else helping, the social information suggests that doing nothing is the appropriate and socially acceptable thing to do.[5] Thus, somewhat ironically, the more people there are available to offer assistance, the less likely it is that anyone will do so, unless someone takes the initiative.

The principle of social proof also helps us understand why foreign cars are sometimes so popular: namely, everyone believes they are good. An article in *The Wall Street Journal* corroborates this argument. It detailed the problems General Motors faced in trying to change its perceptions in the eyes of the car-buying public and recapture market share.[6] As part of the article, the results of a survey conducted by J.D. Power and Associates were displayed. The results represented the percentage of owners of different types of cars (American, Asian, European) who reported being very satisfied with their cars and who would probably buy the same make again, classified by the number of car problems the people had in the previous year. For people with (self-reported) 8 or more defects in the previous year, only 29% of the American car owners reported being very satisfied, while 48% of the owners of Asian cars (who had reported 8 or more defects also) reported being very satisfied. In terms of probably buying the same make of car again, for people who reported 8 or more problems in the past year, 40% of the American car owners said they would buy the same make again, while 66% of the Asian car owners and 48% of the European car owners responded they would buy the same make again. The effect for European cars may be partly commitment—having spent a lot of money on a car, one is reluctant to admit, even to oneself and even when confronted with evidence to the contrary, that one has made a mistake. But the effect for both Asian and European makes is also attributable, in part, to the operation of informational social influence. If everyone tells you that these cars are great, they are, regardless of the evidence you might have acquired through personal experience.

There are many examples of the effects of social proof in organizations, some almost as compelling as the lack of bystander intervention in stabbings. In some instances, social proof was used intentionally to obtain and exercise interpersonal influence; in others, social proof occurred almost accidently, but still can help us understand what happened, and why. The fraudulent transactions of OPM Leasing are a case in point. Some of OPM's victims were among the leading banks and investment bankers in the United States. And though this fact inspires amazement, it also helps explain how such massive fraud could have persisted for so long and on such a scale.

As Gandossy noted, OPM began as a legitimate business, and over the years engaged in thousands of legitimate leasing transactions, many times the number of fraudulent transactions.[7] Thus, many of their associations were totally honest, and these associations may have caused those who suspected fraud to question their own judgment. Moreover, they intentionally used social proof as a strategy:

> Like most executives, Goodman and Weissman were concerned about OPM's corporate image, and they did several things to elevate their standing with outsiders. First they associated with elite, well-known corporations, correctly believing that by doing so, outsiders would see them as bigger and better than they actually were. In their first few years, they hired Big Eight accounting firms and, later,

venerable investment banking houses [Goldman, Sachs] to arrange credit. They didn't employ such firms merely to obtain improved service but simply to establish legitimacy in the marketplace. Whenever possible, they exploited their elite associations. . . . in meetings and correspondence with prospective lessees and lenders, Goodman was quick to mention OPM's relationships with Goldman, Sachs and with Lehman.[8]

OPM used its associations to promote the belief that it was engaged in legitimate business. With no one questioning its methods or its operations—after all, many of the firms were receiving handsome fees—it was difficult for any individual or organization to violate the social consensus and question what was going on. And the longer it went on, the harder it was to question, for there was now a larger set of relationships, and a history of commitment, which made uncovering or disclosing the fraud increasingly unlikely.

Steven Bach, describing how United Artists was undone by its production of *Heaven's Gate*, provides numerous examples of how social proof operated with a vengeance in the movie industry.[9] People who were perceived as "hot" were pursued with little regard to substance or reality—the perception became the reality. Few questions were asked about whether films were actually made on time and within budget, and how well they had performed at the box office. This effect was particularly pronounced at United Artists. It was at that time a division of Transamerica, and thus faced some skepticism about its citizenship in the movie business; it was also run by executives who were not very familiar with the industry. In order to resolve its own uncertainties, and to show that it was one of the group, UA felt especially pressured to run with the pack:

> Every executive . . . tries to convince himself that just a bit more rock turning will yield that holiest of movie grails: a hot property. There results a kind of desperate promiscuity in the executives' relationship to talent. . . . What it really means is avoiding, "How the hell did we lose Brando . . . to UA?" . . . or some other index by which the company in question is perceived as lower on the pecking order than somebody, *any*body else. . . . Often in this scramble for hot material, "Fellas, this book is a piece of *shit*!" becomes lost in the frenzy over "Can we make a deal?"[10]

Or, as a third example, consider Byron's account of how Time Inc. lost more than $50 million in an attempt to launch a weekly magazine of cable television listings.[11] The proposed magazine had virtually no market and was almost certain to be technically impossible to produce because of the information processing requirements. The project itself had little strong leadership. What it did have going for it was some momentum, as well as the reluctance of those with serious reservations to voice them in the face of apparent support for the project (probably pluralistic ignorance) among many top executives. Moreover, the executives were very Ivy League, and had a tendency to favor the young Ivy Leaguers on the staff of the magazine. In a setting in which no one wanted to question the judgment of others, it was difficult, if not impossible, to stop the project until it had consumed enormous amounts of resources.

Because of social influence processes and how they operate, momentum is very important in affecting a decision or accomplishing something. Once a social consensus begins to develop in one direction, it is difficult to change that consensus, not only because people become committed to their positions, but also because the fact of agreement makes each individual believe that his or her own position is probably correct. The implication of this is that affecting how decisions are viewed, very early in the process, is absolutely critical in affecting the outcome.

A second implication is that the very phrase, "decision making," may be somewhat inappropriate. If social proof and social consensus are critical in affecting judgments and decisions, and if the process of building social agreement unfolds over time, it is probably more appropriate to think of decisions as "happening," or "unfolding," rather than being "made."

Finally, it is invaluable to have allies or supporters to provide evidence of social consensus around a particular position. It is crucial to manage the informational environment so that the necessity of what you are trying to accomplish appears to be taken for granted by everyone in the organization. This can be achieved, in part, through the simple repetition of ideas or messages, as well as by pointing out others who agree with you. And it is certainly the case that interpersonal influence is often most effectively exercised in group settings, in which social proof can be brought to bear.

A dramatic illustration of the use of social proof (as well as reciprocity) in achieving a goal can be seen in Henry Kissinger's effort to obtain the position of special assistant for national security affairs in the first Nixon administration.[12] In addition to doing the Nixon campaign the favor of reporting on the progress of the Paris peace negotiations, so that appropriate campaign strategies could be devised, Kissinger made sure that he had many supporters who would speak well of him to the new president—Richard Allen, Nixon's campaign coordinator for foreign policy research, Joseph Kraft, the columnist, John Mitchell, H.R. Haldeman, and Peter M. Flanigan, Nixon's deputy campaign manager. His service to the campaign and his extensive contacts made him the obvious choice for the job. Hersh noted, "Nixon was impressed not only by Kissinger's extensive knowledge and contacts, but also by his willingness to make use of those assets."[13]

LIKING AND INGRATIATION

Cialdini wrote, "Few of us would be surprised to learn that, as a rule, we most prefer to say yes to the requests of people we know and like. What might be startling to note, however, is that this simple rule is used in hundreds of ways . . . to get us to comply with . . . requests."[14] Liking for others is based on a number of factors, including: 1) social similarity (we tend to like people more who resemble us and are from the same social category or group); 2) physical attractiveness (attractive people are more liked and likeable); 3) compliments and flattery (we like people who like us, and who express positive sentiments toward us); 4) contact and cooperation (we tend to like people we know well, especially if we work with them on a common task or toward a common goal); 5) association with other positive things (we like people who bring us good news, and conversely, tend to dislike those who bring us bad news). Liking is important in interpersonal influence because it invokes the reciprocity rule.

Understanding the importance of liking can help explain how it was possible that in 1985, Steve Jobs, the co-founder of Apple Computer and one of its major stockholders, was forced out of all but a ceremonial position in the company. Jobs was "too self-centered to be cynical or calculating or scheming. He was incapable of viewing the world from anyone else's perspective."[15] As we have seen, he never bothered to develop close relationships with the members of the board, who had backed him from the beginning. He also apparently didn't feel it necessary to be considerate to potential allies within the corporation, who might have supported him in the showdown with Sculley. His handling of Del Yocam, a very senior executive who had run the Apple II division and who was in charge of operations and manufacturing, exemplifies an interpersonal style that produces dislike, and as a consequence, reduces influence:

> He went for a long walk around the parking lot with Del, and Del seemed to be agreeing with a lot of what he was saying. At a certain point, however, Steve was just unable to stop himself. He said he wanted to run operations, and he informed Del that he really was a much better operations person than Del was. . . . Del asked him to repeat what he'd just said, so he did. After all, he was just repeating what should have been plain to everyone. But it wasn't plain to Del. Del was upset.[16]

The use of the liking principle in developing and exercising interpersonal influence requires us to build one or more of the bases of liking noted above into our relationship with the targets of the influence. Physical attractiveness is the least malleable factor. But contact, positive association, and particularly, flattery are quite amenable to strategic behavior on the part of those seeking to influence others.

There are numerous examples of the use of liking in sales situations, as well as in other settings in which influence must be developed and exercised. Sales parties, such as those held by Tupperware, Amway, or Mary Kay Cosmetics, operate on the liking principle. The settings use social proof (others are also buying) and commitment (people may be asked to describe how many different uses there are for Tupperware, and even sitting through one of these events builds commitment), but liking is used to draw people into the settings in the first place. I discussed this principle, and the home party example, in an MBA class I was teaching. Somewhat embarrassed (because Stanford MBAs shouldn't be at such events or be taken in so readily), a student described how a co-worker in a former job had invited her to a Mary Kay event. Although she did not particularly want to go, the request came from a friend—how could she refuse without being impolite? Of course, once at the party, surrounded by other acquaintances, she purchased an item—the least expensive one she could. Not surprisingly, the least expensive items typically carry the highest mark-up. The companies know that people will want to purchase at least one thing, and will try to get off as easily as possible. Therefore, the cheapest items tend to be the most profitable for the companies.

Does physical attractiveness promote liking and the ability to exercise interpersonal influence? Ross and Ferris studied the performance evaluations and salaries of accountants in two public accounting firms.[17] They found that physically more attractive accountants (as judged by showing pictures to people who did not work for the accounting firm and who had no knowledge of the study) received higher performance evaluations, even when other factors that might affect performance ratings were statistically controlled. Efran and Patterson, studying the 1974 Canadian federal elections, reported that attractive candidates received more votes than unattractive candidates.[18] Cialdini noted that "Other experiments have demonstrated that attractive people are more likely to obtain help when in need and are more persuasive in changing the opinions of an audience."[19]

Cialdini also summarized experimental research that indicated people were more likely to comply with requests made by someone who was similar to them in terms of dress or other factors such as age, religion, or politics.[20] It is, therefore, not by chance that bank loan officers or branch managers in a place like the Silicon Valley in California tend to be younger, as their clientele is younger. I have often speculated that there is a demographic matching factor that helps to account for instructor ratings in courses and executive programs—your audience is more likely to be enthusiastic if they can identify with you.

Of course, similarity can be, to some extent, created. When Nabisco was merged into RJ Reynolds and Ross Johnson was named president and chief operating officer, he immediately sought to develop an appearance of similarity with the Reynolds crowd:

> Alone among senior Nabisco executives, Johnson moved to Winston-Salem. . . . He was reported to be a thoroughly winning fellow. . . . In his first weeks in Winston-Salem Johnson made an all-out effort to fit in, driving around in a Jeep Wagoneer, inviting people over to dinner, and joining the board of the North Carolina Zoological Society.[21]

Johnson, more than many executives, understood the importance of being well liked to his success, and the role that similarity played in having others like or at least feel comfortable with him.

Flattery or ingratiation is a very effective technique of interpersonal influence.[22] At first, flattery may seem like an obvious strategy to develop liking, and consequently, one might wonder why it is effective. But consider how you may react to receiving a compliment or a flattering remark. You have two options. You can consider the compliment to be sincere, or you can consider it to be instrumental, delivered only to accomplish an ulterior motive. Your own feelings are, obviously, not indifferent to which interpretation you choose to accept. There is, in fact, a motivational bias for you to believe the compliment was sincere. If you believe the flattering remark, you will feel positive about yourself. If, on the other hand, you think the remark was instrumental, you will not feel as good about yourself, you will question the other's opinion of you (what's wrong with you that others think you can be easily taken in by flattery?), and you will not feel positively toward the other person either. Since most of us would rather feel good than bad, we want to see the compliments and flattery as sincere.

Flattery is used particularly in the political realm. Robert Moses's relationship with Mayor LaGuardia, although at times marked by conflict and confrontation, also demonstrated the effective use of ingratiation. Moses pressed LaGuardia to accompany him on inspection tours of projects while they were being built.[23] He played skillfully on LaGuardia's love for pageantry and for being the center of attention. For instance, the opening of a small playground in New

York City was inevitably an occasion for flattering the mayor and making him feel important:

> . . . nearby tenements were draped in red, white, and blue. . . . Flowerpots containing 25,000 chrysanthemums made a bright ring around the playground fence. Flags were everywhere. . . . As the Mayor's limousine pulled up to the curb . . . the bands broke into a tune: incredibly, "Hail to the Chief." And when he reached the . . . speakers' platform he found he was the only speaker, except for Moses, who confined himself to a very brief recitation of playground statistics and then said, "I now introduce the Mayor of the City of New York"—a performance that led LaGuardia to comment that Moses was the ideal master of ceremonies. . . . when the Mayor advanced to cut the ribbon and allow the children to rush into the spray, he found that it was no ordinary ribbon but a braided and tasseled strand colored red, white, and blue, and the shears held out to him by a little girl from the neighborhood were sterling silver shears resting on a cushion of royal velvet.[24]

Moses also saw to it that one playground was named after LaGuardia, and he wrote the mayor, "The best thing about the playground is its name."[25]

Moses cultivated the press, inviting everyone from publishers to reporters to attend lunches, dinners, and ceremonies surrounding the opening of public works, as well as to swimming and dinner outings at Jones Beach.[26] Moses took care of the people who were important to him, and thus it was difficult for them to be critical of him.

Ingratiation is not a technique confined to the public sector. The OPM computer leasing fraud was predicated, in part, on the ability of OPM to win favor in the eyes of important clients and contacts. This was accomplished, in part, through the behavioral skills of Weissman:

> Weissman's interpersonal skills had a great deal to do with OPM's rapid growth. He worked hard to please clients, once paying off a contractor in Florida who was interfering with the installation of a client's computer equipment. He also had a certain charm. . . . Weissman made it his business to get along with people and to nurture his contacts.[27]

But more than behavioral skills were involved in the development of liking. Gandossy reported that OPM provided "services" for their clients that few competitors could or would match, ranging from payoffs for customers and vendors to obtaining prostitutes for the employees of certain corporations, including, apparently, one *Fortune* 500 company.[28]

In the 1960s, the Bechtel Corporation and Steve Bechtel himself used flattery and ingratiation to obtain favors from Henry Kearns, head of the Export-Import Bank. The bank provided below-market, federally guaranteed loans to help U.S. firms do business overseas. For example, the bank might finance a foreign country's purchase of goods and services from U.S. corporations. The access to favorable financing had always been one of the keys to Bechtel's success. Now the Nixon administration wanted to expand the bank's portfolio vastly—which meant that Kearns would have to make a lot of loans. Steve Bechtel, Sr., who already had connections to Kearns, was determined to make the most of this extraordinary opportunity. For as in many other endeavors, particularly those related to construction, the ability to obtain financing was often crucial to winning the contract.

> He [Bechtel] began by flattering Kearns's ego—congratulating him on the fine job he was doing, and offering to help in any way possible. Knowing of Kearns's thirst for publicity . . . Bechtel also began sending along newspaper clips about the bank's activities, attaching to them complimentary notes. He ingratiated himself further by suggesting to Kearns that he commission a film about the bank, in which its president, naturally, would play a starring role.[29]

Bechtel and his firm did many favors for Kearns, the bank, and its clients and staff. There was little that Bechtel would not do for the Export-Import Bank, including testifying on its behalf before Congress. This relationship, cemented through favors and through extensive flattery, paid enormous dividends for Bechtel in terms of access to financing and the business deals such financing provided.

One of the more subtle but effective forms of flattery is being responsive and attentive to others. When this attentiveness is shown by someone who is higher in rank or status, it conveys the flattering impression that your feelings are important enough to concern them. When George Ball was working in the brokerage division of E.F. Hutton (he later became its president, and subsequently president of Prudential-Bache Securities), he focused on building up the spirits of the people in the field. He developed a very strong power base in the retail part of Hutton through his assiduous attention to all of its staff. "Knowing that the little things build loyalty, he left no call unanswered, no request unserved."[30] A major part of Ball's charm came from his ability to flatter people by remembering small details of their lives:

> "George had an uncanny ability to remember everything about you," says a former Hutton account executive. "He charmed you, he flattered you, he made you feel special. A few years after meeting George for the first time, I bumped into him at a sales meeting. Because I was sure he wouldn't recognize me, I headed over to reintroduce myself. But there was no need for that. No sooner does George spot me than he's shaking my hand, saying, 'Hi, how's Betsy and the kids?' "[31]

A good memory helped, but he also studied charts that had pictures and personal details of people he would be meeting on business trips.[32] Even that much effort is flattering, however. He may not have known everyone as well as he seemed to, but he still felt they were important enough to try and memorize their names and some details about their families.

Liking also comes from working with others, toward a common goal and against a common enemy. Apple Computer, during the mid-1980s, effectively used IBM as just such a unifying and motivating external threat. Steve Jobs was fond of saying that IBM had more than 300,000 employees, and Apple had only 6,000. IBM was so large that it threatened total domination of the entire computer industry, and Apple was the only hope for future freedom. The Macintosh team indicated that much of their motivation came from close contact with each other, in a separate facility isolated from the rest of the corporation, and from their shared vision of changing the world, against, always, the competitive threat of IBM, which stood for a different view of computers.

The importance of a common goal in developing positive feelings among those who work toward that goal was demonstrated most clearly in the classic experiments conducted by Muzafer Sherif and his associates.[33] In a boys' summer camp, Sherif and his colleagues first created conflict—letting the boys choose different names for their two groups, assigning the groups to different residence cabins, and introducing competitive activities.[34] To bring the two groups back

together, the experimenters devised tasks that required cooperation in order to achieve some mutually desirable goal.
"Successful joint efforts toward common goals steadily
bridged the rift between the two groups."[35] Contact and familiarity also help to promote liking—just as we tend to like
familiar surroundings, we also tend to like people who are
familiar to us.

Various kinds of pleasure also tend to produce liking. One
of the reasons why donations are solicited over lunch, dinner,
or some other enjoyable social experience is not only that the
norm of reciprocity is activated, but also that the pleasure of
eating a nice meal in a lovely setting is apt to produce liking
for the provider of that experience, which, in turn, makes us
more likely to comply with that person's attempts to influence our behavior.

The most straightforward implication of the liking principle of interpersonal influence has to do with management
style. For a while, the management literature seemed to ven-
erate the cold, often tough numbers-oriented managers such
as Robert McNamara or Harold Geneen. Corporations emphasized discipline, and as the former vice president for human resources at Eastern Airlines stated in the film *Collision
Course,* one got ahead and obtained status from being the
meanest, toughest person on the block. There have certainly
been a number of quite successful managers who were anything but warm or likable. However, the liking principle suggests that managers who are warmer, more humorous, and
less intimidating will, other things being equal, have an easier time exercising influence. It is significant to note that
many managers who were notoriously aloof and intimidating
worked in organizations in which they had a great deal of
formal power, and in which persuasion, as opposed to hierarchy, was less critical in exercising power. Because of shifts
in social norms and values, there are fewer and fewer such
settings.

Another implication of the liking strategy is the importance
of working through friends or mutual acquaintances to influence third parties. Most people are inclined to feel more
warmly toward acquaintances whose attractiveness or reliability has already been vouched for by others they trust.[36]

This is why networks of social relations are useful for exercising interpersonal influence.

INFLUENCE THROUGH EMOTIONS

We are all moved and influenced by our hearts as well as by our minds. Some interpersonal influence strategies rely on the emotional, as well as the cognitive, aspect of social life to affect behavior. Although the study of emotions in organizations is a fairly unexplored domain, there has been some important research that can help us understand the emotional bases of interpersonal influence.

There are three points to the argument that displayed emotions are important techniques of interpersonal influence. The first is that the emotions displayed to others can be managed or controlled. If emotions, at least as experienced by others with whom we interact, were not controllable, then there would be little possibility for using expressed emotions strategically. The second point is that the behavior of others is contingent, at least in part, on the emotions we display, and that consequently, expressed emotions can be effective in influencing their behavior. The implication of the first two facts is that not everyone will have an equal ability to influence others by using emotions tactically. This skill can, in part, be learned or acquired, and it is one of the attributes that helps distinguish comparatively effective from less effective members of organizations.

Can expressed or displayed emotions be employed tactically, or, in other words, are they are under the volitional control of the individual? Certainly organizations think that emotional expressions can be managed and used to affect how clients or customers perceive the organization. When People Express was still in business, it selected its "customer service managers" (flight attendants and gate agents) on the basis of their peppiness and upbeat attitudes. Arlie Hochschild in *The Managed Heart* provides numerous other examples of organizations, such as Delta Airlines, that also used certain expressed emotions as a criterion for selecting prospective employees.[37] Delta (and other airlines) wanted employees who could keep smiling even during a 15-hour flight or under bad weather. Hochschild described the procedure that Pan American Airlines used to select its cheerful flight attendants.

> The recruiter called in a group of six applicants, three men and three women. She smiled at all of them and then said, "While I'm looking over your files here, I'd like to ask you to turn to your neighbor and get to know him or her. We'll take three or four minutes, and then I'll get back to you." Immediately there was bubbly conversation, nodding of heads, expansion of posture, and . . . ripples of laughter. . . . All six looked expectantly at the recruiter: how had they done on their animation test?[38]

Disney World both selects its employees on the basis of personal styles that are positive and upbeat, and works hard to train them to be friendly and polite, and show happiness constantly.

> The example of Disney World employees highlights how role occupants' enduring characteristics and inner feelings can have little influence when they have low discretion over expressed emotions. These employees are trained to follow organizational display rules no matter how they feel. . . . The trainer made a point of telling newcomers that when they are onstage with Disney guests, they must be nice no matter how nasty the guest happens to be and no matter how angry they feel. . . . The trainer . . . told the newcomers: "Everyone treats the guests as VIPs. The only reason we are here is that the guests come to see us and our show. 99% of the guests are nice, but it's that tiny 1% that you can't let get to you." Indeed, Disney employees learn that if they do let the "tiny 1%" get to them, it is grounds for dismissal.[39]

The Southland Corporation, the firm that operates and franchises 7-11 stores, for a time used a variety of tactics to encourage clerks to be friendly and express positive emotions to the customers:

> Clerks in most regions were informed that "mystery shoppers" would be used to observe levels of employee courtesy. In some regions, clerks who were caught displaying the required good cheer to customers received a $25 bonus. In other regions, clerks who were observed greeting, smiling, establishing eye contact . . . could win a new automobile instantly.[40]

The company spent $10 million on a program to reward store operators and clerks who displayed the appropriate positive emotions. Whether the key to getting employees to express such emotions is selection, socialization, rewards, or some combination of the three, there is ample evidence that a wide range of companies believes that emotional expression can be controlled by employees and used to influence clients and customers.

Does this strategy work? Apparently so, in many instances. One review of the effects of expressed emotions by organizational members noted numerous examples in which emotional expression had influence on behavior.[41] For instance, a book used to train police officers in interrogation techniques suggested the silent approach:

> Using this approach, you enter the interrogation room with a slight smile on your face, sit comfortably down in your chair, look him straight in the eye, and say absolutely nothing. . . . The senior author once sat for some 25 minutes without moving or taking his gaze from the suspect's face. The suspect, who was very loud before the interrogation, suddenly broke down and began to cry. Within 3 minutes he gave a full confession.[42]

One study examined the effect of smiling on the tips earned by a cocktail waitress who served 48 male and 48 female customers.[43] Although the number of drinks ordered was not affected by smiling, the amount of tips earned was. Broad smiles brought in $23.20, while a minimal smile earned the waitress only a total of $9.40. In a study of bill collectors, Robert Sutton found that individuals who were able to convey urgency and to use emotional contrast—sometimes being nice, sometimes threatening—succeeded in collecting a surprising amount, even from people who were as much as six months delinquent on their accounts.[44]

Emotions affect behavior through many of the psychological principles we have already considered. For instance, emotional contrast is used by Israeli police interrogators as well as bill collectors.[45] By either having one partner play the good cop and a second partner the bad cop, or having an individual alternate roles himself, the strategy is intended to make nice behavior appear even nicer by contrast. The person exposed to the nice behavior is likely to want to recip-rocate, in this instance, either by paying the bill or by con-fessing to a crime. In addition, the bad cop behavior is experi-enced as aversive, which means that people will want to comply with requests so the pressure will stop. Emotional contrast strategies offer clear proof that expressed emotions can influence others.

Although using expressed or displayed emotion can be an effective technique of interpersonal influence, it is not some-thing everyone can do. There is, in fact, some skill involved in the strategic display of emotions. It requires a tremendous amount of self-control and restraint, as well as a conscious-ness of what effects you want to produce in those with whom you are interacting. And there are costs from trying, over sustained periods of time, to control your emotional displays. Hochschild's book was, in part, about the toll such behavior exacted, particularly from lower-level service employees, who were supposed to be smiling, cheerful, and friendly for long periods of time regardless of the circumstances and how they felt. "In the long term, Hochschild contended, the con-stant pressure of emotional labor may lead to drug use, exces-sive drinking, headaches, absenteeism, and sexual dys-function."[46]

The insights of the work on emotion are excellent, but its focus is often too narrow. Managing one's emotional displays, hiding one's real feelings, and using emotions to influence others is not behavior confined to Disney employees, bill collectors, police interrogators, or flight attendants. Execu-tives and others seeking to exercise influence in organiza-tions often develop skill in displaying, or not displaying, their feelings in a strategic fashion. One thing I have ob-served in teaching MBAs and executives over the years is that how you are doing in your presentation is often more easily discerned with the MBA students. They have not yet mastered the ability, developed in many cases by senior ex-ecutives, to be able to smile, tell you how much they enjoyed the presentation, how much they learned, and how much they appreciated your efforts, even when they were bored out of their minds. Getting along in organizations often in-volves being able to transact business, in a pleasant and effective manner, with people whom you don't like and possibly don't respect, but whose cooperation you need to get things done. The emotions and feelings you display are important, and we all learn from childhood on to "be polite," to "not let our feelings show," and perhaps, even to use emotional displays intentionally to influence others to behave as we want them to. Whether we plan to use expressed emotions, or for that matter, the other strategies of interpersonal influence ourselves, it is helpful to recognize and understand these strategies. If nothing else, it makes us better observers of social influence as it unfolds around us, and helps us to understand and predict organizational outcomes somewhat more accurately.

CONCLUSION

It is tempting, but fundamentally misleading and incorrect, to dismiss the various techniques of interpersonal influence described in the last two chapters as marketing tricks, or at best, as forces that distort our ability to arrive at correct decisions. These are scarcely gimmicks, but rather, are important ideas that we observe at work every day in the world around us. At times they may even be beneficial to organizations. They economize on information processing; every situation we encounter cannot be fully investigated de novo. The only way we and our organizations can get things accomplished is to rely on short cuts in information processing. Thus, the consensus of others is normally taken as a reasonable guide to understanding the situation and hence determining our own behavior. Scarcity normally means that what is scarce is desirable and desired by others. And the principle of consistency saves us from wasting effort in scattered bursts of activity. Interpersonal social influence is an omnipresent part of social life, which can neither be avoided nor wished away.

Moreover, we should not attempt to avoid social influence. The fact that we live in a social world and that organizations are interdependent social systems means that we can get things done only with the help of other people. It is essential that we have the ability to accept another's definition of the situation and to follow rules of behavior that ensure cooperative interaction. The fact that these techniques sometimes can be used to pull the wool over our eyes does not deny their legitimacy—each is based on valid psychological principles and, more important, on valuable social relationships. These strategies of interpersonal influence are the products of a social, interdependent world. As such, they are important factors that can contribute to both personal and organizational effectiveness.

12

Timing Is (Almost) Everything

In utilizing the strategies and tactics of power and influence, it is crucial to determine not only what to do but when to do it. This chapter considers the important but often neglected dimension of timing. Actions that are well-timed may succeed, while the same actions, undertaken at a less opportune moment, may have no chance of success. In considering strategies associated with timing, we will examine the advantages and costs of taking early, first action; strategies associated with delay; how waiting is used to signify and build power; how deadlines affect what is decided; how what is decided depends on the order in which it is considered; and finally, the importance of intervening when the time is ripe.

BEING EARLY AND MOVING FIRST

There are, of course, disadvantages to taking action early. Delay gives you the chance to learn more about other people's points of view and this knowledge can be employed in formulating tactics that will be more successful. Doing something first, taking early action exposes you—to be first is to be visible, to be out front, and therefore a potential target for others.

On the other hand, there are numerous advantages to acting first. By staking out a position, by taking some action that will be difficult to undo, we can compel those who come later to accommodate themselves to our position.[1] Once a project is started, for instance, it is much more difficult to stop; once someone is hired, it is difficult to then fire the person; once something is built, it is often impossible to get it torn down; once a computer is purchased and an information system installed, the possibility of change is severely limited. When it is difficult to undo what you have accomplished, your actions serve as a base for further negotiations. You may set both the terms of the debate and the framework for subsequent action.

Also, being first often provides the advantage of surprise, and the possibility of finding your opponent unprepared. Surprise is, on occasion, determinative in organizational politics. Bill Agee was a master at moving first when he was the chief executive of Bendix, as was evidenced by his clash with William Panny, the president and chief operating officer.[2] Agee fired Panny in September 1980, in a move that left others no time to second-guess him. The specifics of their exchange are not fully known, but the results were unmistakable:

> The final showdown between Panny and Agee . . . may have involved Mary Cunningham. One story going around Detroit has it that a number of Bendix executives went to Panny complaining about the Cunningham-Agee relationship, and that Panny was planning to take the matter to the board. The next day . . . Agee fired him before he had a chance.[3]

Another version of the same story has essentially the same message:

> Panny called her [Cunningham] into his office and chewed her out. . . . Panny and Agee soon had heated words, including some over the relationship between Agee and Cunningham. The next day, Agee asked Panny to resign. Panny refused, but Agee announced his resignation anyway.[4]

Note that in this instance, Agee acted first to get rid of Panny before Panny could cause him serious trouble. Agee also acted swiftly in announcing Panny's resignation. Once the resignation was announced, it would have been almost pointless for Panny to publicly contest it—his reputation and image had already been damaged, and the firing had, in effect, already occurred.

In Agee's battle with the board of directors, briefly mentioned in Chapter 2, he again used early action to his advantage. Because of his presumed relationship with Mary Cunningham and a general loss of confidence in him among senior managers at Bendix, there was a possibility that the board might fire Agee in spite of the company's outstanding financial performance. Three directors from Detroit, Paul Mirabito, CEO of Burroughs, Alan Schwartz, an attorney who served on the boards of nine companies besides Bendix, and Harry Cunningham of Kresge, were particularly troubled by the charges that Agee was playing favorites. Agee also apparently tried to become chairman of Burroughs while still serving as chairman of Bendix. Michael Blumenthal, the former CEO of Bendix and now heir-apparent at Burroughs (he had left Bendix for a cabinet position in the Carter administration) became a significant enemy of Agee's, especially after Agee failed to invite him back onto the Bendix board when he returned to Detroit from Washington. Agee's problem seemed to center around the Detroit directors, who were in many instances tied to Burroughs or to Blumenthal and who were concerned about the growing scandal of his relationship with Cunningham. So Agee decided to move before the directors could get themselves organized.

Agee went to Harry Cunningham, who chaired the committee of the board that set compensation, slated directors, and managed executive succession and selection, and "suggested that since they both sat on Burroughs' board, Mirabito and Schwartz should not be nominated for reelection as Bendix directors at the forthcoming annual meeting."[5] Cunningham put the matter off, but further anonymous letters to him from high-placed Bendix executives caused him growing concern. He told Agee that he planned to hold a meeting of the organization, compensation, and nominating committee on March 6, without Agee in attendance. Agee was not about to wait until that meeting occurred:

> Agee reacted swiftly, calling his own special meeting of the committee for February 25. . . . He opened the session by announcing that Bendix planned to acquire a high-technology company, and those

> Bendix directors who also sat on the Burroughs board could face a conflict of interest. He wanted the committee's approval to ask Mirabito and Schwartz for their resignations. . . . Then Agee suggested that, as Harry Cunningham had once been on the Burroughs board, he too should resign. Caught by surprise, Cunningham angrily replied that he would gladly leave the board.[6]

Overnight, Cunningham decided he had changed his mind. By the time he reached Agee, Agee had already extracted oral resignations from Mirabito and Schwartz, and he told Cunningham that he would not be permitted to change his mind. One more problem remained on the Bendix board—Robert Purcell, a friend of Cunningham who had served on the Kresge board at his invitation. With few allies left on the board, Purcell decided to fight Agee anyway. He fired off a blistering letter to his fellow directors, and then made a major mistake:

> Purcell concluded by requesting a board review of Agee's actions in the Harry Cunningham affair. In a postscript, he asked that the meeting be held after March 16 so a board member then in Europe would be able to attend. . . . Purcell then took off to Sugarbush in Vermont for some skiing.[7]

Agee called a meeting of the board for March 11. With Agee in control of the board and in control of the timing of the meeting, Purcell could not get Agee removed. Agee asked for his resignation. Purcell did not resign immediately, trying again to get Agee removed. However, as he was approaching the mandatory retirement age for directors, he did finally resign in advance of his seventieth birthday.

It is not, of course, invariably the case that nice people finish last. But in political struggles, giving the opposition time to get organized and mobilized is not a very good strategy. Agee's use of surprise was particularly effective, because when surprised, we are likely to react emotionally rather than strategically to the situation.

DELAY

One of the best ways to stop something is to delay it, and a very successful way of delaying something is to call for further study or consideration. Thus, delay is a tactic often used in contests over what will be done in a situation. Delay works for several reasons. First, the proponents of an initiative may simply tire of the effort, particularly if they see it going nowhere. There is a limit to how long and hard people will push for any one project. In addition to simply tiring of the effort, it is possible that the backers of the project may not be around, if the delay is sufficiently long. One reason why permanent staff in government bureaus has comparatively great influence is that it is in place longer than many other groups that may try to influence policies and practices—including even elected leaders.

Third, delay is effective because decisions sometimes have deadlines associated with them, and delay causes rejection. For instance, if the decision is about whether to build some project, the proposal and price quotation undoubtedly have an expiration date associated with them. If the decision can be postponed beyond the point when the bid is still valid, then either the decision is automatically foreclosed or else negotiations must be started anew to determine a new price. Delaying the introduction of a new product can ensure that the firm does not enter the market at all. By the time the firm decides to enter, there may be enough other competitors that entry is foreclosed. Finally, delay may be a signal of the organization's interest in the issue at hand. Delaying making a job offer signals that one is less than completely enthusiastic and certain about the candidate; delaying in making a capital investment or new product decision indicates skepticism about the venture. Such signals tend to undermine the confidence of the proponents, increasing the likelihood that the opponents will prevail by outlasting them.

I have seen delay used to forestall the hiring of a particular job candidate in favor of another, alternate candidate. Under the guise of a complete search, and a full and informed discussion, the search process was prolonged so that the candidate some favored gave up in frustration. The alternate candidate did not give up, because the person was counseled by her advocates that there was an intentional delay to help her get the offer. With this private knowledge of the strategy, the alternate waited until the other candidate withdrew and then got the job.

The engineers of such delays almost always offer justifications for them. It is justified by the press of other matters of more importance. It is justified by the seemingly rational position that more information is desirable, and more time is needed to gather that additional information. More study, more thought, will help us make a better choice. Of course, information and analysis are useful, but what the proponents of delays seldom state publicly is that the passage of time itself changes the decision process, in ways that often favor those advocating the delays.

One of the clearest examples of the use of delay to stop a project is the case of the U.S. supersonic transport program. In 1961, Najeeb Halaby, administrator of the FAA, headed a task force on national aviation goals, which issued a report calling for the development of a supersonic transport. In 1962, the British and French governments jointly announced the Concorde Program, and in June 1963, Pan American World Airways placed an order for six Concorde aircraft. On June 5, 1963, at commencement exercises at the U.S. Air Force Academy, President Kennedy announced that the United States would also have a program to develop a supersonic transport for civilian use. Under the original timetable drawn up in July 1963, there would be three phases, the third involving prototype construction. It was anticipated that this construction of an actual prototype aircraft would occur by mid-1965.

The aircraft manufacturers complained about the proposed cost-sharing arrangement, in which they would incur 25% of the cost and the government would incur 75%. To review the cost-sharing formula as well as to give additional credibility to the SST program, World Bank President Eugene Black and Stanley Osborne, chairman of Olin Matheson, were appointed to review the program. Although Black and Osborne recommended a more generous cost-sharing formula, with the government incurring 90% of the expense, their report set events in motion that inevitably led to the demise of the program. They recommended against a crash program, and more significantly, they suggested that the program be removed from the FAA's oversight, arguing that it was a conflict of interest to have the agency that was licensing aircraft also be involved in developing one. Because a report had been done, it had to be circulated for comment. It was February 1964 before the report was circulated, and although the program was not removed from the FAA, an advisory committee on supersonic transport was established, including Robert McNamara as chairman.

The rest of the history of the program is a story of studies—studies of economic feasibility, studies of the effects of the sonic boom that would be created by supersonic flight, studies of the effects that building, or not building, the SST might have on the balance of trade, studies done by the opponents of the SST. The studies, which of course took time, and the oversight committee headed by McNamara worked to delay the project. In 1965, Halaby resigned his FAA position; Gordon Bain, who had been appointed within the FAA to oversee the SST project, also resigned that year. Delays thus had their first effect, outlasting the original administrators who were sponsoring the project. The delays also pushed the development of the SST into the late 1960s, a time in which protests against the Vietnam War and an active environmental movement made the project politically tenuous. The delays for study and contract letting also extended the project's life over three presidencies—Kennedy's, Johnson's, and Nixon's. The project was finally killed in 1971, without a prototype ever having been constructed. Although the project was, in fact, plagued by economic and technological issues, there have been other things built, particularly under Defense Department sponsorship, that have made less sense than supersonic transport. The difference in this case was the loss of control over the timing of the project, and the studies and delays that cost it momentum. If a prototype had been built quickly, and if representatives and senators had been able to fly in one, the outcome might have been quite different.[8]

Delay is a common and often effective strategy in the legal arena, as one side strives to exhaust both the financial resources and the patience of the other. Delay coupled with the resources to outlast one's opponent has almost always been a guarantee of prevailing. When Robert Moses became parks commissioner in the mid-1920s, one of his first acts was to seize the Taylor Estate, which he intended to turn into a park. Moses had seized the land through a process of appropriation, and although he had drafted the bill giving him broad powers in this arena, he had overstepped even those powers. He had not negotiated with the land owners, nor did he have the appropriated funds to pay for the land available to him at the time. When owners of the land sued, Moses did everything he could to delay the case. Caro noted that "on the day he was scheduled to be examined, he didn't show up in court. . . . his attorneys began a new series of delaying actions in an attempt to stall the proceedings until January."[9] Through the strategy of delay, Moses exhausted his opponents' willingness to spend money; moreover, he completed the park while the case about its construction was being tried.

Another compelling example of delay being used to exhaust an opponent's resources occurred in the Eastern Airlines labor negotiations, during the battle of wits between Frank Lorenzo and Charlie Bryan. Lorenzo's strategy for breaking the machinists' union was quite simple: he would offer the machinists a totally unacceptable contract, they would walk off the job on strike, and he would hire low-wage replacements, much as he had done after declaring bankruptcy at Continental Airlines some years before. To prepare for the strike and the costs that would be incurred until replacements were able to fully operate the airline, Lorenzo built up a war chest, financial reserves that would tide him over. But the war chest was not inexhaustible, and the key to the strategy was the ability to hire lower-wage replacements. One can't hire replacements if there is no strike.

Charlie Bryan understood Lorenzo's strategy, and would not be goaded into a strike. In January 1988, the machinists and the other unions filed a petition with the Mediation Board seeking to have Continental and Eastern declared to be a single carrier for bargaining purposes. Although this was a risky maneuver (Continental was nonunion at the time and it was possible that a combined election at both Eastern and Continental would cost the unions representation in both),

the single-carrier suit stalled the negotiations at Eastern. Bryan knew he couldn't win a strike, and that it still was possible that the pilots might not honor his picket lines. The longer a strike could be delayed, the more cash Lorenzo would lose. . . . Bryan and the mediation board wouldn't permit Lorenzo to engage in the showdown strike he had geared up for.[10]

Bryan continued to stall. Moreover, because of his hardball tactics, Lorenzo could not get the Mediation Board to declare the negotiations at an impasse. When the machinists had to present a counteroffer, Bryan delayed. When he was required to take Lorenzo's proposal to his membership, he put it off as long as possible. Lorenzo was growing short of cash, and he had either to raise money or to sell the airline. The problem was that as long as he was engaged in merger negotiations, the National Mediation Board could not declare an impasse, and whenever he sold a part of Eastern (such as the shuttle), there were suits that consumed more time. The Eastern strike did not finally occur until March 1989. By then, Eastern had operated for more than a year under a growing cloud of negative publicity. Lorenzo's strike contingency fund had long ago been depleted. When the pilots honored the machinists' picket lines, the company declared bankruptcy immediately. Although Bryan's delays had not won the machinists anything, they had cost Lorenzo dearly—the delays and the consequent bleeding of resources from the airline had cost him the airline itself.

THE WAITING GAME

As a tactic in the process of decision making, delay is often made to appear accidental. Delay can also be used deliberately and openly, however, as when we choose to make others wait for our arrival:

> Waiting is patterned by the distribution of power in a social system. This assertion hinges on the assumption that power is directly associated with an individual's scarcity as a social resource and, thereby, with his value as a member of a social unit.[11]

Causing others to wait, or not waiting yourself, is more than a symbol of your own power—it is also a tactic that can be used to increase your power. By being late, you call attention to yourself, and this very fact of visibility can produce influence. Also, making others wait for you forces them to consider your implicit power over them. When you do arrive, others may pay more attention to you in order to convince you to arrive on time in the future, which again reinforces their awareness of their dependence on you:

> To be able to make a person wait is, above all, to possess the capacity to modify his conduct in a manner congruent with one's own interests. To be delayed is in this light to be dependent upon the disposition of the one whom one is waiting for. The latter, in turn, and by virtue of this dependency, finds himself further confirmed in his position of power.[12]

Waiting is also an act of behavioral commitment—you wait and thereby you have to justify waiting. One justification of this waste of time is to cognitively enhance the value of the thing we are waiting for:

> . . . if we regard waiting for a scarce service as an investment or sacrifice in return for a gain, we may measure part of the value of the gain by assessing the degree of sacrifice occasioned on its behalf. . . . The subjective value of the gain is . . . given not only by the objective value . . . but also by the amount of time invested in its attainment. . . . the other's service becomes valuable (and he becomes powerful) precisely because he is waited for.[13]

Thus, a person can emphasize his or her importance by causing others to wait.[14] As head of Standard Brands, Ross Johnson developed a personal style that helped him exercise power, including what was termed the grand entrance:

> Johnson arrived twenty minutes late, punctually, to everything. "If you're on time, no one notices you," he would say. "If you are late, they pay attention."[15]

Changes in waiting arrangements, and who waits for whom, can signify changes in power relations. Even surrounded by the power and glory of the presidency, Harry Truman occasionally enjoyed playing the waiting game:

> Ken Hechler, who was director of research at the White House from 1948 to 1952, recalled the day Mr. Truman kept Winthrop Aldrich, president of the Chase Bank, waiting outside the White House office for 30 minutes. Hechler quoted Mr. Truman as saying: "When I was a United States senator and headed the war investigation committee, I had to go to New York to see this fella, Aldrich. Even though I had an appointment he had me cool my heels for an hour and a half. So just relax. He's got a little while to go yet."[16]

One classic example of arriving late as a tactic employed to acquire more power was Henry Kissinger's behavior in the first days of the Nixon administration. Nixon wanted a centralized and orderly flow of information, so it was clear that his top aides would have a lot of influence. Access was going to be a key. It was also clear that H.R. Haldeman and John Erlichman were going to have a lot of power, so the issue for Kissinger became one of ensuring that he was not subservient to these two aides. In this struggle, he used delay quite effectively:

> Bryce Harlow recalls how Kissinger wriggled his way out of Haldeman's control early in the Nixon administration. During the first few months after the inauguration . . . [Harlow] would join Kissinger, Haldeman, and Erlichman in the President's office every morning and afternoon for meetings. Haldeman, who from the very beginning "wanted to control everything," soon demanded that the meetings with Nixon be preceded by short planning sessions in his office. "Henry started to skip those meetings right away. . . . Well, Bob'd force him in there—but then Henry just began slipping and slipping"—arriving later and later. "Finally, it ended up with Kissinger meeting alone with Nixon."[17]

Kissinger used being late and avoiding meetings to help him get what he wanted and needed to exercise power—private audiences with the president.

DEADLINES

The opposite of delay is the deadline. Deadlines always favor the side that has the momentum or the edge. This is why occasionally in meetings, when the discussion sways in favor of a certain position, an advocate of that point of view will say, "We need to decide now." Deadlines are an excellent means of getting things accomplished. They convey a sense of urgency and importance, and provide a useful countermeasure to the strategy of interminable delay.

If a new plan is proposed near a deadline, it cannot receive as much scrutiny and attention as if it had been proposed earlier. Thus, proposals made near the deadline for a decision are often more likely to pass than they would have been had they surfaced sooner. This fact is well known by the Congress. Some of the most egregious tax preferences for constituents, and many of the single-beneficiary bills, are introduced as the legislature rushes toward adjournment.

In 1924 when Robert Moses drafted bills granting himself extraordinary powers as Long Island state park commissioner, he had a young, naive legislator introduce the bills during the last week of the session, and gave the legislator the bills just before he was to introduce them. There was no debate and they passed unanimously, with the representatives only later discovering the effects of what they had done in such haste as the end of the session approached.

In Alabama in 1975, Act Number 949 created an Interim Committee on Finance and Taxation. Because it altered powers and assumed responsibilities formerly held by other committees, one member at least did not like this committee, and he did something about it. On the last day of the legislative session in 1977, with the Alabama legislature hurrying to adjourn, the following resolution was introduced and passed quickly by a voice vote, with very few of the legislators realizing what had happened. It was the last resolution to go to the governor's office on that day:

H.J.R. 621. COMMENDING AUBURN UNIVERSITY'S HARVEY GLANCE FOR OUTSTANDING ACHIEVEMENT IN TRACK AND FIELD.
WHEREAS, The Legislature of Alabama has noted with pleasure and pride that Auburn University's Harvey Glance, once again has acquitted himself with honor with a spectacular performance in the 45th Southeastern Conference Track and Field Meet; and
WHEREAS, Auburn finished the meet scoring 148 points, with Harvey Glance winning the long jump and contributing in four victories; he also was in three new conference records, winning the 100 and 200 meters in record times, 10.36 and 20.47, and participating for another record, 39.24, in the 440 relay; and
WHEREAS, This outstanding young man, a native of Phenix City, Alabama, and Olympic Gold Medalist, was awarded the Commissioner's Trophy for his 32.5 point total, bringing further honor to himself, his university and to his home state; now therefore
BE IT RESOLVED BY THE LEGISLATURE OF ALABAMA, BOTH HOUSES THEREOF CONCURRING, That this body, once again, recognizes and applauds the outstanding feats accomplished in track and field by champion Harvey Glance; we commend him on his spectacular performance in the 45th SEC Track and Field Meet, in his honor we hereby repeal Act Number Nine Hundred Forty-Nine, adopted October tenth, Nineteen Hundred and Seventy Five, and congratulate him on winning the Commissioner's Trophy, and direct that a copy of this resolution be sent to him that he may know of our pride, our praise and our highest esteem.

On the motion of Mr. Holmes (A), the rules were suspended and the
resolution of H.J.R. 621, was adopted.[18]

Few, if any, members, in the rush to adjourn, read the entire
congratulatory declaration, and I am sure no one bothered to
look up the resolution that was repealed by a phrase buried
deep within this commendation.

Deadlines are often useful in negotiations, as the sale of
Eastern Airlines to Frank Lorenzo and Texas Air illustrates.
Borman and the Eastern board wanted to threaten the unions
with a possible sale of the airline to Lorenzo as a way of
extracting wage concessions. The idea was a pincer play—
wage concessions or the sale of the airline to someone with
a reputation as a notable unionbuster. But in dealing with
Lorenzo, Borman was in over his head. Lorenzo was a master
negotiator, and used a deadline to purchase Eastern Airlines
for a bargain price:

> To block Borman from using him as a club against the unions, Lo-
> renzo added two stipulations to the Merrill Lynch plan. First, East-
> ern had to pay Texas Air a nonrefundable $20 million fee simply to
> make the offer. Second, he wanted an answer in two days, by mid-
> night Sunday, or he'd withdraw. This was a ridiculously short time
> to sell the nation's third-largest airline. But Lorenzo knew exactly
> what he was doing. By setting his own deadline before the one called
> by Eastern's banks, he took control of events.[19]

Borman lost control over the pace and course of events, and
finally, he lost the airline he was running because he was
outmaneuvered by Frank Lorenzo. With time running out,
and with an agreement to purchase already drafted, Lorenzo
was able to dictate terms in his own favor.

ORDER OF CONSIDERATION

In Chapter 10, when I examined the principle of contrast
and its use in framing issues, I noted that the order of consideration can be used to affect decisions. It is unlikely, for
instance, that you will hire the first candidate you see for a
job, even if the person seems quite skilled. You might always
do better, and since he or she is the first candidate, you have

little calibration as to the overall quality of the applicant pool. The same candidate, seen later in the process, might receive a job offer on the spot, particularly if he or she follows a series of very weak candidates. A mortgage offering a 9.5% fixed rate might seem like a bargain today, but barely 20 years ago no one would have considered it. An investment project offering a 15% return will be evaluated depending on the recent projects to which it is being compared.

The order of consideration does not simply affect how we perceive things. Agendas represent a sequence of decisions. These decisions, once taken, may produce behavioral commitments that affect how subsequent decisions are made.[20] Agendas can be used to build commitments to a course of action, which might otherwise be impossible to obtain. Because of the committing and anchoring effects of sequences of choice, the order of presentation becomes an important tactical decision.

Suppose you have two proposals on the same general issue to be discussed and decided, such as two capital budgeting proposals, two new product ideas, two job candidates, two individuals up for tenure or partnership, and so forth. Even the stronger of the two is not a sure bet, but you want them both to obtain favorable decisions. If you present the weaker proposal first, there is likely to be a lot of discussion and debate on its merits. If at the end of the discussion the proposal fails, the implication of this choice for the stronger proposal is limited. The stronger proposal is different, and consequently, people will not feel that their decision to reject the first proposal commits them to also reject the second. In addition, having given you a rough time on the first proposal, people may want to relent and be easier on the second. The second proposal, which is stronger than the first in any event, will look particularly strong by comparison. Time will be getting short, and ideas of fair play and reciprocity will suggest that you should receive something from the meeting. Consequently, it is highly likely that at least the second, stronger proposal will be accepted, and if the first proposal is viewed favorably, both will be approved. Presenting the weaker proposal first will, therefore, tend to ensure that the stronger proposal is favorably received.

If you present the stronger proposal first, there will still be a great deal of discussion. It is first on the agenda, so time is not scarce. Because it is not a sure thing, scrutiny will be intense. If it fails, the second proposal will certainly fail. Having established standards through a process of public decision, one cannot then immediately lower those standards to accept a weaker idea. If the first proposal passes, however, there may be few implications for the second. The group may commit to the standards used in deciding the first issue, and therefore reject the second item, which does not meet those standards. Furthermore, after giving you one thing you wanted, the group may not feel obligated to do you any further favors by approving the second proposal. The order of consideration, then, can have important consequences for what receives approval.

The order of consideration can also affect how things are decided, because decisions are, in some instances, interdependent. Consider a school of business that is going to decide the following issues: 1) cutting student enrollment per faculty member; 2) increasing the student course load per quarter; and 3) broadening the curriculum, to require fewer courses in the student's major and more breadth in other course work. Clearly, there is an optimal order for these proposals. Faculty are more willing to vote for breadth if they have already approved additional courses to be taken. Students can then still be required to take the same number of specialty courses, since there will be more courses to be distributed. Likewise, the proposal to create more courses is going to be viewed more favorably if the number of students has been reduced. Otherwise, creating more courses will serve to increase workload. Thus, in order to get the three changes made, it is necessary or at least useful to first propose the reduction of the number of students, then the increase in the number of courses required per quarter, and finally the requirement for more breadth in the curriculum.

As another example, consider the decision British Steel Corporation faced in the mid-1970s about whether to contract with Korf, a West German engineering firm, to build a new kind of iron ore plant. The plant used a process called direct reduction, which employed natural gas, rather than coal, to turn iron ore into pellets. It was a proprietary process patented by Korf, and it represented an advance in steel-making technology. The decision the corporation faced was whether to buy zero, one, or two plants. The cost of one plant, producing 400,000 tons of iron per year, would be £26 million. A double plant, producing 800,000 tons per year, could be purchased for £43 million, a discount over the cost of buying two separate plants. Because of the capital cost savings from buying the larger plant, the cost of iron ore made from the larger unit would be cheaper than if the smaller, single unit were purchased, with the cost being £63 per ton from the single unit, and £58 per ton from the double unit. One other thing is important in understanding the order of consideration effect. The planning department did some projections that indicated that given the likely demand for steel, and hence iron ore, it was not certain that any direct reduced iron was needed at all.

It is clear that what will be decided in this circumstance depends on the order of consideration. If the first decision is whether the corporation, for strategic reasons, wants to get into this new technology, and if that decision is affirmative, then the likelihood of buying two plants is enhanced. If the corporation is going to be investing in the new technology, then the argument for doing so in a way that reduces its costs is compelling. By contrast, if the first decision is whether to build two plants in order to obtain the additional iron, it is much less likely that the company will vote to purchase them, since the answer to whether the iron is needed is probably, no. Decisions are interdependent and committing, which makes the order of consideration critical.

It should be clear in this discussion that in order to have something approved, it is necessary to have it on the agenda to be considered. Yet this obvious point is often not fully comprehended. The British Steel decision was filmed by Granada Films, which was permitted to follow the participants as they worked toward making the decision. I have used this film frequently in training on the subject of power and influence. At several points in the proceedings, the phrase is repeated, "between one or two plants," and the analysis is an evaluation of one versus two plants. Nevertheless, when I ask the class how many plants are going to be built, there are often at least a few people who answer "none." Although this answer may conform to their view of what the correct decision should be, it is not a likely outcome. Items not on the table for discussion are not likely to be supported or implemented.

Bachrach and Baratz recognized this use of power in the broader political arena.[21] They noted that it is possible to squelch an issue simply by preventing it from becoming a focus of decision making in the first place. Over the years, the power of finance has increased in many U.S. corporations.[22] One reason for this growth in power is that financing has become increasingly important to firms that face a more active market for corporate control, more leverage, and more diversified businesses (in which finance provides the language that permits communication to occur across diverse product lines and markets). But another source of power comes from the agenda at most board of directors meetings. There is always discussion of finances, often in great detail. Financial results are compared against plan and against preceding time periods. Organizational information systems now can readily produce financial information by product line, by region, by line of business, and so forth. There are decisions about capital appropriations, along with audit reports, including, perhaps, reports on inventory losses and depreciation policies and practices. The agenda seldom contains much, if anything, on the organization's personnel or human resource policies. Out of sight, out of mind has validity in this context. Finance exercises power because of what is talked about, and what is not. And this goes on even in firms that are heavily dependent on their work force, and that make regular use of the phrase "people are our most important asset."

PROPITIOUS MOMENTS

During the early stages of the Vietnam War, Robert Johnson of the Policy Planning Council prepared a major study on the advisability of bombing North Vietnam. The group preparing the study had genuine expertise, and no stake in any particular outcome or conclusion. The study was quite negative on the use of bombing:

> Basically the study showed that the bombing would fail because the North was motivated by factors which were not affected by physical change and physical damage. . . . if you threatened the North with escalation you would soon know whether or not it would work because they would have to respond before you started. . . . they would never fold their hands under duress. . . . Nor was anyone particularly optimistic that the bombing would improve South Vietnamese morale. . . . In addition, the study showed that there would be a considerable international outcry if the United States bombed the North. . . . It was an important study because it not only predicted that the bombing would not work, and predicted Hanoi's reaction to the pressure, which was to apply counterpressure, but it forecast that the bombing would affect . . . the American government.[23]

As a piece of policy analysis, the study was brilliant. It was carefully reasoned, extensively documented, and although it was prepared by a number of people, there was remarkable consensus on all of its conclusions. Yet the study was to have virtually no effect on the final decision to proceed with bombing North Vietnam. It was completed at the wrong time:

> The second problem was timing; though the study had been rushed through with the idea of coinciding with the McNamara report on bombing, the President had let McNamara know that he did not want to make any major decisions for the present, and so the bombing was put on hold, and the decision delayed. Similarly, the massive and significant study was pushed aside because it had come out at the wrong time. A study has to be published at the right moment, when people are debating an issue and about to make a decision; then and only then will they read a major paper, otherwise they are too pressed for time.[24]

Issues and events have the quality of ripeness—there is a time to act, and a time to delay. When Al Smith wanted to stir up public support for Robert Moses's possibly illegal seizure of the Taylor Estate to build a park on Long Island, he went on statewide radio. He chose not March or April, but a Sunday night on the first hot, steamy weekend in June, when the citizens of New York City would have just spent two days trying to get out of the metropolis on inadequate roads to reach crowded parks—in other words, when they were particularly likely to want more parks and beaches and to be somewhat less concerned about constitutional niceties. A colleague who had tried for years to get his employer, a large grocery store chain, to pay attention to labor relations issues, pushed one more time just after the company was fined $12 million by the Equal Employment Opportunity Commission for discrimination. This time he found that the senior management and even the board of directors were much more receptive to his ideas. The newly discovered and enthusiastically implemented techniques that form the foundation of the success of Japanese firms operating in the United States are neither new nor particularly Japanese. Based on sound principles of social psychology and organizational behavior, they have been advocated for years in the United States and elsewhere. What is new is only that a competitive threat has forced more attention to these issues and recommendations.

Perhaps the scarcest resource in organizations is attention. Time spent attending to one issue is time not devoted to other concerns. Thus, finding the right set of circumstances to advance one's ideas is critical. A good idea at the wrong time will, like the report on bombing North Vietnam, be ignored and shunted aside. On the other hand, an idea for a new product that would otherwise have languished may be received eagerly if times are tough, the competition keen, and attention focused on promising new products. This is one reason why persistence so often pays off. If one proposes something once, the odds on hitting the right moment are not necessarily great. But if one pushes the same plans, the same objectives, the same actions for a sustained period of time, mere chance suggests that eventually circumstances will make the proposal more apt, and it will get favorable attention.

One of the most important elements of political strategy and tactics is timing. The directors at Bendix might have forced William Agee out had they timed their actions more carefully. The United States might not have bombed North Vietnam and thereby become so deeply enmeshed in that war had the study showing the futility of bombing come out closer to the time the decision on bombing was actually being made. Kissinger might have had less power in the Nixon administration had he been less skilled at taking on the State Department and the other senior Nixon aides early. Although the other strategies and tactics we will consider in subsequent chapters are important, their effectiveness will invariably be enhanced if they are employed at the right moment.

13

The Politics of Information
and Analysis

There is little doubt that information, and the certainty that it can provide, is a source of power. It can be used as part of a very important political strategy—getting one's way through analysis. Perhaps no figure in recent corporate and public life has so exemplified the exercise of power through facts and analysis as Robert McNamara, who was first president of Ford, then secretary of defense under Presidents Kennedy and Johnson, and most recently, prior to his retirement, the head of the World Bank. McNamara's success in rising rapidly through the corporate ranks at Ford came from his mastery of information and analysis:

> Henry Ford was new and unsure of himself, particularly in the field of financial systems. To an uneasy, uncertain Ford, McNamara offered reassurance; when questions arose he always seemed to have the answers, not vague estimates, but certitudes, facts, numbers, and lots of them. Though his critics might doubt that he knew what the public wanted or what it was doing, he could always forecast precisely the Ford part of the equation.[1]

It might seem odd to have a chapter on information and analysis in a book on power in organizations. But as we will see, our belief that there is a right answer to most situations and that this answer can be uncovered by analysis and illuminated with more information, means that those in control of the facts and the analysis can exercise substantial influence.

And facts are seldom so clear cut, so unambiguous, as we might think. The manipulation and presentation of facts and analysis are often critical elements of a strategy to exercise power effectively.

Information and analysis can be useful, but it is important to recognize that, as Peter Drucker once remarked, anyone over the age of 21 can find the facts to support his or her position. Information and analysis are important for getting things done, largely because of our faith in them and in those who seem to have mastered them. But it is not invariably true that they will produce the "right answer," or even a good answer. Halberstam's history of the Vietnam War is the story of a U.S. government filled with brilliant people, who gathered lots of information and formulated analyses that were, unfortunately, not often based on sound judgment, common sense, or reasonable assumptions. It is important to understand the use of information as a political strategy, but it is also important to understand the limits of information and analysis. I particularly like the story of Lyndon Johnson, who inherited Kennedy's brilliant cabinet and set of advisers when Kennedy was assassinated, discussing these people with his friend and mentor, Speaker of the House Sam Rayburn:

> Stunned by their glamour and intellect, he [Johnson] had rushed back to tell Rayburn, his great and crafty mentor, about them, about how brilliant each was, that fellow Bundy from Harvard, Rusk from Rockefeller, McNamara from Ford. On he went, naming them all. "Well, Lyndon, you may be right and they may be every bit as intelligent as you say," said Rayburn, "but I'd feel a whole lot better about them if just one of them had run for sheriff once."[2]

There are four useful points to make about information and analysis as political tactics. First, all organizations strive for the appearance of rationality and the use of proper procedures, which include using information and analysis to justify decisions, even if this information and analysis is mustered after the fact to ratify a decision that has been made for other reasons. In constructing the appearance of legitimate and sensible decision processes, the use of outside experts, particularly expensive outside experts, is especially helpful. Such experts are at once legitimate sources of information and analysis and at the same time likely to be responsive to the needs of their specific clients within the organization. Second, in complex, multidimensional decisions such as those faced by high-level managers, it is very unlikely that processes of straightforward analysis will clearly resolve the issue of what to do. This means that, third, there is room for the advocacy of criteria and information that favor one's own position, or, in other words, there is the opportunity to use information and analysis selectively.

Some might argue that even if information and analysis cannot fully determine the quality of decisions before they are made, decision quality does become known after the fact, leading to a process of learning over time. People who misuse information and analysis for their own political ends, the argument goes, will eventually be "uncovered" when decisions or results turn out badly. This learning will ensure that, over time, better information and better analysis are rewarded and incorporated into the organization's standard operating procedures. As we will see, however, there is little evidence that these assumptions are true, and there are numerous examples of organizations behaving, for quite predictable reasons, in exactly the opposite way. The last point, then, is simply that the discovery of decision quality is both a difficult process and one that is often assiduously avoided in organizations of all types. As a consequence, the opportunity to use information and analysis as potent political weapons is available, and those with the skills and knowledge of how to do so can often, like Robert McNamara, gain substantial power and influence in their organizations.

THE NEED FOR THE APPEARANCE OF RATIONALITY

Power is most effectively employed when it is fairly unobtrusive. Using rational, or seemingly rational, processes of analysis helps to render the use of power and influence less obvious. Perhaps as important, decisions are perceived to be better and are accepted more readily to the extent that they are made following prescribed and legitimate procedures.

John Meyer and his colleagues have argued that the

appearance of bureaucratic rationality is important, if not essential, for making organizations appear legitimate.[3] And this appearance of legitimacy is crucial for attracting support and resources. Thus, in many instances, individuals in organizations do not seek out information in order to make a decision, but rather, they amass information so that the decision will seem to have been made in the "correct" fashion—i.e., on the basis of information rather than uninformed preferences or hunches.[4] Kramer, writing about the analysis of public policies, has made a similar point:

> Apparently analysis is used primarily to justify actions that are based on political predilections. . . . the techniques used and the emphasis on quantification give the results of analysis a "scientific" appearance—an appearance of value-free rationality at work.[5]

A study of a firm's decision to purchase a computer observed that, contrary to the prescriptions of rational choice approaches, information was selectively collected and used in the decision process to provide support for the decision that was already favored.[6] One might reasonably wonder, why bother? Why not just go ahead and purchase the desired computer without going through the exercise of gathering information, selectively and strategically, to favor the choice that had already been made? The answer is that decisions made either without information or simply by directive from above do not have the legitimacy or produce the same level of comfort as decisions that are made on the basis of information and analysis. We rely on facts and analytical technique to produce the "right" choice; how can the right choice be produced in the absence of these comforting certainties?

If information is necessary to get the decisions we want, then it seems obvious that the way to get things done in organizations is to develop skill in obtaining the facts that support our intended course of action. Sometimes we can get the facts we want because of our social ties and alliances, as Donald Frey, former CEO and chairman of Bell and Howell and a former executive at Ford Motor Company, relates:

> I was . . . interested in getting . . . my ideas sold (sometimes against resistance to change), but this meant learning . . . another language. I well remember being asked in the seemingly endless efforts to get

approval for the original "Mustang" . . . what the net, "non substitutional" increase in vehicle sales volume would be with the car—that is, the number of cars that could be sold without cannibalizing our existing market. Since the Mustang was a completely new vehicle concept, no one really knew. One of the corporate market research types was given the question of substitution to answer. He knew from me that the stand-alone break even volume was about 84,000 units. A week later he reported that the increased volume, net of substitution, would be 86,000 units. I called and asked him how he got the number. He said he liked the car and its concept.[7]

In this case, the project turned out to be a big success, as the Mustang sold 400,000 units its first year. Sometimes this process of getting the answers to support the decision produces a less fortuitous result, but the tactics are the same. When the Cadillac division was deciding whether to launch the Allante, the price was set at $55,000. There was some question whether the projected volume and profits could be attained with that price:

Originally, GM's internal staff projected sales of three thousand cars, with a $45,000 price tag. But at that volume and price, the project failed to generate a 15-percent ROI, so the division's answer was to raise both estimates to make the project work on paper.[8]

This internal manipulation of numbers to support one's position is, of course, somewhat unseemly, and besides, one might get caught. A better strategy is to employ an outside expert, such as a consulting firm, to produce the numbers or answers you need. For if you use a third party, at a substantial cost, to produce a report, how can the organization ignore a study on which it has spent a lot of money? Moreover, given that it was done by a legitimate, reputable firm with an aura of expertise, the analysis must be correct. And furthermore, since the work was performed by an outside organization, with apparently no particular political stake in the results, the recommendations must surely be objective and impartial.

In 1981, John Debbink, at the time general manager of the Delco Moraine subsidiary of General Motors, was given the assignment to find out whether it would be possible to organize all the engine plants and engineering into one organization:

The challenge facing Debbink's team was to see if a cultural shift could happen in the process of making the urgent organizational changes that were needed. They began by asking McKinsey and Company, a . . . consulting firm, to help evaluate the options. McKinsey provided the logical format for analyzing GM car operations and formalizing what had already been decided. Their final approach differed little from Debbink's original concept.[9]

The nice thing about using consultants is that they can usually be relied on to further the decision you have in mind. With one exception, I have never seen a consulting firm recommend the abolition of the job or the division that hired them—I think it is called "client relations." Most firms know who brought them in, and provide the answers they are expected to give. The one exception was a firm that recommended the abolition of a department in a long-distance telephone company, even though it was the head of that function who had brought them in to do the study. But this is a rare event. More commonly I have observed that the outside expert recommended the advancement and enhancement of both the individual sponsor and the unit led by that sponsor. Because they are so often used to legitimate choices, I have heard consultants referred to as "hired guns." And we all know where to stand with respect to a gun—behind it, not in front of it.

Consultants, then, can be powerful allies in internal political struggles. After George Ball had left E.F. Hutton for Prudential-Bache Securities, and after the check-kiting scandal at Hutton, Robert Rittereiser was hired as president. Hutton's economic results continued to deteriorate, in part because of general problems in the securities industry, in part because of the legacy of the check-kiting scandal, and in part because of internal management problems, including some attributable to Rittereiser. Hutton desperately needed to raise additional capital, either through a merger with another organization, or by convincing another organization to make a substantial investment in the firm. To protect his own position and to gain influence with the board, Rittereiser decided to make sure that he was in control of bringing in investment bankers to assist in this process. He developed a relationship with Pete Peterson (formerly the managing partner of Lehman Brothers) and his firm, the Blackstone Group:

"The way Ritt saw it, he could borrow from Peterson's prestige to regain the credibility he'd lost with the directors. He thought that if he could say, 'I want to take this particular action, or talk to this particular buyer, and Pete Peterson thinks it's a good idea too,' he could get the board to side with him. In effect, he was hiring Peterson as a corporate ally."[10]

The importance of obtaining seemingly impartial judgments, and the use of outside experts to achieve this end, is also illustrated in an example from Apple Computer. In the late 1980s, Apple Computer was interested in controlling headcount, or the number of permanent employees. John Sculley liked to talk about how high Apple's revenues per employee were, and like many other organizations, Apple believed that it could control its expenses by managing its number of permanent employees. Of course, when work needs to get done and there are not enough people to do it, alternative arrangements are found, which in Apple's case involved using a lot of independent contractors and workers provided by temporary agencies. Particularly in the case of contract employees, Apple may have been violating a number of state and federal labor laws and tax regulations, because the workers were actually legally employees even though they were treated as independent vendors. Apple's human resource staff was concerned about this situation for several reasons: 1) Apple faced some legal risk because of its practices; 2) the hiring of temporary and contract employees bypassed the human resource staff's control over hiring criteria and wage determination—indeed, one problem was that a person would leave Apple as an employee on Friday and return to work on Monday as an independent contractor earning more money than he or she had earned the previous week and than the person's co-workers, who had remained employees, were earning; 3) many of the contract employees, hired in a hurry, would probably not have passed muster as permanent employees; and 4) the use of a large number of contract and temporary workers threatened to weaken the Apple culture (and HR saw itself as a keeper of the culture), as well as exposed the corporation to some strategic risk, since a large fraction of its technical work force, involved in both hardware and software design, had no permanent attachment to the organization.

When the human resource staff broached these issues, their concerns were dismissed. However, the threat of possible legal problems got the corporation to agree to have their outside counsel, Pillsbury, Madison and Sutro, send some labor lawyers to look into these practices. These outside experts found that, at least with respect to the legal and tax issues, the HR department's concerns had been well founded. Based on the legal analysis, a study of part-time, temporary, and contract employees was commissioned. Hiring and compensation practices were changed, and many of the workers were either taken on as regular employees or let go. The role of human resources, the point of contact for the labor attorneys, was strengthened, and the unit acquired various projects and more visibility.

Because of the need for the appearance, if not the reality, of rational decision processes, analysis and information are important as strategic weapons in battles involving power and influence. In these contests, the ability to mobilize powerful outside experts, with credibility and the aura of objectivity, is an effective strategy.

THE LIMITS OF FACTS AND ANALYSIS

It is evident that analysis and outside expertise can be employed strategically to affect decisions and actions. One might argue that such studies are nevertheless desirable—although the numbers and analysis may be used as part of a political contest, they also shed important light on organizational questions. But this is not invariably the case. It turns out in organizational life, common sense and judgment are often more important than so-called facts and analysis. Three examples illustrate this point.

If good decisions were solely the result of intellectual capacity, then few mistakes would have been made during the Vietnam War. McNamara exerted tremendous influence over the war and the policies that were adopted toward it. And McNamara believed wholeheartedly in facts, in analysis, in data. The issue, of course, in this as in any other decision situation, is not whether it is right to gather information, but the more subtle question of what are the correct indicators and the appropriate information to consider. If you can find the facts to support virtually any decision, then your only concern is how to sort and weigh the information you obtain. There is also a bigger danger. In the absence of facts and analysis, you may admit that you are uncertain. But surrounded by information, even useless, misleading information, you will no longer feel uncertain or uninformed. In this sense, bad or misleading information is much worse than no information at all.

McNamara went to Vietnam to see things for himself. The man who loved and trusted data wanted to get it firsthand:

> And there was that confidence which bordered on arrogance, a belief he could handle it. Perhaps . . . the military weren't all that good; still, they could produce raw data, and McNamara, who *knew data,* would go over it carefully and extricate truth from the morass. . . . Talking with reporters and telling them that all the indices were good. He could not have been more wrong; he simply had all the wrong indices, looking for American production indices in an Asian political revolution. . . . he scurried around Vietnam, looking for what he wanted to see. . . . He was so much a prisoner of his own background. . . . memories of him still remain: McNamara in 1962 going to Operation Sunrise, the first of the repopulated villages, the villagers obviously filled with bitterness and hatred, ready, one could tell, to slit the throat of the first available Westerner, and McNamara not picking it up, innocently firing away his questions. How much of this? How much of that?[11]

When he finally turned against the war, McNamara was bitter about the generals who he thought had misled him. But he had obtained the data he wanted, and had it analyzed by the very best systems analysts around. The problem wasn't the numbers or the analysis—the problem was interpretation.

> Thus did the Americans ignore the most basic factor of the war, and when they did stumble across it, it continued to puzzle them. McNamara's statistics and calculations were of no value at all, because they never contained the fact that if the ratio was ten to one in favor of the government, it still meant nothing, because the one man was willing to fight and die and the ten were not.[12]

We apparently learned little from the limits of analysis in Vietnam in the 1960s, because the same type of mistakes occurred in business corporations in the 1970s. During the 1970s, the Xerox Corporation's finance staff and president came from Ford Motor Corporation and the Robert McNamara school of systems analysis and quantification.[13] Archie McCardell was hired in 1966 as group vice president of finance and control, and became president in 1971. With McColough, the CEO, increasingly preoccupied with external relations, McCardell and his numbers orientation came to dominate the Xerox culture. The question that might be posed, however, is whether any of the numbers and the decisions based upon them made sense. Xerox's failure to respond to the threat posed by small Japanese copiers, which was discussed in Chapter 10, is yet another example of the limits of numbers and analysis.

Xerox adopted a strategy of grouping customers "by the volume of their copying needs, then designed, built, and sold machines with copying speeds to match each segment."[14] Because of the segmentation by market, when the Japanese entered the small machine, low copy-volume segment, Xerox did not react. Savin/Ricoh quickly outflanked Xerox, distributing their machines through office equipment dealers, dealing with the service issue by building machines that broke down one-third as often and were easier to repair because of modular parts, and designing standardized components in the machines to reduce manufacturing costs. Moving first into the low end of the market, away from the centralized reprographics department, Savin/Ricoh was able to get machines installed in the facilities of virtually all of Xerox's customers. Moving upmarket, with an established reputation for reliability, product innovation, and dependability, was simple. Xerox lost one-third of its market share in five years, between 1972 and 1977, simply by following analysis that suggested the part of the market it was losing was not of concern anyway.

When Xerox finally began to see its margins erode, analysis again tried to provide the answer—cut manufacturing costs. The problem with this strategy, as Ford was learning about the same time, is how to measure costs. Manufacturing costs are, of course, only part of the costs of installing and maintaining a product—warranty and service costs are important as well, as are customer good will and market acceptance. In

Xerox's drive to cut manufacturing costs, in part by substituting cheaper components, warranty and service costs increased at a rate that almost completely eroded any "savings" in manufacturing. This was not captured in the cost analysis, which focused only on what it cost to get the machine out the door. And, Xerox's market share continued to erode under the pressure of poor product quality; a market share of 95% in 1972 had fallen to 65% in 1977, 54% in 1978, and 46% in 1979.[15] Xerox had lost half its market in seven years, all the while paying attention to the numbers and being dominated by financial analysis. This example does not mean that numbers and analysis will invariably produce poor results—but it shows that good results don't necessarily follow, either.

We have seen that information and analysis cannot really help one weigh the importance of alternative perspectives. We have also seen that numbers, particularly numbers from traditional cost accounting systems, can be misleading in terms of developing and implementing sound manufacturing and marketing strategy.[16] Our final example illustrates that the rapture of information and analysis can, in the end, mislead even those who are gathering the information and doing the analysis, and who ought to know better.

Time Inc.'s ill-fated attempt to launch *TV-Cable Week* was based on an analysis done by two Harvard MBAs. The concept involved system-specific listings for each cable system, which would be costly to edit and produce, especially because the editor, Richard Burgheim, was committed to doing only a quality product. The magazine would probably be marketed by the cable system operators, and the question was how high a market penetration the magazine would need in each cable system to make money:

Neither one knew, so they started experimenting with various penetration assumptions. At 3 percent . . . (roughly what *Time* Magazine enjoyed in its own markets), losses . . . ran far into the millions annually without letup. . . . if one raised the penetration assumption to 8 percent? Still a loss. . . . Go for 15 percent. No deal. Try 20 percent. At 60 percent penetration, the numbers at last showed a profit . . . as it happened, 60 percent market penetration, while admittedly a level unheard of in mass magazine marketing, equaled almost exactly the level of penetration enjoyed by HBO in its own cable markets. . . . the players reasoned thus: if HBO can get such penetration, then why not a listings guide that tells viewers what HBO is showing? The thinking was logical, the mathematics impeccable. But the conclusion was totally out of touch with reality. For no mass market magazine had ever gotten more than one-fifth the market penetration their project now seemed to require to show a profit.[17]

Once reduced to black and white, once pro formas had been done, the analysis took on a life of its own. Regardless of the absurdity of the underlying assumptions, the analysis became reality, and the magazine was eventually launched. Of course, its penetration never even approached 3%.

SELECTIVE USE OF INFORMATION

Because of the need for a rationalized decision process, when such processes are inherently ambiguous, there is room for individuals to selectively advocate criteria that favor their own interests and units. Almost all decisions involve not only choosing among the available alternatives but also selecting the appropriate criteria. Because organizations are inevitably confronted with multiple, occasionally competing, objectives, the assessment of the effects of organizational choices is inherently ambiguous and uncertain.[18]

Given the availability of multiple bases for making a decision, one strategic use of power and influence involves advocating the employment of standards that favor one's own position. A study of resource allocation at the University of Illinois found that:

> There is support in the data for the idea that when asked what the criteria for budget allocations should be, respondents replied with criteria that tended to favor the relative position of their own organizational subunit. . . . To the extent the department head perceived a comparative advantage in terms of his department's obtaining grants and contracts and to the extent his department actually did receive more restricted funds, the department head tended to favor grants and contracts as a basis of budget allocation. . . . Preferences for basing budget allocation on the number of undergraduate students taught was correlated .34 . . . with the proportion of undergraduate instructional units taught. . . . Preferences for basing budget allocations on the national rank [prestige] of the department was correlated .43 . . . with the national rank of the department in 1969. . . . The

data indicate that departments with a comparative advantage in a particular area favored basing budget allocations more on this criterion.[19]

Using data selectively comes from simple self-interested behavior. But, it is more than self-interest that produces the selective use of both data and a particular perspective. Through a process of commitment, individuals come to believe in what they do. And under conditions of uncertainty, which often characterize managerial decision making, individuals would prefer to use both data and decision-making processes with which they are comfortable.[20] Thus, it is not surprising that finance types, often unfamiliar with engineering or with manufacturing processes, rely on quantitative indicators of operations and forecasts of economic return,[21] while engineers rely more on technical factors and on their sense of the product design or the design of the operating system. We do what we know how to do, and we make choices according to the criteria that are most familiar to us.

Not all of us, however, are equally sensitive to the strategic purposes served by selectively favoring certain data, nor are we all equally skilled at the process involved. One study examined the effects of three factors on resource allocations at the University of Illinois, once departmental power and objective factors were taken into account: 1) the accuracy with which the department head perceived his unit's relative standing on various criteria used for resource allocation; 2) the extent to which the department head advocated basing resource allocations on criteria on which the department scored relatively well; and 3) the accuracy of the department head's perceptions of the distribution of departmental power in the university.[22] The study found that advocating criteria that favored the department, and having an accurate understanding of where the department stood on the potential criteria for resource allocations, were both positively related to the department's ability to obtain resources, with the effects being particularly strong for less critical and scarce resources and for higher power departments. The evidence suggests that power is effectively employed, in part, through advocating the use of decision rules that favor one's own department, and the use of this strategy requires that departmental representatives understand their relative benefit from the use of alternative criteria.

The use of analysis and information to favor one's own position is enhanced by having certain technical skills. I remember talking to a former student who had taken a job with the *Washington Post*, a newspaper that had hired a number of MBAs, some from schools with less of a quantitative orientation than Stanford. I asked him how he was doing, particularly in his interactions with his colleagues from other schools. He replied that he was doing very well, and that he had found he was particularly effective in winning acceptance for proposals he favored. When I asked how he did this, he explained that his knowledge of both statistics and operations research and quantitative analysis was helpful, in that he could develop elaborate and sophisticated presentations and rationales for his point of view. Of course, he stated, he did not use the analysis to decide what course of action to pursue, but rather, to convince others of the validity of his ideas. In this sense, knowledge of analytic techniques is very helpful, if not critical, in the exercise of power and influence in organizations. The key is to understand what form of argument will be convincing in one's particular environment, and to have the ability to formulate an argument in the appropriate fashion, using whatever analysis or data are accepted in that context.

Of course, employing information selectively means strategically ignoring information that does not advance one's own point of view. We are particularly likely to ignore or distort information when it is inconsistent with our biases and with the course of action we have already undertaken. The following example from the Second World War, concerning the Allied decision to attack Germany through Holland in 1944, is particularly striking:

> The whole enterprise depended upon an absence of strong German forces both in the Arnhem area and on the approach route from the south. Hence it came as something of a jolt when SHAEF received reports from the Dutch underground that two S.S. Panzer divisions which had mysteriously "disappeared" some time previously had now reappeared almost alongside the dropping zone. . . . since these ugly facts did not accord with what had been planned they fell upon

a succession of deaf ears. . . . When one of his intelligence officers showed him the aerial photographs of German armour, General Browning, at First British Airborne H.Q., retorted: "I wouldn't trouble myself about these if I were you. . . . they're probably not serviceable at any rate." The intelligence officer was then visited by the Corps medical officer who suggested he should take some leave because he was so obviously exhausted.[23]

WHY THERE IS OFTEN NO LEARNING

The final issue to be considered in our discussion of the political strategy of information and analysis is the question of learning. If the distortion of data occurs so routinely, why don't people treat analyses with greater wariness? And why doesn't feedback tend to correct some of these errors? For instance, if data are tabulated according to criteria that promote someone's favored decision, and that decision does not work out, he or she might be expected to suffer the consequences. In fact, however, such consequences are rarely visited on those who use information strategically. There are several reasons for their rarity.

First, there is often no possible way of knowing whether the right decision has been made, because as I noted in Chapter 7, the right decision is a construct with almost no meaning in many circumstances. For instance, say a government agency or department head such as Robert Moses uses information and analysis to show that his unit is comparatively more deserving of resources, and as a consequence, receives a disproportionate share of the budget. How can one know if that was a correct or incorrect decision? How can one know whether New York City has too many parks and not enough firehouses, if San Francisco has spent too much on public health and not enough on roads, if the University of Illinois has spent too much on its physics department and not enough on its romance languages? Different people will have different points of view. There are a number of ways of measuring the effects of budget allocations and other decisions, but there is no way of completely resolving the uncertainty.

But surely things are clearer in private, for-profit organizations—the profit goal must provide a yardstick against which to evaluate judgments, so that people who use information strategically will be in trouble if their particular perspective turns out not to be the best for the organization's profitability.

Not necessarily.

In the first place, many decisions have remote or highly indirect connections to the outcomes that are measured or measurable in organizations. For instance, we saw in Chapter 5 that many people like to help their allies obtain positions of power, or alternatively, to have other executives beholden to them—allies are a critical source of power in organizations. But, unless your allies are egregiously incompetent, it is not likely that appointing your friends and supporters to positions of power will have a visible effect on organizational performance.

A related point is that outcomes in organizations are overdetermined in the sense that they have multiple causes. It is difficult, if not impossible, to ascertain which of the possible causes is the true source of the result. Consider Xerox's loss of market share and potential profitability during the 1970s. To what should we attribute this—Peter McColough's appointment of McCardell as president and the consequent dominance of Ford-trained finance types? The location of PARC in Palo Alto, away from the rest of Xerox, so that integrating the results of its research into product development was more difficult? McColough's preoccupation with external relations and organizations? The strategic insights of the Japanese, who saw both a market opportunity (in the low-end copiers) and a way of exploiting that opportunity? Or one of a number of other factors?[24] With multiple causation, assigning of the blame for a failure is itself a political process, rather than an inferential one.

There are three other factors that also tend to prevent the kind of feedback that might constrain both the operation of power and influence and the strategic use of information, analysis, and outside expertise. The first factor is the length of time many decisions take to have consequences that are ascertainable, even if such consequences can be evaluated at all. Building a nuclear power plant takes more than a decade, and many capital construction projects extend over many years. The launching of a new product, expansion geographically, and alterations in product strategy are all actions that take time both to implement and to produce consequences. This time lag before decisions come to fruition makes it less likely that who is responsible will be clearly remembered.

It is also the case that the very nature of most organizational decision making involves building up some degree of collective responsibility, which means that it is difficult to assign blame to individuals when plans go awry. Most of the notable failures we have discussed so far did not have single architects who could be called to account for their mistakes. For instance, Time Inc.'s decision to launch *TV-Cable Week* was essentially a group decision. There were several executive committee meetings held, many people were involved in the process, and finally, even the board of directors gave approval to pursuing the project. And if it is difficult to determine responsibility for what has been done, it is nearly impossible to find those responsible for what has not been done. There were a number of people at Xerox, including some at PARC, who did not push for the rapid commercialization of their personal computer technology, thus permitting other companies, such as Apple, to gain first-mover advantages.

Just as there is collective responsibility for decisions, there is a collective unwillingness to determine the causes of past failures. Organizations are notorious for avoiding evaluation and avoiding looking backward. They are incredibly nonintrospective, if I can use that term. It is only under extreme public pressure, for instance, that either schools or hospitals have recently begun to publish outcome measures—in the case of schools, student scores on standardized tests, and in the case of hospitals, data on costs and morbidity and mortality outcomes. For years both types of institutions resisted not only publishing such data but even collecting it for internal use.

My colleague Jim Baron sat on a panel considering the implementation of pay-for-performance in the Civil Service System. It occurred to him that over the years there had been literally hundreds of innovations in personnel practices, both in the government and in the private sector. Yet the amount of evaluation of these innovations, to see whether they had any effect at all, let alone the desired effect, was trivial, in either the public or the private sector. I suspect many readers of this book will have been in organizations in which performance evaluation systems were changed, compensation practices altered, organizations restructured, work organization reformed, and so forth. In how many instances was the evaluation of any of these changes undertaken or even contemplated? Although we often think that the avoidance of evaluation and assessment is particularly likely in so-called institutionalized organizations such as those in the public sector,[25] I often see the same reluctance to evaluate the results of changes in private sector firms.

We should consider what happened to various executives involved in ventures that were clearly unsuccessful—a clarity that is, in fact, quite rare in complex organizations. Under the McCardell presidency, Xerox lost half its market share, lost its lead in technology (in the high end of the copier business to Kodak, in the low end to Savin/Ricoh), developed a reputation for poor-quality products, failed to keep pace with the manufacturing efficiencies of the Japanese, and failed to take advantage of the digital technologies being developed at the Palo Alto Research Center. In 1977, International Harvester hired Archie McCardell to be its chief executive officer, with a multiyear compensation package worth more than $6 million.[26]

After *TV-Cable Week* was closed down, having cost Time Inc. approximately $50 million:

> Saving face proved to be a major thirty-fourth floor concern. . . . When a television reporter asked Grunwald to comment on the failure, Time Inc.'s Editor-in-Chief said, "Well, everybody's entitled to one Edsel." . . . When a trade reporter asked Executive Vice President Clifford Grum which management official had been responsible for overseeing the project, Time Inc.'s second-in-command answered, "There was no *one* man in charge; it was a group effort," then looked ready to end the interview if the reporter should press further. . . . In his three years as the company's president and CEO, Munro failed at virtually every new venture he authorized, eventually accumulating losses that totaled nearly 10 percent of Time Inc.'s entire net worth. . . . corporate debt increased, earnings per share stagnated, and investment analysts began to view the company as lacking in direction. Yet his weak performance did not stop Time Inc.'s five-man Compensation and Personnel Committee . . . from bestowing on him regular annual salary and stock bonus increases anyway.[27]

Furthermore, Munro elevated the head of the Video Group and the head of the Magazine Group, each of them closely involved with the failure, to the corporation's board of directors even as the magazine was closing.[28]

When Eastern Airlines was in severe financial trouble in the mid-1980s and the employees had lost confidence in Frank Borman, the CEO, the board of directors rejected Borman's resignation, offered in return for promised additional wage concessions on the part of the employees. Rather, they preferred to sell the company to Frank Lorenzo, with Borman receiving a $1 million severance package shortly thereafter. And, of course, in 1990, as he retired after presiding over General Motors' loss of about one-third of its market share, Roger Smith was awarded an increased pension in excess of $1 million per year by the board of directors.

Such outcomes are not inevitable, and I am certainly not arguing that the road to success is through corporate failure and disaster. But it is important to recognize that the connection between results and what happens to people inside large organizations is quite tenuous, for all the reasons that I have presented. What this means is that we should probably not hesitate to use information and analysis to exercise power in organizations, since the strategy is an effective one and the likelihood of our being called to account for our actions is not very great.

14

Changing the Structure to Consolidate Power

In earlier chapters, we saw that structure can be a source of power. Your position in the organization can provide access to information, and this provides power. Your position in the hierarchy can provide formal authority. And the particular issues that fall within your jurisdiction in the division of labor can provide power if those issues are particularly critical for the organization.

Given the links between structure and power, it is not surprising that structural changes are often undertaken as one of the more important strategies for exercising power. Structure can be used to divide and conquer the opposition. It can be used to consolidate your own power, by placing yourself or your allies in a position to exercise more control over resources and information. To the extent that structure entails the identification of responsibilities, it can be used to co-opt others and to ensure that they support our initiatives. Skilled managers understand the importance of structure and employ it to tactical advantage. The examples in this chapter provide some illustrations of the use of organizational design and re-design to develop and exercise influence.

This view of structure is at variance with others that see organizational design as the consequence of a process in which rational decisions are made about how to organize activities to ensure the efficient operation of the enterprise. It is quite likely that the grouping of positions and the allocation of responsibilities entailed in organizational design do have effects on the effectiveness and efficiency of organizational operations. But, it is also clear that structures are designed and used to produce and implement political power, and that they need to be understood, at least in part, on that basis.

DIVIDE AND CONQUER: MANAGING INDEPENDENT POWER CENTERS

John Sculley's victory in the power struggle with Steve Jobs illustrates the role that independent power centers played at Apple Computer. As general manager of the Macintosh division, Jobs had emphasized the independence of Macintosh employees. The division had been run much like a cult, occupying a separate building with a skull and crossbones flag flying overhead to symbolize the roguish, out-of-the-mainstream nature of the group, staffed by employees working exceptionally long hours, who shared a vision of both the product they were building and loyalty to the team that was doing the design.

They were also loyal, of course, to Steve Jobs, and the independence of the Macintosh division might have been problematic after Jobs's ouster, had Sculley not undertaken a reorganization of the company the previous year. Apple had begun as a functional organization, and had evolved into a product line, divisionalized organization with the development of the Macintosh. One of the lessons Jobs drew from the success of the Macintosh development effort was the advantage of using largely self-contained teams to do product design and modification. But product line organizations develop strong identification with the product divisions, and one of those divisions was Macintosh. Sculley moved to reestablish a functional structure, arguing for economies of scale in engineering and manufacturing, as well as the ability to develop more depth of expertise. During 1984 and 1985, Apple evolved back toward a functional organization. By the time Jobs was out of the organization, Macintosh personnel had been reassigned to the new functional divisions, to other projects, and to other activities. Although many of the reorganizations and reassignments may have been made in the interests of efficiency, their effort was, nevertheless, pronounced. Some Macintosh team members had left rather than be reassigned, and even those who remained were now dispersed to create much less threat to Sculley's power and position.

A similar story of the erosion of the power of product divisions through a reorganization occurred at General Motors. The creation of the General Motors Assembly Division (GMAD) in 1965 was ostensibly intended, at least in part, to forestall antitrust action to break up the corporation. The theory was that, if each product division had its own engineering and dedicated manufacturing facilities, it would be comparatively easy to split the company apart along product division lines. If, however, assembly, for instance, was integrated across product divisions, the feasibility of splitting the organization would be reduced, because it would be too difficult to assign distinct manufacturing and assembly units to the various newly created companies.

Whatever the motivation, the reorganization of General Motors did diminish the power of the product divisions. One consequence was the increasing sameness of cars produced by the various divisions—a centralized assembly operation led to demands for interchangeability of parts in order to achieve economies of scale. The establishment of the assembly division "also had the effect of creating another autonomous bureaucracy . . . and another hurdle in the tedious process of getting a car from the design studio to the showroom."[1] The erosion of power of the car divisions, whether intentionally or not, increased the power of the central administrative staff and the corporate hierarchy on the fourteenth floor of the headquarters building.

Breaking up independent units or reducing their power almost always tends to increase the power of those in more centralized positions. Sometimes this effect is not intended, but it occurs nevertheless. The U.S. House of Representatives was organized for many years by a strict seniority system—committee chairmanships and positions on committees were apportioned according to length of service in the House. During the 1960s and early 1970s, there was growing restiveness among the younger, less senior members, who had to devote decades to reaching positions of influence. There was also concern about the competence of some of the more elderly chairmen, and frustration that their power was blocking the reform of Congress and the passage of numerous bills. For instance, the power of the Southern committee chairmen had hindered the passage of civil rights legislation in the early 1960s, and it was only through Lyndon Johnson's political skill and determination that such legislation was eventually passed. The election in 1974 of a large new freshman class of Democratic party legislators (following the Watergate scandal that drove Richard Nixon from the presidency) precipitated a revolt that changed the rules governing the organization of the House and drastically limited the power of committee chairmen. But these reforms, by reducing the autonomy of the independent centers of power, the committee chairs, at the same time substantially increased the power of the Speaker of the House:

> . . . the same reforms that seemed to atomize power also vastly strengthened the Speaker's hand. The revolt had been not against the Speaker, but against chairmen. . . . The Speaker gained the power to appoint Rules Committee members, to set deadlines for committees to report out legislation—so chairmen could not block his will and the will of the Caucus—and other political weapons. Ways and Means lost the power to make members' committee assignments; that went to the Democratic Steering and Policy Committee, and the Speaker dominated that committee.[2]

Although some Speakers, such as Carl Albert and Tip O'Neill, would not use this new power forcefully, Jim Wright would. And having seen how the elimination of independent power centers gave him, in the central position, more control, Wright would be unwilling to have new centers of power, perhaps hostile to him, emerge in the structure of the House. Thus, for instance, when Dan Rostenkowski, chairman of the Ways and Means committee and a competitor for leadership positions and for power, tried to add a new structural element, Wright resisted:

> Rostenkowski tried one last maneuver to create a power base for himself, pushing for the creation of a council of committee chairmen. If such a "chairmen's council" were set up, it would immediately become a power center independent of the Speaker . . . Wright would not agree to its creation.[3]

Power is created and used by having a separate, somewhat protected domain of activity established in the structure of the organization as a base for gathering information and resources. Those in central positions often strive to keep such subdivisions weak or under their control, while the creation of separate domains is imperative for those seeking to gain power in bureaucratic political infighting. The importance of having a separate domain with defined responsibilities for exercising influence is beautifully illustrated by the difficulties that Asian affairs personnel faced in the State Department in the late 1940s and early 1950s. The U.S. foreign policy establishment was looking toward Europe, and important events in the Pacific region, such as the takeover of China by the Communists, the instability in Indochina, and the reemergence of Japan were going unnoticed. U.S. policy toward the region was ill-formed and often reactive. The problem was that Asian affairs experts had no structural power:

> The very organization of the Department in those days was the basic problem for the Asian officers. Asia was not a separate area; instead the colonies were handled through the European nations, and concurrent jurisdiction was required for policy changes. That meant that on any serious question involving territory supposedly emerging from colonialism, both the European and the Asian divisions had to agree before the question could go to a higher official. . . . The result . . . was that this favored the status quo and the European division.[4]

THE EXPANSION OF ONE'S DOMAIN

Structural power is developed by obtaining control of a unit rich in resources, information, and formal authority, on the one hand, and by preventing your opponents from gaining structural bases of power, on the other. Once you have gained control of a unit, structural reorganizations can be employed to expand your unit's sphere of influence, thereby enhancing power at the expense of competing units in the organization. Territory is one source of power, and organizational territory—the reach or span of activities—is something that structural modifications can profoundly affect.

As nursing gained power at Stanford University Hospital, the individual who is now the chief operating officer of the hospital became the director of nursing. But, recall that nursing was increasingly powerful because of its impact on the hospital's financial position (since so much of the staff was in nursing or related activities) and on the delivery of patient care. It was, therefore, a natural and logical extension to soon appoint the director of nursing to a newly created position, vice president of patient care services, which included responsibility for the operation of the emergency room, operating rooms, physical therapy department, and respiratory therapy department—in other words, departments in which nonphysicians delivered services (physical, occupational, respiratory therapy) and facilities that were organized and scheduled by nursing and related personnel. Once that reorganization occurred, and once the former nursing director now exhibited good ability to operate in this expanded domain, her continued rise to even more senior management levels was almost assured. The reorganization brought a simplified administrative structure to the hospital, but also expanded the domain and influence of the person in charge.

One of the ways in which Jim Wright was to wield power as Speaker of the House of Representatives was to use every appointment, every position he controlled or could conceivably control, as a lever for gaining additional influence. Expanding a domain may involve taking on new activities and new responsibilities, as the director of nursing did at Stanford. But another way of expanding your domain is not to undertake new activities, but rather just to get full value out of those domains already ostensibly under your control. Until Wright assumed the speakership, previous Speakers had either been less interested in wielding power or had based their influence on friendship and personal obligation networks. Wright was not as well liked as the previous Speaker—he was more of a loner, and would not be able to wield the kind of influence he wanted solely through personal style and relationships. So, he turned to the formal structure.

The whip organization was responsible for providing intelligence to the Democratic leadership by counting votes and for persuading members to adhere to party policy in their voting.[5] Although the whip was now elected by the members, the chief deputy whip was appointed by the Speaker. Wright appointed someone to the job whom he could trust, and did not even inform the whip until after the appointment was announced. Wright took over the whip organization:

> Coelho might be the whip, but the whip organization belonged to Wright. Coelho might manage the organization, but only as a delegate. A final indignity came after the Caucus elected Coelho whip; while the members were still applauding, interrupting the applause, killing it, was the announcement of the ten deputy whips.[6]

Wright also moved to exercise his control over the Democratic Steering and Policy Committee. The committee made standing committee assignments to all other committees except Rules. Since committee assignments were important to members' political futures, the Steering and Policy Committee had substantial power:

> Thirty-one members sit on Steering and Policy; the Speaker chairs it, and the entire leadership plus the chairmen of Appropriations, Budget, Rules, and Ways and Means committees automatically have seats. Eight other members are appointed by the Speaker; another twelve are elected by region.[7]

Steering and Policy was a source of power for Rostenkowski, chairman of Ways and Means and a rival to Wright. Wright made sure that this powerful committee would fall under his domain. In some of his discretionary appointments, he named people from Rostenkowski's own Ways and Means Committee. "Wright was invading Rostenkowski's own lair, forcing his committee members to split their loyalties."[8] He also picked his own people to run for the various elected positions. "Steering and Policy belonged to Wright."[9]

In part by using appointments strategically, and in part by making aggressive use of his formal powers, Wright made sure that his influence was consolidated in as many domains of the House leadership as possible. The theme that runs through these examples is the same one we have seen in other contexts: power is built by ensuring that you control as much territory as possible, and this control is obtained by placing your allies in key positions and by expanding the activities over which you have formal responsibility.

TASK FORCES AND COMMITTEES

It is often the case that exercising power creates enemies who constitute a threat to your long-term organizational survival. Thus, in developing and exercising power it is important to use structural mechanisms that institutionalize your power and diffuse responsibility for decisions and actions. Task forces and committees, as vehicles for co-opting others, can be quite useful in this regard.

The concept of co-optation is an important idea. Developed originally in studies of boards of directors,[10] the idea is that if I appoint you to some board, committee, or task force, you will develop some loyalty to the organization to which that group is attached, and some commitment to the ideas it proposes. Although influence is exercised in both directions—as a board or committee member, you obviously can influence what is decided—the idea of co-optation is that you become, to some extent, "captured" by your affiliations. Moreover, decisions taken by such representative bodies come to be seen as collective decisions. Powerful executives thus strive to have their decisions made or ratified by boards or committees in order to avoid acquiring personal enemies as they exercise their power.

Consider the case of an individual in charge of labor relations, among other functions, at a large Jesuit university in which both faculty and support staff are represented by labor unions. One tendency would be to centralize negotiating authority in the labor relations office, and control the handling of grievances and other contractual issues. But collective bargaining was particularly problematic in this academic institution. To begin with, there was the usual problem of the faculty being professionals and at the same time union members. The university was usually under some degree of financial stress, so there was pressure not to give too much away; at the same time it was located in a strong union town, so it could not be perceived as being a union-busting organization and still derive the support it wanted from the community. The Jesuit leaders had ambivalent feelings about labor organizations, on the one hand, having some tendencies to favor the working person, but on the other hand, having to deal with budget constraints. Because so much of the university's budget was salaries, and such a high proportion of the employees were unionized, the person responsible for managing labor relations had, potentially, a great deal of power. If the issues were not handled properly, however, he could also become a target for the many groups that invariably lose something in the bargaining and compromising process necessary to reach agreement. How could this head of labor relations use structure to his advantage?

His plan is represented in Figure 14-1. He established a series of groups and committees to participate in the process. In the act of establishing these groups, he also outlined a formal set of responsibilities for those involved in the labor relations process. Moreover, he controlled the selection of people for the various teams and committees, which gave him the power to stack the groups when he wanted to co-opt people who might otherwise give him trouble. And since almost without exception the members of these groups had little expertise or, for that matter, interest in labor relations matters, it was fairly easy to control the process. Thus, the head of labor relations was able to exercise power in a fairly unobtrusive fashion. Even more important, because of the legitimacy and formality of the process, and the involvement of numerous interested parties, labor relations results were institutionally owned and there was collective responsibility for the outcomes. Thus, it was more difficult for opponents or political enemies to successfully mount an attack. They would be attacking, not a single individual, but rather an entire legitimated process with extensive involvement by many people.

I have seen other instances in which committees were established to institutionalize and legitimate changes that the individual in charge of the committee wanted to accomplish without drawing fire. To use this as an effective strategy for wielding power, you need to staff the committees quite carefully; it is also helpful if your interest and expertise in the issues being addressed is greater than that of the committee members, so you can more readily guide the process. If you fail to meet these two conditions, it is quite possible to establish a committee or board structure that will get out of hand and become an independent center of power, or at least a powerful unit not reliably under your control.

Figure 14-1
Labor Relations Organization

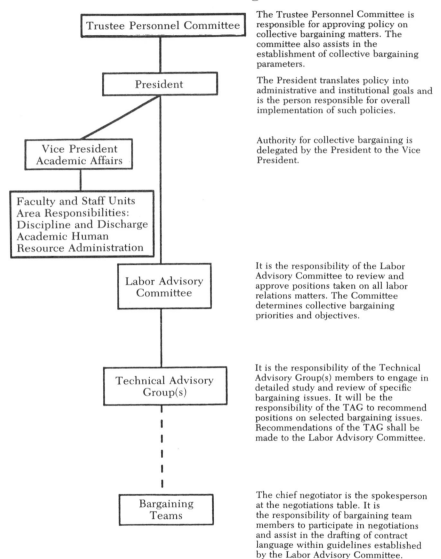

Trustee Personnel Committee	The Trustee Personnel Committee is responsible for approving policy on collective bargaining matters. The committee also assists in the establishment of collective bargaining parameters.
President	The President translates policy into administrative and institutional goals and is the person responsible for overall implementation of such policies.
Vice President Academic Affairs	Authority for collective bargaining is delegated by the President to the Vice President.
Faculty and Staff Units Area Responsibilities: Discipline and Discharge Academic Human Resource Administration	
Labor Advisory Committee	It is the responsibility of the Labor Advisory Committee to review and approve positions taken on all labor relations matters. The Committee determines collective bargaining priorities and objectives.
Technical Advisory Group(s)	It is the responsibility of the Technical Advisory Group(s) members to engage in detailed study and review of specific bargaining issues. It will be the responsibility of the TAG to recommend positions on selected bargaining issues. Recommendations of the TAG shall be made to the Labor Advisory Committee.
Bargaining Teams	The chief negotiator is the spokesperson at the negotiations table. It is the responsibility of bargaining team members to participate in negotiations and assist in the drafting of contract language within guidelines established by the Labor Advisory Committee.

Henry Kissinger was a master at exercising power through intervention in the structure, particularly in the task forces and committees that were already in place. When he was named special assistant for national security affairs for President Nixon in 1968, he and the president wanted to consolidate power over foreign policy in the White House. In particular, they did not trust the State Department to share their point of view and interests; nor did Nixon trust the CIA, which he believed was staffed by Ivy League liberal intellectuals. Thus, Kissinger's first task was to get control of the foreign policy apparatus.

Kissinger asked Morton Halperin, a 30-year-old deputy assistant secretary of defense, to join his staff and to prepare a paper on systems analysis techniques and their use in foreign policy:

> Halperin, seizing the opportunity, took it upon himself to draft a broad memorandum that placed nearly all the power in the hands of the national security advisor. Halperin understood the needs of his master as well as Kissinger understood the needs of his. The projected system gave Kissinger the power to decide the agenda for the National Security Council meetings and also made him chairman of the review group that considered the various option papers prepared by the bureaucracy. . . . In addition, Halperin's memorandum gave Kissinger direct authority to order State and other agencies to prepare option papers on specific subjects.[11]

The Halperin memorandum became, when issued under Kissinger's name, the structure that President Nixon approved.

Not only had Kissinger been given direct authority over much of the foreign policy apparatus, but in an apparently unimportant sentence buried at the end of the memorandum, competition from a State Department-led group was eliminated:

> At the end of my memorandum appeared an innocuous sentence: "The elaborated NSC machinery makes the continued functioning of the existing Senior Interdepartmental Group unnecessary." . . . The Senior Interdepartmental Group . . . had been established in 1967. It was composed of the highest officials of the government just below Cabinet level. . . . It was chaired by the Under Secretary of State. Its role was to review the options to be presented to the National Security Council and to follow up on decisions reached. . . . Needless to say, the State Department considered this structure a major bureaucratic triumph because it formally enshrined the Department's preeminence in foreign policy.[12]

The elimination of the SIG gave Kissinger's proposed organizational arrangements no competition in the control of the foreign-policy determination process. Moreover, Kissinger immediately began asking for National Security Study Memoranda, as permitted by the new structure.

The first batch of "requests" seemed to have three goals: First, they were a sincere effort to get the bureaucracy to begin thinking in terms of different options to foreign policy questions; second, they asserted the ascendancy of the Kissinger apparatus; and finally, with their requirements of lengthy studies and impossibly short deadlines, they were intended to overwhelm the "faceless civil servants." . . . In the first month in office, Kissinger's staff issued twenty-two NSSMs requesting broad studies on every important issue before the new administration. Yet . . . the most important decisions were made without informing the bureaucracy, and without the use of NSSMs.[13]

Kissinger changed the committee structure to give him more procedural and substantive control, and simultaneously overwhelmed the existing competitors for influence with busywork. He had power because of his relationship to Nixon; he was able to further develop and exercise that power by being a sophisticated player in the game of bureaucratic politics. In this effort, he understood the importance of task forces, committees, and the design of formal structures.

We have seen in this chapter that a sensitivity to the importance of the formal structure of the system and the ability to use design and redesign are important strategies for the exercise of power and influence in organizations ranging from the U.S. House of Representatives to Apple Computer. Awareness of the role of organizational design in the exercise of power can sensitize us to the hidden agendas that may underlie restructurings undertaken for seemingly straightforward reasons. It can also help us gauge how we are faring in these redesigns. Skill in understanding and using structure is a valuable complement to our arsenal of strategies and tactics for developing and exercising power to get things accomplished.

15

Symbolic Action: Language, Ceremonies, and Settings

Given the choice of influencing you through your heart or your head, I will pick the heart. It's your head that sends you off to check *Consumer Reports* when you are thinking of purchasing a new car. It's your heart that buys the Jaguar, or the Porsche. It's your head that tells you that political campaign speeches cannot be believed or trusted, but it's your heart that responds to the best oratory, and makes you refuse to vote for people who come across as "dull," as though that were a reason to vote or not vote for a governmental representative. "People are persuaded by reason, but moved by emotion."[1] We exercise power and influence, when we do it successfully, through the subtle use of language, symbols, ceremonies, and settings that make people feel good about what they are doing. A friend once remarked that it is management's job to make people want to do what they need or have to do in order to make the organization prosper. In a similar fashion, it is the job of people interested in wielding power and influence to cause others to feel good about doing what we want done. This involves the exercise of symbolic management.[2]

Symbolic management operates fundamentally on the principle of illusion, in that using political language, settings, and ceremonies effectively elicits powerful emotions in people, and these emotions interfere with or becloud rational analysis. Murray Edelman noted, "It is not uncommon to give the rhetoric to one side and the decision to the other."[3] Edelman further noted that political speech was a ritual that dulled the critical faculties rather than sharpening them.[4] But it would be incorrect to think that using symbolism and language to make others feel good about the actions or decisions you require of them is somehow acting against their interests. If, after all, the actions or decisions are important and necessary, they might just as well feel good about them as not.

In this chapter, I begin by considering rational versus emotional approaches to persuasion and the exercise of power. I then describe and provide examples of each form of symbolic management in turn, beginning with the important issue of language, and subsequently discussing the use of settings and ceremonies in the exercise of power and influence.

RATIONALITY AND EMOTION

In all types of administration and in many organizations, training and skill building at all levels have been focused on the development of better decision-making capabilities. Moreover, decision-making capacity is assessed in terms of conformance to a rational model of choice. The rational analyst, with a command of facts, figures, logic, and analytical technique, has come to be revered in our society. We use phrases like "rocket scientist" to express both our wonder and our respect for these (often young) analytic wizards. The "whiz kids" of Ford Motor Company and the Defense Department's systems analysis unit were among the first of the new breed of analyst, who spread this approach to management through a number of organizations. Robert McNamara at Ford Motor, and Tex Thornton at Litton Industries, were among the early practitioners and advocates. The following passage about McNamara, from David Halberstam's book, *The Best and the Brightest,* well illustrates the features of the super analyst:

> If the body was tense and driven, the mind was mathematical, analytical, bringing order and reason out of chaos. Always reason. And reason supported by facts, by statistics—he could prove his rationality with facts, intimidate others. He was marvelous with charts and

statistics. Once, sitting at CINCPAC for eight hours watching hundreds and hundreds of slides flashed across the screen showing what was in the pipe line to Vietnam and what was already there, he finally said, after seven hours, "Stop the projector. This slide, number 869, contradicts slide 11." Slide 11 was flashed back and he was right, they did contradict each other. Everyone was impressed and many a little frightened. No wonder his reputation grew; others were in awe. . . .[5]

One problem in exercising power in this manner is apparent already in the passage quoted from Halberstam. Power is exercised by a mastery of the facts, and by leaving others intimidated, awestruck at one's brilliance and ability. But being in awe of someone does not always cause us to feel warmly about that person. We may admire the mental capacity and be struck with the acuity of the mind, but liking is not necessarily one of the feelings elicited. Forgetting for the moment our discussion about how facts can be produced to justify almost any decision, it is also the case that exercising power through intimidation, by overwhelming our opponents, is not likely to produce allies, or as many friends as we would like.

Humans are not computers, and emotion and feelings are important components of our choices and our activities. Our unwillingness to confront this reality about ourselves, as well as a fear of the emotional side of life, helps to explain why people are often uncomfortable reading about or discussing the use of political language, ceremonies, or settings. This is a part of us that somehow embarrasses us, something we would like to pretend doesn't exist. But this very denial makes us more susceptible to emotional appeals. We are off guard, and therefore more easily swayed. My experience has been that people with training in engineering or business are more readily seduced by emotional appeals than people trained in literature or drama, who understand exactly the techniques being employed, and who therefore admire them but are not necessarily taken in.

We cannot see the dynamics of organizations just in terms of who wins, who loses, and the associated costs. These are important considerations, but we must remember that the consequences of actions and choices often have their origin in the symbolic, political actions that are taken to affect how people feel about the situation. Murray Edelman explained the complexity of political analysis:

> Political analysis must, then, proceed on two levels simultaneously. It must examine how political actions get some groups the tangible things they want . . . and at the same time it must explore what these same actions mean to the mass public and how it is placated or aroused by them. In Himmelstrand's terms, political actions are both instrumental and expressive.[6]

POLITICAL LANGUAGE

I am reasonably certain that no readers of this book living in the United States will ever again face a tax increase. We may be subject to "revenue enhancement," the reduction or elimination of "tax preferences" (such as deductions for mortgage interest, medical expenses, and so forth), or, best of all, we may once again experience the joys of "tax equity and reform." Herbert Stein provided a lovely list of the magnitude of the tax increases passed under the Reagan administration, but never called "taxes" or "tax increases" at all:

> Tax Equity and Fiscal Responsibility Act, 1982—$55.7 billion
> Social Security Amendments, 1983—$30.9 billion
> Budget Reconciliation Act, 1987—$13.9 billion
> Tax Reform Act of 1986—$24.4 billion[7]

Who can be opposed to "tax equity and fiscal responsibility"? Perhaps all of us, once we see how much such lofty words are taking out of our pockets. How was Reagan able to do all this and keep his image as a fiscal conservative?

> Mr. Reagan retained his title as the world's champion enemy of taxes, despite all the tax increases enacted with his concurrence during his regime. . . . The lesson for politicians seems to be that you can get away with raising taxes if you talk as if you didn't do it.[8]

Language is a powerful tool of social influence, and political language is frequently vital in the exercise of power in organizations of all types. We perceive things according to how they are described in conversation and debate. This is why it is reported that Confucius, upon being asked what he would do if he were appointed to rule a country, replied, "The first thing I would do is to fix the language." Morris noted, "Sharing a language with other persons provides the subtlest and most powerful of all tools for controlling the behavior of these other persons to one's advantage."[9]

Another classic example of the use of political language in national politics is the Windfall Profits Tax, passed in the waning days of the Carter administration—after the start of the tax revolt in California and just as Ronald Reagan was to be elected president on a program of less taxation and less government. The tax, which at the time of its passage was predicted to raise about $227 billion over ten years, was designed to capture for the government some of the economic benefits derived by the U.S. oil companies when the price of domestic oil was decontrolled and rose to the world market price. The tax, however, was not based on the profits of the oil companies, defined in the conventional way as revenues minus expenses. Rather, the tax was a sales or excise tax, based on the price of oil. This is why there has recently been talk of repealing the tax—oil prices have fallen so far that they have occasionally been below the trigger price, or the price at which the tax generates any revenue. Although there is some dispute among economists about whether corporate income taxes are shifted to consumers, there is more agreement that, depending on one's assumptions about the elasticities of supply and demand, excise taxes fall heavily on the consumer.

How, then, could a $227 billion tax on consumers of oil and oil products be passed? Certainly not by calling the tax an excise tax, or an oil sales tax, or even the "Hard-Earned Profits Tax." The successful passage of the tax depended in important respects on what it was called—the Windfall Profits Tax." In a society in which public opinion polls show that many citizens do not understand the role of profits in the economic system, windfall profits are particularly odious. "Windfall" is defined as "an unexpected sudden gain or advantage,"[10] and how could anyone object to taxing something that was not really expected in the first place? Of course, many people well understood that this was not a tax on profits at all. *The Wall Street Journal* in numerous editorials called attention to the precise nature of the tax. But if you call something the "Windfall Profits Tax" often enough and long enough, the connotations of that name have effects emotionally, even if not intellectually, and these effects are potent.

Language is important in exercising influence, and it is the job of leaders and managers in organizations to get things done. It is, consequently, not surprising that many writers have noted the importance of using symbols and political language in the management task. Karl Weick wrote:

> Managerial work can be viewed as managing myths, images, symbols, and labels. The much touted "bottom line" of the organization is a symbol, if not a myth. . . . Because managers traffic so often in images, the appropriate role for the manager may be evangelist rather than accountant.[11]

Tom Peters argued that "symbols are the very stuff of management behavior. Executives, after all, do not synthesize chemicals or operate lift trucks; they deal in symbols."[12] Nixon commented, "The leader necessarily deals to a large extent in symbols, in images, and in the sort of galvanizing idea that becomes a force of history."[13] In writing about leadership, Lou Pondy noted that one of the important tasks of leaders entails providing labels for activities and making them meaningful for organizational members:

> . . . the effectiveness of a leader lies in his ability to make activity meaningful for those in his role set . . . to give others a sense of understanding what they are doing and especially to articulate it so they can communicate about the meaning of their behavior. . . . This dual capacity to make sense of things and to put them into language meaningful to large numbers of people gives the person who has it enormous leverage.[14]

One of the important questions raised by our discussion of symbolic action and political language concerns the value of proposing actions or choices using factual, rational analysis. Most of us believe we are well served by backing up our proposals with extensive quantitative rationales and analysis. In watching the videotape of British Steel making an important capital investment decision, executives and students often comment on how the project champion never seems to have or use any numbers, but instead relies on a variety of emotional appeals and interpersonal influence techniques. There are some situations that are, however, best handled in precisely that way. Particularly if the emotions tapped are potent, and if the project, or at least a decision that irrevocably commits the organization to the project, can be completed quickly, there are many advantages to arguing not with numbers but with symbols. Numbers can always be debated and disputed. If your numbers are challenged, studies may be proposed to try to determine whose assumptions are the more reasonable. The problem is that while this is going on, the project is losing momentum and time. It is easier to argue about numbers than about symbols, which provides at least one reason to use symbols either alone or in conjunction with analyses.

When Time Inc. considered launching *TV-Cable Week,* the people involved on the startup team felt that they needed a way to explain, succinctly and concisely, what the project was about in terms of its market potential. Preparing for a major presentation to the corporation's highest-ranking executives, the five business-side players tried to come up with a simple way of presenting the project. One of them, a Harvard MBA graduate, suggested, "Why don't we play this game we used to play at the B-School—If You Could Tell Them Just One Thing?"[15] Then:

> . . . one of the group . . . no one quite remembers who . . . drew two lines on a sheet of scratch pad paper, and set in motion a deal worth $100 million. First, a vertical line, then bisecting it a horizontal line . . .

4.	1.
3.	2.

> To the right of the vertical line was the "free market," in which magazines reached the reader by traditional means, such as newsstand sales. . . . To the left was the market for magazines co-marketed

with cable operators. Above the horizontal line were the weeklies, below were the monthlies. . . . Then . . . one came to Quadrant 4, the co-marketed weeklies—with no competitors in there at all. A whole empty quadrant for the taking. . . . the ultimate executive memo: a document with no words at all, just two crossed lines on a piece of paper.[16]

The importance of finding that simple presentation of the concept for the magazine cannot be exaggerated; it was used at meetings of the corporation's executive committee and the board of directors, and the ability to give symbolic representation to the concept was a potent force in pushing the project forward. Of course, no one in the company asked the obvious question: If there is one quadrant unoccupied, why? Maybe that quadrant is not commercially feasible (which turned out to be the case, at least at that time).

At about the same time, across the continent at another corporation, the importance and power of language was also being demonstrated. Fall of 1983 was a tough time for Apple Computer. At the end of September, the cover story of *Business Week* proclaimed IBM the winner in the personal computer wars. The Apple III had failed, Lisa was not selling well, and even Apple II sales had fallen, in anticipation of IBM's launching of the Peanut, to be known as the PCjr. The sales force was concerned, and morale was low. In computer sales, moreover, "forecasts became self-fulfilling, for lost credibility meant fewer sales, and fewer sales meant bigger losses, and bigger losses meant lowered credibility, and on and on in what could only result in the whole business going spiraling down the drain."[17] At the fall sales meeting, motivating the sales force and the independent distributors in attendance was critical:

Jobs and Murray were sprawled on the floor of a hallway outside, writing Jobs' speech. . . . Macintosh was an artificial arrangement of silicon and metal designed to manipulate electrons according to the strict rules of logic; but its appeal transcended logic, and so would his pitch for it. This was no mere "productivity tool" but a machine to free the human spirit. . . . It was a mystical experience. All you needed to use it—all you needed to *respond* to it—was your own intuition. And to sell it, Jobs had only to play to the emotions.[18]

Jobs's speech, repeated at the 1984 annual meeting in January at which Macintosh was announced, focused on IBM's mistakes—in not buying the rights to xerography, in not taking either minicomputers or personal computers seriously. Then, it turned to the hard times in the personal computer industry, and the fact that IBM wanted it all:

> "Will Big Blue dominate the entire information age?" he cried at last. "Was George Orwell *right?*" "No!" they screamed. . . . And as they did so, an immense screen descended from the ceiling. In a sixty-second microburst [the 1984 commercial] the drama unfolded. . . . The sales conference was transformed in that moment—all defeatism banished, euphoria in its place.[19]

No change in Apple's market position, no change in its technology, no change in its substantial bank account occurred because of that masterful use of symbolic management, either at the sales conference or at the annual meeting in Cupertino. What was changed was the organization, and how its employees (and competitors and potential customers) felt about it. That was all, and that was enough.

The skillful use of language tends to be rewarded in organizations. Having your own proposal seen as "clean," "tight," and "forward-looking," and the alternatives viewed as "messy" and "indecisive," will almost assuredly guarantee the success of what you have proposed. Language is also often used to take the sting out of what might otherwise be painful or difficult transitions in organizations. An automobile sales manager never talks about firings, only about "career readjustments." At Stanford in 1990, we did not have administrative cutbacks with accompanying layoffs, but rather, "repositioning." In a large medical care organization, there are no mistakes or malpractice, just PCEs (potentially compensable events).

Lyndon Johnson was a master at using symbols and language to make otherwise unpalatable situations appear better, and to motivate those around him. As Congressman Kleberg's secretary, he had two assistants, one of whom was Gene Latimer. Latimer had wanted to come to Washington to be near his fiancée, but the work schedule of the office under Johnson's direction left little time for romance. "He was allowed time off from the office to see her on Sundays after three p.m.—and only on Sundays after three p.m."[20] Johnson paid Latimer very poorly, as the money he saved on his assistants he could keep for himself. But when Latimer seemed at one point to be near rebellion, Johnson understood how to placate him with a symbolic gesture:

> "He listened with sympathetic concern . . . then told me he had been thinking for some time on how to reward the excellent work I had been doing. He had finally decided that I merited having my name put on the office stationery as assistant secretary. As he described the prestige and glory of such an arrangement, I could see the printing stand out six inches."[21]

The use of a title or some other symbolic reward to make people feel better about their position in the organization and about what the organization is doing is quite common, and also quite often successful, as Johnson's efforts were with Latimer, who worked for him virtually all his life.

Political language works, in part, by calling "the attention of a group with shared interests to those aspects of their situation which make an argued for line of action seem consistent with the furthering of their interests."[22] And political language is often effective because people are judged by their intent, by the symbolism of what they are seeking to accomplish, rather than by the reality of what they are doing. George Gallup noted, "People tend to judge a man by his goals, by what he's trying to do, and not necessarily by what he accomplishes or by how well he succeeds."[23]

Language is such a powerful tool of influence that I often advise people to diagnose the language in their own organizations. It can tell them a lot about how the organization thinks about itself and its activities. As a consequence, language can be a potent predictor of behavior.

One of the more interesting diagnostics is the form of pronouns that one sees used in organizations. There are "I" and "me" organizations, and organizations that emphasize "we" and "us." There are also organizations in which other persons and units within the firm are referred to as "they" or "them." Not only can this language tell you something about the organization's culture and health, the language itself can be important in exercising influence.

Consider the case of the split of a large Cleveland-based law firm, Jones, Day, Reavis and Pogue (JDR&P). A substantial part of the Washington office broke off when the managing partner of the firm, Alan Holmes, tried to remove Eldon Crowell and his government contracts group from the Washington office. The events that followed after Crowell was told he had to leave the partnership have many interesting aspects, but the use of language is particularly instructive. Both the Holmes group and the Crowell group distributed memoranda to partners and associates, trying to muster support and recruit for their side. Partners could, of course, either remain with JDR&P, or join the new firm, Crowell and Moring. I have obtained copies of both memoranda, and the differences in the use of language are striking. Recall that this is a contest for the loyalty and support of highly educated professionals in a firm that exists to sell professional services.

The Holmes or Cleveland group memorandum is addressed, "To the Washington Partners," and it begins:

> Appended hereto is a copy of the position paper we have this morning delivered to the members of the Washington Office Executive Committee.
>
> Most of us . . . plan to be in the Washington Office for much of the day and we would be glad to talk . . . with anyone who would like to discuss further our national firm program.

The next page, headed "To the Partners of JDR&P," reads, in part, as follows:

> At the partnership meeting of the Cleveland office . . . I reported on the discussions. . . . Since that time I have been away . . . but I asked . . . to give consideration during my absence to all aspects of the problems raised. I now have their views . . . and believe it is appropriate now to give you my considered judgement of the situation.
>
> I believe most of our partners recognize the dramatic changes in the nature of the demand for legal services. . . . Those corporate law firms which are limited to providing such conventional services will not, in my judgement, successfully survive the changes occurring in the modern corporate practice. Only those large firms which, because

of their ability to respond on what I would term a transaction basis . . .
will flourish in the future.

There are seven uses of a first person pronoun on the first
page (six in the first paragraph), and nine by the end of the
paragraph that continues from the first page to the top of page
2. Can you guess how the firm was managed—by an elected
executive committee, or by a strong managing partner with
virtual CEO powers? The answer is in the language. Perhaps
more important, how would the language make you feel if
you were an undecided Washington partner? Is a hand being
extended to you, or are you being told by a parental figure
about the world of law practice as he sees it?

By contrast, the Crowell group's memorandum is headed,
"To Our Partners in JDR&P." It begins:

> During the past three weeks, the members of the Washington Execu-
> tive Committee and most of the partners located in Washington have
> spent considerable time discussing the relationship between the
> Washington Office and the remainder of our firm. The focus of those
> discussions has uniformly been on steps which might be taken to
> strengthen existing relationships . . . and move forward together with
> our friends and partners . . . to achieve more fully our common goal
> of building the best law firm in the United States. . . . our partners
> resident in Washington take great pride in their association with
> Jones, Day. . . . We expressed these views at a breakfast meeting. . . .
> We expressed also our sincere hope that this would be the first of
> many meetings. . . . We were disappointed to be told by Mr. Holmes
> of his conclusion . . . that the "Governments Contracts Group" is
> incompatible with his concept of the national firm.

The Cleveland memo is signed by five attorneys (named),
with Alan Holmes listed first. The Crowell group memorandum is signed, "Washington Executive Committee." There
is no use of "I" or "my" in the Crowell group memo, and the
tone is much more of reaching out, and less of lecturing.
There are many reasons why Crowell and his colleagues did
so well at attracting both partners and associates to go with
them, but their use of language and the attitude it implied
was clearly a significant factor that contributed to their success. These two memoranda provide a nice illustration both
of how language can be used to diagnose power and gover-

nance structures, and how the use of language is a critical tactic in the exercise of power and influence.

CEREMONIES

Ceremonies provide the opportunity to mobilize political support as well as to quiet opposition. Ceremonies are occasions to help organizational members feel better about doing what needs to be done. They can also be used as part of larger political battles within organizations. There are a number of ceremonies, or ceremonial events, which occur regularly in organizations, ranging from annual meetings, sales meetings, training sessions, conventions, and other such gatherings to the replacement of high-level executives, retirement events, and celebrations of accomplishments. In each instance, the issue is what use is made of the ceremony. If symbolic reassurance is offered to a group to be co-opted, or if the ceremony is used as part of a political struggle, we need to ask whether it is successful in disarming the opposition.

Apple Computer's 1984 annual meeting was, as we have noted, an example of the successful use of political language. It was a ceremony with significance on many levels. By closing down all of the facilities in northern California and providing transportation for all employees to attend the meeting, Apple signalled that this was an important event. The meeting was intended to build a sense of community in the company, by means of a celebration of the Macintosh. At that moment, however, with the Macintosh not yet introduced, Lisa doing poorly, and the Apple III withdrawn, Apple II was, obviously, carrying the company, and this fact was not recognized in the ceremony. By putting the Macintosh team at the front of the hall, having videos and other special recognition of the Macintosh team, and by focusing exclusively on the new machine, the ceremony further signalled to members of the Apple II division their second-class status and their diminished power in the organization.

Meetings are often held to reassure some group in the organization that it is important. The very holding of the meeting dedicated to that group provides some symbolic reassurance, but what occurs at the meeting is also important. Under Robert Fomon's leadership at E.F. Hutton, the retail brokerage part of Hutton became increasingly dissatisfied with the direction of the firm. The division felt left out, unimportant, and ignored. Some years before, George Ball had established the Directors Advisory Council (DAC), "an elite group of successful Hutton brokers. . . . In theory, the DAC was meant to keep the Hutton board informed of the brokers' thinking and lobby for changes on their behalf."[24] Of course, what it really involved was an attempt to make the brokers feel important and included in the organization's governance. Unhappy with Fomon, the DAC called a meeting and demanded that he attend. The potential for a ceremony to cause the brokers to feel better both about him and the organization was there, but Fomon missed the opportunity:

> By using the DAC meeting as a platform to appoint Miller as head of the field, Fomon would have diffused much of the anger and demonstrated he could be responsive to the field. But . . . Fomon had a different response. He simply turned around and left the meeting. He walked out. It was as if he couldn't be bothered with these lowly stockbrokers and their petty whining.[25]

Conventions and special meetings can, if used properly, both co-opt interests in the organization and signify relative power and status to everyone involved. Similar outcomes often occur in corporate training activities. Smart organizations involve their highest-level executives in training, evening discussions, or informal social events. Such ceremonies signify to the managers at the session that they are important to the organization. Even if they are not really considered in the organization's top-down decision making, they will feel flattered by their contact with top-level people and their inclusion in events attended by important executives. What functions or what executives actually attend such events also helps to symbolize power and status in the organization. If quality is an issue and quality control personnel are rising in prominence, one would expect to see them at the training sessions as instructors or executives in residence, not just as participants. If the company is dominated by finance, then one can be sure that there will be financial presentations on the company's reception by investors, and perhaps even explanations of how the capital markets work and how the company is valued. This latter focus has been a major theme at Westinghouse training, and it reflects that corporation's conglomerate structure and highly financial orientation. In companies that face public affairs and public relations problems, such as insurance companies, representatives from those functions will play a larger role. In short, participation at training activities not only signifies the relative power of various groups, but from this very signification, helps to enhance that power at the expense of competing units.

Regular, ongoing meetings, such as those involved in budget, performance, or product review, likewise have ceremonial aspects, in which power, both departmental and hierarchical, can be displayed. Harold Geneen's monthly review sessions with the business unit managers in International Telephone and Telegraph were notorious. By putting managers on the spot for their performance, Geneen maintained his own power. And in order to look good in front of their peers, the managers engaged in a competition to provide better results, at least as measured by ITT's systems.

Hierarchical power, and loyalty to the boss, were displayed at meetings held in General Motors. De Lorean noted that high-level committee meetings became occasions for the top two or three people to demonstrate their power and authority:

> In Fourteenth Floor meetings, often only three people, Cole, Gerstenberg, and Murphy would have anything substantial to say, even though there were 14 or 15 executives present. The rest of the team would remain silent. . . . When they did offer a comment, . . . it was just to paraphrase what had already been said by one of the top guys.[26]

Often, top executives would obtain precise facts and use them to intimidate subordinates during meetings, again reaffirming their power in the organization. A master of this was Frederic Donner:

> One time in an Administrative Committee meeting he asked the head of GM Truck and Coach Division:
>
> "How many buses did you build last month?"
>
> The executive replied: "Approximately three thousand."

Donner scowled and snapped back . . . "Last month you built three thousand, one hundred and eighty-seven vehicles." Whatever the figure was, it was precise. . . . Donner was trying to make the point, "Look how I know this business. . . . Look what a mind I have!"[27]

Understanding that meetings are ceremonial occasions can help us gain the patience to sit through them, and even to obtain some enjoyment from the experience. Paying attention to the symbolic, as well as the substantive, content of meetings of all types can help us diagnose organizational power and influence and become more sensitive to the way it is played out in various settings.

Executive replacement and succession is often another important ceremonial occasion. For companies caught doing something illegal or improper, the replacement of executives can provide reassurance that the corporation as a whole does not tolerate such behavior and that things will be different in the future. In the early 1970s when illegal contributions to political campaigns and bribes to foreign governments to obtain business were discovered, the chief executives of both Gulf Oil and Northrop resigned. When E.F. Hutton was discovered writing bad checks and earning interest on the float, two high-level executives were forced out, although not the CEO. Someone had to be held accountable for the misdeeds, and this individual, in turn, had to be removed from the organization, as a form of ritual purification.

It is seldom the case that accountability for corporate misdeeds can truly be attributed to one or a few individuals. Corporations have shared cultures and standard operating procedures, which makes me skeptical that the firing of one or two people really makes much substantive difference. And indeed, in some of the organizations (such as aerospace firms) in which ritual firings occurred once, there were ritual firings again (and again) as additional instances of misconduct came to light. Firing high-level executives, particularly the president or CEO, can also signal to the world that things in the company are going to improve. It is said that managers in professional sports are hired to be fired—to shake things up and to assure the public that the ownership will not tolerate poor performance forever. A similar function is served by managers in business firms and other organizations as well.

Indeed, recent studies show that at poorly performing smaller firms the replacement of the CEO by an outsider actually causes the stock price to advance compared to the market.[28] Thus, the market at least believes that replacement is a consequential event in the life of a corporation.

Succession is indeed a ceremony. If the company is to take advantage of the ceremony, it must release lots of information indicating that the problems are the fault of the individual being replaced. The choice of the successor, and his or her installation, should be accompanied by much public comment and display. The successor should be given a wonderful biography, so that the promise for the future seems very bright indeed. Although, as we have seen, Archie McCardell left the Xerox Corporation in poor financial shape, the announcements of his arrival at International Harvester made him appear as though he were the greatest business genius of the twentieth century. Companies never admit to hiring losers at the time they are hired, but always admit to hiring deficient executives at the time those executives are terminated.

The event of succession is also an occasion for the various political divisions within the organization to show their influence. Which particular group will the new executive represent? Because of the symbolic as well as substantive importance of the choice of organizational leaders, this decision is often highly political and hotly contested.[29] When E.F. Hutton stopped appointing brokers as its CEO, there was concrete evidence that power in the firm had shifted away from the retail side. The appointment of John Sculley at Apple Computer was a signal not only that the company had grown up, but also that marketing and organization were seen as comparatively more important than technology. The appointment of an accountant to head Bethlehem Steel in the 1970s signalled that the company was now perceived as a collection of financial assets; passing over a contender from the steel side of the business conveyed the decline of steel not only in industrial America but also at this particular firm.

There are many occasions for ceremonies, and these events are important because of their connotations about power and influence in the organization and their effect on various organizational constituencies. The importance of ceremonies and

language in the development and use of power has sometimes led me to recommend acting, literature, or English
classes to aspiring managerial leaders. Some of my colleagues think that Stanford MBA students are only looking
for an easy grade when they take drama as an elective, but I
often think these courses have more utility than many traditional alternatives.

SETTINGS

We have already discussed the way in which settings and
physical space can be used to diagnose power distributions.
The physical representation of power and influence can take
on a life of its own, helping those in power to stay there and
forming a bar to the aspirations of the less powerful. Even
more interesting, however, is the way in which physical
space can be used as a tool for the exercise of power and
influence.

General Motors was, and probably still is, a very hierarchical organization. Power was concentrated at the top, with
relatively little influence being exercised by lower-level participants. This concentration of power at the top was ratified
by the design of the headquarters building:

> In General Motors the words "The Fourteenth Floor" are spoken
> with reverence. This is Executive Row. . . . To most GM employees,
> rising to the Fourteenth Floor is the final scene in their Horatio
> Alger dream. . . . The atmosphere on the Fourteenth Floor is awe-
> somely quiet. . . . The omnipresent quiet projects an aura of great
> power. The reason it is so quiet must be that General Motors' power-
> ful executives are hard at work in their offices. . . . It is electrically
> locked and is opened by a receptionist who actuates a switch under
> her desk in a large, plain waiting room outside the door. . . . GM
> executives usually arrive at and leave their offices by a private eleva-
> tor located just inside Executive Row.
>
> They [executive offices] are arranged in order of importance. . . .
> There is great jealousy among some executives about how close their
> offices are to the chairman and president. . . . All [offices] were uni-
> formly decorated in blue carpet, beige walls, faded oak paneling and
> aged furniture . . . except for those of a few uppermost executives,
> who could choose their own office decoration.[30]

By contrast, Apple Computer was a less hierarchical organization, and power was less concentrated at the top. This was reflected in the office arrangements for the chief executive, John Sculley:

> Sculley's office was as unassuming and informal as his new wardrobe. A small, square room in the rear corner of the Pink Palace, it overlooked the car wash on one side and parking lot on the other. The furnishings were standard issue for Apple executives. . . . The wall that overlooked the area where his secretary sat was all glass, creating an illusion of openness.[31]

Hierarchical power differences are at once symbolized and created by physical settings. Think about the description of the two office environments—Apple Computer and General Motors. At which one are you, as an average manager, going to feel more like speaking with the CEO? At which are you more likely to feel as if you can challenge or question decisions? At which will you feel closer and more similar to the top executives? If you confront an imposing, intimidating physical setting, you will probably feel less powerful and influential than you otherwise would. In this way space creates power and influence as well as reflecting it.

Thomas Foley, the Democratic majority leader in the House of Representatives during Jim Wright's tenure as Speaker, also had an office that he carefully constructed to reflect his view of his job:

> The office was laid out like a living room, with a small desk, no larger than what a child might have in a bedroom, against a window; Foley's job was to listen and he believed that a large desk, which conveyed authority and served as moat between listener and visitor, interfered with people speaking freely. He did not impose himself; he listened.[32]

Physical settings mark horizontal power struggles as well. When the Macintosh division was in the ascendancy at Apple, and the Apple II division was falling in influence, Apple II was exiled from Bandley Drive, corporate row, to a leased building a mile away, as Macintosh occupied their old space. And while that space had held some 200 employees when the Apple II division occupied it, the space was reconfigured for the Macintosh division to hold about half that many.[33] The rise in power of the Macintosh group under Jobs was physically apparent, and the luxury of the division's physical location, particularly its nearness to headquarters, gave it advantages in the struggle for corporate resources and attention.

At the interpersonal level, once again, space can be used to exercise power. There are power positions, such as at the head of the table, that tend to convey power immediately to the occupant. Having a large office, an imposing desk and desk chair, and an office arrangement that separates you from your visitors are all ways of subtly increasing your power.

Like language and ceremonies, settings, too, are important in the exercise of power and influence. As such, settings should be considered carefully and used strategically. Occupying space because it is available, convenient, or cheap seldom produces good results. It is necessary to be sensitive to the physical environment, not only for its effects on position in the network of interaction, but also for the impression of power or powerlessness that it conveys.

One reason that language, ceremonies, and settings are so important in the exercise of influence is because we are often scarcely conscious of their effects on us. The influence of appropriately chosen language, well-conducted ceremonies, and carefully designed settings can escape our conscious attention. And because of our focus on the rational and the analytic, we are likely to downplay their potency. How many of us would request another meeting place, or ask to have terminology corrected, in an important discussion over issues of great substance? But if we are not sensitive to the language, the ceremonies, and the settings, we may find ourselves at a power disadvantage without even being aware of it.

Power Dynamics: How Power Is Lost and How Organizations Change

It is easy to get caught up in the micro-level descriptions of sources of power, the diagnoses of power and of situations, and the discussions of the strategies and tactics for employing power, and lose sight of what this book is really about—getting things done in organizations. We are interested in power as a means to make both ourselves and our organizations more effective and successful. This final section of the book begins by providing some cautionary ideas about how power is lost. One way of understanding power and its dynamics is by considering how power erodes. We will see in the first chapter of this section how even the mighty fall, and consider what this means for us as we think about our own personal relationship to power and influence.

The penultimate chapter considers, in some detail, how power dynamics can be productive or unproductive for the organization. This book is about managing with power, and it is also about managing power. It is important to consider how power dynamics affect organizations, and perhaps even more critical to understand the problems and potential in managing power dynamics productively.

The final chapter reminds us that power is of more than academic interest. Freeways get built, or don't, the blood supply becomes contaminated, or not, products are introduced, or technological skills are wasted, depending on our ability to get things done. But more than ability is involved. It is not only political skill, it is also political will, the desire or at least the willingness to be "in the arena," to use Richard Nixon's phrase, that matters for affecting the world around us. In the first chapter I discussed our ambivalence about power, the tendency to think of power as something somehow evil or dirty, something to be avoided. This ambivalence must certainly be increased when we do, as we have done in this book, a detailed, clinical diagnosis of power, its sources, and how it is used. A useful analogy is looking at almost anyone through a magnifying glass. Anyone, regardless of how beautiful, will appear less attractive if we examine the individual with enough magnification to see the pores, the small imperfections, that at a distance form part of an overall gestalt. In much the same way, social interaction can appear to be unattractive when we consider in detail the various ways in which power and influence are developed and exercised.

This last section, and particularly the last chapter, remind us that in the world as it exists, for the many reasons we have examined in this book, getting things done requires understanding and using power and influence. Thus, the book closes by noting that perhaps there is a greater sin than making mistakes or influencing others—the sin of doing nothing, of being passive in the face of great challenges and opportunities, and even great problems. It is insufficient to understand power, and where it comes from, how it is used, and why. This knowledge should increase your own power, and with that empowerment, your willingness to get involved. Look around. The problems of your organization or, for that matter, your city, are more likely to result from failures in implementation or failures to take action than from doing too much, too quickly. Being personally effective requires at least two things: knowing how to get things done and being willing to do them.

16

Even the Mighty Fall:
How Power Is Lost

Organizational change often, if not inevitably, involves changes in the distribution of power. For Apple Computer to crack the corporate market and to build individual products and systems that were compatible, it was necessary for power to pass from counterculture computer jocks to someone like John Sculley, with his Wharton MBA degree and traditional corporate career at Pepsico—to someone, in other words, who understood corporate America and who saw the company more as a business and less as a cause or mission. For Xerox to regain its lost momentum and solve its quality problems in the copier and office products business, power had to pass from the finance types to David Kearns, an ex-IBM executive who understood the importance of serving the customer well and who was willing to do whatever it took to fix the corporation's problems. For Ford to undergo organizational transformation in the 1980s, becoming the most profitable of the large U.S. automobile manufacturers, required a passage of power from the financial people who had largely controlled the company since the days of McNamara to Donald Petersen, an engineer and product person by both training and inclination, and someone who, as a line manager, understood the critical importance of involving all of the work force in efforts to improve the company. In some organizations, such changes in power and perspective proceed smoothly, while in others they are delayed or are contested.

But in any event, power dynamics are inextricably linked with organizational dynamics, and understanding how power is lost is essential for understanding how organizations change.

The difference between the interests of the larger system and the interests of the individual is probably nowhere clearer than in examining instances of the loss of power. For the person, the loss of power and position can be painful, even devastating. For the organization, shifts in power are more often than not therapeutic, permitting new ideas, new information, and new skills to take over and solve critical problems that may have developed under the previous regime. Of course, there is no guarantee that the succession in power will bring better times, but such shifts in influence are almost inevitably associated with change and at least the potential for adaptation.

Shifts in power are virtually guaranteed, and the likelihood is great that after acquiring power we will eventually lose it. To be noticed and at the center of things often cause others to compete with us, and at a minimum focus public attention on us and our actions. Jim Wright's biographer noted perceptively, "By rising he exposed himself, made himself a target, and exposed his weaknesses. Now those weaknesses would be explored, probed, stressed, tested, to see if they could withstand the pressure."[1] Think about putting your financial affairs, your tax returns, through the scrutiny that the financial records of elected officials now receive in the United States. To be in power is to be watched more closely, and this surveillance affords one the luxury of few mistakes. The purpose of this chapter, then, is not just to help the reader maintain power once it has been acquired—although that is one goal. Rather, by understanding the almost inevitable dynamics that result in the loss of power, we can, perhaps, be both forewarned about and more at peace with the evolution of influence within our own organizations.

TIMES CHANGE—PEOPLE DON'T

On December 21, 1977, President Carter overturned a Civil Aeronautics Board ruling from October that had awarded the

Dallas-to-London route to Pan Am, instead giving the route to Braniff. The Pan Am chairman, William Seawell, was outraged by the decision, which he saw as the result of political pressure brought to bear on the president by the Texas congressional delegation. During a party at about this time in the home of Averell Harriman, William Coleman, a former secretary of transportation and a Pan Am board member, took aside Berl Bernhard, a 48-year-old Washington lawyer active in politics, and asked him if his firm would be interested in representing Pan Am. Further discussions were held, and on January 1, 1978, Pan Am "officially switched its Washington legal account from the firm of Jones, Day, Reavis & Pogue to the firm of Verner, Liipfert, Bernhard & McPherson."[2] At the time of the switch, Pan Am was the largest client of the Washington office of Jones, Day, in 1977 paying the firm $966,275 in fees out of total revenues of around $10 million.[3]

The loss of Pan Am meant that the head of the Washington office, Welch Pogue, was no longer the biggest income producer in the firm. There was more frequent talk about choosing Pogue's successor, as Pogue was in his seventies at the time. Welch Pogue was a gentleman, and he believed in a gentlemanly view of the practice of law. He had been chairman of the Civil Aeronautics Board in the early 1940s before leaving to go into private practice, founding a firm called Pogue and Neal. In 1967 that firm had merged with the small Washington office of Jones, Day, and the new, larger firm had been created. In 1978, Jones, Day was the sixth-largest law firm in the country, with headquarters in Cleveland and offices in Los Angeles as well as in Washington. Pogue did not ordinarily lobby on Capitol Hill. "He did not peddle influence. It was his belief that that kind of work—political work—inevitably led to a lessening of a lawyer's respect in the community."[4]

The conflict that ensued over the succession in the Washington office was a major factor in the split of that office, which was discussed in Chapter 15. Pogue was forced out as managing partner, replaced by an elected executive committee in the months just prior to the split. In spite of the genuine respect and affection many of the firm's attorneys felt for Pogue, he had lost a major base of his power in losing the Pan Am account. Moreover, his loss of that account reflected something more fundamental—the practice of law in Washington had changed, and Welch Pogue hadn't. Pogue and the Cleveland office of Jones, Day had a single-minded devotion to a few large clients, a business based on long-standing relationships. In Washington, things now worked differently:

> . . . Pan Am's interests were being looked after at a party given by Pan Am's arch-rival, the primary purpose of which was to muster the support of people interested in Pan Am, people interested in Braniff, and many others, for a government policy. The ability of all those people to do business with one another transcended their connections of the moment to one or another private or public interest group; no doubt long after they had all switched jobs and clients, they would still be friends.[5]

The way law was practiced in Washington had evolved, but Pogue still clung to his old ideas about legal work. One of the important ways in which power is lost is just this—as environments and problems change, they require new approaches, new skills, and new relationships. Although individuals may have flexibility, and some obviously have more than others, it is nevertheless true that people in general tend to resist innovation. We learn how to do things a certain way, grow committed to our choices and our actions, become trapped by our particular form of expertise and by our particular networks of contacts and friendships, and in short, are limited in our ability to even recognize the need for change, let alone to accomplish it. Power is lost, then, because circumstances are often more changeable than we are.

Fiorello LaGuardia served three terms as mayor of New York City. During his tenure, he cleaned up one of the most corrupt cities in America, built vast public works, and put in place social services and programs that left New York the envy of many cities in the country. He had taken what was thought to be an ungovernable city, a city choking from an absence of adequate public services, and had made it a model of urban reform. By the mid-1940s, however, LaGuardia was out of favor. He declined to run for a fourth term, but polls showed him running far behind two other candidates. It is doubtful he could have won, even if he had run. What had happened? Times had changed, and the LaGuardia style and perspective were now no longer appropriate:

But his style of government was pitched to a different time and a different sensibility. He felt deeply for the poor and the needy, and he had been so comforting and effective to the huge population displaced by the Depression. But he had little to offer postwar boom America bent on each making his own. He had emphasized old values, but as Americans made ready to break free of the restrictions that depression and war had placed upon them, his demand for attention to the poor and the hurt sounded less appealing, especially as they would be a small minority again. . . . There he was favoring rent control, while free enterprisers were preparing to charge what an undersupplied market would bear for apartments.[6]

Lyndon Johnson also lost power in large measure because he did not change his approach or style as the environment changed around him. Mired in the Vietnam War, he announced in the spring of 1968 that he would not seek to run for president that year. His problem, however, was more than the war and his inability to extricate the United States from a set of commitments that made little sense from a foreign policy perspective. Johnson had built his career on making private, secret deals, on telling one thing to one group, and another thing to another, on getting things done surreptitiously. But the 1960s ushered in the age of television news. The war was on America's televisions every night, and it was difficult to keep the real progress of the war far from the American public. Johnson had obtained congressional approval for the escalation of the war with the Gulf of Tonkin Resolution, so named because of an incident in the waters off Vietnam in which North Vietnamese boats ostensibly attacked U.S. warships, escalating the conflict. In subsequent hearings on the incident, the evidence seemed to indicate that the event was largely fabricated to provoke the U.S. Congress into taking the action that Johnson wanted. Johnson had prevailed on his friend, Senator William Fulbright from Arkansas, not to hold real hearings on the resolution, and to push it through the Senate with only two dissenting votes. Subsequently, Fulbright discovered that he had been deceived, and became one of the major leaders of the opposition to the war.

. . . if the Senate and Fulbright had been noted for their lack of assertiveness in the serious questioning of American foreign policy, then that era ended with the Tonkin Resolution. A new age would dawn, in which all the major assumptions of American foreign policy would be challenged, and Bill Fulbright, the least likely adversary for Johnson, feeling personally betrayed, would become the leader of a hostile and bitter opposition which no longer believed anything emanating from the White House. . . . The old order, the assumption that the executive branch knew better because it was privy to better inside information, would end, as would the corollary, that the President of the United States could be trusted.[7]

In this and other episodes, the issue was not just the war, but Johnson's credibility. A political style that had worked wonderfully in the days of backroom politics and private arrangements served Johnson poorly when the task became convincing the American people, through the medium of television, of his sincerity and trustworthiness. And why should Johnson have done anything differently? He had risen from the hill country of Texas to the presidency using exactly the same behaviors, the same approach, that would now cause him to lose credibility, allies, and power. He had even won on the Tonkin Resolution itself, but the short-term victory had been purchased at a terrific long-term cost.

To avoid losing power we need to be sensitive to sometimes subtle changes in the environment, and to understand how a particular style, a particular set of activities, and a particular approach are effective because they fit the customs and concerns of a specific era. We also need the flexibility to adjust our behavior to accommodate the new reality, even if this means abandoning well-worn habits. People in power are seldom challenged or given bad news, and even when challenged, they have a tendency to reject the discrepant information. Having developed particular skill at one way of doing things or thinking about problems, they are not always skilled with alternative approaches. It is no wonder, then, that changing circumstances often produce, with some lag, a dynamic that causes those in power to lose that power.

EASY COME, EASY GO

People who arrive at powerful positions without working their way up, without experience in acquiring and holding onto power, often lose power simply because they lack insight about its dynamics. Although it may seem a stroke of good fortune to be installed in a high-level, powerful position without having to struggle to reach it, the good fortune is occasionally short-lived. In working your way into a job, you build networks of relations and gain a lot of specific institutional knowledge that an outsider would lack. This phenomenon helps us understand why the entrepreneurs who start organizations are often displaced from power as the organizations grow and develop. Beginning the organization, they started at the top, and often lack sensitivity to the nuances of power relationships that pose a threat to them later.

In the fall of 1967, Semon E. (Bunkie) Knudsen, head of General Motors' nonauto and overseas operations, lost to Edward Cole in the competition to become president of the company. Although a high-level executive and a multimillionaire, Knudsen was disappointed at being passed over for the top job, and he let his feelings be known. Henry Ford, working largely in secret and behind the scenes, met with Knudsen and offered him the job of president of Ford Motor Company, which Knudsen assumed in February of 1968. Knudsen, whose father had been fired from Ford in 1921 before taking over the Chevrolet division at GM and triumphing over Ford in the automobile market, had worked at GM for some 29 years. As a visible, high-level executive with historical as well as personal ties to the automobile industry, he was, in many ways, a trophy executive for Ford.

Knudsen's abrupt firing 19 months later occurred with little public explanation. The evidence indicates, however, that Knudsen had two problems: 1) he ran the company with a strong hand, bothering both Ford and other high-level executives, and 2) he was quite unsuccessful in managing his political relationships with Lee Iacocca and other Ford executives who reported to him. Knudsen came in as an outsider to the organization, and he had little knowledge of the established power centers, virtual fiefdoms, which were jealously guarded by the executives to whom they belonged. Moreover, the Ford executives, although in some sense rivals with each other for power, were nevertheless bound together by long associations and working relationships. Knudsen, as an outsider, was an easy target.

From all the descriptions of General Motors, it is an organization in which hierarchy matters a great deal, and orderly succession and planning is the byword. Ford was much more tumultuous, much less likely to have planned, orderly executive successions, and much more political. Knudsen, with the title of president, thought he had the formal authority that went with that title. In major conflicts over styling with Iacocca, the person responsible for the Mustang and the Maverick, Knudsen took on a man who belonged to the board of directors and who had the advantage over him in the area of conflict.

And, we might ask—why was he hired by Ford in the first place? To take a swipe at GM? To show GM that Ford could hire one of their senior executives? To redress a historical error—to hire from GM the son of the man who had been forced out of Ford and had helped build GM? To the extent any of these explanations are accurate, Ford's objectives were largely achieved by the act of hiring Knudsen. After that, he was on his own, and would have to make his own way through the corporate minefields. It is not clear Knudsen even understood this, nor did he have the ties and experience that would give him power, beyond his title, in the organization.

Why would a 31-year-old justice department lawyer be named counsel to the president, and be given major responsibility for issues of profound sensitivity, including actually running the Watergate cover-up? In other words, what made John Dean such an attractive candidate to the Nixon White House? Possibly it was his very lack of experience and of political contacts. He depended for his job on the men who hired him, Haldeman and Erlichman, and thus, they could certainly count on his subservience and his loyalty. Dean's lack of an independent power base, his tremendous awe of and dependence on Nixon and the White House staff, made it difficult for him to resist being drawn into a lot of illegal activities, for which he ultimately received a criminal conviction and served time in jail. He didn't work his way up through the staff, or even through the Washington political establishment. This left him without allies or supporters to take care of him in a highly politicized and difficult working environment.

In earlier chapters we saw how Steve Jobs, because of his

position as founder of Apple, felt as though he did not have to build alliances with board members or even his senior management. This pattern is quite common among founders of firms, particularly the technological stars, who are often removed as the firm develops. Some observers have attributed this to the need for different skills and capabilities as the firm develops. They argue that in the beginning, you need a product, which often entails some technical breakthrough. Later on, financing, marketing, and general management skills become more critical. There is clearly an evolution in terms of the competencies required as organizations develop, but my view is that the real problem with the entrepreneur is the failure to understand the importance of developing power bases within the organization. It is this, rather than the change in business issues, that seems to explain why some entrepreneurs survive and others lose their jobs as their firms develop.

The lesson here is that first of all, if someone offers you a position of more prestige or power than you thought you had any right to expect, you should ask what their motives are, and what the pitfalls of the situation are. Sometimes we are brought in, without a power base of relationships or organization-specific knowledge, to serve an agenda. It behooves us to be aware of what that agenda is. Second, one should never assume that the formal position, be it founder, president, or White House counsel, is sufficient to maintain power over a protracted period of time. Power has many sources, and position, as we have seen, is only one. Those who plan for long-term survival are quick to use their position to build other sources of power, and never believe that the position itself gives them more security than it really does.

PRIDE, PRIVILEGE, AND PATIENCE

Power is lost because changed circumstances render previous skills or networks obsolete and because people may acquire positions without learning enough about power dynamics in their organization. Power is also lost because once in a position of power, it is sometimes irresistibly tempting for

us to reap the benefits of our position immediately. We sometimes let power go to our heads, forgetting that authority is
always the consequence of a relationship between those with
power and those who grant that power. Pride, the seizure of
privilege, and the lack of patience occasionally combine to
cause the downfall of those in power.

In 1990, Larry Horner was ousted as chairman of KPMG
Peat Marwick, one of the largest accounting firms in the
world. His replacement, Jon C. Madonna, had little international experience, even though Peat Marwick's international
business is an important part of its operations and a major
source of future growth. Why was Horner ousted? His pride
and his pursuit of privilege play a large role in the explanation. Horner made $1.2 million in his last year as chairman,
more than 10 times what the lowest-level Peat Marwick partner made in that year, and indeed, almost 10 times the earnings that the average partner in the firm earned in 1989. The
firm granted him a $1 million loan at prime plus one percent-
age point to help him purchase a $2 million apartment in
New York when he moved there from California in 1984 to
become chairman. Whenever he travelled on business, the
firm paid for a chauffeur-driven gray Cadillac. And, in 1987,
the partners had agreed to a change that permitted retiring
Peat partners to receive up to 40% of their pay with the maxi-
mum payment no longer capped at $200,000.[8]

But the privileges, though lavish, were not the sole problem. Peat Marwick has had a history of deposing its chairmen, and a strong populist streak runs through the firm.
Horner had added three vice chairmen to the nine already
in place, so there were now 12 well-paid vice chairmen in
the firm. Of the 1,850 Peat partners at the time of the election
for chairman, some 751 had become partners in just the past
six years.[9] This tended to increase populist sentiment in the
firm. There were many in the firm not likely to pay deference
to seniority, since they had little of it themselves. Horner
named a task force to study the firm's governance structure,
but he apparently packed the committee, which wound up
recommending no change. And, instead of picking Madonna,
the person who eventually succeeded him, as his running
mate in the partnership election, Horner chose K. Dane
Booksher, "who seemed far less promising and certainly not

as charismatic, or so the partners said."[10] In spite of being
urged by partners around the country to choose a different
running mate, Horner stubbornly refused, and at the last minute, pulled out of the race for chairman when it was quite
clear he would not be elected. Horner, in an organization
with an elected chairman, had done little to cater to his constituents' feelings. It was difficult for him, and understand-
ably so, to let partners, many of whom were quite young,
force him to choose a running mate that was not his first
choice, and to compel a reorganization he did not agree with.
He was the chairman of the firm, he had done great things
for the organization, and he was reluctant to take actions that
symbolically showed his dependence on his partners. This
sense of pride was costly in his quest to maintain power.

To be proud is to think that you are almost invariably right,
and to fail to bend to the needs of others. It is to set yourself
above and apart from others, and thus to forfeit their support.
It is a way of behaving that leaves you vulnerable to attack,
as Robert Moses discovered near the end of his career. The
undoing of Robert Moses began with an incident concerning
the building of a parking lot for a restaurant, the Tavern-on-
the-Green, in Central Park in New York City, in 1956. The
restaurant was owned by Arnold Schleiffer, under a lease
from the city that provided that he pay 5% of his gross income
to the city. The restaurant charged high prices and was in an
excellent location. Moreover, Schleiffer's lease provided that
he could repair and renovate the restaurant, and deduct the
costs of these improvements from his rent payments. In a
four-year period, the restaurant had collected $1,786,000, but
after offsetting costs of improvements, had paid the city only
$9,000, less than half of 1%.[11] The arrangement was typical
with Moses's favored concessionaires, as it enabled him to
partly bypass the cumbersome city budgeting machinery for
capital improvements and to circumvent other budgetary restrictions. The concessionaires knew that they owed Moses
handsomely for their profits, and as a consequence, they were
more than willing to throw huge parties, lavish dinners and
receptions, and in general, to spend money in ways that Moses directed.

A group of mothers, including some very prominent and
rich mothers, learned of the plans to build a parking lot and

thereby destroy a small glen, by finding some plans left lying around when a group of workers went for lunch. The mothers immediately began organizing a protest. Although this protest would turn out to be different, Moses, inured to park protests and accustomed to getting his way, was both insensitive and imprudent in his handling of the situation:

> Local protest over a park "improvement" . . . was an old one [story] to Moses—old and boring. Ever since he had become Park Commissioner he had kept such protest to a minimum by keeping the "improvements" secret, so that . . . it was already under way, and by ignoring protest and going ahead with the "improvement" as if it didn't exist. . . . On the seismograph on which Moses recorded public tremors, in fact, the Tavern-on-the-Green protest had barely registered. Twenty-three mothers? He had just finished evicting hundreds of mothers rather than shift a section of his Cross-Bronx Expressway a single block! He was at that very moment in the process of displacing *five thousand* mothers for Manhattantown, *four thousand* for Lincoln Center![12]

But this protest was to be different. The opponents were wealthy and sophisticated, and they knew how to use the media. The 1950s were not the 1930s and 1940s—times had changed, and along with them, people's attitudes toward large-scale public construction projects that covered over open space and displaced people. And this was an issue not about public housing, or about building a road, but rather, about building a parking lot, for an expensive private restaurant, in Central Park. Moses was going to cut down trees. And the opponents, skilled in staging a protest, made sure that mothers with baby carriages were there to be photographed by the news media. The newspapers called it the Battle for Central Park.

Moses would win out, but only temporarily. He had a fence built in the middle of the night, so that when construction started on April 24, the mothers and their children could not get close to the construction site. He controlled police, construction crews, and contractors who knew that they owed him their livelihood. The construction began under the cover of darkness, as had many of his other improvements, but this time it served to provoke an angry and outraged reaction from the media and even from his supporters.

Thirty years before, Robert Moses had leapt on the front pages in a single bound—in stories that portrayed him as a fighter for parks, as a faithful, selfless, public servant. . . . The image would never be whole again. Tuesday, April 24, 1956, the day that Robert Moses sent his troops into Central Park, was Robert Moses' Black Tuesday. For on it, he lost his most cherished asset: his reputation. The Moses Boom had lasted for thirty years. Now it was over.[13]

Robert Moses had won so many battles, fought so many opponents over his 30 years in public life, that he had become disdainful of opposition, and overconfident of his own capabilities. He left for a 24-day trip to Spain with his wife even as the controversy was raging. Of course, the cost to him was not just in the loss of this battle. He eventually retreated, and built a playground rather than a parking lot. The cost was in his reputation, a reputation as a public servant, and a reputation as someone who was invincible, and therefore one to avoid in a fight:

The aura of invincibility, the aura that had been so important to him in the past, the aura that had lasted for thirty years, was gone, destroyed in a day just as the aura of infallibility had been destroyed.[14]

After that, it was never the same for Robert Moses, who had let his pride and his arrogance, his belief in his own powers, cause him to disdain his opponents. Never underestimate your opponents. If you prepare too carefully, and take too many precautions, you may waste some effort. But if you underestimate what you are up against, you can lose, and losing even one battle may signal the decline of your power.

Power can also be lost through a lack of patience—through trying to do too much, too soon, and being too greedy in seizing the spoils of a recent victory. This was essentially what happened to Lew Glucksman, after he ousted Pete Peterson from Lehman Brothers. Glucksman obtained full control of the firm on July 26, 1983. Beginning in July, the operating committee, with Glucksman in charge, began meeting to distribute bonuses and shares of the firm's stock. Glucksman had long resented what he considered the disproportionate share of the profits that went to the investment banking side of Lehman. As a person from sales and trading, he thought that side of the house, which had recently brought in income at a greater rate than banking, deserved more of the profits. And now, as CEO, he moved quickly—perhaps too quickly—to put his friends in power and to distribute rewards to himself and his allies.

By the fall of 1983, Glucksman had placed his own person at the head of most of the firm's 12 departments. This included making some strange management changes. Richard Fuld, Jr., who had been running the fixed income division, became supervisor of both the fixed income and equities division. He was just 37 years old, and a stranger to most of the partners because he was said to be "defiantly antisocial."[15] Glucksman named Sheldon Gordon, whose career had been entirely in sales and trading, to run the investment banking division. Although he delayed formally naming Robert Rubin president and his righthand man, he did begin the process of moving him into the highest management ranks by putting him on the seven-person operating committee that ran the day-to-day affairs of the firm. Rubin was also not widely liked by the other partners, for although he was known as a brilliant man, he was also considered to be prickly and private.

Glucksman brought in two outside partners, giving them a substantial number of shares, without the board's full knowledge or consent. And he was particularly greedy with respect to bonuses and shares for himself and his friends. At the board meeting on September 21, barely two months after taking over, Glucksman's plans for the firm and its profits were clear:

> Lew Glucksman and four other senior executives received 25 percent of the total bonus pool. Glucksman's bonus jumped from $1.25 million to $1.5 million. . . . Sheldon Gordon went from $400,000 to $1 million. . . . in September 1983, Glucksman's shares rocketed from 3,500 to 4,500. Rubin went from 2,500 to 2,750 shares; Shel Gordon and Dick Fuld went from 2,500 to 2,750 shares. . . . What appeared to be a disproportionately large number of bankers had their slice of the pie reduced and reapportioned among the trading departments.[16]

The board went along, but many partners were angry. In a partnership, trust is everything, and Glucksman had, in less than three months, destroyed the trust of the investment banking side of the house and even dismayed some of his own allies. By the end of the year, six partners had announced their intention to leave the firm, and with their departure would go their capital, so desperately needed in the increasingly competitive 1980s securities business. The threat over the flight of capital, and the capital question, would finally cause the firm to be sold to American Express. But it was Glucksman's hasty actions that discomfited the partnership and ultimately led both to the sale of the firm and to Glucksman's departure. He had worked hard to climb up the ladder at Lehman, and had struggled to get rid of his co-CEO, Peterson. Once in power, he had rushed to enjoy the fruits of his victory, and as a consequence the firm he had taken over was sold out from under him. By April 1984, Lehman had ceased being a private partnership, and was now part of Shearson and American Express.

The lessons from Glucksman's loss of power were summed up by a former partner: "If you were Machiavelli . . . you would have been modest in your own bonus and stock. You would have shored up your weaknesses in banking."[17] Organizations entail interdependence. Regardless of your power or your position, your dependence on others remains. How tempting it is to gloat or to revel in the power you have worked so hard to obtain, and to receive some payoff from your efforts. But, seeking too many benefits too early will invariably undermine the foundations of your power.

TIME PASSES

According to Smith's biography of William Paley of CBS, as he grew older and more infirm, Paley asked, "Why do I have to die?"[18] Armand Hammer, of Occidental Petroleum, died at the age of 92 still holding his position as CEO. Robert Moses finally lost power when he threatened to resign from his positions and Governor Nelson Rockefeller took him up on the threat. Moses was annoyed that he had to ask Rockefeller to sign a special waiver exempting him from the state's mandatory retirement laws, because he was in his 70s at the time. Welch Pogue was still the managing partner of the Washington office of Jones, Day at the age of 79. Aging is inevitable, and thus at its limit, it is inevitable that regardless of our wealth, or fame, or brilliance, we will finally lose power, if not from mandatory retirement, which is now against the law for many positions, then from infirmity and death.

A discussion of the psychology of letting go is beyond the scope of this book, but it is easy to see why, having worked hard to attain a position of power and the perquisites that come with it, one is not likely to go quietly. There are a few exceptions, however. Arjay Miller, former president of Ford and dean of Stanford's business school, used to quote the advice of another former Stanford dean and corporate executive, Ernie Arbuckle, to the effect that after ten years in a position, it was time to move on. Arbuckle was a senior executive at Wells Fargo, dean at Stanford, and then chairman of Saga Foods for a time. Although we might applaud such sentiments, it is not wise to count on our leaders having them.

Therefore, perhaps the best way to deal with losing power is to institutionalize the process. By fixing the terms of office, by fixing mandatory replacement mechanisms, in other words, by regularizing succession, we reduce the stigma of losing power and make it part of the normal course of events. As such, the trauma is less, both for the individuals involved and for their organizations. Eldon Crowell, the government contracts lawyer who precipitated the split at Jones, Day, and who founded Crowell and Moring, a firm that now has more than 150 attorneys, learned something from Welch Pogue. The new firm is governed by an elected executive committee, with the stipulation that no person can serve more than three successive one-year terms without going off the governing body for at least a year. Did Crowell, the named partner and co-founder, follow this rule? Absolutely. And in forcing himself to share power, he built a healthier organization, which was less dependent on a single person, and also a somewhat healthier life for himself.

What we want to learn, then, is both how to avoid losing power prematurely and how to leave our positions gracefully. Understanding our role in the system by which organizations operate and are governed will help us to achieve both of these goals.

17

Managing Political Dynamics
Productively

After Xerox had lost half of its market share in the copier business, it should have been clear that change was needed. Yet when David Kearns came to power in the early 1980s, he faced skepticism and resistance. General Motors lost one-third of its market share in the 1980s. Again, however, there was reluctance to change—reluctance to learn from its joint venture with Toyota,[1] reluctance to cede control to a new breed of manager, and reluctance to reform the culture. The change that brought John Sculley to Apple Computer and the company to a different product strategy was wrenching, in spite of evidence of problems in the direction of the company. Change and adaptation come only after great internal, customarily political, struggle. Why is change so difficult? And if, indeed, adaptation and innovation normally come about only through the operation of power and political dynamics, what does this fact reveal about the dysfunctions of power and the trade-offs and judgments involved in managing political dynamics productively? These are the topics for this chapter.

THE POLITICS OF CAREER DYNAMICS

People enter organizations, and some of them subsequently do better than others, in terms of promotion to higher-level positions and in terms of informal power and status.[2] Organizations, whether or not they recognize it, have in place career systems that tend to reward and encourage some activities and skills more generously than others. For instance, as we have seen, in the U.S. automobile industry for much of the 1960s and 1970s, financial and analytical skills were venerated, while knowing something about actually building and selling cars was considered somewhat less valuable. On Wall Street at about the same time, many firms, including E.F. Hutton, were losing their retail focus, chasing after the merger and acquisitions market and creating new, sophisticated financial instruments largely sold to institutions. Sometimes the careers and skills to be rewarded were consciously chosen as part of an organization's strategy, and sometimes not. It hardly matters, since inevitably and invariably, all organizations have a career system in which some kinds of activities and abilities are more highly rewarded.

Therefore, those who rise to positions of influence and who benefit from this career system have a particular set of skills and have engaged in a particular set of activities—those favored by that system. What happens when a change is needed, when the old ways, the old career system, fail to produce the competencies necessary to cope with changing environmental circumstances? It is not likely that those promoted and rewarded by a particular career system for a specific set of competencies are now going to turn their back on that system—particularly because, except for the person at the very top, these individuals are, in fact, still climbing the organizational ladder. To change the rules is to discredit the very source of their success, and to make their chances of rising any farther unlikely. Even if the person at the top (who, after all, has the least to lose in terms of future promotion possibilities) wants to change, those in the ranks immediately below have nothing to gain and much to lose from changing the criteria for success.

And even if they were not wedded to the past by what put them in their present position, they might not be able to change anyway. Education and experience both enrich and deepen our understanding, but they also leave us with a particular set of blinders. There is an old saying that goes, "Education means you know more and more about less and less," and the same can be said for experience in an organization.

This is the compelling lesson learned by considering Robert McNamara and the other brilliant people in the Kennedy and then Johnson administrations who were so mistaken about Vietnam. They were successful because they had developed a particular form of analytical insight. Not only were they not likely to discredit that ability in favor of some other, of which they possessed less, but they were blinded by their own skills and capabilities to the possibility of another way of decision making.

If this is true, then where does change in organizations come from? Not from the insiders, with their intellectual blinders and their vested interests. Rather, innovation, adaptation, and change almost always come from someone at least partly outside the mainstream. Sometimes the person will be, literally, an outsider, such as John Sculley at Apple, or Ross Johnson at Nabisco. After Standard Brands merged with Nabisco and Ross Johnson became president and chief operating officer of the combined firm, he immediately began to change the company's culture and its method of operation. Nabisco was a company that was living on its past successes:

> In the seventies, Nabisco was run by decent, slow-moving executives who fostered a culture that venerated past glories. Good men all, but change agents they weren't. . . . Nabisco stagnated. No one was fired. No one worked past five. No one raised a voice. . . . Then along came Ross Johnson.[3]

Johnson and his Standard Brands people challenged presentations at meetings, questioned how people were spending their time and what was the focus of attention, and imparted a spirit of change:

> Nabisco executives prided themselves on the company's elaborate planning procedures, compiled in thick, multiyear projections and operations outlooks. Johnson chucked them all. "Planning, gentlemen, is 'What are you going to do next year that's different from what you did this year?' " he told them.[4]

On occasion the agent of change will be someone just slightly removed from the main power structure such as Donald Petersen at Ford, David Kearns at Xerox, or Robert Stempel, the most recent CEO at General Motors. For instance, it was said of Stempel:

> Stempel had a history of being more nontraditional. . . . he possessed the rare talent of being able to raise objections without sounding critical. . . . He was known as a boss who really listened to his people.[5]

Sometimes, of course, the outsiders are so far outside the mainstream of their organization that the only way they can get their ideas implemented is to leave, either to found their own company or to join another that recognizes their point of view. Thus, for instance, Renn Zaphiropoulos had an idea, while working at Varian, for the development of an electrostatic printer that transformed information from a computer tape into graphical form and made it visible on paper. When Varian was uninterested in the idea, Zaphiropoulos formed Versatec, which Xerox purchased in the late 1970s. The last time I checked, Versatec itself was larger than Varian, the company that had been the home of its founder. Many of the startups in the Silicon Valley, as well as elsewhere, were formed not because their founders were greedy to get rich, but because they could find no other way to get their ideas implemented.

The question, then, is how to incorporate new perspectives and new ideas, which often involve shifting the power distribution in the organization, without so much trauma and turmoil that the organization is destroyed in the process. Power dynamics are critical for organizational adaptation and change. The ideal is to manage the dynamics so that change is produced, without either squelching political processes and thereby destroying the capacity for adaptation, or on the other hand, letting conflict get so out of control that the organization self-destructs. Needless to say, as in most instances in which a balance is required, general rules are not available. We can certainly consider some of the issues and trade-offs, but the application of these ideas is highly contingent on the specific circumstances.

PROBLEMS WITH POWER DYNAMICS

Just as hierarchy and common vision have difficulties associated with them as ways of getting things done, so, too, do power and influence. In considering potential difficulties with power dynamics in organizations, we can come to appreciate more fully how important power is as a source of adaptation, and what the trade-offs may be in inhibiting political processes.

One problem with power dynamics is that it takes time, energy, and effort to engage in attempts at intraorganizational influence, and some see these efforts as a waste of organizational resources. For instance, two economists wrote:

> The time and effort spent on influence activities (and in dealing with them) are resources with valuable alternative uses. Yet to the extent that influence activities are aimed at shifting the distribution of the net benefits of decisions among the members of the organization, these activities need bring no efficiency gain to the organization that offsets the costs involved.[6]

The problems that economists highlight are so-called agency problems in organizational decision making. Some people are empowered to make decisions, but to do so, they must often rely on information supplied by others within the organization. These others may be affected by the decisions that are made, and as a consequence, have an interest in distorting the information they supply so that it favors their interests. Since each party affected by a decision has similar incentives to engage in this political activity, a lot of energy may be spent on politicking, without anything very productive being accomplished.

One way of ameliorating this problem is to reduce the incentives or reasons to engage in political activity. This can be done by dividing organizational rewards more evenly. If there is nothing substantial to be gained from attempts at influence, because everyone fares about the same in any event, the influence attempts should diminish. For instance, it may be efficient to reduce the variation in wages among organizational members; this will lessen influence attempts to affect career outcomes such as promotions and wages. In general, distributing organizational resources (such as capital budgets, additional personnel, and so forth) more equally can be an effective way to reduce influence activities and the time and effort consumed by them.

There is little doubt that influence activities waste time and energy. The struggle for control of Lehman Brothers entailed a string of partner meetings, negotiations over Peterson's financial settlement, and meetings of the Lehman board of directors. While partners gossiped in the halls, work was not being done. And after Glucksman took over, there was more politicking over the division of the firm's shares and profits, which entailed more meetings and more informal discussion. This fighting over compensation was intensified by the fact that Glucksman was going to change past practice and also consolidate the rewards. The stakes were substantial. In much the same way,

> "Hutton's compensation system, if you can call it that, was run like a combination beauty contest and tug-of-war," Neal Eldridge [an outside consultant] recalls. . . . "It was the squeaky-wheel system of corporate compensation."[7]

The problem with the squeaky-wheel system is that the production of the squeaking diverts efforts from other activities, potentially of more benefit to the firm. Indeed, under Fomon, there was so much politicking over succession at all levels that the management system of E.F. Hutton virtually ground to a halt, with adverse consequences for the organization.

The difficulty with more equal allocations as a means to minimize such struggles for influence is that it precludes the possibility of using contingent allocation schemes. An equal distribution of capital budgets across operating divisions will hinder the reallocation of assets to the most productive uses. The allocation of salaries on a more equal basis will gratify those who would otherwise be lower in the salary distribution, but the outstanding performers, who might otherwise have received higher salaries, will be unhappy with the results and may leave the organization in consequence. There may, however, be less extreme examples of rules that can benefit the organization by being readily understood and unambiguously applied. To the extent that organizations can agree on goals and on measures of progress toward goal attainment, influence activities can be reduced. In the absence of this condition, however, influence costs may be a form of "transaction" cost—a cost of governance inherent in making decisions under conditions of uncertainty and heterogeneity.

In determining how much conflict can exist in a healthy organization, we would do well to remember that not all conflict is harmful. Differences of opinion are useful and important for forming judgments that take all available information and points of view into account. The story is told that Alfred Sloan, when he ran General Motors in the 1920s and 1930s, would refuse to make a decision at a meeting if no one could argue a strong case against what was being proposed. He felt that if no one had any objections to what was being decided, it was because they had not thought long and hard enough about the question under consideration. Sloan recognized that all important issues in organizations have multiple dimensions, and he wanted to be sure that all sides of a question had been thoroughly examined before something was decided. Sometimes conflict takes on a personal tone, however, and no longer concerns issues or substance, but rather winning a fight or harming the other person or group. Conflict can be bitter, focused on personalities, and unproductive rather than illuminating. To the extent that power struggles result in destructive conflict, organizations are harmed.

When Robert P. Rittereiser was hired from Merrill Lynch to become president of Hutton, and Fomon's heir apparent, he brought in his own people to staff the major functions. But he drew these people from numerous organizations, ranging from Salomon Brothers to American Express to Citicorp to Deloitte, Haskins, and Sells, the Big Eight accounting firm. Rittereiser was not a strong leader, and the various people hired had no history with each other, no common perspective, and no shared vision for the firm. Consequently, there was a lot of jockeying for position:

> "It was a fever for power—all the guys on Rittereiser's executive committee suffered from it. They spent more time battling each other for rank and position and clout than in trying to turn the firm around."[8]

At Xerox, the people at the Palo Alto Research Center were rivals with the people from Scientific Data Systems (SDS), acquired by Xerox to help the firm enter the computer industry:

> SDS belittled the very idea of PARC and lacked the capacity to develop inventions into products; many of PARC's computer scientists scoffed at SDS's talents. . . . PARC and SDS antagonized each other from the outset.[9]

When people at PARC developed a time-sharing system using a competitor's computer, SDS was furious and the hostility intensified. Needless to say, this ill-will did not help interunit cooperation or the development of viable products for the computer industry.

Interdepartmental conflict is not inevitable even when there is both interdependence and diversity in perspective. The interdepartmental conflict at Apple was encouraged by the attitude of Steve Jobs toward the other divisions.[10] In Lehman, Peterson's preoccupation with external relations and his lack of interaction with his partners helped to provoke Glucksman's resentment and also left the firm prone to internecine conflict. The conflict between the Washington and Cleveland offices of Jones, Day occurred partly because methods of operation in the two offices had never truly meshed. The Washington office had been brought into the firm through a merger, and, initially, had a different name, different compensation, and a different management structure, as well as a different type of legal practice. Little was done to bridge these differences.

In some instances, interdepartmental conflict arose from the particular personal idiosyncrasies of the various members and executives. Such conflicts were worse when no efforts were made to manage them constructively and to unite the organization around a common vision and a common set of external threats. In that regard, it is perhaps not surprising that Apple Computer, Lehman Brothers, Xerox, and even Jones, Day all seemed to share two characteristics—a lack of strong, unifying leadership, and a munificent [Generous] economic environment that did not pose the kind of threat that would motivate people within the firm to work together.

A second problem that can arise if power dynamics are not managed successfully is delay. Power and influence processes take time, and this can result in delays in decisions and actions. I recall doing some executive training for a large grocery store chain. At that time, the organization was filled with internal dissent. One group consisted of the traditional grocery store management and operations people. They saw experience in the stores as critical to success and were interested in making operations a stronger focus of the company. There were finance types who disagreed. The financial community, they argued, viewed the grocery business as a nice, stable cash-generating activity, but one in which margins were low, competition intense, and growth limited. If the firm remained so focused on its core grocery business, it would be ripe for a hostile bid of some kind (a forecast that, in retrospect, turned out to be quite prescient, given the leveraged buyouts and hostile takeovers that have occurred in the industry). The finance people wanted to do lots of strategic analyses and diversify the firm into other businesses, such as pharmacies, nurseries, and other retail businesses that might be located in the same centers as the firm's grocery stores, as well as the manufacture of food and dairy products. The firm was also divided geographically. It had a very strong presence in California, but operated in other areas of the United States and overseas as well. The various divisions contended with each other for capital funds. The California division claimed that it was supporting the losses and capital expenditures of other parts of the operation, and wanted to keep more of the profits for itself. Other territories argued that they operated in less competitive environments and offered the firm the opportunity for growth. The firm had a very strong legal department, which tended to evaluate all potential actions in terms of their impact on antitrust and labor law. And, the real estate division argued that the firm, in fact, enjoyed most of its competitive success from its outstanding real estate locations. Given this strength in the firm, the division thought there should be more activity in shopping center and retail development, to capitalize on the real estate expertise in the organization.

Each point of view had merit, and each point of view was represented by strong advocates in the highest councils of the firm. The problem was that while the debate about what to do went on, and on, and on, lower-level managers were afraid to take almost any action at all. It was at this firm that I first heard the expression, "When the elephants fight, the ants get stepped on." The ants, indeed, scurried for cover, and didn't do anything that could be postponed. Decisions on store remodelling were put off, decisions on expansion were made only after long delays, and the organization lost potential locations because it could not decide if, and where, it was going to expand. It was paralyzed by the conflict among the various interests.

As one might guess from this description, the organization did not have a strong president at the time. The president was young, comparatively inexperienced, and had obtained his job in part because his family owned a lot of stock in the company. That made the jockeying for position at the next level down even worse. Lacking a sense of what it was trying to do and a clear vision or strategic intent, the organization lost profits and opportunities for business development, as the fighting continued.

A third problem that can emerge in power dynamics is incomplete analysis. I am not convinced that analysis can resolve all business or organizational decision issues. On the other hand, data and information are often useful and necessary for making informed and intelligent decisions about what to do. As we saw in Chapter 13, power and influence in organizations sometimes cause the development of a pathology in which information is either ignored, or else sought in such a strategic, focused fashion that the process does not produce valid data.

There is perhaps no context that so clearly illustrates the problems of politics and influence supplanting analysis as the purchase and deployment of military goods and services in the United States. Nick Kotz has written a penetrating analysis of the military procurement system in general, and the B-1 bomber in particular.[11] To get support for the B-1 bomber from Michigan congressmen, the Air Force threatened to close Wurtsmith Air Force Base in northern Michigan. At a luncheon meeting of the Chamber of Commerce in Oscoda, Michigan, Lieutenant General Earl O'Loughlin, vice commander of the Air Force Logistics Command, warned:

"We have legislators in Michigan who have not defended the B-1 program—and those states with B-1 opponents will be the first to be cut!" . . . General O'Loughlin urged the chamber . . . to sponsor a letter-writing campaign to [Senators] Levin and Riegle protesting their positions on the B-1 . . . .[12]

The pressure apparently worked:

In press conferences and committee hearings, Levin sent his own message back home: "I may have been against building the B-1's, but they are being built and Wurtsmith is the right place to base them." . . . The only thing missing from that political process was any serious debate about what would be best for the national defense.[13]

The bombers were eventually based at Dyess Air Force Base in Texas, as a reward for John Tower's intervention and for his support of the Air Force; at McConnell Air Force Base near Wichita, Kansas, because of the influence and intervention of Senator Robert Dole; and at two other bases in the United States that made more sense militarily. The Texas base would require complex refueling of the bombers to reach the Soviet Union. The Kansas base was also not well located strategically, being near a major population center as well as a busy runway used by the Boeing Aircraft Company. Moreover, basing the B-1 bombers at McConnell would cost an extra $40 million, as the base had no facilities for storing nuclear weapons. But after Dole made it clear that his support for both military procurement and Reagan's tax reform were in jeopardy, McConnell got its B-1s.

The entire history of the B-1 bomber is a history of politics overriding (if not totally submerging) analyses of strategic needs, costs, and alternatives. The bomber was built in spite of, not because of, strategic analysis of its necessity. And the history of the program repeatedly demonstrated the willingness to suppress or forgo analysis to push through a decision based on the power of various interests. Numerous examples from the arena of military procurement illustrate the problems that can arise when analysis is either not done or is ignored.

Yet, these situations, too, involve trade-offs. The strategic, military consequences of bomber siting are, after all, only one of a set of consequences that arise from where and how much the country spends on military weapons systems. Bombers and military procurement provide economic benefits that, in some small communities, constitute virtually the lifeblood of the community. It is possible that the siting of the bombers was the least expensive way to jointly obtain the benefits of military deterrence as well as economic benefit for some communities. The point is that most decisions involve multiple dimensions, and when decisions incorporate dimensions that we believe are irrelevant, we sometimes claim that they are fundamentally flawed. They aren't flawed—they are just different from what an analysis that optimized along only one dimension might suggest was the right thing to do. As we learned earlier, numbers can be used to show almost anything. It is necessary, however, to have the numbers, even if your response is only to treat them skeptically. Trade-offs invariably need to be made—it is important to know the costs.

The competition among interests and perspectives, which creates challenges for managing political dynamics productively, springs out of exactly those conditions that we learned create power and influence situations in the first place. To remove the role of power—by equalizing distributions of organizational rewards, creating homogeneity in point of view, submerging differences of opinion—has its own costs. Managing power in organizations requires the ability to compromise.

There is one final point about managing political dynamics. A friend at Strategic Decisions Group, a management consulting firm, noted that one difficulty in managing organizations is that there is sometimes confusion about what stage the organization is in, or needs to be in. There are times when the firm needs to make a decision, times when change is required, and times when implementation is needed. The skills required to get something implemented are different from those required to change direction and policy, and both of these situations require skills that are different from those needed to figure out what to do in the first place. One of the critical tasks, then, in managing power dynamics productively, is to figure out what phase the organization ought to be in and how to get it operating effectively in the particular decision and action mode that is required. A second critical task is moving the organization from one stage or phase to another.

Some organizations get stuck in an implementation mode, and never re-evaluate what they are implementing. This was the problem with the Parks Commission under Robert Moses. Some organizations have difficulty in getting things implemented, even in the presence of great technical insights and analysis. Xerox in the 1970s possibly provides an example. Some organizations are great at making decisions using good information, and even skilled at implementing those decisions, but have difficulty in recognizing changed circumstances and in accomplishing fundamental change. Many organizations fit here, but certainly General Motors provides a classic case.

It is important to recognize that the political dynamics, and their potential problems and dysfunctions, differ across the different stages and processes. The types of influence skills necessary to accomplish change are somewhat different than the skills required to motivate great analysis, or to implement something that is basically agreed upon. Sensitivity to the potential problems that arise from power and influence, consideration of the various trade-offs, and an awareness of the stage of the organization's decision making can help, but certainly cannot guarantee, that we will have the insights necessary to manage these dynamics productively.

POWER AND PERFORMANCE

The potential problems that arise from political processes in organizations make it important to assess the relationship between power and influence processes and performance. Is it the case that in organizations with less power and influence in action, performance is better? Or is the relationship between power and performance more complex and contingent?

I should note at the outset that the most common assumption is that organizational power and influence processes impede performance. Tom Peters borrowed a copy of my earlier book on power.[14] Although he clearly attempted to restrain himself, when it was returned I noticed at several points in the margin the notation, "not in effective organizations." The conflict and politics described were not evident, he thought, in the most excellent organizations. And he was probably right, which is why many of them were no longer considered to be so excellent in a few years.[15] As Pascale has noted, there is a paradox. On the one hand, there are prescriptions for congruence among organizational systems, staffing, structure, strategy, and so forth. On the other hand, if there is too much congruence, too much complementarity among all of the organizational components, the organization may not be able to change or adapt to new circumstances.[16] This dilemma provoked Pascale to do detailed case studies of Ford, Honda, General Electric, and other large corporations to understand how organizations changed or transformed themselves.

Pascale's analysis focuses on planned efforts, albeit not always comprehensively planned. There is a sense of people seeing a problem and trying to figure out what to do about it; there is also, on occasion, a sense of luck helping to determine both success and failure. What there is not in this otherwise excellent analysis is any sense of individual or collective motives or interests, which must surely operate to help determine both what is attempted and what is finally implemented.

If fundamental change, including change in strategy, technology, approach to the market, and management of the work force, is not required—if, in other words, the organization's existing management and culture are successful and will continue to be so for the foreseeable future—then power and influence processes are at once unnecessary and inefficient. This is the situation implicitly assumed by economists and others who approach power and politics from an agency theory perspective. The presumption is that there is some intelligent, well-motivated principal who makes decisions on behalf of the organization. That individual may lack information or analytical capability, which is why he or she must rely on agents—the same agents who may seek to present information strategically to further their own interests or the interests of their units. But the principal himself is presumed to be interested in economic efficiency and organizational well-being. The problem is that in the real world, who is a principal and who is an agent is less than perfectly clear, and even chief executive officers often act not in the interests of the organization but in their own interests, to maintain power or control, to build an organization or a building that will serve as their legacy, and so forth. It is not clear that actual organizations possess the dispassionate efficiency maximizer we find in some models of organizations. If decision making is not problematic, in the sense that the motives or interests of the decision maker can be trusted, and if the environment is stable, then political infighting is a waste of time and energy.

Kathleen Eisenhardt and Jay Bourgeois studied eight small, high-tech firms in the microcomputer industry.[17] The largest firm had about 500 employees, the smallest had 50. They studied specific, important decisions concerning strategic direction and product development. They found that there were more politics when decision making was highly centralized in an authoritarian chief executive. They noted that "the more powerful a CEO, the greater the tendency among remaining executives to consolidate power and engage in alliance and insurgency behaviors."[18] Examining the relationship between politics and performance, they found that "the top management teams of the effective firms avoided politics, whereas the management teams of poor performers tended to use politics."[19] This was because: 1) politics consumed time and dissipated executive energy; 2) politics restricted the flow of information; and 3) in politically active top-management teams, perceptions about the opinions of others became distorted.

The carefully executed Eisenhardt and Bourgeois study is one of the very few to examine empirically the link between politics and performance in organizations. Consequently, its results should be carefully considered. First, as the authors note, it is possible that in addition to politics causing poor performance, poor performance may produce political behavior. Poor performance is likely to cause executives to feel insecure (and probably rightfully so) about their positions, which may produce more jockeying for position and attempts to avoid blame. Second, in this study, politics and authoritarian management were almost perfectly correlated. Authoritarian management is not likely to be effective in a rapidly changing, technologically complex environment. These were small firms without established market positions, operating in an area in which personal mobility to other firms was easy. It is likely that the authoritarian management style produced higher turnover and less-motivated performance from the technically critical employees. We cannot, then, tell whether the relationship between poor performance and politics is a direct one, or whether it springs indirectly out of the association of politics in this sample with authoritarian management, which is the real cause of the poor performance. But most important, these firms provide a context closest to that assumed in the models of economists. These are small organizations in which the principal is most likely to be the top manager, who probably has a significant ownership position. There is little of the incentive we saw in Hutton or Xerox to maintain power for its own sake; rather the very competitive nature of the environment and the strong equity interest would make the CEO quite likely to take actions in the organization's best interests. In that context, politics and information distortion work against making the highest-quality decisions. These are competitive, rapidly changing environments in which outcomes are likely to be known fairly quickly.

By contrast, consider the development of a weapons system for national defense, such as the Polaris system. The Polaris has been hailed as one of the most successful and effective of the weapons development programs undertaken in the United States. It had few critics, was considered to be a model of good management practice, and produced a weapons system important to the development of the country's nuclear deterrent capability. The development of a weapons system is not as readily evaluated in terms of its success or effectiveness as is a microcomputer firm. Sapolsky, who wrote an excellent case study of Polaris, suggested that "absence of criticism . . . can be taken as a mark of success, for it means that no one views the operation of a particular program or organization as inimical to his own interests or goals and that some may even perceive it as beneficial."[20]

The success of Polaris was not preordained at the time the program began. The three armed services were competing for a role in strategic offensive missiles, so the program faced "problems of jurisdictional competition and interagency coordination."[21] The question is, what was the role of politics in the performance of the Polaris program? Did it make the program less effective, as in the organizations observed by Eisenhardt and Bourgeois? Was the success of the Polaris program the result of an absence of struggles for power and influence?

Not according to Sapolsky, who concluded that it was the skill in bureaucratic politics of the backers and managers of the Polaris program that largely accounted for its success. Congressional and administrative support was obtained; interservice rivalry was managed; scientific expertise was mustered for the program as needed; and the network of interagency and interorganizational contracting relationships was successfully managed.

> The success of the Polaris program depended upon the ability of its proponents to promote and protect the Polaris. Competitors had to be eliminated; reviewing agencies had to be outmaneuvered; congressmen, admirals, newspapermen, and academicians had to be co-opted. Politics is a system requirement. What distinguishes programs in government is not that some play politics and others do not, but rather, that some are better at it than others.[22]

Sapolsky noted that even the famed management methods developed for the program, such as PERT charts and critical path analysis, were used largely for window dressing and to garner support. These methods of analysis did not necessarily have any substantive importance for evaluating or managing the program:

> Though the program innovativeness in management methods was, as I have tried to show, as effective technically as rain dancing, it was, nevertheless, quite effective politically. The Special Projects Office quickly learned that a reputation for managerial efficiency made it difficult for anyone to challenge the . . . development plans.[23]

A different environment meant that skill in politics was essential for success. And a similar result emerges from Finn Borum's study of organizational development in a hospital.[24] Borum's study was done as part of an organization development intervention. Eschewing the typical OD approach, which assumes common goals and consensus and which works with the upper strata of the organization, Borum and his colleagues worked with the personnel of a surgical unit to improve its effectiveness—first and foremost, by increasing the power of lower-level personnel. The intervention strategy began with the assumption that nothing would change until those who were suffering under the current system had enough power to force a change. He noted, "The strategy contains a stage in which the weaker party in the conflict improves its position of power vis-à-vis the stronger opponent. This can be accomplished either by strengthening the power base of the weaker party or by weakening the power bases of the stronger party."[25]

The problems of the surgical unit included: 1) variations in work load that did not correspond well to variations in staffing patterns; 2) poor relations between the unit (which was comprised of almost all female support personnel) and the (male) surgeons; and 3) a poor organizational climate, characterized by stress and discontent. The consultants' efforts focused on building up the power of the unit, so it could enter negotiations with others, particularly the surgeons, to change working arrangements. The intervention was successful. But not only was the surgical unit staff happier at the end, so too were the surgeons, and by most measures, the unit functioned more effectively.

Borum's study reminds us that problems of performance and effectiveness are problems of power and politics—power imbalances, powerlessness, and the inability of some groups to get their ideas or suggestions taken seriously. These problems are, of course, more likely to occur in a setting, such as a hospital, in which performance outcomes are difficult to assess at the total organizational level and there is not as much competitive pressure and emphasis on short-term results as one finds in the microcomputer firms.

The relationship between politics and performance is, then, a contingent one. Obviously, problems emanating from the dynamics of power interfere with effectiveness, and to the extent that steps are taken to alleviate them, performance will be enhanced. But beyond that, we can say it is probably the case that in larger organizations with more centralized control and institutionalized power, the skills of power and influence are critical to getting change accomplished. In smaller organizations, with owner-managers, with clearly measurable results, and with short feedback cycles, power and influence may get in the way of performance. The critical issue is whether in the absence of political activity the organization will both register and respond to its environment, or whether such activity is an integral part of the process of organizational change.

But, sadly, there are no guarantees. There are no assurances that the power and influence processes, even in a large organization, will result in making the organization effective. All investor-owned electric utilities have faced a vastly changed environment over the past several decades, and in all of them, there has been a rise in the power of law and finance. Few, however, have come to be as dominated by law and finance as Pacific Gas and Electric, as we have seen. PG&E changed its corporate objectives, implemented new financial planning and control systems, and became an organization in which many operating departments were headed by attorneys. Has this change helped PG&E effectively cope with its new environment?

The evidence from a case study is necessarily not going to be definitive, but the data do not support a picture of a vastly more effective corporation. Compare PG&E to Southern California Edison, a company operating in the same state regulatory environment, benefiting from many of the same favorable economic trends and conditions, but never coming to be dominated by attorneys to the same degree. In 1977, Southern California Edison had revenues of $2.06 billion and earnings per share of $1.90. By 1985, revenues had increased to $5.17 billion and earnings per share had grown to $3.26, a gain of 71.6%. In 1977, PG&E had revenues of $3.5 billion and earnings per share of $3.15. PG&E's revenues also increased dramatically over the period, growing to $8.4 billion by 1985. Its earnings per share, however, decreased to $2.65. I chose this period because the time from 1979 through 1984 was the time during which the lawyers gained substantial control over PG&E—it was a period of transition, and it is interesting to see the consequences of that transition.

Some will say the comparison isn't fair, and there is some validity to that point of view. One reason for PG&E's poor financial results is problems with its nuclear power plants. For instance, in 1983, PG&E decided to decommission Unit 3 at the Humboldt Bay Nuclear Power Plant. The state regulatory commission did not allow the company to recover all of its costs, resulting in an accounting loss of $37 million.

Also, its problems with Diablo Canyon Nuclear Power Plant were legendary. There was substantial opposition to granting the plant an operating license, and there were numerous delays in putting the plant in service, as well as tremendous cost overruns. Surely one cannot blame the regime of lawyers and finance types for difficulties that arose from an overzealous commitment to the problematic technology of nuclear power, which was made years before they arrived on the scene.

But it is not clear that they are totally blameless. Electric power, and particularly nuclear power, is a very political issue. One of the presumed advantages of attorneys is their ability to operate effectively in a politically charged regulatory environment. In the mid-1980s, staff members of the California Public Utilities Commission (CPUC) indicated that a new view of utility regulation was growing in prominence. This new position argued for more emphasis on the engineering and economic justification for capital investments and operating procedures, and a closer interface with more utility staff to discuss technical, economic, and environmental problems. The CPUC staff members, almost without exception, expressed dissatisfaction with PG&E's approach, explicitly mentioning that they preferred the relationship they had with Southern California Edison. Does this different perception of the two utilities fully account for their difference in financial problems? I doubt it. But it probably does have some effect on the relative profitability of the two otherwise quite similar companies.

This case indicates that change in large organizations is often the result of a political process, in which power dynamics play a prominent role. But such change does not guarantee a favorable outcome for the organization. Power and politics may be useful and necessary to align the organization with its environmental contingencies, but there are no guarantees that the process will inevitably work out well. Much depends on the distribution of political skills and interests among the various participants. We can say that power dynamics are often useful for organizational adaptation; we can say with much less assurance whether the changes they produce will be beneficial for organizational effectiveness or performance.

18

Managing with Power

It is one thing to understand power—how to diagnose it, what are its sources, what are the strategies and tactics for its use, how it is lost. It is quite another thing to use that knowledge in the world at large. And putting the knowledge of power and influence into action—managing with power—is essential for those who seek to get things accomplished:

> "There's a thing you learn at Data General, if you work here for any period of time," said West's lieutenant of hardware, Ed Rasala, "that nothing happens unless you push it."[1]

Computers don't get built, cities don't get rebuilt, and diseases don't get fought unless advocates for change learn how to develop and use power effectively. We saw that in the early 1980s the blood banks resisted testing for transfusion-transmitted AIDS, and even denied that a contaminated blood supply was a serious health risk. The 1980s saw an increase in the political skill of the AIDS lobby, and its tactics are now being borrowed by others:

> Women with breast cancer are taking a lesson from AIDS advocacy groups and using political action to urge the Federal and state governments to pay more attention to their disease. "They showed us how to get through to the government. . . . They took on an archaic system and turned it around while we have been quietly dying."[2]

Women's health issues are sorely underfunded compared to the proportion of women in the population, a situation that is likely to change if, and only if, power and influence are brought to bear on, and more importantly, *in* those organizations that fund medical research and regulate the pharmaceutical and medical industries.

In corporations, public agencies, universities, and government, the problem is how to get things done, how to move forward, how to solve the many problems facing organizations of all sizes and types. Developing and exercising power require having both will and skill. It is the will that often seems to be missing. Power and influence have a negative connotation. We hound politicians from office, and try to bring down those institutions or individuals that seek to do things differently or better. I wonder how many of us would have had the nerve or the courage to do what the young Henry Ford II did when the company that bears his name was in trouble in the 1940s?

Ford Motor Company was founded by Henry Ford II's grandfather. Although the elder Ford had tremendous engineering genius, and the Model T truly transformed the country, in his later years he was rigid, inflexible, autocratic, and virtually destroyed the company by failing to incorporate new technology and styling. Ford saw a criticism of the Model T as a criticism of him personally, so the competitive threat of Chevrolet was met with price cutting—eight times from 1920 to 1924, twice more in 1926.[3] Even after the Model A was introduced in 1927, the company continued to decline. Henry Ford, originally surrounded by bright engineers and innovative managers, soon surrounded himself with bodyguards and strongmen, including the notorious Harry Bennett, who carried a gun and who would, on occasion, take target practice while talking with visitors.

Even the brief triumph of the Model A did not halt the downward spiral of the company. Henry Ford remained locked in the past. He grew more erratic and finally senile. At the end of his life he believed that World War II did not exist, that it was simply a ploy made up by the newspapers to help the munitions industry. . . . It was a spectacular self-destruction, one that would never again be matched in a giant American corporation.[4]

By the time of World War II, the federal government actually considered taking over the company, because it was in such desperate managerial and financial condition that it could fail at any time, and the government badly needed its wartime production capabilities. In 1943, Secretary of the Navy Frank Knox discharged a 26-year-old Henry Ford II from the Navy. He had a bigger, more important job to do—to take over and then save the Ford Motor Company. Henry's father, Edsel Ford, had died of stomach cancer that same year at the age of 49. Although described as both gentle and brilliant, he had been totally dominated by the elder Ford, and had never played a major role in the company. The company had destroyed the second generation of Fords, and there were people who would have been quite happy to do the same thing with the third generation.

As Ford had grown older and more senile, effective control of the company had passed to the hands of Harry Bennett, head of the dreaded Ford Service Department, which was effectively a secret police force of hoodlums, gangsters, and ex-policemen, who exercised control through physical force. One story had it that when an employee violated the company's policy against smoking, Bennett personally shot the cigar from the man's mouth. With Edsel gone, and Henry Ford increasingly infirm, the only thing keeping Bennett from control of Ford was Henry Ford II.

Although Ford was in the company, with the title of vice president, Bennett constantly belittled him (as he had his father, Edsel). Moreover, the elder Ford had drawn up a codicil to his will, which stipulated that at his death, control of the company would pass to a 10-person board of directors, not including Henry Ford II, for 10 years. Henry was incensed, and threatened to resign unless the will was changed. He also warned that he would inform the company's dealers about the firm's sorry condition. Henry's mother (Edsel's widow), Eleanor Clay Ford (related to the Hudson department store family), insisted that Henry II be given control of the company or she would sell her stock. Henry's grandmother (and the elder Ford's wife), Clara Bryant Ford, backed Eleanor. On September 20, 1945, Henry Ford II became president of Ford Motor Company. The next day this decision was ratified by the board of directors.

Henry Ford immediately fired Bennett—after 29 years in the company, much of it as its effective boss, he was out. Inheriting a company with no financial controls and in managerial disarray, losing $10 million a month, Ford hired financial experts, including Arjay Miller, to straighten out the company's books and records, and Ernie Breech, from Bendix, to help with the management. In the first several months in control, Ford fired more than 1,000 executives, including many of Bennett's cronies. By 1949, Ford had instituted a pension plan with the United Auto Workers Union, the first in the industry, and brought out an all-new automobile. In 1950, the company earned a profit of $265 million. Ford and his recent hires had turned the company around, but it had taken courage and a willingness to take on some pretty tough people inside the organization to do it. Henry Ford II had managed with power.

What does it mean, to manage with power?

First, it means recognizing that in almost every organization, there are varying interests. This suggests that one of the first things we need to do is to diagnose the political landscape and figure out what the relevant interests are, and what important political subdivisions characterize the organization. It is essential that we do not assume that everyone necessarily is going to be our friend, or agree with us, or even that preferences are uniformly distributed. There are clusters of interests within organizations, and we need to understand where these are and to whom they belong.

Next, it means figuring out what point of view these various individuals and subunits have on issues of concern to us. It also means understanding why they have the perspective that they do. It is all too easy to assume that those with a different perspective are somehow not as smart as we are, not as informed, not as perceptive. If that is our belief, we are likely to do several things, each of which is disastrous. First, we may act contemptuously toward those who disagree with us—after all, if they aren't as competent or as insightful as we are, why should we take them seriously? It is rarely difficult to get along with those who resemble us in character and opinions. The real secret of success in organizations is the ability to get those who differ from us, and whom we don't necessarily like, to do what needs to be done. Second, if we think people are misinformed, we are likely to try to "inform" them, or to try to convince them with facts and analysis. Sometimes this will work, but often it will not, for their disagreement may not be based on a lack of information; it may, instead, arise from a different perspective on what our information means. Diagnosing the point of view of interest groups as well as the basis for their positions will assist us in negotiating with them and in predicting their response to various initiatives.

Third, managing with power means understanding that to get things done, you need power—more power than those whose opposition you must overcome—and thus it is imperative to understand where power comes from and how these sources of power can be developed. We are sometimes reluctant to think very purposefully or strategically about acquiring and using power. We are prone to believe that if we do our best, work hard, be nice, and so forth, things will work out for the best. I don't mean to imply that one should not, in general, work hard, try to make good decisions, and be nice, but that these and similar platitudes are often not very useful in helping us get things accomplished in our organizations. We need to understand power and try to get it. We must be willing to do things to build our sources of power, or else we will be less effective than we might wish to be.

Fourth, managing with power means understanding the strategies and tactics through which power is developed and used in organizations, including the importance of timing, the use of structure, the social psychology of commitment and other forms of interpersonal influence. If nothing else, such an understanding will help us become astute observers of the behavior of others. The more we understand power and its manifestations, the better will be our clinical skills. More fundamentally, we need to understand strategies and tactics of using power so that we can consider the range of approaches available to us, and use what is likely to be effective. Again, as in the case of building sources of power, we often try not to think about these things, and we avoid being strategic or purposeful about employing our power. This is a mistake. Although we may have various qualms, there will be others who do not. Knowledge without power is of remarkably little use. And power without the skill to employ it effectively is likely to be wasted.

Managing with power means more than knowing the ideas discussed in this book. It means being, like Henry Ford, willing to do something with that knowledge. It requires political savvy to get things done, and the willingness to force the issue.

For years in the United States, there had been demonstrations and protests, court decisions and legislative proposals attempting to end the widespread discrimination against minority Americans in employment, housing, and public accommodations. The passage of civil rights legislation was a top priority for President Kennedy, but although he had charisma, he lacked the knowledge of political tactics, and possibly the will to use some of the more forceful ones, to get his legislation passed. In the hands of someone who knew power and influence inside out, in spite of the opposition of southern congressmen and senators, the legislation would be passed quickly.

In March 1965, the United States was wracked by violent reactions to civil rights marches in the South. People were killed and injured as segregationists attacked demonstrators, with little or no intervention by the local law enforcement agencies. There were demonstrators across from the White House holding a vigil as Lyndon Johnson left to address a joint session of Congress. This was the same Lyndon Johnson who, in 1948, had opposed federal antilynching legislation, arguing that it was a matter properly left to the states. This was the same Lyndon Johnson who, as a young congressional secretary and then congressman, had talked conservative to conservatives, liberal to liberals, and was said by many to have stood for nothing. This was the same Lyndon Johnson who in eight years in the House of Representatives had introduced not one piece of significant legislation and had done almost nothing to speak out on issues of national importance. This was the same Lyndon Johnson who, while in the House, had tried instead to enrich himself by influencing colleagues at the Federal Communications Commission to help him both obtain a radio station in Austin, Texas, and change the operating license to make the station immensely profitable and valuable. This was the same Lyndon Johnson who, in 1968, having misled the American people, would decide not to run for reelection because of both his association with the Vietnam War and a fundamental distrust of the presidency felt by many Americans. On that night Johnson was to make vigorous use of his power and his political skill to help the civil rights movement:

> With almost the first words of his speech, the audience . . . knew that Lyndon Johnson intended to take the cause of civil rights further than it had ever gone before. . . . He would submit a new civil rights bill . . . and it would be far stronger than the bills of the past. . . . "their cause must be our cause, too," Lyndon Johnson said. "Because it is not just Negroes, but really it is all of us, who must overcome the crippling legacy of bigotry and injustice. . . . And we shall overcome."[5]

As he left the chamber after making his speech, Johnson sought out the 76-year-old chairman of the House Judiciary Committee, Emmanuel Celler:

> "Manny," he said, "I want you to start hearings tonight."
> "Mr. President," Celler protested, "I can't push that committee or it might get out of hand. I am scheduling hearings for next week."
> . . . Johnson's eyes narrowed, and his face turned harder. His right hand was still shaking Celler's, but the left hand was up, and a finger was out, pointing, jabbing.
> "Start them *this* week, Manny," he said. "And hold night sessions, too."[6]

Getting things done requires power. The problem is that we would prefer to see the world as a kind of grand morality play, with the good guys and the bad ones easily identified. Obtaining power is not always an attractive process, nor is its use. And it somehow disturbs our sense of symmetry that a man who was as sleazy, to use a term of my students, as Lyndon Johnson was in some respects, was also the individual who almost single-handedly passed more civil rights legislation in less time with greater effect than anyone else in U.S. history. We are troubled by the issue of means and ends. We are perplexed by the fact that "bad" people sometimes do great and wonderful things, and that "good" people sometimes do "bad" things, or often, nothing at all. Every day, managers in public and private organizations acquire and use power to get things done. Some of these things may be, in retrospect, mistakes, although often that depends heavily on your point of view. Any reader who always does the correct thing that pleases everyone should immediately contact me—we will get very wealthy together. Mistakes and opposition are inevitable. What is not inevitable is passivity, not trying, not seeking to accomplish things.

In many domains of activity we have become so obsessed with not upsetting anybody, and with not making mistakes, that we settle for doing nothing. Rather than rebuild San Francisco's highways, possibly in the wrong place, maybe even in the wrong way, we do nothing, and the city erodes economically without adequate transportation. Rather than possibly being wrong about a new product, such as the personal computer, we study it and analyze it, and lose market opportunities. Analysis and forethought are, obviously, fine. What is not so fine is paralysis or inaction, which arise because we have little skill in overcoming the opposition that inevitably accompanies change, and little interest in doing so.

Theodore Roosevelt, making a speech at the Sorbonne in 1910, perhaps said it best:

> It is not the critic who counts; not the man who points out how the strong man stumbles, or where the doer of deeds could have done them better. The credit belongs to the man who is actually in the arena, whose face is marred by dust and sweat and blood; who strives valiantly; who errs, and comes short again and again; because there is not effort without error and shortcoming; but who does actually strive to do the deeds; who knows the great enthusiasms, the great devotions; who spends himself in a worthy cause, who at the best knows in the end the triumphs of high achievement and who at the worst, if he fails, at least fails while daring greatly, so that his place shall never be with those cold and timid souls who know neither victory nor defeat.[7]

It is easy and often comfortable to feel powerless—to say, "I don't know what to do, I don't have the power to get it done, and besides, I can't really stomach the struggle that may be involved." It is easy, and now quite common, to say, when confronted with some mistake in your organization, "It's not really my responsibility, I can't do anything about it anyway, and if the company wants to do that, well, that's why the senior executives get the big money—it's their responsibility." Such a response excuses us from trying to do things; in not trying to overcome opposition, we will make fewer enemies and are less likely to embarrass ourselves. It is, however, a prescription for both organizational and personal failure. This is why power and influence are not the organization's last dirty secret, but the secret of success for both individuals and their organizations. Innovation and change in almost any arena require the skill to develop power, and the willingness to employ it to get things accomplished. Or, in the words of a local radio newscaster, "If you don't like the news, go out and make some of your own."

NOTES

Chapter 1

[1] Randy Shilts, *And the Band Played On: Politics, People, and the AIDS Epidemic* (New York: St. Martin's Press, 1987).
[2] Ibid., 207.
[3] Ibid., 220.
[4] Ibid., 308.
[5] Ibid., 411.
[6] Ibid., 599.
[7] Douglas K. Smith and Robert C. Alexander, *Fumbling the Future: How Xerox Invented, Then Ignored, the First Personal Computer* (New York: William Morrow, 1988).
[8] Richard M. Nixon, *Leaders* (New York: Warner Books, 1982), 5.
[9] Norton E. Long, "The Administrative Organization as a Political System," *Concepts and Issues in Administrative Behavior*, eds. S. Mailick and E.H. Van Ness (Englewood Cliffs, NJ: Prentice-Hall, 1962), 110.
[10] Nixon, *Leaders*, 330.
[11] John W. Gardner, *On Leadership* (New York: Free Press, 1990).
[12] Michael T. Hannan and John Freeman, *Organizational Ecology* (Cambridge, MA: Harvard University Press, 1989).
[13] Gardner, *On Leadership*, 55–57.
[14] Warren Bennis and Burt Nanus, *Leaders: The Strategies for Taking Charge* (New York: Harper and Row, 1985), 6.
[15] Ibid., 15–17.
[16] Nixon, *Leaders*, 324.
[17] Rosabeth Moss Kanter, "Power Failure in Management Circuits," *Harvard Business Review* 57 (July–August 1979): 65.
[18] Jeffrey Gandz and Victor V. Murray, "The Experience of Workplace Politics," *Academy of Management Journal* 23 (1980): 237–251.
[19] Tim Reiterman with John Jacobs, *Raven: The Untold Story of the Rev. Jim Jones and His People* (New York: E.P. Dutton, 1982), 305–307.
[20] Nixon, *Leaders*, 326.

[21] Abraham Zaleznik and Manfred F.R. Kets de Vries, *Power and the Corporate Mind* (Boston: Houghton Mifflin, 1975), 109.

[22] Henry Kissinger, *The White House Years* (Boston: Little, Brown, 1979), 39.

[23] Elliot Aronson, *The Social Animal* (San Francisco: W.H. Freeman, 1972), chapter 4; Barry M. Staw, "Rationality and Justification in Organizational Life," *Research in Organizational Behavior,* eds. B.M. Staw and L.L. Cummings (Greenwich, CT: JAI Press, 1980), vol. 2, 45–80; Gerald R. Salancik, "Commitment and the Control of Organizational Behavior and Belief," *New Directions in Organizational Behavior,* eds. Barry M. Staw and Gerald R. Salancik (Chicago: St. Clair Press, 1977), 1–54.

[24] Leon Festinger, *A Theory of Cognitive Dissonance* (Stanford: Stanford University Press, 1957).

[25] Nixon, *Leaders,* 329.

[26] Alok K. Chakrabarti, "Organizational Factors in Post-Acquisition Performance," *IEEE Transactions on Engineering Management* 37 (1990): 259–268.

[27] Ibid., 259.

[28] Ibid., 266.

[29] D. Purkayastha, "Note on the Motorcycle Industry—1975," #578-210. Boston: Harvard Business School, 1981.

[30] Richard T. Pascale, "Perspectives on Strategy: The Real Story Behind Honda's Success," *California Management Review* 26 (1984): 51.

[31] Ibid., 54.

[32] Ibid., 55.

[33] William A. Pasmore, *Designing Effective Organizations: The Sociotechnical Systems Perspective* (New York: John Wiley, 1988); David L. Bradford and Allan R. Cohen, *Managing for Excellence* (New York: John Wiley, 1984).

[34] Mark Stevens, *Sudden Death: The Rise and Fall of E.F. Hutton* (New York: Penguin, 1989), 98.

[35] Ibid., 121.

[36] Thomas J. Peters and Robert H. Waterman, Jr., *In Search of Excellence* (New York: Harper and Row, 1982); Terrence Deal and Allan A. Kennedy, *Corporate Cultures* (Reading, MA: Addison-Wesley, 1982); Stanley Davis, *Managing Corporate Culture* (Cambridge, MA: Ballinger, 1984).

[37] Richard T. Pascale, "The Paradox of 'Corporate Culture': Reconciling Ourselves to Socialization," *California Management Review* 26 (1985): 26–41; Charles O'Reilly, "Corporations, Culture, and Commitment: Motivation and Social Control in Organizations," *California Management Review* 31 (1989): 9–25.

[38] Sanford M. Dornbusch, "The Military Academy as an Assimilating Institution," *Social Forces* 33 (1955): 316–321.

[39] Richard Harvey Brown, "Bureaucracy as Praxis: Toward a Political Phenomenology of Formal Organizations," *Administrative Science Quarterly* 23 (1978): 365–382.

[40] Janice Lodahl and Gerald Gordon, "The Structure of Scientific Fields and the Functioning of University Graduate Departments," *American Sociological Review* 37 (1972): 57–72.

[41] Thomas S. Kuhn, *The Structure of Scientific Revolutions,* 2d ed. (Chicago: University of Chicago Press, 1970).

[42] Irving L. Janis, *Victims of Groupthink* (Boston: Houghton Mifflin, 1972).

[43] Frank Rose, *West of Eden: The End of Innocence at Apple Computer* (New York: Viking Penguin, 1989), 81.

[44] Ibid., 85.

[45] Ibid., 97.

[46] Thomas J. Peters, "Symbols, Patterns, and Settings: An Optimistic Case for Getting Things Done," *Organizational Dynamics* 7 (1978): 3–23.

[47] Jeffrey Pfeffer, *Power in Organizations* (Marshfield, MA: Pitman Publishing, 1981), Kanter, "Power Failure in Management Circuits", Richard M. Emerson, "Power-Dependence Relations," *American Sociological Review* 27 (1962): 31–41.

Chapter 2

[1] John P. Kotter, "Power, Success, and Organizational Effectiveness," *Organizational Dynamics* 6, no. 3 (1978): 27–40; and *Power and Influence: Beyond Formal Authority* (New York: Free Press, 1985).

[2] Martin Patchen, "The Locus and Basis of Influence in Organizational Decisions,"*Organizational Behavior and Human Performance* 11 (1974): 195–221.

[3] Jeffrey Gandz and Victor V. Murray, "The Experience of Workplace Politics," *Academy of Management Journal* 23 (1980): 237–251.

[4] Dan L. Madison et al., "Organizational Politics: An Exploration of Managers' Perceptions," *Human Relations* 33 (1980): 79–100.

[5] Jeffrey Pfeffer and Gerald R. Salancik, *The External Control of Organizations: A Resource Dependence Perspective* (New York: Harper and Row, 1978), 40.

[6] Douglas K. Smith and Robert C. Alexander, *Fumbling the Future: How Xerox Invented, Then Ignored, the First Personal Computer* (New York: William Morrow, 1988), 14.

[7] Ibid., 148.

[8] M. Ann Welsh and E. Allen Slusher, "Organizational Design as a Context for Political Activity," *Administrative Science Quarterly* 31 (1986): 389–402.

[9] Rosabeth M. Kanter, *Men and Women of the Corporation* (New York: Basic Books, 1977).

[10] Gerald R. Salancik and Jeffrey Pfeffer, "The Bases and Use of Power in Organizational Decision Making: The Case of a University," *Administrative Science Quarterly* 19 (1974): 453–473.

[11] Frederick S. Hills and Thomas A. Mahoney, "University Budgets and Organizational Decision Making," *Administrative Science Quarterly* 23 (1978): 454–465.

[12] Jeffrey Pfeffer and William L. Moore, "Power in University Budgeting: A Replication and Extension," *Administrative Science Quarterly* 25 (1980): 637–653.

[13] Ibid., 650–651.

[14] James D. Thompson and Arthur Tuden, "Strategies, Structures and Processes of Organizational Decision," *Comparative Studies in Administration*, eds. J.D. Thompson et al. (Pittsburgh: University of Pittsburgh Press, 1959): 195–216.

[15] David Halberstam, *The Reckoning* (New York: William Morrow, 1986).

[16] J. Patrick Wright, *On a Clear Day You Can See General Motors* (Grosse Point, MI: Wright Enterprises, 1979), 33.

[17] Salancik and Pfeffer, "Bases and Use of Power."

[18] Chris Argyris, *Behind the Front Page* (San Francisco: Jossey-Bass, 1974).

[19] Diana Tillinghast, "The Los Angeles *Times:* Weakening of Territorial Imperative," *Newspaper Research Journal* 1 (1980): 18–26.

[20] Herbert E. Meyer, "Shootout at the Johns-Mansville Corral," *Fortune* (October 1976): 146–154.

[21] Ibid., 154.

[22] Hugh D. Menzies, "The Boardroom Battle at Bendix," *Fortune* (January 11, 1982): 54–64.

[23] John P. Kotter, *The General Managers* (New York: Free Press, 1982), "Power, Success, and Organizational Effectiveness," and *Power and Influence.*

Chapter 3

[1] Andrew M. Pettigrew, *Politics of Organizational Decision-Making* (London: Tavistock, 1973), 240.

[2] David Krackhardt, "Assessing the Political Landscape: Structure, Cognition and Power in Organizations," *Administrative Science Quarterly* 35 (1990): 342–369.

[3] Jeffrey Pfeffer and Gerald R. Salancik, "Administrator Effectiveness: The Effects of Advocacy and Information on Resource Allocations," *Human Relations* 30 (1977): 641–656.

[4] Mark Stevens, *Sudden Death: The Rise and Fall of E.F. Hutton* (New York: Penguin, 1989), 52–53.

[5] Ibid., 51–52.

[6] Ibid., 215.

[7] Henri Tajfel and Joseph P. Forgas, "Social Categorization: Cognitions, Values and Groups," *Social Cognition: Perspectives on Everyday Understanding,* ed. Joseph P. Forgas (New York: Academic Press, 1981), 113–140.

[8] Marilynn B. Brewer and Roderick M. Kramer, "The Psychology of Intergroup Attitudes and Behavior," *Annual Review of Psychology* 36 (1985): 219–243.

[9] Charles Perrow, "Departmental Power and Perspectives in Industrial Firms," *Power in Organizations,* ed. Mayer N. Zald (Nashville, TN: Vanderbilt University Press, 1970), 59–89.

[10] C.R. Hinings et al., "Structural Conditions of Intraorganizational Power," *Administrative Science Quarterly* 19 (1974): 22–44.

[11] Jeffrey Pfeffer and Gerald R. Salancik, "Organizational Decision Making as a Political Process: The Case of a University Budget," *Administrative Science Quarterly* 19 (1974): 135–151; Jeffrey Pfeffer and William L. Moore, "Power in University Budgeting: A Replication and Extension," *Administrative Science Quarterly* 25 (1980): 637–653.

[12] Martin Patchen, "The Locus and Basis of Influence in Organizational Decisions," *Organizational Behavior and Human Performance* 11 (1974): 195–221.

[13] Nelson W. Polsby, "How to Study Community Power: The Pluralist Alternative," *Journal of Politics* 22 (1960): 474–484.

[14] Pfeffer and Salancik, "Organizational Decision Making"; Pfeffer and Moore, "Power in University Budgeting."

[15] Stevens, *Sudden Death,* 160.

[16] T.L. Whisler et al., "Centralization of Organizational Control: An Empirical Study of Its Meaning and Measurement," *Journal of Business* 40 (1967): 10–26.

[17] Michael Lewis, *Liar's Poker: Rising through the Wreckage on Wall Street* (New York: Penguin, 1990), 59.
[18] John R.P. French, Jr., and Bertram Raven, "The Bases of Social Power," *Group Dynamics*, eds. Dorwin Cartwright and Alvin Zander, 3rd ed. (New York: Harper and Row, 1968), 259–269; Patchen, "Locus and Basis of Influence," 210.
[19] Stevens, *Sudden Death.*

Chapter 4

[1] Michael L. Tushman, William H. Newman, and Elaine Romanelli, "Convergence and Upheaval: Managing the Unsteady Pace of Organizational Evolution," *California Management Review* 29 (1986): 29–44.
[2] R.E. Nisbett and L. Ross, *Human Inferences: Strategies and Shortcomings of Social Judgment* (Englewood Cliffs, NJ: Prentice-Hall, 1980).
[3] Linda E. Ginzel, "The Impact of Biased Feedback Strategies on Performance Judgments," Research Paper #1102 (Palo Alto, CA: Graduate School of Business, Stanford University, 1990).
[4] Ibid., 26.
[5] Robert W. Allen et al., "Organizational Politics: Tactics and Characteristics of Its Actors," *California Management Review* 22 (1979): 77–83.
[6] David G. Winter, "Leader Appeal, Leader Performance, and the Motive Profiles of Leaders and Followers: A Study of American Presidents and Elections," *Journal of Personality and Social Psychology* 52 (1987): 196–202.
[7] Ibid., 200.
[8] Christopher H. Achen, *The Statistical Analysis of Quasi-Experiments* (Berkeley: University of California Press, 1986).
[9] Andrew M. Pettigrew, *Politics of Organizational Decision-Making* (London: Tavistock, 1973), 17.
[10] Ibid., 31.
[11] D.J. Hickson et al., "A Strategic Contingencies' Theory of Intraorganizational Power," *Administrative Science Quarterly* 16 (1971): 216–229.
[12] Martin Patchen, "The Locus and Basis of Influence in Organizational Decisions," *Organizational Behavior and Human Performance* 11 (1974): 209.
[13] Ibid., 213.
[14] George Strauss, "Tactics of Lateral Relationship: The Purchasing Agent," *Administrative Science Quarterly* 7 (1962): 161–186.
[15] Michael L. Tushman and Elaine Romanelli, "Uncertainty, Social Location and Influence in Decision Making: A Sociometric Analysis," *Management Science* 29 (1983): 12–23.
[16] Gerald R. Salancik, Jeffrey Pfeffer, and J. Patrick Kelly, "A Contingency Model of Influence in Organizational Decision Making," *Pacific Sociological Review* 21 (1978): 239–256.
[17] Ibid., 253.
[18] Bernard M. Bass, "Evolving Perspectives on Charismatic Leadership," *Charismatic Leadership*, eds. Jay A. Conger, Rabindra N. Kanungo and Associates (San Francisco: Jossey-Bass, 1988), 40–77.
[19] Robert J. House, William D. Spangler, and James Woycke, "Personality and Charisma in the U.S. Presidency: A Psychological Theory of Leader-

ship Effectiveness," unpublished, Wharton School, University of Pennsylvania, 1989.

[20] Ibid.; Robert J. House, "A 1976 Theory of Charismatic Leadership," *Leadership: The Cutting Edge*, eds. J.G. Hunt and L.L. Larson (Carbondale: Southern Illinois University Press, 1977).

[21] House, Spangler, and Woycke, "Personality and Charisma."

[22] Nancy C. Roberts and Raymond Trevor Bradley, "Limits of Charisma," *Charismatic Leadership*, eds. Jay A. Conger, Rabindra N. Kanungo and Associates (San Francisco: Jossey-Bass, 1988), 253–275.

[23] Ibid., 254.

[24] Ibid., 260.

[25] Ibid., 263.

[26] Ibid.

[27] Ibid., 264.

[28] Ibid., 269.

[29] Ibid.

[30] Ibid., 268.

Chapter 5

[1] Robert A. Caro, *The Power Broker: Robert Moses and the Fall of New York* (New York: Random House, 1974).

[2] Robert A. Caro, *The Path to Power: The Years of Lyndon Johnson* (New York: Alfred A. Knopf, 1982), 261.

[3] Ibid., 263.

[4] Ibid., 264–265.

[5] David Halberstam, *The Reckoning* (New York: William Morrow, 1986); Maryann Keller, *Rude Awakening: The Rise, Fall, and Struggle for Recovery of General Motors* (New York: William Morrow, 1989).

[6] Douglas K. Smith and Robert C. Alexander, *Fumbling the Future: How Xerox Invented, Then Ignored, the First Personal Computer* (New York: William Morrow, 1988).

[7] Max Holland, *When the Machine Stopped* (Boston: Harvard Business School Press, 1989).

[8] Jeffrey Pfeffer and Gerald R. Salancik, *The External Control of Organizations: A Resource Dependence Perspective* (New York: Harper and Row, 1978), 48–49.

[9] Richard C. Edwards, *Contested Terrain: The Transformation of the Workplace in the Twentieth Century* (New York: Basic Books, 1979).

[10] Sanford M. Jacoby, *Employing Bureaucracy: Managers, Unions, and the Transformation of Work in American Industry, 1900–1945* (New York: Columbia University Press, 1985).

[11] John M. Barry, *The Ambition and the Power* (New York: Viking, 1989).

[12] Ibid., 68.

[13] Ibid., 69.

[14] Ibid., 70.

[15] Ibid.

[16] Richard M. Emerson, "Power-Dependence Relations," *American Sociological Review* 27 (1962): 31–41; Peter M. Blau, *Exchange and Power in Social Life* (New York: John Wiley, 1964).

[17] Otto A. Davis, M.A.H. Dempster, and Aaron Wildavsky, "A Theory of the Budgeting Process," *American Political Science Review* 60 (1966): 529–547;

Jeffrey Pfeffer and Gerald R. Salancik, "Organizational Decision Making as a Political Process: The Case of a University Budget," *Administrative Science Quarterly* 19 (1974): 135–151; Jeffrey Pfeffer and William L. Moore, "Power in University Budgeting: A Replication and Extension," *Administrative Science Quarterly* 25 (1980): 637–653.

[18] Daniel Kahneman and Amos Tversky, "Choices, Values, and Frames," *American Psychologist* 39 (1984): 341–350.

[19] Gerald R. Salancik and Jeffrey Pfeffer, "The Bases and Use of Power in Organizational Decision Making: The Case of a University," *Administrative Science Quarterly* 19 (1974): 135–151; Pfeffer and Moore, "Power in University Budgeting."

[20] Janice Lodahl and Gerald Gordon, "Funding the Sciences in University Departments,"*Educational Record* 54 (1973): 74–82.

[21] Paul J. DiMaggio and Walter W. Powell, "The Iron Cage Revisited: Institutional Isomorphism and Collective Rationality in Organizational Fields," *American Sociological Review* 48 (1983): 147–160.

[22] Robert P. Gandossy, *Bad Business: The OPM Scandal and the Seduction of the Establishment* (New York: Basic Books, 1985), 5.

[23] Ibid., 11.

[24] Ibid., 38–39.

[25] Ibid., 39.

[26] Ibid., 41.

[27] Ibid., 44.

[28] Ibid., 52.

[29] Ibid., 53.

[30] Ibid., 215.

[31] Jeffrey Pfeffer and Alison Konrad, "The Effects of Individual Power on Earnings," *Work and Occupations* (in press, 1991).

[32] Halberstam, *The Reckoning.*

[33] Ibid., 136.

[34] Ibid., 141.

[35] Ibid., 148.

[36] Ibid., 156.

[37] Ibid., 183.

[38] Barry, *The Ambition and the Power,* 18.

[39] Bryan Burrough and John Helyar, *Barbarians at the Gate: The Fall of RJR Nabisco* (New York: Harper and Row, 1990), 35.

[40] Barry, *The Ambition and the Power,* 71.

[41] Ibid., 76.

[42] Ibid., 84.

[43] J. Patrick Wright, *On a Clear Day You Can See General Motors* (Grosse Point, MI: Wright Enterprises, 1979), 41.

[44] Donald L. Helmich and Warren B. Brown, "Successor Type and Organizational Change in the Corporate Enterprise," *Administrative Science Quarterly* 17 (1972): 371–381.

[45] Alvin W. Gouldner, "The Norm of Reciprocity: A Preliminary Statement," *American Sociological Review* 25 (1960): 161–178.

[46] Caro, *The Power Broker.*

[47] Burrough and Helyar, *Barbarians at the Gate,* 33.

[48] Ibid., 37.

[49] Hugh D. Menzies, "The Boardroom Battle at Bendix," *Fortune* (January 11, 1982): 62.

[50] Burrough and Helyar, *Barbarians at the Gate,* 63.

[51] Ibid., 64.

[52] Frank Rose, *West of Eden: The End of Innocence at Apple Computer* (New York: Viking Penguin, 1989), 132.

[53] Ken Auletta, "Power, Greed and Glory on Wall Street: The Fall of Lehman Brothers," *New York Times Magazine* (February 17, 1985): 34.

Chapter 6

[1] Linton C. Freeman, "Centrality in Social Networks: Conceptual Clarifications," *Social Networks* 1 (1979): 215–239; Daniel J. Brass, "Being in the Right Place: A Structural Analysis of Individual Influence in an Organization," *Administrative Science Quarterly* 29 (1984): 518–539.

[2] Freeman, "Centrality in Social Networks."

[3] Alex Bavelas, "Communication Patterns in Task Oriented Groups," *Journal of Acoustical Society of America* 22 (1950): 725–730; Harold J. Leavitt, "Effects of Certain Communication Patterns on Group Performance," *Journal of Abnormal and Social Psychology* 46 (1951): 38–50.

[4] Kenneth D. Mackenzie, *A Theory of Group Structures* (London: Gordon and Breach, 1975).

[5] Jay R. Galbraith, *Designing Complex Organizations* (Reading, MA: Addison-Wesley, 1973).

[6] Ibid.

[7] Hickson et al., "A Strategic Contingencies' Theory of Intraorganizational Power," *Administrative Science Quarterly* 16 (1971): 216–229.

[8] Andrew M. Pettigrew, "Information Control as a Power Resource," *Sociology* 6 (1972): 190–191.

[9] Brass, "Being in the Right Place," 519.

[10] Ibid., 525.

[11] Ibid., 532.

[12] David Krackhardt, "Assessing the Political Landscape: Structure, Cognition and Power in Organizations," *Administrative Science Quarterly* 35 (1990): 342–369.

[13] Jeffrey Pfeffer and Alison Konrad, "The Effects of Individual Power on Earnings," *Work and Occupations* (in press, 1991).

[14] Frank Rose, *West of Eden: The End of Innocence at Apple Computer* (New York: Viking Penguin, 1989), 244–245.

[15] Ibid., 298.

[16] Robert A. Caro, *The Path to Power: The Years of Lyndon Johnson* (New York: Alfred A. Knopf, 1982), 266.

[17] Mark Stevens, *Sudden Death: The Rise and Fall of E.F. Hutton* (New York: Penguin, 1989), 161.

[18] Henry Kissinger, *The White House Years* (Boston: Little, Brown, 1979), 47.

[19] David Halberstam, *The Reckoning* (New York: William Morrow, 1986); Neil Fligstein, "The Intraorganizational Power Struggle: Rise of Finance Personnel to Top Leadership in Large Corporations, 1919–1979," *American Sociological Review* 52 (1987): 44–58.

[20] Maryann Keller, *Rude Awakening: The Rise, Fall, and Struggle for Recovery of General Motors* (New York: William Morrow, 1989), 58.

[21] Ibid., 60–61.

[22] L. Festinger, S. Schacter, and K. Back, *Social Pressures in Informal Groups* (Stanford, CA: Stanford University Press, 1950).

[23] John P. Kotter, "Power, Success, and Organizational Effectiveness," *Organizational Dynamics* 6, no. 3 (1978): 27–40.

[24] Christopher Byron, *The Fanciest Dive* (New York: W.W. Norton, 1986).
[25] J. Patrick Wright, *On a Clear Day You Can See General Motors* (Grosse Point, MI: Wright Enterprises, 1979).
[26] Rosabeth M. Kanter, *Men and Women of the Corporation* (New York: Basic Books, 1977).

Chapter 7

[1] *New York Times* (July 15, 1978): 23.
[2] Sally Bedell Smith, *In All His Glory: The Life of William S. Paley* (New York: Simon and Schuster, 1990), 397.
[3] David Mechanic, "Sources of Power of Lower Participants in Complex Organizations," *Administrative Science Quarterly* 7 (1962): 349–364.
[4] John W. Gardner, *On Leadership* (New York: Free Press, 1990), 24.
[5] Stanley Milgram, *Obedience to Authority* (New York: Harper and Row, 1974).
[6] Max Weber, *The Theory of Social and Economic Organization* (New York: Free Press, 1947).
[7] Steven Bach, *Final Cut: Dreams and Disaster in the Making of Heaven's Gate* (New York: William Morrow, 1985), 54.
[8] Lynne G. Zucker, "The Role of Institutionalization in Cultural Persistence," *American Sociological Review* 42 (1977): 726–743.
[9] R.C. Jacobs and D.T. Campbell, "The Perpetuation of an Arbitrary Tradition Through Successive Generations of a Laboratory Microculture," *Journal of Abnormal and Social Psychology* 62 (1961): 649–658.
[10] Zucker, "The Role of Institutionalization," 732.
[11] Ibid., 732–733.
[12] J. Sterling Livingston, "Pygmalion in Management," *Harvard Business Review* 47 (July–August 1969): 81–89; W. Peter Archibald, "Alternative Explanations for Self-Fulfilling Prophecy," *Psychological Bulletin* 81 (1974): 74–84.
[13] Mark Snyder, "Self-fulfilling Stereotypes," *Psychology Today* 16 (July 1982): 60–68.
[14] Lloyd H. Strickland, "Surveillance and Trust," *Journal of Personality* 26 (1958): 200–215.
[15] Rosabeth M. Kanter, *Men and Women of the Corporation* (New York: Basic Books, 1977).
[16] David E. Berlew and Douglas T. Hall, "The Socialization of Managers: Effects of Expectations on Performance," *Administrative Science Quarterly* 11 (1966): 207–223.
[17] Maryann Keller, *Rude Awakening: The Rise, Fall, and Struggle for Recovery of General Motors* (New York: William Morrow, 1989), 66–67.
[18] Ibid., 67.
[19] Smith, *In All His Glory*, 150.
[20] Ibid., 152.
[21] Ibid., 153.
[22] Ibid., 156.
[23] Henry Kissinger, *The White House Years* (Boston: Little, Brown, 1979), 45.
[24] Ibid., 47.
[25] David Halberstam, *The Best and the Brightest* (New York: Random House, 1972), 79.
[26] Ibid., 80.

[27] M.J. Lerner and C.H. Simmons, "Observer's Reaction to the 'Innocent Victim': Compassion or Rejection?" *Journal of Personality and Social Psychology* 4 (1966): 203–210.

[28] John M. Barry, *The Ambition and the Power* (New York: Viking, 1989), 154.

[29] Joseph W. Harder, *Play for Pay: Salary Determination and the Effects of Over- and Under-Reward on Individual Performance in Professional Sports* (Stanford, CA: Stanford University, unpublished doctoral dissertation, 1989).

[30] Robert A. Caro, *The Power Broker: Robert Moses and the Fall of New York* (New York: Random House, 1974), 463.

[31] James G. March and John P. Olsen, *Ambiguity and Choice in Organizations* (Bergen, Norway: Universitetsforlaget, 1976).

[32] Gardner, *On Leadership*, 8.

[33] Martha S. Feldman and James G. March, "Information in Organizations as Signal and Symbol," *Administrative Science Quarterly* 26 (1981): 171–186.

Chapter 8

[1] Michael Lewis, *Liar's Poker: Rising through the Wreckage on Wall Street* (New York: Penguin, 1990), 61.

[2] William L. Moore and Jeffrey Pfeffer, "The Relationship Between Departmental Power and Faculty Careers on Two Campuses: The Case for Structural Effects on Faculty Salaries," *Research in Higher Education* 13 (1980): 291–306.

[3] Jeffrey Pfeffer and Alison Davis-Blake, "Understanding Organizational Wage Structures: A Resource Dependence Approach," *Academy of Management Journal* 30 (1987): 437–455.

[4] John E. Sheridan et al., "Effects of Corporate Sponsorship and Departmental Power on Career Tournaments," *Academy of Management Journal* 33 (1990): 578–602.

[5] John M. Barry, *The Ambition and the Power* (New York: Viking, 1989), 29.

[6] Janice Lodahl and Gerald Gordon, "The Structure of Scientific Fields and the Functioning of University Graduate Departments," *American Sociological Review* 37 (1972): 57–72.

[7] Janice Lodahl and Gerald Gordon, "Funding the Sciences in University Departments," *Educational Record* 54 (1973): 74–82.

[8] Jeffrey Pfeffer and William L. Moore, "Power in University Budgeting: A Replication and Extension," *Administrative Science Quarterly* 25 (1980): 637–653.

[9] Rosabeth M. Kanter, *Men and Women of the Corporation* (New York: Basic Books, 1977).

[10] Gerald R. Salancik, Barry M. Staw, and Louis R. Pondy, "Administrative Turnover as a Response to Unmanaged Organizational Interdependence," *Academy of Management Journal* 23 (1980): 422–437; Jeffrey Pfeffer and William L. Moore, "Average Tenure of Academic Department Heads: The Effects of Paradigm, Size, and Departmental Demography," *Administrative Science Quarterly* 25 (1980): 387–406.

[11] Alison M. Konrad and Jeffrey Pfeffer, "Do You Get What You Deserve? Factors Affecting the Relationship Between Productivity and Pay," *Administrative Science Quarterly* 35 (1990): 258–285.

12 Janice M. Beyer and Thomas M. Lodahl, "A Comparative Study of Patterns of Influence in United States and English Universities," *Administrative Science Quarterly* 21 (1976): 104–129.

13 Pfeffer and Moore, "Average Tenure of Academic Department Heads"; Salancik, Staw, and Pondy, "Administrative Turnover."

14 D.J. Hickson et al., "A Strategic Contingencies' Theory of Intraorganizational Power," *Administrative Science Quarterly* 16 (1971): 216–229.

15 Setsuo Miyazawa, "Legal Departments of Japanese Corporations in the United States: A Study on Organizational Adaptation to Multiple Environments," *Kobe University Law Review* 20 (1986): 97–162.

16 Ibid., 135.

17 Ibid., 126.

18 John Dean, *Blind Ambition* (New York: Simon and Schuster, 1976), 30.

19 Ibid., 38.

20 Ibid., 40.

21 Richard M. Emerson, "Power-Dependence Relations," *American Sociological Review* 27 (1962): 31–41; Peter M. Blau, *Exchange and Power in Social Life* (New York: John Wiley, 1964).

22 Michel Crozier, *The Bureaucratic Phenomenon* (Chicago: University of Chicago Press, 1964).

23 Robert A. Caro, *The Power Broker: Robert Moses and the Fall of New York* (New York: Random House, 1974), 464.

24 Ibid., 464–465.

25 Hickson et al., "A Strategic Contingencies' Theory"; C.R. Hinings et al., "Structural Conditions of Intraorganizational Power," *Administrative Science Quarterly* 19 (1974): 216–229.

Chapter 9

1 John P. Kotter, *The General Managers* (New York: Free Press, 1982).

2 Hedrick Smith, *The Power Game: How Washington Works* (New York: Ballantine, 1988), 61–62.

3 Robert Caro, *The Path to Power: The Years of Lyndon Johnson* (New York: Alfred A. Knopf, 1982), 218.

4 Ibid., 226.

5 Ibid., 235.

6 Robert Caro, *The Power Broker: Robert Moses and the Fall of New York* (New York: Random House, 1974), 227.

7 Sally Bedell Smith, *In All His Glory: The Life of William S. Paley* (New York: Simon and Schuster, 1990), 394.

8 John W. Gardner, *On Leadership* (New York: Free Press, 1990), 48.

9 Robert Caro, *Means of Ascent: The Years of Lyndon Johnson* (New York: Alfred A. Knopf, 1990).

10 Caro, *The Path to Power*.

11 Caro, *The Power Broker*, 229.

12 Kotter, *The General Managers*.

13 Smith, *In All His Glory*, 395.

14 John M. Barry, *The Ambition and the Power* (New York: Viking, 1989), 20.

15 Douglas K. Smith and Robert C. Alexander, *Fumbling the Future: How Xerox Invented, Then Ignored, the First Personal Computer* (New York: William Morrow, 1988), 50.

16 Ibid., 131–132.

[17] Gardner, *On Leadership*, 1.

[18] Jeanne M. Brett, Stephen B. Goldberg, and William L. Ury, "Designing Systems for Resolving Disputes in Organizations," *American Psychologist* 45 (1990): 162–170; Roger Fisher and William Ury, *Getting to Yes: Negotiating Agreements Without Giving In* (Boston: Houghton Mifflin, 1981).

[19] Max H. Bazerman and Margaret A. Neale, "Heuristics in Negotiation: Limitations to Dispute Resolution Effectiveness," *Negotiating in Organizations*, eds. M.H. Bazerman and R.J. Lewicki (Beverly Hills, CA: Sage, 1983), 51–67.

[20] Gardner, *On Leadership*, 50–51.

[21] Barry, *The Ambition and the Power*, 12.

[22] Paul Clancy and Shirley Elder, *TIP: A Biography of Thomas P. O'Neill Speaker of the House* (New York: Macmillan, 1980), 4.

[23] Smith, *In All His Glory*, 391.

[24] Ibid.

[25] Ibid., 404.

[26] Caro, "My Search for Coke Stevenson," *The New York Times Book Review* (February 3, 1991), 28.

[27] Gardner, *On Leadership*, 53.

[28] Aaron Bernstein, *Grounded: Frank Lorenzo and the Destruction of Eastern Airlines* (New York: Simon and Schuster, 1990), 167.

[29] Richard Christie and Florence L. Geis, *Studies in Machiavellianism* (New York: Academic Press, 1970), 312.

[30] Gerald R. Salancik and Jeffrey Pfeffer, "Who Gets Power—and How They Hold on to It: A Strategic-Contingency Model of Power," *Organizational Dynamics* 5 (1977): 3–21.

[31] James D. Thompson and Arthur Tuden, "Strategies, Structures and Processes of Organizational Decision," *Comparative Studies in Administration*, eds. J.D. Thompson et al. (Pittsburgh: University of Pittsburgh Press, 1959), 195–216.

[32] Robert L. Khan et al., *Organizational Stress: Studies in Role Conflict and Ambiguity* (New York: John Wiley, 1964).

[33] Thomas C. Schelling, *The Strategy of Conflict* (New York: Oxford University Press, 1963,), 13.

[34] Hedrick Smith, *The Power Game: How Washington Works* (New York: Ballantine, 1988), 61.

[35] David Halberstam, *The Best and the Brightest* (New York: Random House, 1972), 30.

[36] Caro, *The Power Broker*, 448.

[37] Ibid., 449.

[38] Ibid., 448.

[39] Bryan Burrough and John Helyar, *Barbarians at the Gate: The Fall of RJR Nabisco* (New York: Harper and Row, 1990), 19.

[40] Ibid., 21.

[41] Ibid., 34.

[42] Ken Auletta, "Power, Greed and Glory on Wall Street: The Fall of Lehman Brothers," *The New York Times Magazine* (February 17, 1985).

[43] Ibid., 36.

[44] Smith, *In All His Glory*, 408.

[45] Laton McCartney, *Friends in High Places: The Bechtel Story* (New York: Simon and Schuster, 1988), 170.

[46] Ibid.

[47] Ibid., 172.

[48] Ibid., 179.
[49] Ibid.
[50] Ibid., 180.

Chapter 10

[1] Robert B. Cialdini, *Influence: Science and Practice,* 2d ed. (Glenview, IL: Scott, Foresman, 1988).
[2] Ibid.
[3] Douglas K. Smith and Robert C. Alexander, *Fumbling the Future: How Xerox Invented, Then Ignored, the First Personal Computer* (New York: William Morrow, 1988).
[4] Gerald R. Salancik, "Commitment and Control of Organizational Behavior and Belief," *New Directions in Organizational Behavior,* eds. Barry M. Staw and Gerald R. Salancik (Chicago: St. Clair Press, 1977).
[5] Daryl J. Bem, "Self-Perception Theory," *Advances in Experimental Social Psychology,* ed. Leonard Berkowitz, vol. 6 (New York: Academic Press, 1972), 1–62.
[6] E. Aronson and J. Mills, "The Effect of Severity of Initiation on Liking for a Group," *Journal of Abnormal and Social Psychology* 59 (1959): 177.
[7] John W. Gardner, *On Leadership* (New York: Free Press, 1990).
[8] Barry M. Staw and Jerry Ross, "Commitment in an Experimenting Society: An Experiment on the Attribution of Leadership from Administrative Scenarios," *Journal of Applied Psychology* 65 (1980): 249–260.
[9] Steven Bach, *Final Cut: Dreams and Disaster in the Making of Heaven's Gate* (New York: William Morrow, 1985), 181.
[10] Ibid., 187.
[11] Ibid., 189.
[12] Ibid., 191.
[13] Ibid., 192.
[14] Ibid., 196.
[15] Tracy Kidder, *Soul of a New Machine* (Boston: Atlantic-Little, Brown, 1981), 65–66.
[16] Christopher Matthews, *Hardball: How Politics Is Played—Told By One Who Knows The Game* (New York: Summit Books, 1988), 60.
[17] Ibid., 62–63.
[18] Aaron Bernstein, *Grounded: Frank Lorenzo and the Destruction of Eastern Airlines* (New York: Simon and Schuster, 1990), 133.
[19] Ibid., 134.
[20] Ibid., 136.
[21] Ibid., 137.
[22] Jack W. Brehm, *A Theory of Psychological Reactance* (New York: Academic Press, 1966).
[23] Cialdini, *Influence: Science and Practice,* 232.
[24] Ibid.
[25] Frank Rose, *West of Eden: The End of Innocence at Apple Computer* (New York: Viking Penguin, 1989), 78.
[26] David Halberstam, *The Best and the Brightest* (New York: Random House, 1972), 78.
[27] Ibid., 410.
[28] Ibid., 245.

Chapter 11

[1] Leon Festinger, "A Theory of Social Comparison Processes," *Human Relations* 7 (1954): 117–140.

[2] Ellen Berscheid and Elaine Hatfield Walster, *Interpersonal Attraction* (Reading, MA: Addison-Wesley, 1969); D. Byrne, "Attitudes and Attraction," *Advances in Experimental Social Psychology*, ed. Leonard Berkowitz, vol. 4 (New York: Academic Press, 1969), 35–89.

[3] Robert B. Cialdini, *Influence: Science and Practice*, 2d ed. (Glenview, IL: Scott, Foresman, 1988), 112.

[4] Ibid., 123.

[5] Bibb Latane and John M. Darley, "Group Inhibition of Bystander Intervention in Emergencies," *Journal of Personality and Social Psychology* 10 (1968): 215–221.

[6] Joseph B. White and Gregory A. Patterson, "GM Begins Quest to Win Back Consumer Confidence," *The Wall Street Journal* (May 4, 1990): B1.

[7] Robert P. Gandossy, *Bad Business: The OPM Scandal and the Seduction of the Establishment* (New York: Basic Books, 1985), 11.

[8] Ibid., 12–13.

[9] Steven Bach, *Final Cut: Dreams and Disaster in the Making of Heaven's Gate* (New York: William Morrow, 1985).

[10] Ibid., 76–77.

[11] Christopher Byron, *The Fanciest Dive* (New York: W.W. Norton, 1986).

[12] Seymour M. Hersh, *The Price of Power: Kissinger in the Nixon White House* (New York: Summit Books, 1983).

[13] Ibid., 24.

[14] Cialdini, *Influence: Science and Practice*, 157.

[15] Frank Rose, *West of Eden: The End of Innocence at Apple Computer* (New York: Viking Penguin, 1989), 274.

[16] Ibid., 276.

[17] Jerry Ross and Kenneth R. Ferris, "Interpersonal Attraction and Organizational Outcomes: A Field Examination," *Administrative Science Quarterly* 26 (1981): 617–632.

[18] M.G. Efran and E.W.J. Patterson, "The Politics of Appearance," University of Toronto, 1976.

[19] Cialdini, *Influence: Science and Practice*, 162. Cialdini also cites P.L. Benson, S.A. Karabenic, and R.M. Lerner, "Pretty Pleases: The Effects of Physical Attractiveness on Race, Sex, and Receiving Help," *Journal of Experimental Social Psychology* 12 (1976): 409–415; and S. Chaiken, "Communicator Physical Attractiveness and Persuasion," *Journal of Personality and Social Psychology* 37 (1979): 1387–1397.

[20] Cialdini, *Influence: Science and Practice*.

[21] Bryan Burrough and John Helyar, *Barbarians at the Gate: The Fall of RJR Nabisco* (New York: Harper and Row, 1990), 69.

[22] Camille B. Wortman and Joan A. Linsenmeier, "Interpersonal Attraction and Techniques of Ingratiation in Organizational Settings, *New Directions in Organizational Behavior*, eds. Barry M. Staw and Gerald R. Salancik (Chicago: St. Clair Press, 1977), 133–178.

[23] Robert A. Caro, *The Power Broker: Robert Moses and the Fall of New York* (New York: Random House, 1974), 454.

[24] Ibid., 455.

[25] Ibid., 457.

[26] Ibid., 458.

[27] Gandossy, *Bad Business*, 19.

[28] Ibid., 26.

[29] Laton McCartney, *Friends in High Places: The Bechtel Story* (New York: Simon and Schuster, 1988), 156.

[30] Mark Stevens, *Sudden Death: The Rise and Fall of E.F. Hutton* (New York: Penguin, 1989), 81.

[31] Ibid., 82–83.

[32] Ibid., 84.

[33] M. Sherif et al., *Intergroup Conflict and Cooperation: The Robbers' Cave Experiment* (Norman: University of Oklahoma Institute of Intergroup Relations, 1961).

[34] Cialdini, *Influence: Science and Practice*, 171.

[35] Ibid., 172.

[36] Fritz Heider, *The Psychology of Interpersonal Relations* (New York: John Wiley, 1958).

[37] Arlie Hochschild, *The Managed Heart* (Berkeley: University of California Press, 1983).

[38] Ibid., 96–97.

[39] Anat Rafaeli and Robert I. Sutton, "The Expression of Emotion in Organizational Life," *Research in Organizational Behavior*, ed. Barry M. Staw, vol. 11 (Greenwich, CT: JAI Press, 1989), 15–16.

[40] Robert I. Sutton and Anat Rafaeli, "Untangling the Relationship Between Displayed Emotions and Organizational Sales: The Case of Convenience Stores," *Academy of Management Journal* 31 (1988): 465.

[41] Anat Rafaeli and Robert I. Sutton, "Expression of Emotion as Part of the Work Role," *Academy of Management Review* 12 (1987): 23–37.

[42] R.O. Arther and R.R. Caputo, *Interrogation for Investigators* (New York: William C. Copp and Associates, 1959), 75–76.

[43] K.L. Tidd and J.S. Lockard, "Monetary Significance of the Affiliative Smile," *Bulletin of the Psychonomic Society* 11 (1978): 344–346.

[44] Robert I. Sutton, "Maintaining Organizational Norms About Expressed Emotions: The Case of Bill Collectors," *Administrative Science Quarterly* 36 (1991): 245–268.

[45] Anat Rafaeli and Robert I. Sutton, "Emotional Contrast Strategies as Means of Social Influence: Lessons from Criminal Interrogators and Bill Collectors," *Academy of Management Journal* (in press).

[46] Rafaeli and Sutton, "Expression of Emotion," 31.

Chapter 12

[1] Thomas C. Schelling, *The Strategy of Conflict* (New York: Oxford University Press, 1963).

[2] Peter W. Bernstein, "Upheaval at Bendix," *Fortune* (November 1, 1980): 48–56.

[3] Ibid., 52–53.

[4] Hugh D. Menzies, "The Boardroom Battle at Bendix," *Fortune* (January 11, 1982): 56.

[5] Ibid., 60.

[6] Ibid., 62.

[7] Ibid.

[8] M. Horwitch, "Managing the U.S. Supersonic Transport Program (A)," 678-040. Boston: Harvard Business School, 1977.

[9] Robert A. Caro, *The Power Broker: Robert Moses and the Fall of New York* (New York: Random House, 1974), 203.

[10] Aaron Bernstein, *Grounded: Frank Lorenzo and the Destruction of Eastern Airlines* (New York: Simon and Schuster, 1990), 84–85.

[11] Barry Schwartz, "Waiting, Exchange, and Power: The Distribution of Time in Social Systems," *American Journal of Sociology* 79 (1974): 843–844.

[12] Ibid., 844.

[13] Ibid., 857.

[14] Ibid., 859.

[15] Bryan Burrough and John Helyar, *Barbarians at the Gate: The Fall of RJR Nabisco* (New York: Harper and Row, 1990), 24.

[16] *Chicago Daily News* (December 27, 1972): 4.

[17] Seymour M. Hersh, *The Price of Power: Kissinger in the Nixon White House* (New York: Summit Books, 1983), 44.

[18] *Journal of the House*, Alabama State Legislature (1977): 2698.

[19] Bernstein, *Grounded*, 42.

[20] Gerald R. Salancik, "Commitment and the Control of Organizational Behavior and Belief," *New Directions in Organizational Behavior*, eds. Barry M. Staw and Gerald R. Salancik (Chicago: St. Clair Press, 1977), 1–54.

[21] Peter Bachrach and Morton S. Baratz, "Two Faces of Power," *American Political Science Review* 56 (1962): 947–952.

[22] Neil Fligstein, "The Intraorganizational Power Struggle: Rise of Finance Personnel to Top Leadership in Large Corporations, 1919–1979," *American Sociological Review* 52 (1987): 44–58.

[23] David Halberstam, *The Best and the Brightest* (New York: Random House, 1972), 435–436.

[24] Ibid., 437.

Chapter 13

[1] David Halberstam, *The Best and the Brightest* (New York: Random House, 1972), 285.

[2] Ibid., 53.

[3] John W. Meyer and Brian Rowan, "Institutional Organizations: Formal Structure as Myth and Ceremony," *American Journal of Sociology* 83 (1977): 340–363; John W. Meyer and W. Richard Scott, *Organizational Environments: Ritual and Rationality* (Beverly Hills, CA: Sage, 1983).

[4] Martha S. Feldman and James G. March, "Information in Organizations as Signal and Symbol," *Administrative Science Quarterly* 26 (1981): 171–186.

[5] Fred A. Kramer, "Policy Analysis as Ideology," *Public Administrative Review* 35 (1975): 509.

[6] Richard M. Cyert, Herbert A. Simon, and Donald B. Trow, "Observation of a Business Decision," *Journal of Business* 29 (1956): 237–248.

[7] Donald Frey, "The Techies' Challenge to the Bean Counters," *The Wall Street Journal* (July 16, 1990): A12.

[8] Maryann Keller, *Rude Awakening: The Rise, Fall, and Struggle for Recovery of General Motors* (New York: William Morrow, 1989), 216.

[9] Ibid., 105.

[10] Mark Stevens, *Sudden Death: The Rise and Fall of E.F. Hutton* (New York: Penguin, 1989), 277.

[11] Halberstam, *The Best and the Brightest*, 304–305.

[12] Ibid., 562–563.

[13] Douglas K. Smith and Robert C. Alexander, *Fumbling the Future: How Xerox Invented, Then Ignored, the First Personal Computer* (New York: William Morrow, 1988).

[14] Ibid., 134.

[15] Ibid., 218.

[16] H. Thomas Johnson and Robert S, Kaplan, *Relevance Lost: The Rise and Fall of Management Accounting* (Boston: Harvard Business School Press, 1987).

[17] Christopher Byron, *The Fanciest Dive* (New York: W.W. Norton, 1986), 56–57.

[18] Jeffrey Pfeffer and Gerald R. Salancik, *The External Control of Organizations: A Resource Dependence Perspective* (New York: Harper and Row, 1978).

[19] Gerald R. Salancik and Jeffrey Pfeffer, "The Bases and Use of Power in Organizational Decision Making: The Case of a University," *Administrative Science Quarterly* 19 (1974): 462–463.

[20] Rosabeth M. Kanter, *Men and Women of the Corporation* (New York: Basic Books, 1977).

[21] David Halberstam, *The Reckoning* (New York: William Morrow, 1986); Max Holland, *When the Machine Stopped* (Boston: Harvard Business School Press, 1989).

[22] Jeffrey Pfeffer and Gerald R. Salancik, "Administrator Effectiveness: The Effects of Advocacy and Information on Resource Allocations," *Human Relations* 30 (1977): 641–656.

[23] N. Dixon, *On the Psychology of Military Incompetence* (New York: Basic Books, 1976), 147.

[24] Smith and Alexander, *Fumbling the Future*.

[25] Meyer and Rowan, "Institutional Organizations."

[26] Smith and Alexander, *Fumbling the Future*, 190.

[27] Byron, *The Fanciest Dive*, 274–275.

[28] Ibid., 277.

Chapter 14

[1] Maryann Keller, *Rude Awakening: The Rise, Fall, and Struggle for Recovery of General Motors* (New York: William Morrow, 1989), 50.

[2] John M. Barry, *The Ambition and the Power* (New York: Viking, 1989), 67.

[3] Ibid., 99.

[4] David Halberstam, *The Best and the Brightest* (New York: Random House, 1972), 105.

[5] Barry, *The Ambition and the Power*, 78.

[6] Ibid., 81.

[7] Ibid., 82.

[8] Ibid., 83.

[9] Ibid.

[10] Philip Selznick, *TVA and the Grass Roots* (Berkeley: University of California Press, 1949).

[11] Seymour M. Hersh, *The Price of Power: Kissinger in the Nixon White House* (New York: Summit Books, 1983), 29.

[12] Henry Kissinger, *The White House Years* (Boston: Little, Brown, 1979), 42.

[13] Hersh, *The Price of Power*, 35.

Chapter 15

[1] Richard M. Nixon, *Leaders* (New York: Warner Books, 1982), 4.

[2] Jeffrey Pfeffer, *Power in Organizations* (Marshfield, MA: Pitman Publishing, 1981).

[3] Murray Edelman, *The Symbolic Uses of Politics* (Urbana: University of Illinois Press, 1964), 39.

[4] Ibid., 124.

[5] David Halberstam, *The Best and the Brightest* (New York: Random House, 1972), 217.

[6] Edelman, *The Symbolic Uses of Politics*, 12.

[7] Herbert Stein, "Confessions of a Tax Addict," *The Wall Street Journal* (October 2, 1989): A14.

[8] Ibid.

[9] C.W. Morris, *Signs, Language and Behavior* (New York: Prentice-Hall, 1949), 214.

[10] Merriam-Webster, Inc., *Webster's Third New International Dictionary* (Springfield, MA: Merriam-Webster, Inc., 1981), 2619–2620.

[11] Karl E. Weick, "Cognitive Processes in Organizations," *Research in Organizational Behavior*, ed. Barry M. Staw, vol. 1 (Greenwich, CT: JAI Press, 1979), 42.

[12] Thomas J. Peters, "Symbols, Patterns, and Settings: An Optimistic Case for Getting Things Done," *Organizational Dynamics* 7 (1978): 10.

[13] Nixon, *Leaders*, 4.

[14] Louis R. Pondy, "Leadership Is a Language Game," *Leadership: Where Else Can We Go?*, eds. Morgan W. McCall, Jr., and Michael M. Lombardo (Durham, NC: Duke University Press, 1978), 94–95.

[15] Christopher Byron, *The Fanciest Dive* (New York: W.W. Norton, 1986), 63.

[16] Ibid., 64–65.

[17] Frank Rose, *West of Eden: The End of Innocence at Apple Computer* (New York: Viking Penguin, 1989), 124.

[18] Ibid., 130.

[19] Ibid., 131.

[20] Robert A. Caro, *The Path to Power: The Years of Lyndon Johnson* (New York: Alfred A. Knopf, 1982), 235.

[21] Ibid., 236.

[22] Edelman, *The Symbolic Uses of Politics*, 123.

[23] Ibid., 78.

[24] Mark Stevens, *Sudden Death: The Rise and Fall of E.F. Hutton* (New York: Penguin, 1989), 191.

[25] Ibid., 194.

[26] J. Patrick Wright, *On A Clear Day You Can See General Motors* (Grosse Point, MI: Wright Enterprises, 1979), 39.

[27] Ibid., 44.

[28] Marc R. Reinganum, "The Effect of Executive Succession on Shareholder Wealth," *Administrative Science Quarterly* 30 (1985): 46–60; Stewart D. Friedman and Harbir Singh, "CEO Succession and Stockholder

Reaction: The Influence of Organizational Context and Event Content," *Academy of Management Journal* 32 (1989): 718–744.
[29] Mayer N. Zald, "Who Shall Rule? A Political Analysis of Succession in a Large Welfare Organization," *Pacific Sociological Review* 8 (1965): 52–60.
[30] Wright, *On a Clear Day*, 16–18.
[31] Rose, *West of Eden*, 139.
[32] John M. Barry, *The Ambition and the Power* (New York: Viking, 1989), 77.
[33] Rose, *West of Eden*, 98.

Chapter 16

[1] John M. Barry, *The Ambition and the Power* (New York: Viking, 1989), 5.
[2] Nicholas Lemann, "The Split: A True Story of Washington Lawyers," *Washington Post Magazine* (March 23, 1980): 20.
[3] Ibid., 19.
[4] Ibid.
[5] Ibid., 20.
[6] Thomas Kessner, *Fiorello H. La Guardia and the Making of Modern New York* (New York: McGraw-Hill, 1989), 570.
[7] David Halberstam, *The Best and the Brightest* (New York: Random House, 1972), 511.
[8] Alison Leigh Cowan, "The Partners Revolt at Peat Marwick," *New York Times* (November 18, 1990).
[9] Ibid., 10.
[10] Ibid.
[11] Robert A. Caro, *The Power Broker: Robert Moses and the Fall of New York* (New York: Random House, 1974), 998.
[12] Ibid., 986.
[13] Ibid., 996.
[14] Ibid., 1003.
[15] Ken Auletta, "The Fall of Lehman Brothers: The Men, The Money, The Merger," *New York Times Magazine* (February 24, 1985): 37.
[16] Ibid., 40.
[17] Ibid.
[18] Sally Bedell Smith, *In All His Glory: The Life of William S. Paley* (New York: Simon and Schuster, 1990).

Chapter 17

[1] Richard T. Pascale, *Managing on the Edge* (New York: Simon and Schuster, 1990).
[2] Robert A. Burgelman, "Intraorganizational Ecology of Strategy Making and Organizational Adaptation: Theory and Field Research," *Organization Science* (in press).
[3] Bryon Burrough and John Helyar, *Barbarians at the Gate: The Fall of RJR Nabisco* (New York: Harper and Row, 1990), 32.
[4] Ibid., 33.
[5] Maryann Keller, *Rude Awakening: The Rise, Fall, and Struggle for Recovery of General Motors* (New York: William Morrow, 1989), 228.
[6] Paul Milgrom and John Roberts, "An Economic Approach to Influence

Activities in Organizations," *American Journal of Sociology* 94 (supplement, 1988): S156–S157.

[7] Mark Stevens, *Sudden Death: The Rise and Fall of E.F. Hutton* (New York: Penguin, 1989), 160.

[8] Ibid., 219.

[9] Douglas K. Smith and Robert C. Alexander, *Fumbling the Future: How Xerox Invented, Then Ignored, the First Personal Computer* (New York: William Morrow, 1988), 144.

[10] Frank Rose, *West of Eden: The End of Innocence at Apple Computer* (New York: Viking Penguin, 1989), 92.

[11] Nick Kotz, *Wild Blue Yonder: Money, Politics, and the B-1 Bomber* (New York: Pantheon Books, 1988).

[12] Ibid., 11.

[13] Ibid., 14.

[14] Jeffrey Pfeffer, *Power in Organizations* (Marshfield, MA: Pitman Publishing, 1981).

[15] Pascale, *Managing on the Edge*, 16.

[16] Ibid.

[17] Kathleen M. Eisenhardt and L.J. Bourgeois, "Politics of Strategic Decision Making in High-Velocity Environments: Toward a Midrange Theory," *Academy of Management Journal* 31 (1988): 737–770.

[18] Ibid., 742–743.

[19] Ibid., 760.

[20] Harvey M. Sapolsky, *The Polaris System Development* (Cambridge, MA: Harvard University Press, 1972), 232.

[21] Ibid., 242.

[22] Ibid., 244.

[23] Ibid., 246.

[24] Finn Borum, "A Power-Strategy Alternative to Organization Development," *Organization Studies* 1 (1980): 123–146.

[25] Ibid., 129.

Chapter 18

[1] Tracy Kidder, *Soul of a New Machine* (Boston: Atlantic-Little, Brown, 1981), 111.

[2] Jane Gross, "Turning Disease Into a Cause: Breast Cancer Follows AIDS," *New York Times* (January 7, 1991): A1.

[3] David Halberstam, *The Reckoning* (New York: William Morrow, 1986), 90.

[4] Ibid., 91.

[5] Robert A. Caro, *Means of Ascent: The Years of Lyndon Johnson* (New York: Alfred A. Knopf, 1990), xix–xx.

[6] Ibid., xxi.

[7] Richard M. Nixon, *Leaders* (New York: Warner Books, 1982), 345.

BIBLIOGRAPHY

Achen, Christopher H. 1986. *The Statistical Analysis of Quasi-Experiments.* Berkeley: University of California Press.

Allen, Robert W., et al. 1979. "Organizational Politics: Tactics and Characteristics of Its Actors." *California Management Review,* 22: 77–83.

Archibald, W. Peter. 1974. "Alternative Explanations for Self-Fulfilling Prophecy." *Psychological Bulletin,* 81: 74–84.

Argyris, Chris. 1974. *Behind the Front Page.* San Francisco: Jossey-Bass.

Aronson, Elliot. 1972. *The Social Animal.* San Francisco: W. H. Freeman.

Aronson, E., and J. Mills. 1959. "The Effect of Severity of Initiation on Liking for a Group." *Journal of Abnormal and Social Psychology,* 59: 177–181.

Arther, R.O., and R.R. Caputo. 1959. *Interrogation for Investigators.* New York: William C. Copp and Associates.

Auletta, Ken. 1985a. "Power, Greed and Glory on Wall Street: The Fall of Lehman Brothers." *New York Times Magazine,* February 17, 1985.

———. 1985b. "The Fall of Lehman Brothers: The Men, The Money, The Merger." *New York Times Magazine,* February 24, 1985.

Bach, Steven. 1985. *Final Cut: Dreams and Disaster in the Making of Heaven's Gate.* New York: William Morrow.

Bachrach, Peter, and Morton S. Baratz. 1962. "Two Faces of Power." *American Political Science Review,* 56: 947 952.

Barry, John M. 1989. *The Ambition and the Power.* New York: Viking.

Bass, Bernard M. 1988. "Evolving Perspectives on Charismatic Leadership" in *Charismatic Leadership:* 40–77. Jay A. Conger, Rabindra N. Kanungo and Associates (eds.). San Francisco: Jossey-Bass.

Bavelas, Alex. 1950. "Communication Patterns in Task Oriented Groups." *Journal of Acoustical Society of America,* 22: 725–730.

Bazerman, Max H., and Margaret A. Neale. 1983. "Heuristics in Negotiation: Limitations to Dispute Resolution Effectiveness" in *Negotiating in Organizations:* 51–67. M. H. Bazerman and R. J. Lewicki (eds.). Beverly Hills, CA: Sage.

Bem, Darly J. 1972. "Self-Perception Theory" in *Advances in Experimental Social Psychology,* vol. 6: 1–62. Leonard Berkowitz (ed.). New York: Academic Press.

Bennis, Warren, and Burt Nanus. 1985. *Leaders: The Strategies for Taking Charge.* New York: Harper and Row.

Benson, P.L., S.A. Karabenic, and R.M. Lerner. 1976. "Pretty Pleases: The Effects of Physical Attractiveness on Race, Sex, and Receiving Help." *Journal of Experimental Social Psychology,* 12: 409–415.

Berlew, David E., and Douglas T. Hall. 1966. "The Socialization of Managers: Effects of Expectations on Performance." *Administrative Science Quarterly,* 11: 207–223.

Bernstein, Aaron. 1990. *Grounded: Frank Lorenzo and the Destruction of Eastern Airlines.* New York: Simon and Schuster.

Bernstein, Peter W. 1980. "Upheaval at Bendix." *Fortune,* November 1, 1980: 48–56.

Berscheid, Ellen, and Elaine Hatfield Walster. 1969. *Interpersonal Attraction.* Reading, MA: Addison-Wesley.

Beyer, Janice M., and Thomas M. Lodahl. 1976. "A Comparative Study of Patterns of Influence in United States and English Universities." *Administrative Science Quarterly,* 21: 104–129.

Blau, Peter M. 1964. *Exchange and Power in Social Life.* New York: John Wiley.

Borum, Finn. 1980. "A Power-Strategy Alternative to Organization Development." *Organization Studies,* 1: 123–146.

Bradford, David L., and Allan R. Cohen. 1984. *Managing for Excellence.* New York: John Wiley.

Brass, Daniel J. 1984. "Being in the Right Place: A Structural Analysis of Individual Influence in an Organization." *Administrative Science Quarterly,* 29: 518–539.

Brehm, Jack W. 1966. *A Theory of Psychological Reactance.* New York: Academic Press.

Brett, Jeanne M., Stephen B. Goldberg, and William L. Ury. 1990. "Designing Systems for Resolving Disputes in Organizations." *American Psychologist,* 45: 162–170.

Brewer, Marilynn B., and Roderick M. Kramer. 1985. "The Psychology of Intergroup Attitudes and Behavior." *Annual Review of Psychology,* 36: 219–243.

Brown, Richard Harvey. 1978. "Bureaucracy as Praxis: Toward a Political Phenomenology of Formal Organizations." *Administrative Science Quarterly,* 23: 365–382.

Burgelman, Robert A. 1991. "Intraorganizational Ecology of Strategy-Making and Organizational Adaptation: Theory and Field Research." *Organization Science* (in press).

Burrough, Bryan, and John Helyar. 1990. *Barbarians at the Gate: The Fall of RJR Nabisco.* New York: Harper and Row.

Byrne, D. 1969. "Attitudes and Attraction" in *Advances in Experimental Social Psychology*, vol. 4: 35–89. Leonard Berkowitz (ed.). New York: Academic Press.

Byron, Christopher. 1986. *The Fanciest Dive*. New York: W.W. Norton.

Caro, Robert A. 1974. *The Power Broker: Robert Moses and the Fall of New York*. New York: Random House.

———. 1982. *The Path to Power: The Years of Lyndon Johnson*. New York: Alfred A. Knopf.

———. 1990. *Means of Ascent: The Years of Lyndon Johnson*. New York: Alfred A. Knopf.

———. 1991. "My Search for Coke Stevenson." *The New York Times Book Review*, February 3, 1991, 1 and following.

Chaiken, S. 1979. "Communicator Physical Attractiveness and Persuasion." *Journal of Personality and Social Psychology*, 37: 1387–1397.

Chakrabarti, Alok K. 1990. "Organizational Factors in Post-Acquisition Performance." *IEEE Transactions on Engineering Management*, 37: 259–268.

Christie, Richard, and Florence L. Geis. 1970. *Studies in Machiavellianism*. New York: Academic Press.

Cialdini, Robert B. 1984. *Influence: How and Why People Agree to Things*. New York: William Morrow.

———. 1988. *Influence: Science and Practice*, 2d ed. Glenview, IL: Scott, Foresman.

Clancy, Paul, and Shirley Elder. 1980. *TIP: A Biography of Thomas P. O'Neill Speaker of the House*. New York: Macmillan.

Cowan, Alison Leigh. 1990. "The Partners Revolt at Peak Marwick." *New York Times*, November 18, 1990.

Crozier, Michel. 1964. *The Bureaucratic Phenomenon*. Chicago: University of Chicago Press.

Cyert, Richard M., and James G. March. 1963. *A Behavioral Theory of the Firm*. Englewood Cliffs, NJ: Prentice-Hall.

Cyert, Richard M., Herbert A. Simon, and Donald B. Trow. 1956. "Observation of a Business Decision." *Journal of Business*, 29: 237–248.

Davis, Otto A., M.A.H. Dempster, and Aaron Wildavsky. 1966. "A Theory of the Budgeting Process." *American Political Science Review*, 60: 529–547.

Davis, Stanley. 1984. *Managing Corporate Culture*. Cambridge, MA: Ballinger.

Deal, Terrence, and Allan A. Kennedy. 1982. *Corporate Cultures*. Reading, MA: Addison-Wesley.

Dean, John. 1976. *Blind Ambition*. New York: Simon and Schuster.

DiMaggio, Paul J., and Walter W. Powell. 1983. "The Iron Cage Revisited: Institutional Isomorphism and Collective Rationality in Organizational Fields." *American Sociological Review*, 48: 147–160.

Dixon, N. 1976. *On the Psychology of Military Incompetence*. New York: Basic Books.

Dornbusch, Sanford M. 1955. "The Military Academy as an Assimilating Institution." *Social Forces*, 33: 316–321.

Edelman, Murray. 1964. *The Symbolic Uses of Politics*. Urbana: University of Illinois Press.

Edwards, Richard C. 1979. *Contested Terrain: The Transformation of the Workplace in the Twentieth Century*. New York: Basic Books.

Efran, M.G., and E.W.J. Patterson. 1976. "The Politics of Appearance." Unpublished manuscript, University of Toronto.

Eisenhardt, Kathleen M., and L.J. Bourgeois. 1988. "Politics of Strategic Decision Making in High-Velocity Environments: Toward a Midrange Theory." *Academy of Management Journal*, 31: 737–770.

Emerson, Richard M. 1962. "Power-Dependence Relations." *American Sociological Review*, 27: 31–41.

Feldman, Martha S., and James G. March. 1981. "Information in Organizations as Signal and Symbol," *Administrative Science Quarterly*, 26: 171–186.

Festinger, Leon. 1954. "A Theory of Social Comparison Processes." *Human Relations*, 7: 117 140.

———. 1957. *A Theory of Cognitive Dissonance*. Stanford, CA: Stanford University Press.

Festinger, L., S. Schacter, and K. Back. 1950. *Social Pressures in Informal Groups*. Stanford, CA: Stanford University Press.

Fisher, Roger, and William Ury. 1981. *Getting to Yes: Negotiating Agreements without Giving In*. Boston: Houghton Mifflin.

Fligstein, Neil. 1987. "The Intraorganizational Power Struggle: Rise of Finance Personnel to Top Leadership in Large Corporations, 1919–1979." *American Sociological Review*, 52: 44–58.

Freeman, Linton C. 1979. "Centrality in Social Networks: Conceptual Clarifications." *Social Networks*, 1: 215–239.

French, John R.P., Jr., and Bertram Raven. 1968. "The Bases of Social Power" in *Group Dynamics*, 3rd ed.: 259–269. Dorwin Cartwright and Alvin Zander (eds.). New York: Harper and Row.

Frey, Donald. 1990. "The Techies' Challenge to the Bean Counters." *The Wall Street Journal*, July 16, 1990: A12.

Friedman, Stewart D., and Harbir Singh. 1989. "CEO Succession and Stockholder Reaction: The Influence of Organizational Context and Event Content." *Academy of Management Journal*, 32: 718–744.

Galbraith, Jay R. 1973. *Designing Complex Organizations*. Reading, MA: Addison-Wesley.

Gandossy, Robert P. 1985. *Bad Business: The OPM Scandal and the Seduction of the Establishment*. New York: Basic Books.

Gandz, Jeffrey, and Victor V. Murray. 1980. "The Experience of Workplace Politics," *Academy of Management Journal*, 23: 237–251.

Gardner, John W. 1990. *On Leadership*. New York: Free Press.

Ginzel, Linda E. 1990. "The Impact of Biased Feedback Strategies on Performance Judgments." Palo Alto, CA: Graduate School of Business, Stanford University, Research Paper No. 1102.

Gouldner, Alvin W. 1960. "The Norm of Reciprocity: A Preliminary Statement." *American Sociological Review*, 25: 161–178.

Gross, Jane. 1991. "Turning Disease Into a Cause: Breast Cancer Follows AIDS." *New York Times*, January 7, 1991: A1, A10.

Hackman, Judith Dozier. 1985. "Power and Centrality in the Allocation of Resources in Colleges and Universities." *Administrative Science Quarterly,* 30: 61–77.

Halberstam, David. 1972. *The Best and the Brightest.* New York: Random House.

———. 1986. *The Reckoning.* New York: William Morrow.

Hannan, Michael T., and John Freeman. 1984. "Structural Inertia and Organizational Change." *American Sociological Review,* 49: 149–164.

———. 1989. *Organizational Ecology.* Cambridge, MA: Harvard University Press.

Harder, Joseph W. 1989. *Play for Pay: Salary Determination and the Effects of Over- and Under-Reward on Individual Performance in Professional Sports.* Unpublished doctoral dissertation, Stanford University.

Heider, Fritz. 1958. *The Psychology of Interpersonal Relations.* New York: John Wiley.

Helmich, Donald L., and Warren B. Brown. 1972. "Successor Type and Organizational Change in the Corporate Enterprise." *Administrative Science Quarterly,* 17: 371–381.

Hersh, Seymour M. 1983. *The Price of Power: Kissinger in the Nixon White House.* New York: Summit Books.

Hickson, D.J., et al. 1971. "A Strategic Contingencies' Theory of Intraorganizational Power." *Administrative Science Quarterly,* 16: 216–229.

Hills, Frederick S., and Thomas A. Mahoney. 1978. "University Budgets and Organizational Decision Making." *Administrative Science Quarterly,* 23: 454–465.

Hinings, C.R., et al. 1974. "Structural Conditions of Intraorganizational Power." *Administrative Science Quarterly,* 19: 22–44.

Hochschild, Arlie R. 1983. *The Managed Heart.* Berkeley: University of California Press.

Holland, Max. 1989. *When the Machine Stopped.* Boston: Harvard Business School Press.

Horwitch, M. "Managing the U.S. Supersonic Transport Program (A)," 678–049. Boston: Harvard Business School, 1977.

House, Robert J. 1977. "A 1976 Theory of Charismatic Leadership" in *Leadership: The Cutting Edge.* J.G. Hunt and L.L. Larson (eds.). Carbondale: Southern Illinois University Press.

House, Robert J., William D. Spangler, and James Woycke. 1989. "Personality and Charisma in the U.S. Presidency: A Psychological Theory of Leadership Effectiveness." Unpublished manuscript, Wharton School, University of Pennsylvania.

Jacobs, R.C., and D.T. Campbell. 1961. "The Perpetuation of an Arbitrary Tradition Through Successive Generations of a Laboratory Microculture." *Journal of Abnormal and Social Psychology,* 62: 649–658.

Jacoby, Sanford M. 1985. *Employing Bureaucracy: Managers, Unions, and the Transformation of Work in American Industry, 1900–1945.* New York: Columbia University Press.

Janis, Irving L. 1972. *Victims of Groupthink.* Boston: Houghton Mifflin.

Johnson, H. Thomas, and Robert S. Kaplan. 1987. *Relevance Lost: The Rise and Fall of Management Accounting*. Boston: Harvard Business School Press.

Kahn, Robert L., et al. 1964. *Organizational Stress: Studies in Role Conflict and Ambiguity*. New York: John Wiley.

Kahneman, Daniel, and Amos Tversky. 1984. "Choices, Values, and Frames." *American Psychologist*, 39: 341–350.

Kanter, Rosabeth M. 1977. *Men and Women of the Corporation*. New York: Basic Books.

———. 1979. "Power Failure in Management Circuits." *Harvard Business Review*, 57 (no. 4): 65–75.

Keller, Maryann. 1989. *Rude Awakening: The Rise, Fall, and Struggle for Recovery of General Motors*. New York: William Morrow.

Kessner, Thomas. 1989. *Fiorello H. La Guardia and the Making of Modern New York*. New York: McGraw-Hill.

Kidder, Tracy. 1981. *Soul of a New Machine*. Boston: Atlantic-Little, Brown.

Kissinger, Henry. 1979. *The White House Years*. Boston: Little, Brown.

Konrad, Alison M., and Jeffrey Pfeffer. 1990. "Do You Get What You Deserve? Factors Affecting the Relationship Between Productivity and Pay." *Administrative Science Quarterly*, 35: 258–285.

Kotter, John P. 1978. "Power, Success, and Organizational Effectiveness." *Organizational Dynamics*, 6 (no. 3): 27–40.

———. 1982. *The General Managers*. New York: Free Press.

———. 1985. *Power and Influence: Beyond Formal Authority*. New York: Free Press.

Kotz, Nick. 1988. *Wild Blue Yonder: Money, Politics, and the B-1 Bomber*. New York: Pantheon Books.

Krackhardt, David. 1990. "Assessing the Political Landscape: Structure, Cognition and Power in Organizations." *Administrative Science Quarterly*, 35: 342–369.

Kramer, Fred A. 1975. "Policy Analysis as Ideology." *Public Administration Review*, 35: 509–517.

Kuhn, Thomas S. 1970. *The Structure of Scientific Revolutions*, 2d. ed. Chicago: University of Chicago Press.

Latane, Bibb, and John M. Darley. 1968. "Group Inhibition of Bystander Intervention in Emergencies." *Journal of Personality and Social Psychology*, 10: 215–221.

Lax, David A., and James K. Sebenius. 1986. *The Manager as Negotiator*. New York: Free Press.

Leavitt, Harold J. 1951. "Effects of Certain Communication Patterns on Group Performance." *Journal of Abnormal and Social Psychology*, 46: 38–50.

———. 1986. *Corporate Pathfinders*. Homewood, IL: Dow Jones-Irwin.

Lemann, Nicholas. "The Split: A True Story of Washington Lawyers." *Washington Post Magazine*, March 23, 1980.

Lerner, M.J., and C.H. Simmons. 1966. "Observer's Reaction to the 'Innocent Victim': Compassion or Rejection?" *Journal of Personality and Social Psychology*, 4: 203–210.

Lewis, Michael. 1990. *Liar's Poker: Rising Through the Wreckage on Wall Street*. New York: Penguin.

Livingston, J. Sterling. 1969. "Pygmalion in Management." *Harvard Business Review*, 47 (July–August): 81–89.

Lodahl, Janice, and Gerald Gordon. 1972. "The Structure of Scientific Fields and the Functioning of University Graduate Departments." *American Sociological Review*, 37: 57–72.

———. 1973. "Funding the Sciences in University Departments." *Educational Record*, 54: 74–82.

Long, Norton E. 1962. "The Administrative Organization as a Political System," in *Concept and Issues in Administrative Behavior*. S. Mailick and E.H. Van Ness (eds.). Englewood Cliffs, NJ: Prentice-Hall.

Mackenzie, Kenneth D. 1975. *A Theory of Group Structures*. London: Gordon and Breach.

Madison, Dan L., et al. 1980. "Organizational Politics: An Exploration of Managers' Perceptions." *Human Relations*, 33: 79–100.

March, James G., and John P. Olsen. 1976. *Ambiguity and Choice in Organizations*. Bergen, Norway: Universitetsforlaget.

Matthews, Christopher. 1988. *Hardball: How Politics Is Played—Told By One Who Knows The Game*. New York: Summit Books.

McCartney, Laton. 1988. *Friends in High Places: The Bechtel Story*. New York: Simon and Schuster.

McClelland, D.C. 1975. *Power: The Inner Experience*. New York: Irvington.

McClelland, D.C., and R.E. Boyatzis. 1982. "Leadership Motive Pattern and Long-term Success in Management." *Journal of Applied Psychology*, 67: 737–743.

McClelland, D.C., and D. Burnham. 1976. "Power Is the Great Motivator." *Harvard Business Review*, 54 (no. 2): 100–111.

Mechanic, David. 1962. "Sources of Power of Lower Participants in Complex Organizations." *Administrative Science Quarterly*, 7: 349–364.

Menzies, Hugh D. 1982. "The Boardroom Battle at Bendix." *Fortune*, January 11, 1982: 54–64.

Merriam-Webster, Inc. 1981. *Webster's Third New International Dictionary*. Springfield, MA: Merriam-Webster, Inc.

Meyer, Herbert E. "Shootout at the Johns-Manville Corral." *Fortune*, October 1976: 146–154.

Meyer, John W., and Brian Rowan. 1977. "Institutional Organizations: Formal Structure as Myth and Ceremony." *American Journal of Sociology*, 83: 340–363.

Meyer, John W., and W. Richard Scott. 1983. *Organizational Environments: Ritual and Rationality*. Beverly Hills, CA: Sage.

Milgram, Stanley. 1974. *Obedience to Authority*. New York: Harper and Row.

Milgrom, Paul, and John Roberts. 1988. "An Economic Approach to Influence Activities in Organizations." *American Journal of Sociology*, 94 (Supplement): S154–S179.

Miyazawa, Setsuo. 1986. "Legal Departments of Japanese Corporations in the United States: A Study on Organizational Adaptation to Multiple Environments." *Kobe University Law Review*, 20: 97–162.

Moore, William L., and Jeffrey Pfeffer. 1980. "The Relationship Between

Departmental Power and Faculty Careers on Two Campuses: The Case for Structural Effects on Faculty Salaries." *Research in Higher Education,* 13: 291–306.

Morris, C.W. 1949. *Signs, Language and Behavior.* New York: Prentice-Hall.

Nisbett, R.E., and L. Ross. 1980. *Human Inferences: Strategies and Short-comings of Social Judgment.* Englewood Cliffs, NJ: Prentice-Hall.

Nixon, Richard M. 1982. *Leaders.* New York: Warner Books.

O'Reilly, Charles. 1989. "Corporations, Culture, and Commitment: Motivation and Social Control in Organizations." *California Management Review,* 31: 9–25.

Pascale, Richard T. 1984. "Perspectives on Strategy: The Real Story Behind Honda's Success." *California Management Review,* 26: 47–72.

———. 1985. "The Paradox of 'Corporate Culture': Reconciling Ourselves to Socialization." *California Management Review,* 27: 26–41.

———. 1990. *Managing on the Edge.* New York: Simon and Schuster.

Pasmore, William A. 1988. *Designing Effective Organizations: The Socio-technical Systems Perspective.* New York: John Wiley.

Patchen, Martin. 1974. "The Locus and Basis of Influence in Organizational Decisions." *Organizational Behavior and Human Performance,* 11: 195–221.

Perrow, Charles. 1970. "Departmental Power and Perspectives in Industrial Firms," in *Power in Organizations:* 58–89. Mayer N. Zald (ed.). Nashville, TN: Vanderbilt University Press.

Peters, Thomas J. 1978. "Symbols, Patterns, and Settings: An Optimistic Case for Getting Things Done." *Organizational Dynamics,* 7: 3–23.

Peters, Thomas J., and Robert H. Waterman, Jr. 1982. *In Search of Excellence.* New York: Harper and Row.

Pettigrew, Andrew M. 1972. "Information Control as a Power Resource." *Sociology,* 6: 187–204.

———. 1973. *Politics of Organizational Decision-Making.* London: Tavistock.

Pfeffer, Jeffrey. 1981. *Power in Organizations.* Marshfield, MA: Pitman Publishing.

Pfeffer, Jeffrey, and Alison Davis-Blake. 1987. "Understanding Organizational Wage Structures: A Resource Dependence Approach." *Academy of Management Journal,* 30: 437–455.

Pfeffer, Jeffrey, and Alison Konrad. 1991. "The Effects of Individual Power on Earnings." *Work and Occupations.* In press.

Pfeffer, Jeffrey, and William L. Moore. 1980a. "Average Tenure of Academic Department Heads: The Effects of Paradigm, Size, and Departmental Demography." *Administrative Science Quarterly,* 25: 387–406.

———. 1980b. "Power in University Budgeting: A Replication and Extension." *Administrative Science Quarterly,* 25: 637–653.

Pfeffer, Jeffrey, and Gerald R. Salancik. 1974. "Organizational Decision Making as a Political Process: The Case of a University Budget." *Administrative Science Quarterly,* 19: 135–151.

———. 1977. "Administrator Effectiveness: The Effects of Advocacy

and Information on Resource Allocations." *Human Relations*, 30: 641–656.

––––––. 1978. *The External Control of Organizations: A Resource Dependence Perspective*. New York: Harper and Row.

Polsby, Nelson W. 1960. "How to Study Community Power: The Pluralist Alternative." *Journal of Politics*, 22: 474–484.

Pondy, Louis R. 1978. "Leadership is a Language Game" in *Leadership: Where Else Can We Go?:* 87–99. Morgan W. McCall, Jr., and Michael M. Lombardo (eds.). Durham, NC: Duke University Press.

Purkayastha, D. 1981. "Note on the Motorcycle Industry—1975." #578-210. Boston: Harvard Business School.

Rafaeli, Anat, and Robert I. Sutton. 1987. "Expression of Emotion as Part of the Work Role." *Academy of Management Review*, 12: 23–37.

––––––. 1989. "The Expression of Emotion in Organizational Life," in *Research in Organizational Behavior*, vol. 11: 1–42. Barry M. Staw (ed.). Greenwich, CT: JAI Press.

––––––. 1991. "Emotional Contrast Strategies as Means of Social Influence: Lessons from Criminal Interrogators and Bill Collectors." *Academy of Management Journal*. In press.

Reinganum, Marc R. 1985. "The Effect of Executive Succession on Shareholder Wealth." *Administrative Science Quarterly*, 30: 46–60.

Reiterman, Tim, and John Jacobs. 1982. *Raven: The Untold Story of the Rev. Jim Jones and His People*. New York: E.P. Dutton.

Roberts, Nancy C., and Raymond Trevor Bradley. 1988. "Limits of Charisma" in *Charismatic Leadership*: 253–275. Jay A. Conger, Rabindra N. Kanungo and Associates (eds.). San Francisco: Jossey-Bass.

Rose, Frank. 1989. *West of Eden: The End of Innocence at Apple Computer*. New York: Viking Penguin.

Ross, Jerry, and Kenneth R. Ferris. 1981. "Interpersonal Attraction and Organizational Outcomes: A Field Examination." *Administrative Science Quarterly*, 26: 617–632.

Salancik, Gerald R. 1977. "Commitment and the Control of Organizational Behavior and Belief" in *New Directions in Organizational Behavior*: 1–54. Barry M. Staw and Gerald R. Salancik (eds.). Chicago: St. Clair Press.

Salancik, Gerald R., and Jeffrey Pfeffer. 1974. "The Bases and Use of Power in Organizational Decision Making: The Case of a University." *Administrative Science Quarterly*, 19: 453–473.

––––––. 1977. "Who Gets Power—and How They Hold on to It: A Strategic Contingency Model of Power." *Organizational Dynamics*, 5: 3–21.

Salancik, Gerald R., Jeffrey Pfeffer, and J. Patrick Kelly. 1978. "A Contingency Model of Influence in Organizational Decision Making." *Pacific Sociological Review*, 21: 239–256.

Salancik, Gerald R., Barry M. Staw, and Louis R. Pondy. 1980. "Administrative Turnover as a Response to Unmanaged Organizational Interdependence." *Academy of Management Journal*, 23: 422–437.

Sapolsky, Harvey M. 1972. *The Polaris System Development*. Cambridge, MA: Harvard University Press.

Schelling, Thomas C. 1963. *The Strategy of Conflict.* New York: Oxford University Press.

Schwartz, Barry. 1974. "Waiting, Exchange, and Power: The Distribution of Time in Social Systems." *American Journal of Sociology,* 79: 841–870.

Selznick, Philip. 1949. *TVA and the Grass Roots.* Berkeley: University of California Press.

Sheridan, John E., et al. 1990. "Effects of Corporate Sponsorship and Departmental Power on Career Tournaments." *Academy of Management Journal,* 33: 578–602.

Sherif, M., et al. 1961. *Intergroup Conflict and Cooperation: The Robbers' Cave Experiment.* Norman: University of Oklahoma Institute of Intergroup Relations.

Shilts, Randy. 1987. *And the Band Played On: Politics, People, and the AIDS Epidemic.* New York: St. Martin's Press.

Smith, Douglas K., and Robert C. Alexander. 1988. *Fumbling the Future: How Xerox Invented, Then Ignored, the First Personal Computer.* New York: William Morrow.

Smith, Hedrick. 1988. *The Power Game: How Washington Works.* New York: Ballantine.

Smith, Sally Bedell. 1990. *In All His Glory: The Life of William S. Paley.* New York: Simon and Schuster.

Snyder, Mark. 1982. "Self-fulfilling Stereotypes." *Psychology Today,* 16 (July): 60–68.

Staw, Barry. 1980. "Rationality and Justification in Organizational Life" in *Research in Organizational Behavior,* vol. 2: 45–80. B.M. Staw and L.L. Cummings (eds.). Greenwich, CT: JAI Press.

Staw, Barry M., and Jerry Ross. 1980. "Commitment in an Experimenting Society: An Experiment on the Attribution of Leadership from Administrative Scenarios." *Journal of Applied Psychology,* 65: 249–260.

Stein, Herbert. 1989. "Confessions of a Tax Addict." *The Wall Street Journal,* October 2, 1989: A14.

Stevens, Mark. 1989. *Sudden Death: The Rise and Fall of E.F. Hutton.* New York: Penguin.

Strauss, George. 1962. "Tactics of Lateral Relationship: The Purchasing Agent." *Administrative Science Quarterly,* 7: 161–186.

Strickland, Lloyd H. 1958. "Surveillance and Trust." *Journal of Personality,* 26: 200–215.

Sutton, Robert I. 1991. "Maintaining Organizational Norms About Expressed Emotions: The Case of Bill Collectors." *Administrative Science Quarterly,* 36: 245–268.

Sutton, Robert I., and Anat Rafaeli. 1988. "Untangling the Relationship Between Displayed Emotions and Organizational Sales: The Case of Convenience Stores." *Academy of Management Journal,* 31: 461–487.

Tajfel, Henri, and Joseph P. Forgas. 1981. "Social Categorization: Cognitions, Values and Groups" in *Social Cognition: Perspectives on Everyday Understanding:* 113–140. Joseph P. Forgas (ed.). New York: Academic Press.

Thompson, James D., and Arthur Tuden. 1959. "Strategies, Structures and

Processes of Organizational Decision" in *Comparative Studies in Administration:* 195–216. J.D. Thompson, et al. (eds.). Pittsburgh: University of Pittsburgh Press.

Tidd, K.L., and J.S. Lockard. 1978. "Monetary Significance of the Affiliative Smile." *Bulletin of the Psychonomic Society,* 11: 344–346.

Tillinghast, Diana. 1980. "The Los Angeles *Times:* Weakening of Territorial Imperative." *Newspaper Research Journal,* 1: 18–26.

Tushman, Michael L., William H. Newman, and Elaine Romanelli. 1986. "Convergence and Upheaval: Managing the Unsteady Pace of Organizational Evolution." *California Management Review,* 29: 29–44.

Tushman, Michael L., and Elaine Romanelli. 1983. "Uncertainty, Social Location and Influence in Decision Making: A Sociometric Analysis." *Management Science,* 29: 12–23.

Weber, Max. 1947. *The Theory of Social and Economic Organization.* New York: Free Press.

Weick, Karl E. 1979. "Cognitive Processes in Organizations" in *Research in Organizational Behavior,* vol. 1: 41–74. Barry M. Staw (ed.). Greenwich, CT: JAI Press.

Welsh, M. Ann, and E. Allen Slusher. 1986. "Organizational Design as a Context for Political Activity." *Administrative Science Quarterly,* 31: 389–402.

Whisler, T.L., et al. 1967. "Centralization of Organizational Control: An Empirical Study of Its Meaning and Measurement." *Journal of Business,* 40: 10–26.

White, Joseph B., and Gregory A. Patterson. 1990. "GM Begins Quest to Win Back Consumer Confidence." *The Wall Street Journal,* May 4, 1990: B1.

Winter, David G. 1987. "Leader Appeal, Leader Performance, and the Motive Profiles of Leaders and Followers: A Study of American Presidents and Elections." *Journal of Personality and Social Psychology,* 52: 196–202.

Wortman, Camille B., and Joan A. Linsenmeier. 1977. "Interpersonal Attraction and Techniques of Ingratiation in Organizational Settings" in *New Directions in Organizational Behavior:* 133–178. Barry M. Staw and Gerald R. Salancik (eds.). Chicago: St. Clair Press.

Wright, J. Patrick. 1979. *On a Clear Day You Can See General Motors.* Grosse Point, MI: Wright Enterprises.

Zald, Mayer N. 1965. "Who Shall Rule? A Political Analysis of Succession in a Large Welfare Organization." *Pacific Sociological Review,* 8: 52–60.

Zaleznik, Abraham, and Manfred F.R. Kets de Vries. 1975. *Power and the Corporate Mind.* Boston: Houghton Mifflin.

Zucker, Lynne G. 1977. "The Role of Institutionalization in Cultural Persistence." *American Sociological Review,* 42: 726–743.

INDEX

About the Author

Jeffrey Pfeffer is Thomas D. Dee II Professor of Organizational Behavior in the Graduate School of Business, Stanford University. He received his B.S. and M.S. from Carnegie-Mellon University and his Ph.D. in business administration from Stanford. Dr. Pfeffer has served on the business school faculties at the University of Illinois, the University of California at Berkeley, and as a visiting professor at the Harvard Business School. He has directed executive programs and management development programs and has taught executive seminars around the world, in addition to lecturing in management development programs in companies, associations, and universities in the United States. He is also a member of many professional organizations, has served on the editorial boards of scholarly journals, and is the author of *Organizations and Organization Theory, Power in Organizations, Organizational Design,* and co-author of *The External Control of Organizations: A Resource Dependence Perspective,* as well as more than eighty articles and book chapters.